Charles Evans, American Bibliographer

Illinois Contributions to Librarianship, No. 7

CHARLES EVANS
American Bibliographer

   Edward G. Holley

University of Illinois Press   *Urbana, 1963*

Dedicated to Robbie Lee Gault Holley

234293

Acknowledgments

Any substantial work of a historical nature necessarily involves the help of many people. The biography of Charles Evans is no exception to this rule, and I am happy to have this opportunity to express my appreciation to my family, friends, fellow doctoral students, and professional colleagues upon whose lives this work has intruded during the past five years. They have listened, criticized, suggested, and advised with a tolerance which is a tribute to their good natures.

Three, however, are of special importance and it would be difficult to say whose contribution has been most valuable. Each has been invaluable in his own way, and without their aid and encouragement my task would have been an almost impossible one.

Dr. Leslie W. Dunlap originally suggested the writing of the life of Charles Evans and was responsible for my initial contact with the Evans family. His own conviction that the biography would be an important contribution to library literature has often spurred me on when my research seemed to move at a snail's pace. Thanks to his constructive criticism, I have avoided many pitfalls, and I am sincerely grateful for the personal interest he has taken in my work.

Mr. Eliot H. Evans, elder son of Charles Evans, has manifested an interest and helpfulness in the progress of the biography which was beyond all expectation. When the proposal that I write the biography of his father was first mentioned to him, he entered into the project with the full determination that I should be offered every assistance. Through his efforts the family papers were shipped to the University of Illinois for my research, and he has invariably responded promptly and cheerfully to my numerous requests for additional data or for another personal interview. The openhanded way in which he has made available his own personal papers bearing upon his father's life has been gratifying. He provided a grant for a research trip in May, 1958, to the major eastern libraries in which Charles Evans did much of his work. Although he and other members of the family have taken great interest in my research and have read the manuscript while in progress, they have granted me complete freedom in the use of the papers and have not suggested how I should use them in interpreting the bibliographer to my readers. For all these reasons my indebtedness to Eliot Evans is great and I am happy to record my appreciation here.

Most writers pay perfunctory tribute to their wives in the preface of their work. There is nothing perfunctory about the genuine appreciation I feel for Robbie Lee Holley's help on this thesis. As I look back upon the period it has taken to bring the biography to completion, I am amazed that she has been able to read the original drafts, make suggestions, and type the reading draft despite the appearances of Gailon Boyd in 1957, Edward Jens in 1959, Amy Lin in 1960, and Beth Alison in 1961. The inroads on her life have been many during this period, and I am all the more grateful that her patience and perseverence continued to the end.

In addition to the above three, Charles Evans, Jr., and Mrs. Gertrude Evans Jones, the other two surviving children of Charles Evans, have cooperated with me in a fine way. Dean Robert B. Downs has borne with me sympathetically as I attempted to complete the thesis while carrying a full-time job as Librarian of the Education, Philosophy, and Psychology Library at the University of Illinois. To my staff, Pearce Grove, Ralph Stenstrom, Mrs. Grace Yeatter, and Mrs. Barbara Meador, I am grateful for relieving me of some of the more tedious and time-consuming aspects of day-to-day library work without complaint.

My thanks also go to many other people: to Dr. Clifford K. Shipton and Dr. Clarence S. Brigham of the American Antiquarian Society, Dr. Lawrence C. Wroth and Mr. Thomas R. Adams of the John Carter Brown Library, and Dr. Walter M. Whitehill of the Boston Athenaeum, whose willingness to talk with me about Evans and his work added much to the completeness of the biography. The late Arthur Parsons, Jr., first of the Omaha Public Library and then of the Enoch Pratt Free Library, answered my plea for help from those institutions when I would otherwise have failed. About midway in the writing of the biography it was my privilege to meet Dr. William L. Williamson, whose biography of William Frederick Poole is easily one of the outstanding biographies of a librarian now available. I value highly my correspondence and conversation with him. In almost all of the libraries with manuscript materials as listed in the bibliography, there are at least two or three staff members to whom I am indebted. Although I do not mention them personally here, I hope each will feel that he or she is personally covered in this final word of sincere gratitude.

Abbreviations Used in the Footnotes

A. A. S.	American Antiquarian Society
A. B.	*American Bibliography*
A. L. A.	American Library Association
ALS	autograph letter signed
B. A.	Boston Athenaeum
C. E.	Charles Evans
C. H. S.	Chicago Historical Society
C. S. B.	Clarence Saunders Brigham
I. P. L.	Indianapolis Public Library
J. C. B.	John Carter Brown Library
L. E.	Lena Evans
M. A. B.	Mary Abbie Bean
M. H. S.	Massachusetts Historical Society
MS draft	rough autograph draft of a letter
TDS	typed document signed
TL	typed letter unsigned
TLS	typed letter signed
Typed carbon	typed carbon of original letter
Typed copy	copy transcribed from original letter
W. F. P.	William Frederick Poole

Brookline and Worcester in the text or footnotes always refer to cities in Massachusetts. Except where otherwise noted, all autograph letters, newspaper clippings, etc., are in the Evans Papers at the University of Illinois Library.

Preface

Five years ago the name Charles Evans meant to me what it means to most people in the library profession—a name which conjured an image of twelve massive volumes, uniformly bound in rich crimson buckram, covering the first 160 years of printing in America. Beyond that not much was known about the man, his background, his method of work, or the real meaning of his efforts. When it was suggested that the library world needed a good biography of Charles Evans, I immediately became interested.

As Jesse H. Shera pointed out sixteen years ago, one of the most neglected areas of research in the field of American library history has been that of biography.[1] Until thorough and comprehensive biographies of pioneer librarians have been written, American library history will continue to be handicapped by an inadequate conception of one of the motivating forces behind the rise of the library movement. Except for the sketchy treatment of seven individuals in the American Library Pioneers series, there have been few attempts to evaluate the contributions of men like Melvil Dewey, Samuel Swett Green, or William I. Fletcher. Despite Shera's appeal for "scholarly monographs that will really interpret the lives of American library pioneers," only three such monographs in the form of

[1] Jesse H. Shera, "The Literature of American Library History," *Library Quarterly*, XV (Jan., 1945), 1–24.

doctoral dissertations have appeared since 1945.[2] It is apparent that Shera's appeal has been largely ignored.

One of the leading figures in early librarianship in this country was the same Charles Evans who became one of the greatest American bibliographers. At the age of twenty-two he became the first librarian of the Indianapolis Public Library, an institution he quickly raised to the front rank among American public libraries. He was the first treasurer of the American Library Association, attended the International Conference of Librarians at London in 1877, and held various positions of importance in libraries of the late nineteenth century. However, his real contribution to scholarship is his *American Bibliography,* which he subtitled, *A Chronological Dictionary of All Books, Pamphlets, and Periodical Publications Printed in the United States of America from the Genesis of Printing in 1639 down to and Including the Year 1820, with Bibliographical and Biographical Notes.* Although Evans did not reach his original goal, his efforts resulted in the publication of a twelve-volume record of American printing from 1639 to 1799. Almost singlehandedly he accomplished what one of his colleagues has hailed as "one of the greatest bibliographical compilations of all time." [3]

In the last decade there has been a revival of interest in Evans' bibliographical work, and currently the American Antiquarian Society is engaged in a project to reproduce all the books, pamphlets, and broadsides in the *American Bibliography* in microprint form. Since this project has as a subsidiary goal the correction of errors in Evans' work, the provision of a list of additions, and eventually a short-title revision of the entire bibliography, a biographical study of Charles Evans appeared timely. Despite an awareness of Evans' bibliographical work, the significance of his contributions to librarianship and bibliography are not well known. It is the purpose of this biography to remedy that deficiency.

[2] Joseph A. Borome, "The Life and Letters of Justin Winsor" (Unpublished Ph.D. dissertation, Columbia University, 1950); Lewis C. Branscomb, Jr., "A Bio-bibliographical Study of Ernest Cushing Richardson, 1860–1939" (Unpublished Ph.D. dissertation, University of Chicago, 1954); William L. Williamson, "William Frederick Poole and the Modern Library Movement" (Unpublished Ph.D. dissertation, University of Chicago, 1959).

[3] Clarence S. Brigham, "Report of the Council," A. A. S. *Proceedings,* n.s., LXV (April, 1955), 4.

Contents

Fitted for Useful Labor

1

The year 1876 marked a turning point for American librarianship, as it did for many American institutions. Although the public library movement had developed very rapidly in the previous quarter of a century, American librarians had as yet created no professional organization through which they could communicate with each other.

Early in the centennial year, the United States Bureau of Education prepared a giant volume on the status of public libraries in America.[1] This ambitious project, requiring as it did the cooperative efforts of many practitioners, focused attention on the need for a conference where librarians could discuss their common problems. Since many other scholarly groups planned to use the centennial exposition at Philadelphia as an occasion for conferences, it was an appropriate time for librarians to do likewise.

After a bit of maneuvering in the late spring, three distinguished librarians—Justin Winsor, of the Boston Public Library, William F. Poole, of the Chicago Public Library, and Lloyd P. Smith, of the Library Company of Philadelphia—joined with a younger colleague, Melvil Dewey, to form a conference committee which issued a call for a three-day library conference to assemble at Philadelphia on October 4, 1876. The response to the call was gratifying and

---

[1] U.S. Department of the Interior, Bureau of Education, *Public Libraries in the United States of America; Their History, Condition, and Management*, Special Report, pt. 1 (Washington: Government Printing Office, 1876). Cited hereafter as *Public Libraries in the U.S.*, 1876.

103 librarians descended upon Philadelphia from the major public and university libraries in the United States. Among the conferees who gathered in the hall of the Historical Society of Pennsylvania was a tall, slender young man with red hair. Not yet twenty-six, he was in many ways one of the most remarkable personalities in a group notable for its promising young men. An enthusiastic promoter of the conference from the beginning, this librarian of the Indianapolis Public Library had come to Philadelphia to read a paper on "The Sizes of Printed Books." Though a very quiet person, he favorably impressed many of the delegates and made many professional friends. On the third day of the conference, when the time came to organize a professional association and place it on a firm basis, he was sitting next to the irrepressible Melvil Dewey. The call came for all those who wanted to join the association to sign the register. Dewey, with characteristic flourish, took the register and wrote "Number One." He then passed the register to his neighbor, who quietly signed "Number Two, Charles Evans." [2] The manner in which the shy but determined Evans entered into the spirit of the occasion illustrated two characteristics which dominated his life: the reserved manner and the sense of history.

In almost twenty-six years, Charles Evans had come a long way. Certainly nothing in his background had promised a notable library career. Born on November 13, 1850, the second son of Charles Peter and Mary Ewing Evans, Charles Theodore Evans early underwent several unsettling experiences.[3] His father, a mariner either of

---

[2] William Stetson Merrill, "Early Days at the Newberry Library; Reminiscences of Persons and Events, 1889 to 1894," typewritten MS, Oconomowoc, Wis., March 15, 1954, p. 23, verso, in the Newberry Library.

[3] Much confusion exists in the records of the parentage and early life of Charles Evans. In searching the Boston birth records Dr. C. S. Brigham discovered that both Charles Peter and Mary Ewing Evans came from Ireland, but he was not sure that they were not English people living temporarily in Ireland. See C. S. B. to Eliot H. Evans, TLS, May 18, 1936, in possession of Mr. Evans. Gifford Ernest, who later worked on the genealogy of Charles Evans, believed that Charles Peter Evans was Danish, that he was born in 1814, and that he came to this country in 1836. Although I am personally inclined to doubt this, Ernest found a declaration of American citizenship for a Charles Peter Evans recorded in the Archives Division, Records of Naturalization, vol. 28, p. 270, at Boston, dated October 22, 1858. Presumably this record gives Denmark as his place of birth. There is no question of Mary Ewing. A certified copy of the death certificate states that Mary Ewing Evans, age forty-five, married, born in Ireland, died in Boston on April 1, 1859. See copy of Commonwealth of Massachusetts, Division of Vital Statistics, vol. 131, no. 817, p. 19, in possession of Eliot H. Evans. Charles Evans himself always believed that he was Welsh and communicated this fact to many people, including his family and his profes-

Danish or Welsh descent, had come to America by way of Ireland, where he had married Mary Ewing. Life in America was not a very stable one for the Evanses, for in an eight-year period the family lived at five different locations in the city of Boston. Tragedy also came to Charles Evans in early life; in the space of his first nine years both parents died. The combination of these emotionally disturbing experiences, subsequently extended and reinforced, left young Charlie with a sense of insecurity which lasted throughout his life.

The death of both parents required an additional uprooting. On July 13, 1859, Charles was placed in the Boston Asylum and Farm School for Indigent Boys, where he was joined by his brother, Thomas John Evans, the following year.[4] Thus in the period of nine years Charles Evans had known neither the security of a stable family unit nor cultural advantages which might have given him a literary bent. Orphaned at nine, he might well have become one of the hundreds of apprentices who were often attached to tradesmen in the Boston area. Fortunately, Evans was admitted to the Farm School, and it was that institution that supplied the sense of direction and training which would lead to opportunities for his life's work.

At the time Evans entered, the Boston Asylum and Farm School for Indigent Boys was one of the city's distinguished charitable institutions. Situated on a 157-acre island in Boston Harbor, the school regularly enrolled about 100 boys from eight to sixteen years of age.[5]

---

sional associates at the Enoch Pratt Free Library, although his reply to the questionnaire for the *National Cyclopedia of American Biography*, dated July 2, 1914, disclaims any knowledge of his paternal ancestry. See Eliot H. Evans, "Charles Evans, 1850–1935," scrapbook, in possession of Mr. Evans. In view of Charles Evans' later antiquarian interests and his trips to Boston and London, it is strange that he did not check these points.

[4] *Alphabetical List of Boys Admitted to the Boston Asylum and Farm School for Indigent Boys, from June 1835 to January 1883* (Boston: Farm School, 1883) gives the date of admission of Thomas John Evans as July, 1863, and the date of discharge as April, 1864. However, a memorial resolution of the alumni association of the Farm and Trades School, dated June 16, 1934, in the Evans Papers, gives the date of admission as 1860. The printed record is strong evidence but I am inclined to think that the earlier date is more accurate. Thomas J. Evans had an interest in the Farm School that would be difficult to secure from only nine months on the island. He was the first alumnus to serve on the board of managers and held that position for many years.

[5] Most of the data which follow are taken from Boston Asylum and Farm School, *Reports of the Superintendents and Teachers* (Boston: John Wilson

The result of a merger of two similar institutions in 1835, the Boston Farm School provided both a home and education for boys "who from loss of parents or other causes, were exposed to extraordinary temptations and in danger of becoming vicious and dangerous or useless members of society." [6] Its aim was simple: to teach and discipline the boys in residence so that they would "be fitted for useful labor." To further this purpose, the boys were not only provided with strict academic instruction in a year-round school program; they were also required to work on the island farm and to do other manual labor in connection with the housing, feeding, and clothing of the island's 100 residents. An essential feature of the school's program was the belief in the dignity and value of hard work.

Thompson's Island was an ideal setting for a boys' home. The island had good land, which provided much of the produce needed to feed its residents. The surrounding water provided for small boys the delight of the sea and at the same time a means of keeping them on the island without the psychological disadvantage of brick walls and iron gates. Not that the restraint was ever apparent to the boys; Charles Evans later remembered with pleasure the wholesome freedom he had enjoyed on the island.[7]

The southern section of the island, then devoted to farming, also contained an old Indian graveyard and the foundation stones of the house of David Thompson, in the late seventeenth century one of the most pretentious houses in Boston. A short distance from these stones stood the remains of a barn, "blackened, weather-beaten . . . roofless, nearly boardless. Its rough-hewn oak timbers stood as they had stood for over a hundred years, a grim reminder of the sturdy manner in which our forefathers built it." [8] Between the old foundation and the barn was what remained of the orchard, perhaps half a dozen apple trees. There was a sense of history about the island which Charles Evans imbibed early.

The land sloped gently from the southern tip of the island to a

and Son, 1858), p. 1, and *Report of the Board of Managers of the Boston Asylum and Farm School for Indigent Boys, Thompson's Island, for the Year 1866* (Boston: J. H. Eastburn's Press, 1867), p. 8.

[6] Boston Asylum and Farm School for Indigent Boys, *Report of the Board of Managers* (Boston: Farm School Printing Department, 1896), p. 11.

[7] C. E. to L. E., ALS, June 27, 1904.

[8] Charles Evans, "Address," in *The Farm and Trades School, 1814–1914; One Hundredth Anniversary* (Boston, 1914), p. 18. Cited hereafter as Evans, "One Hundredth Anniversary Address."

point called Mansion Hill, which was sixty-five feet above mean high water. Here stood the solitary three-story brick building designed in 1833 by the celebrated Boston architect Charles Bulfinch. In singular majesty this main building with its four white columns dominated the island and housed all the boys, the personnel of the school, and the classroom. On the first floor were the dining hall and the school offices, on the second the schoolroom and staff quarters, and on the third floor a large open room where all the boys slept.

As each boy arrived at the school, he was given a sack and sent to the barn at the foot of Mansion Hill to fill the sack with corn shucks. When he returned to the main building with his sack of shucks, he was told to sit upon it until he had spread the shucks evenly through the sack. He was then assigned one of the wooden bunks in the giant dormitory room on the third floor and his sack of shucks was placed upon it to serve as a mattress. In addition to a bunk each boy was also assigned a drawer into which he could put his personal belongings, the drawer furnishing the only segment of privacy in a highly communal organization.

One of the disadvantages of Bulfinch's building was its lack of adequate heating. Despite the provision of a "furnace" in the east wing of the building in 1857, the heat was by no means uniform throughout the three floors. The furnace heated the dining room on the first floor quite well and kept the schoolroom on the second floor moderately warm. The third floor sleeping quarters received little heat, however, for by the time the air reached the third floor the heat had largely been dissipated. Despite this lack of heat in the sleeping quarters and a mean winter temperature of 26 to 28 degrees, the boys seemed to thrive under the rigorous conditions. Superintendent Morse was always careful to note that "their regular habits, with abundance of fresh air and wholesome food, under the eye of directors and teachers devoted to their welfare, lead to almost unbroken health." [9] Agreeing with the cheery optimism of the superintendent's reports on the health at the school, Charles Evans years later called attention to the great number of octogenarians and nonagenarians among the alumni. This fact he took to be a wonderful tribute to the healthful life the boys enjoyed during their youth. "There is no reason why a Farm School boy who continues to live the same clean, wholesome, active life in his after years should not

---

[9] Farm School, *Report*, 1867, p. 9.

live to be a centenarian on such a sturdy well-built foundation." [10]

Coupled with the spartan living conditions and the outdoor life provided by work on the farm, the institution maintained a strict schedule of academic work. During the summer and autumn the boys attended classes from 8:30 to 12:00 noon and from 2:00 to 5:30 P.M. Regularly, five days a week, they did their homework and recited during the evenings. In the winter, the classes were cut to six hours per day but scheduled for an additional one and a half to two hours in the evening. Saturdays and Sundays were special days. The teachers read to the boys from some instructive book or paper on Saturday evenings, while Sunday evenings were normally devoted to moral instruction.

The teachers provided systematic study in reading, spelling, writing, arithmetic, geography, and grammar. In addition to this program of formal study the boys had the privilege of reading from the few hundred books in the school library. These books, largely donations, were shelved in a bookcase in the schoolroom and were reportedly written "in an attractive and didactic style." That the collection left much to be desired is intimated in the reports of 1857 and 1866 when the teachers issued a plea for additional library materials. At the time of Evans' arrival in 1859, the library had about 300 volumes. While the boys were permitted to select their own books, they had to read them in the schoolroom. If Evans' single comment on a title possessed by the school can be regarded as typical, the collection tended toward the ponderous. At the age of ten he began reading a copy of Marshall's *Life of Washington.* Although persistence was later one of his notable traits, Evans never finished the set and characterized it as "the dullest work a great man ever wrote." [11]

To complete the instructional program, Sundays were devoted to Sabbath school and religious services. Occasionally visiting clergymen spoke to the boys. More often the services were conducted by the teachers who also taught in the Sabbath school, which was kept up with "energy and good results." [12] Though a private school not associated with any denominational group, the managers stressed religious values. Continuous moral instruction would provide a sound program for fitting the boys "for useful labor."

---

[10] C. E. to Arthur Adams, MS draft, Nov. 13, 1934.
[11] C. E. to William Alcott, typed copy, May 7, 1926.
[12] Farm School, *Report,* 1858, p. 2.

These Sabbath school sessions gave Charles Evans a good foundation in knowledge of the Bible, although his application of this knowledge was far different from anything his teachers could have imagined. He found his Sabbath school training chiefly valuable in working with early American printed books whose authors delighted in adorning their title pages with long Biblical quotations. Although he was never a churchman, he learned his lessons well. The school's religious training program instilled in him a sense of moral integrity which nothing could shake.

Despite a schedule that was strict and rigorous, students appreciated their training and developed strong loyalty to the school. Superintendent Morse proudly told his board in 1858 that he had received many visits from graduates who spoke of the months and years spent on Thompson's Island as the most agreeable of their lives. Moreover, he had yet to hear of the first boy who even attempted to escape. He was especially pleased with his efforts in developing dependability and self-respect. With a sense of the moral rectitude often associated with New England, Morse reported: "We also often send boys with keys to the different rooms in the house, and not unfrequently have dispatched our boatboys to the city and other places, sometimes with money to pay bills; and they have always proved themselves trustworthy. I should not expect to inspire boys with confidence in themselves, unless they saw me willing to confide in their integrity."

At least for one alumnus the superintendent did not underestimate the results of his efforts for the boys on Thompson's Island. Charles Evans held Morse in high esteem and subscribed heartily to his total program for the school. Morse's many kindnesses and genuine affection for his boys instilled in Charles Evans a fierce sense of loyalty, and he maintained a keen interest in the activities and welfare of the school throughout his life. Always a subscriber to the school newspaper, the *Beacon,* he repeatedly contributed to alumni drives for funds, even when his own personal financial position was precarious.

Evans even sent the school a copy of each volume of his *American Bibliography,* with the inscription from "an old Farm School boy." This contribution of Evans indicates his devotion to the school, for one can scarcely imagine anything less useful to such a school than the twelve volumes of the *American Bibliography.* Though he justified his actions by a belief that the school should keep examples of the work of its graduates to inspire the future students, he knew that the primary value to the school would be monetary. The limited edition would soon go out of print, and as the years passed, the set would grow increasingly valuable.

By 1914, when Charles Evans had become distinguished as an American bibliographer, the Farm School considered him the logical alumnus to address the students and their guests at the hundredth anniversary celebration. In keeping with the historic nature of the occasion the ceremonies were to be held in the Old South Church in Boston, where Evans would share the platform with President A. Lawrence Lowell of Harvard and the Right Reverend William Lawrence, Episcopalian Bishop of Massachusetts.

Evans willingly accepted the invitation to represent the alumni, although he disliked public speaking. Perhaps no other alumnus had the keen sense of history that Evans did, and his address had the tone of the historian and the solemnity of a clergyman.[13] Comparing the Farm School to the great English schools as charity foundations, he noted that although the school on Thompson's Island had not yet given the nation such famous people as John Wesley, Blackstone, Addison, and Thackeray as had her sister institutions, still she was young. Perhaps in the future there would be graduates who would distinguish themselves in literature, the arts, and government, just as the graduates of the old world institutions had done. Moreover, one should remember that democracy gives its rewards sparingly; it was at least noteworthy that the school had given the nation more than 2,000 solid citizens in the humbler walks of life.

In his capacity as representative of the alumni, Evans called the foundation of the Farm School an "expression of the conscience of Boston towards its orphan children," and paid tribute to the men who had served the school so well as trustees during its first 100 years. In a more personal vein he expressed his own appreciation in these solemn tones:

The cardinal virtues taught at the School, as I understand it, are obedience, fidelity, individual character and industry. Possessed of these, there is nothing which may not be obtained in life. Genius is only the capacity for patient labor. Character is credit, and credit is capital at any bank. Fidelity is the sum of other virtues, and before you can command others you must learn to be obedient yourself. To these must be added something

---

[13] Evans, "One Hundredth Anniversary Address," pp. 16–17.

of the saving grace of a New England conscience. Mine came to me in the form of one of the wisest and best of men . . . and if I have accomplished anything, it has been because it would please him.[14]

After further remarks about Dr. Samuel Eliot, member of the board of managers for many years, Evans closed with a description of the island as he knew it in his boyhood days:

> You may travel far and into many strange lands, but nowhere will you see a more beautiful sight than, when the lengthening shadows fall on Thompson's Island, you see the sun resting like a golden crown over the fair city of Boston. Drink in this beautiful sight while you may. Fill your mind and soul with the brilliant coloring of the great master painter. God gave this privilege to you when he gave you the privilege of being a Farm School boy.[15]

That Evans had learned his own lessons well was demonstrated especially in the force which these New England virtues gave to his own life. Self-discipline, fidelity to what he believed to be right, and above all the capacity for patient labor were the tools out of which he fashioned his *American Bibliography*. Whatever other men might later say about the inflexibility which grew out of this training, none ever suggested that Charles Evans did not give his best efforts to any group with which he was associated.

So impressed were the trustees with Evans' address in 1914 that they called upon him again four years later for a memorial address for Alfred Bowditch, President of the Board of Managers from 1905 to 1918. At the graduation exercises on June 14, 1918, he spoke on "The Indebtedness of the Farm and Trades School to its Board of Managers, as Exemplified in the Service of Its Late President, Alfred Bowditch." [16] The ceremony was held on the sloping lawn overlooking Boston Harbor. The boys had decorated the area with pennants, the natural shrubbery added to the beauty of the scene, and the school band provided music for the occasion. The event touched Evans deeply and he delivered what one Boston newspaper called a "noteworthy memorial." Fifteen years later, when Evans had to refuse an invitation to speak at another celebration, he wrote a description of the island as it appeared to him on that June day in 1918: "Of all the days of the year, when earth and sea, and air and sky join to make our Island home a paradise, June is the rarest in beauty—unless it be those glorious days in late September and early

---

[14] *Ibid.*, pp. 18–19.
[15] *Ibid.*, p. 19.
[16] Newspaper clipping, Boston *Daily Globe*, June 14, 1918.

October—and the setting for your exercises will linger long in the memories of those so fortunate as to attend them." [17]

After spending seven years on Thompson's Island, Charles Evans was given an unusual opportunity which determined his life's work. Dr. Samuel Eliot, a member of the board of managers of the Farm School and also a trustee of the Boston Athenaeum, selected him as an assistant in the library of the latter institution. Most of the boys who graduated from the Farm School were apprenticed to farmers or to such tradesmen as wheelrights, bakers, shoemakers, and carpenters in the Boston area.[18] Very few went to positions from which they could enter a profession. The interest of Dr. Eliot and the need of the Athenaeum for an assistant combined to make Evans one of those fortunate few. Eliot also accepted the responsibility of guardianship for the young man until he should come of age.

Despite a beginning beset with poverty and tragedy, Evans had developed diligence, obedience, and industry at the Farm School. Now, under the guidance of one of Boston's most prominent citizens, he was to build upon this solid foundation. Fundamental as Evans' education at the Farm School had been, it still did not provide him with much knowledge of life outside the island. This would come in part through his work and association with the patrons of the Athenaeum, where a young man could come to know "the full humanity of the present and the past." [19]

---

[17] C. E. to Arthur Adams, MS draft, May 14, 1933.

[18] Farm School, *Report,* 1858, p. 2. The Farm School *Alphabetical List* gives the names, dates of admission and discharge (only month and year), and the reason for discharge of all the boys admitted from 1835 to 1883.

[19] Barrett Wendell, "The Influence of the Athenaeum on Literature in America," in *The Athenaeum Centenary* (Boston: The Boston Athenaeum, 1907), p. 7.

The Full Humanity of the Present
and the Past

2

When Charles Evans entered the door of the Boston Athenaeum on June 12, 1866, he came into contact with an institution which was to provide him with cultural and professional opportunities to enrich a lifetime. Located almost at the center of Boston, the Athenaeum drew to its libraries and art galleries some of the most prominent scholars, statesmen, and literary figures of the nineteenth century. Among the proprietors was Charles Sumner, then the senior United States Senator from Massachusetts, a man who was to become one of young Evans' best friends. The historians Francis Parkman and John Lothrop Motley used the library facilities regularly; and, from their example, Evans would observe the patience and labor involved in historical research. Ralph Waldo Emerson, in company with his daughter, paid a weekly visit to the Athenaeum, where he met other distinguished Boston literary figures and talked about the issues of the day. Names famous not only in New England but also throughout America were commonplace among that distinguished coterie which frequented the Boston Athenaeum in the mid-nineteenth century.

In later years Evans called the Boston Athenaeum "the alma mater of my bibliographical life." [1] "Alma mater" was an appro-

---

[1] Charles Evans, *The American Bibliography* (Chicago: Privately printed for the author by the Blakely Press, 1904), II, dedication.

11

priate term, for the Athenaeum became his liberal arts college and graduate professional school as well. Association with the great and near-great provided Evans with an opportunity known to few American college students in the mid-nineteenth century. College students of that day concentrated primarily upon the "wisdom of antiquity." [2] There was no instruction in modern languages and little in the social sciences except history. The college student viewed experimental science with disdain. Furthermore, he was not encouraged to use the college library, and if he had wanted to do so, he would have found it very inadequate. The library of Columbia University as late as 1876 was open only an hour and a half daily. The college librarian of the mid-nineteenth century regarded his function as one of collecting and conserving books, not one of making books accessible to readers.

In contrast to the sterility of formal education, Evans could learn on the job what the leading American minds thought about politics, economics, and the current status of the arts and sciences. With his ear attuned to the conversations taking place in front of the circulation desk, Evans might hear a spirited discussion between such persons as Ralph Waldo Emerson and Julia Ward Howe. By noting the books the proprietors read he could learn not only the catholicity of taste of the general reader but also the depth and narrowness of the specialist-scholar. Again in contrast to the inadequate collections of the American college library, Evans had access to one of the finest libraries and art galleries in America. Moreover, he was encouraged by his guardian, Dr. Samuel Eliot, to read widely, to study on his own, and to develop his mind while he was young. If liberal education at its best is self-education under competent direction, the six years Evans spent at the Athenaeum resulted in a more truly liberal education than most young men of his day received.

To encourage Evans to make the most of his opportunities at the Athenaeum was primarily the task of two men: Dr. Samuel Eliot and William Frederick Poole, Librarian of the Athenaeum from 1856 to 1869. Dr. Eliot was a Boston gentleman of the old school, who used the leisure which a private fortune afforded to devote himself to the public welfare.[3] Involved as he was with a number of

---

[2] William H. Cowley, "College and University Teaching, 1858–1958," *Educational Record,* XXXIX (Oct., 1958), 312–313.

[3] Dr. Eliot was a member of a prominent and wealthy Boston family. He had tried writing with some success, and then teaching. After serving as President of Trinity College he then returned to Boston in 1864, where he became a member

important and time-consuming trusteeships, he might well have overlooked the young lad he had placed in the library of the Boston Athenaeum. However, Eliot gave careful attention to Evans' development. Indicative of his interest in Evans' welfare was a letter he wrote from Paris in 1870. Not having heard from Evans for some time, he asked a series of searching personal questions: how was Evans getting along, where was he boarding, what salary was he receiving, who was working in the library, and how did matters go there? [4] Having given advice about the importance of self-improvement before he left for Europe, he especially encouraged the young man in keeping up with his studies.

Despite Eliot's interest in Evans' intellectual development, he did not exert any effort to help the young man obtain formal academic training. The knowledge which he hoped Evans would obtain was to come through self-study. However, Charles Evans very much wanted a college education and a college degree. The patrons of the Athenaeum demonstrated the advantages of formal education. How to secure such training was the problem. Without sufficient funds to attend college his best possibility seemed to be enrollment at a service academy. Pursuing his dream in 1869 Evans asked Dr. Eliot if he had any objection to his applying for an appointment to West Point.[5] Although Dr. Eliot agreed that West Point would be an excellent place to receive such instruction, he noted that it was difficult to obtain an appointment. Appointments were largely in the hands of the politicians, with whom he had no influence. If Evans thought Senator Sumner might help him, it would be all right to write him; but before he proceeded further, he should explore the matter with his guardian personally.

After Dr. Eliot gave Charles Evans permission to apply for a West Point cadetship, the young man wrote to Senator Sumner about

---

of so many boards and committees that one biographer called him a "quasi-professional trustee and chairman of boards." George Harvey Genzmer, "Samuel Eliot," *Dictionary of American Biography,* eds. Allen Johnson and Dumas Malone (New York: Scribners, 1931), VI, 80. Among the more prominent institutions with which he was connected were Harvard University as overseer, 1866–72; the Boston Athenaeum as trustee, 1866–79, and as president, 1880–98; the Massachusetts General Hospital as trustee, 1866–98, and as chairman of the trustees, 1874–98. In 1865 he became a member of the Massachusetts Historical Society and was elected a fellow of the American Academy of Arts and Sciences. As a devout Episcopalian he participated in many activities of his church in the Boston area.

[4] Samuel Eliot to C. E., ALS, March 19, 1870.
[5] Samuel Eliot to C. E., ALS, Feb. 16, 1869.

his aspirations. The senator responded that there was not much he could do, since it was the representative of each district who had the right to nominate a candidate. If seriously interested, Evans should write Samuel Hooper, United States Representative from Boston. However, Sumner was not impressed with the type of education Evans would receive from the academy. In a postscript to his letter he advised against the application: "Books are better than guns. Pardon me if I say: stick to your books." [6]

Despite Sumner's friendly warning Evans made application and began to study for the competitive examination which determined the appointment from Boston. Although he studied diligently throughout the spring and summer, his efforts were not enough; he was unsuccessful. Attempting to cheer him up, Dr. Eliot wrote that Charlie had learned a great deal from taking the exam which in itself should provide consolation for his disappointment.[7] In a similar vein, another friend wrote that his lack of success was no reason for despair; all the self-education he could obtain would help him along in life and "open the doors of good society" to him.[8]

This was the only attempt Charles Evans ever made to obtain formal academic training, though throughout his life he held such training in high regard. All of his education subsequent to the Farm and Trades School came from his own program of reading, listening to public lectures, and association with the patrons of the Athenaeum. He early mastered the art of good writing and his sentences flowed with a grace which made a later correspondent suggest that one of his great achievements was the thousands of beautiful letters he penned in longhand throughout his life.[9] Young Evans no doubt had received the same advice from Eliot that the old gentleman later gave to Evans' daughter Gertrude: "If you read the best books, and write often yourself, and always study to be simple in subject, you will write good stories, and perhaps something better still. I hope you will." [10]

If Dr. Eliot exerted little effort to see that Evans secured formal college training, he did counsel with him about the books to read, about high standards of workmanship, and about morality. In his address on the one hundredth anniversary of the Farm and Trades

[6] Charles Sumner to C. E., ALS, March 8, 1869.
[7] Samuel Eliot to C. E., ALS, March 19, 1870.
[8] M. A. B. to C. E., ALS, Oct. 31, 1869.
[9] Interview with C. S. Brigham, Worcester, May 12, 1958.
[10] Samuel Eliot to Gertrude Evans, ALS, Dec. 31, [1897?].

School, Evans paid tribute to Dr. Eliot for providing him with the opportunity to develop into a librarian and bibliographer. In the nostalgia of the moment he credited Eliot with whatever he had accomplished, since the guiding principle in his life had been to reflect credit upon his guardian.[11] A reflection of his debt to Eliot is found in the dedication of the fourth volume of the *American Bibliography:* "To the memory of Samuel Eliot, L.L.D., scholar, educator, philanthropist, historian of liberty, who added lustre to a name illustrious in the annals of New England and bore through life the white flower of a Christian gentleman and died in peace and honor."

The second person who profoundly influenced Evans' career was William F. Poole. By the time Evans entered the employment of the Athenaeum, Poole had been the librarian for ten years. He had contributed much toward strengthening the library's resources and was known throughout the country for his *Index to Periodical Literature,* which had already gone through two editions. One of America's leading librarians, Poole took great interest in developing young assistants along genuinely professional lines. At a time when librarianship was largely a trade which young assistants learned through apprenticeship, Poole was already thinking in terms of librarianship as a profession.[12] Another librarian later commented that the Boston Athenaeum under Poole had been noted as a training school for librarians and that Poole had sent out a number of graduates to important library positions.[13] Four such apprentices were working at the Athenaeum in 1866: William I. Fletcher, Harriet H. Ames, Mary Abbie Bean, and Charles Evans. All four subsequently achieved some prominence in the library profession. All except Miss Ames came to Poole at a very early age: Miss Bean at fifteen, Evans at sixteen, and Fletcher at seventeen. Indicative of their appreciation for the years of apprenticeship under Poole was the fierce loyalty they developed toward his ideas. Fletcher, in speaking of his five years with Poole at the Athenaeum, summarized well the character of Poole's training:

These five years were for me both an apprenticeship and a liberal education. Dr. Poole was everything that was kindly and stimulating, and I had no other ambition than to become like him, energetic and resourceful, able

---

[11] Charles Evans, "One Hundredth Anniversary Address," p. 19.

[12] W. F. P. to C. E., ALS, Feb. 15, 1871.

[13] Melvil Dewey, "Apprenticeship of Librarians," *Library Journal,* IV (May 31, 1879), 148.

to mark out my own path guided by the light of common sense. In this sentence I have perhaps given a hint of Mr. Poole's ways of dealing with his subordinates, which was to set them at a task with a fair amount of instruction, and then leave them to show what was in them. He won the loyal affection of us all by showing a personal interest in us, and by trusting us to do our best without close supervision.[14]

Each of the other three would have subscribed heartily to Fletcher's summary. Some twenty years afterward, Miss Bean, in gently chiding Evans for his seeming neglect in writing Poole, reminded him that it was Poole who started all of them on the road to library success. She noted that Poole took great pride in their progress and "has always a good word for us and a kindly corner in his heart. . . ."[15] "Beanie," as Charlie was accustomed to call her, knew that he was not lacking in appreciation, but she thought men often became too busy and let slip the courtesies of life.

Whatever may have been Evans' occasional neglect of life's amenities, he, too, had great admiration for Poole. In his later career he consciously imitated many of Poole's best-known characteristics: his dogmatism, his indefatigable efforts, his large plans, his impatience with discussion of the trivial in library administration, his rigidity toward those guilty of infraction of library rules, and his conception of bibliography as the foundation stone of librarianship.[16] That his application of Poole's techniques was sometimes unsuccessful did not deter him from striving toward the master's ideals. In the dedication to his third volume of the *American Bibliography,* Charles Evans voiced his appreciation of Poole's contribution to his own development. After a lengthy recitation of Poole's accomplishments, Evans placed on the same page a quotation from Dante suggesting that Poole had been his teacher and the person from which he took the beautiful style by which he had eventually honored himself:

> Tu se' lo mio maestro e' l mio autore:
> Tu se' solo colui, da cu' io tolsi
> Lo bello stile, che m' ha fatto onore.
> —Dante Alighieri

---

[14] William I. Fletcher, "Some Recollections of the Boston Athenaeum, 1861–1866," *Library Journal,* XXXIX (Aug., 1914), 582.

[15] M. A. B. to C. E., ALS, Jan. 1, 1885.

[16] William L. Williamson, "William Frederick Poole and the Modern Library Movement" (Unpublished Ph.D. dissertation, University of Chicago, 1959), pp. 160, 221, 227, 397–398, 419, 486, 520, 741. Williamson's biography of Poole is an excellent work and his treatment of Poole's relationship with his junior assistants very thorough. I have found this biography especially valuable as background for chapters 2 and 8.

If Evans had purposely chosen a library in America in 1866 where he could develop strong bibliothecal tastes, he could not have chosen better than the Athenaeum. Poole was a library administrator who gave trustees and even businessmen a sense of the dynamism of librarianship. Also a historian and bibliographer, he inspired his junior assistants to imitation of his best qualities. The library collection at the Athenaeum was distinguished long before Poole had become librarian, but he added substantially to its strength. Despite the fact that the library was maintained largely as a good collection of the best American and European literature, the Athenaeum contained many excellent research collections.

Poole's chief contribution in building the research collection was his unflagging interest in obtaining a comprehensive collection of materials published in the South during the Civil War. Taking up a task begun by Francis Parkman in June, 1865, Poole pursued vigorously the contacts the former had made. He inserted advertisements in local southern newspapers; he enlisted the aid of Union generals in the army of occupation; and he made his cousin, Charles H. Poole, the Athenaeum agent for Alabama, instructing him to collect everything he could lay his hands on: "What you call 'the smaller fry of ballads, songs, speeches and sermons' is precisely the fry we would tote into our net. We are willing to pay for anything of this sort. Everything printed at the South during the war that goes to illustrate the state and action of the Southern mind we desire to preserve in the Boston Athenaeum." [17]

By October 20, 1865, Poole reported that he had about twenty-five correspondents at different points in the South, all scouring the country for newspaper files, story books, song books, school books, and manuscripts which would be grist for the historian's mill. As W. M. Whitehill has remarked, with such material pouring into the library in increasing quantity it is not surprising that a letter of Poole's dated December 25, 1865, stated, "I have come to town to spend my Christmas in the library." [18] With the example of such an avid bibliographer and historian before him, it would have been surprising if a serious-minded young man had not developed the same characteristics.

One serious deficiency of the Boston Athenaeum was its lack of an

---

[17] Walter Muir Whitehill, "Introduction," in Marjorie Lyle Crandall, *Confederate Imprints; a Checklist Based Principally on the Collection of the Boston Athenaeum* (Boston: The Boston Athenaeum, 1955), I, xvii.

[18] *Ibid.,* p. xviii.

adequate catalog, although work on a comprehensive catalog had been under way for ten years. Until it could be completed and printed, the proprietors had to use a catalog of separate and disjointed strips, often insecurely attached to the insecure sheets of sundry loose and unwieldly volumes. Under heavy use some of the strips were torn; often the most important information was lost altogether. The lack of an adequate catalog meant that a great amount of information had to be kept in the head of the librarian or his assistants. Under these conditions it was very important that an assistant working in the Athenaeum have a good memory.

Although Charles Evans never worked on the catalog, the lack of a good catalog at the Athenaeum had a positive effect upon his thinking. He came to appreciate the worth of an adequate guide to the collections, and one of his first tasks in any new library situation was to develop a catalog for the public. In this respect he also followed the advice and practice of Poole, whose public library catalogs were title-a-line lists designed to make the collection easily accessible to great numbers of users. These finding lists could be printed cheaply and revised often. While this title-a-line approach worked very well for Poole and Evans in public libraries, it would have been hopelessly inadequate for scholarly libraries such as the Athenaeum. When Cutter finally completed the fifth and last volume of the Athenaeum catalog in 1882, it was one of the truly great bibliographic contributions to American libraries in the nineteenth century.

Evans began work in the Athenaeum as an assistant hired to perform all types of duties. However, his chief work soon became the location and circulation of books. The Athenaeum collection numbered almost 100,000 volumes in 1866.[19] These books were arranged roughly by subject in the library rooms on the second floor. Hawthorne described the library as "a noble hall . . . with its splendid vista of alcoves."[20] "Noble" was the proper adjective. The main library room—109 feet long, forty feet wide, and twenty feet high—was finished in the Italian style. There were tables and

---

[19] Library statistics for this period are notoriously inadequate, but Justin Winsor in 1868, two years after Evans' employment, said that the Boston Athenaeum had 100,000 volumes and 70,000 pamphlets. Boston Public Library, *Sixteenth Annual Report of the Trustees* (Boston: Alfred Mudge and Son, 1868), pp. 31–32.

[20] Quoted from Nathaniel Hawthorne, *The American Note Books*, in Charles K. Bolton, "The First One Hundred Years of Athenaeum History," in *The Athenaeum Centenary*, p. 38.

chairs for the patrons in the middle of the hall and in the thirteen alcoves on each side. Massive plaster columns divided the alcoves; shelving in each alcove reached a height of about twenty feet, the upper shelves being made accessible by a light iron mezzanine running the entire length of the room on either side. Five cast-iron spiral staircases led from the reading room floor to the mezzanine. Additional book collections on the first and third floors of the Athenaeum could be reached by separate staircases from the main reading room.

At a circulation desk at one end of the room sat the young assistant, waiting for opportunities to be of assistance to the proprietors. To keep him busy when he was not helping the patrons, the librarian assigned various small tasks such as collating new books. As has previously been indicated, the location of books in the Athenaeum was not always an easy matter. With such a large collection and an inadequate catalog, the proprietors depended either upon their own knowledge of the collection or upon that of the young assistants. The alcoves were each designated with a letter of the alphabet, and new books were assigned an alcove number and a shelf number. They were then shelved by size on a specific shelf in the alcove, from tallest to shortest. With Evans' remarkable memory and his practice in reshelving and searching for volumes, he quickly became noted for his ability to locate books, both for the proprietors and for the annual inventory. Poole once said that if Charles could not find a book, no one could. Forty years later Evans still remembered Poole's confidence in his ability to ferret out the books.[21]

After Charles Evans had become familiar with the Athenaeum collection, the patrons began to call upon him for various services. In addition to their requests for help in locating books, they asked for recommendations on what books to read, and for aid with genealogical research. With his phenomenal memory and remarkable energy Evans developed into a good circulation and reference librarian at the Athenaeum. A tangible indication of appreciation for his services came from the trustees as they regularly and systematically raised his salary. Evans had received his first check on September 29, 1866, for $105.20, covering his work from June 12, 1866.[22] In November, 1868, they raised his salary to $500 per year,

---

[21] Clarence S. Brigham, "Charles Evans," A. A. S. *Proceedings,* n.s., XLV (April, 1935), 14.
[22] For Evans' successive salary increases see Boston Athenaeum, "Librarian's General Account, May 1, 1856–July 1, 1866," III, MS, entry for Sept. 29, 1866;

and the following July he was granted three weeks of vacation instead of the usual two. By 1870 his salary was reported as $600, a good salary for a library assistant of that day. Both in 1871 and 1872 Evans received $100 per year increments. Such steady increases for one so young were tributes to his conscientious and exact performance of duty.

Financial reward alone did not tell the story. The appreciation of the proprietors for a job well done came in a special tribute when Evans resigned from his position on November 25, 1872, to become the first librarian of the Indianapolis Public Library.[23] Six self-appointed "shareholders and habitués of the Boston Athenaeum" distributed a printed letter asking for a one dollar donation from each proprietor.[24] This fund was to be used to purchase a gold watch and chain for Charles Evans, who had given "six years of polite and faithful service." The response was prompt and widespread. Frank R. Blake, Jr., appointed to receive the funds, received also numerous notes and letters which testified to Evans' kindness, courtesy, and thoughtfulness. James Freeman Clarke wrote to Blake: "I enclose with much pleasure, my contribution— with many thanks to the gentlemen who have had 'the happy thought' of expressing in this manner our common feeling toward Mr. Chas. T. Evans." [25] James T. Fields, distinguished Boston publisher and literary entrepreneur, suggested that Evans' place would not be easily filled and asked if the Athenaeum could not double his salary and keep him in Boston.[26] There were contributions from some of the most famous Athenaeum proprietors: Josiah Quincy, Charles Francis Adams, Jr., Gamaliel Bradford, Francis Parkman, Andrew P. Peabody, Oliver Wendell Holmes, and Justin Winsor. By December 16 there were 270 responses to the appeal. Since the committee had received more than enough for the 14k vest chain and the "18k gold open face stemwinder" watch, they bought a

---

"Records of the Library Committee, 1859–1892," MS, entries for Nov. 9, 1868, and July 18, 1869; *Trustees Report,* Dec. 31, 1870, and broadside, Dec. 31, 1871; "Records of the Library Committee, 1859–1892," MS, entry for Feb. 19, 1872, all in B. A. Archives.

[23] C. E. to the library committee, ALS, Nov. 25, 1872, in Boston Athenaeum, "Records of the Library Committee, 1859–1892," B. A. Archives.

[24] Printed letter, Boston, Nov. 30, 1872. Copy in B. A., "Scrapbook," Evans Papers. The following men constituted the committee: Josiah Quincy, Thomas Russell, Edmund Quincy, N. S. Dodge, Alexander Young, and F. Blake, Jr.

[25] James Freeman Clarke to F. Blake, Jr., ALS, Dec. 3, 1872, B. A., "Scrapbook."

[26] James T. Fields to F. Blake, Jr., ALS, Nov. 30, 1872, B. A., "Scrapbook."

gentleman's stone locket and sent Evans the remainder of the fund: $4.55. Blake had personally bought a steel plate engraving of George Washington to put in the locket, but he expressed the hope that Evans would not keep it in "its present position to the exclusion of the face or hair of any fine friend." [27]

The Boston newspapers on December 7 carried short notices of Evans' resignation and his thanks for the gold watch and chain which had been presented to him on the previous evening. One newspaper reported: "Mr. Evans retires from his position to-day, after six years of arduous and valuable service, and carried with him the good wishes of every visitor of the Athenaeum." [28]

The impression of courtesy, kindness, and consideration for others was the facet of his personality which Evans continuously presented to the proprietors of the Athenaeum. Usually it was also the side of his personality which he presented to his associates. His colleague, Mary Abbie Bean, wrote that "at your happiest moments you have rare kindliness and geniality—Keep always up to the *high water mark* of that quality. . . ." [29] Normally Evans was "fair haired bright faced Charlie Boy" with the "merry twinkle in his eye." However, there was another side to Evans' personality. This side developed early in his life and probably was the result of a feeling of inferiority and insecurity in the highly literary and moneyed world in which he moved. When that particular side came to the fore, Evans' colleagues were not pleased. Miss Bean spoke of the "one cloud which used to obscure the sunlight for days" and of "the Bad Charlie who sometimes tries to rule over you." She and others tried to help Evans overcome his moodiness, his withdrawal into himself, and his sulking when things did not go his way. This was a deficiency in personality which Evans never overcame. It remained to haunt him throughout his years of eminence as a librarian and contributed to his persistent difficulties in the profession.

Among Evans' closest friends at the Athenaeum were Harriet H. Ames and Mary Abbie Bean, who worked on the catalog. Harriet Ames was sixteen years older than Evans and took a motherly interest in the orphan. Charlie was "her boy" and she called herself "votre mère Amesie." She took great interest in Evans' professional

---

[27] Francis Blake, Jr., to C. E., ALS, Dec. 16, 1872.
[28] Newspaper clipping, B. A., "Scrapbook."
[29] M. A. B. to C. E., ALS, Jan. 1, 1885, Sept. 5, 1869, Nov. 27, 1870, and Jan. 9, 1884.

development and felt that she had contributed much to his progress by her good training.

Miss Bean, ten years older than Evans, took an even greater interest in him than did Miss Ames. The Bean family lived in Everett, where Mary Bean's father worked in the local bank; Evans visited the family frequently. One of Mary Bean's sisters was also a librarian and the two tried to help Evans both in the library profession and personally. The Beans had a Sabbath school in their home at Everett which Charles Evans attended regularly. This weekly gathering provided him with a refuge from his loneliness and a continuation of the moral training he had received at the Farm School. Miss Bean described the weekly scene in a nostalgic letter which she wrote Evans from Annapolis in 1869: "Today—I fancy you and all my many and dear friends gathered once more in our Sabbath home; glad to return, glad to meet again; how I would like to be of the number; as I think of you all I seem to hear the familiar hymns, and the pleasant service in the 'Manual,' I hear the pleasant greetings—see the friendly faces—and it makes School St. with its friends—more than ever dear." [30]

Evans became so fond of Miss Bean and of her family that he asked her to let him call her "sister," a suggestion to which she readily agreed with the stipulation that she occasionally scold him as an older sister should. A sense of the moral virtues of New England ran strong in Mary Abbie Bean, and she did not hesitate to admonish Charlie about his moral duty. "Excelsior" should be his motto. He should never be discouraged about his lack of success, but should ever keep striving toward his goal.

The Bean home became a haven for Evans, a place of stability during his young years. Yet even there he did not completely let down his guard and become a part of the family. That reserve which was so much a part of his later life had its seeds in the young man who would not allow himself to be too close to anyone. Upon his return to Boston for a visit in 1876 he did not spend the time with the Bean family which his earlier association might have warranted. In fact Mary Abbie felt keenly disappointed that he had not made Everett his headquarters, for the family wanted him to consider their house his home whenever he was in the East.

Evans also had other friends among the young people of the Boston area. Even though he developed work habits more strongly

---

[30] M. A. B. to C. E., ALS, Sept. 5, 1869.

than social habits and he sometimes let absorption with his work overcome his social qualities, he still had a variety of associates with whom to enjoy the pleasures nineteenth-century Boston provided the young. Of girl friends there were quite a bevy, as indicated by the early Boston photographs that he kept. In addition to the Beans, who really did not count romantically, there were the sisters Ames and a young lady named Viola Ryan, whom he had once accompanied on a variety of church socials, including a Sunday school picnic. Out at Winchester also were a number of lady friends. Whatever periods of moodiness or self-pity descended upon Evans, he often shook himself loose for a round of activities with the young ladies.

Simple outings, walks around Boston, lectures, art exhibits, and occasional evenings at the theater were Charles Evans' normal pleasures. However, with such male friends as G. E. Channing, an employee of a local construction firm, he could also enjoy the rugged outdoor life. In the summer of 1869 he and Channing went to the White Mountains to fish and hunt. His description of this vacation indicated a thorough love of the outdoors, and his realism in describing the hunting brought forth a letter of sorrow from "Beanie," who pitied the poor little squirrels. Charles Evans loved New England and regarded its mountains, hills, rivers, and streams as a part of "God's country." Beside New England the West always seemed crude and unfinished. The beauty of the countryside and the beauty of Boston were two different sides of the same coin, and Charles Evans loved them both. Even after years of living in the Midwest Charles Evans was still a New Englander at heart.

Poole, Bean, and Ames left the Athenaeum in 1869 to organize the library of the Naval Academy at Annapolis, and Charles A. Cutter took Poole's place as librarian of the Boston Athenaeum. Although Evans did get along with Cutter well enough to gain several increases in salary, the relationship was not a happy one. It is probable that Evans' fierce loyalty to Poole made him completely unsympathetic to another man's approach to library problems. Poole and Bean both asked Evans to do numerous favors for them after they left the Athenaeum. Poole wanted some samples of the pegs used to hold the wooden shelves in place at the Athenaeum and reported that there were about half a peck lying around. Bean wanted specimen sheets of shelf list paper when she went to Annapolis and later when she removed to St. Johnsbury, Vermont. Out of his desire to do the bidding of his friends and former master, Evans supplied whatever they requested. This led to trouble with Cutter, who was understandably irritated with the depletion of his supplies, however noble the cause. To tighten up his control of the institution Cutter apparently made the employees sign for various items, including door keys. This irritated Evans and caused him to write a letter to Bean calling Cutter "the king of the goats." At another time Bean admonished Evans not to "borrow" stamps from the Athenaeum to write to her or he would get into trouble.

Poole's protégés did not care for Cutter or his ideas. Miss Bean in her letters to Evans called Cutter "his majesty" and respectfully declined to send him greetings. She asked Evans to defend her and Harriet Ames from Cutter, indicating that Cutter did not have a high opinion of the work which had been done before he arrived. In July, 1869, Miss Bean asked the question, "Do the new brooms still sweep clean?" Her pique with Cutter was further demonstrated in 1870, when she asked Evans to show Mr. Thayer, Librarian of the Athenaeum of St. Johnsbury, Vermont, around the Boston Athenaeum and to tell him about library administration. If Evans could arrange it, Thayer ought also to meet Poole, if the latter were in town. She depended upon Charlie to do the honors at the Boston Athenaeum since any letter of introduction should by courtesy go to the head librarian, and Mary Abbie Bean had no intention of writing Cutter a letter of any kind.

Though Evans remained a good assistant at the Athenaeum under Cutter's direction, he sought opportunities to move and communicated his desire to his friend and mentor W. F. Poole. In 1871 Poole had become librarian of the Cincinnati Public Library. He was rapidly making that library one of the outstanding public libraries in the country. In a letter written from Cincinnati on February 9, 1871, Poole encouraged Evans in his ambitions:

> This is a big world, Charlie, and my advice to you is—make yourself as useful as you can, learn all you can in your profession (for it is a profession) & there will be an opening for you when you can command good wages. There is a great dearth of skilled and competent librarians. Character, dignity of deportment, and worldly wisdom are as essential to success as knowledge of books. I am always your friend and never hesitate to ask a favor of W. F. Poole.[31]

In July of the same year Poole wrote Evans and asked if he were free to accept a position at the Cincinnati Public Library. He

---

[31] W. F. P. to C. E., ALS, Feb. 9, 1871.

wanted Evans to supervise the delivery department, have charge of the attendants, and keep the financial accounts of the library. Poole added a note at the end of the letter, "You see I am looking out for you." Although Poole was unable to secure this position for Evans, he promised to keep Evans in mind and was sure that something good would turn up before long.

In early 1872 Evans had an offer of a position at Cleveland which Poole urged him to turn down because of a political controversy then being waged in that city. At the same time, Poole had been appointed consultant to a new board which was charged with the responsibility for creating a new public library in Indianapolis. Would Evans be interested in becoming librarian of the new institution? Poole had recommended Evans to the board, and he thought the board would accept his recommendation. The West was a big place, growing rapidly, and the possibilities for building a name for himself were very good. This was just the opportunity for which Evans had been waiting. He would have Poole to advise him and could operate more independently than he would ever be able to do in the Boston area.

Poole's encouragement and recommendations were overwhelming. Though Evans' years at the Athenaeum had been pleasant and profitable, the position under Cutter did not hold much for the future. Evans would always have fond memories of the Athenaeum and would acknowledge his debt to the institution for the training he received there, but he readily yielded to Poole's persuasive powers and began negotiations with Indianapolis. Just short of twenty-three years, Evans was suddenly catapulted into a position which he would soon make one of the most promising in the American library world.

The Boston Import

3

The movement for a free public library in Indianapolis had been under way for several years prior to 1872. Its origin was similar to that of other libraries which came into existence in the mid-nineteenth century. Professional people, whose background and training made them appreciative of the value of books and reading, provided the initial stimulus while the prevalent American desire for self-culture gave the movement momentum. Finally the politicians were persuaded and the public library became a reality.[1]

Direct action for the library had come at a meeting in December, 1870, when Abraham C. Shortridge, Superintendent of Public Schools, had laid before seven prominent citizens certain proposals for strengthening the school system, among which was a provision for a free public library to be controlled by the board of school commissioners.[2] Backing for Shortridge's proposals was quickly obtained, and the forty-seventh session of the Indiana Assembly passed enabling legislation.

---

[1] Sidney H. Ditzion, *Arsenals of a Democratic Culture; a Social History of the American Public Library Movement in the New England and the Middle States from 1850 to 1900* (Chicago: American Library Association, 1947), chap. II. In separate chapters Ditzion presents the various factors involved in the library movement, but it is apparent that without the influence of such leading citizens as Wayland, Ticknor, and Everett in Massachusetts, the movement would not have been very successful. Public libraries in Indianapolis and elsewhere owed most of their progress to the unremitting efforts of the few.

[2] Jacob P. Dunn, *Greater Indianapolis; the History, the Industries, the Institutions, and the People of a City of Homes* (Chicago: The Lewis Publishing Company, 1910), I, 274, 512.

Indianapolis quickly took advantage of the law, and the following spring a committee composed of Dr. H. G. Carey, Dr. T. B. Elliott, Austin H. Brown, and Addison L. Roache visited St. Louis and Cincinnati to view their public library operations.[3] In the latter city they were so impressed with the success of William F. Poole, the librarian, that they immediately employed him to prepare an acquisitions list of 8,000 volumes for the new public library in Indianapolis. Poole was also asked to serve as library consultant to the committee with special advisory functions on the arrangement of the library and an efficient system for loaning books.

Poole went to Indianapolis in late June, 1872, and talked with the entire school board about their plans for a public library. On June 29 he wrote his young protégé, Charles Evans, his impressions of the embryo library.[4] According to Poole the city had 50,000 inhabitants, it was growing rapidly, and the public library would have about $8,000 per year to spend. Although he did not say so explicitly, the Cincinnati librarian obviously thought that one of the chief virtues of the job was the willingness of the board to listen to sound advice, which in this case meant his. The Midwest was a wonderful place in which to work, and how ideal it would be if the right young man could be persuaded to take the position of librarian! Without consulting Evans he had recommended him for the job and wondered if he would be interested in it at a salary of $1,000 per year. Poole thought the board would accept his recommendation if Evans indicated an interest in the job.

Poole's appointment as adviser to the board was confirmed on July 5, 1872, and he began immediately to work on two projects: first, to compile a suitable list of books for the library, and second, to get the board to appoint Charles Evans as their first librarian. In his reply to Poole, Evans displayed the normal interest of a bright young man ready for additional responsibility.[5] The Cincinnati librarian had already given a strong recommendation to Dr. T. B. Elliott, who arrived in Boston on July 11 to interview Evans for the job. The first flush of enthusiasm was high in both Evans and

---

[3] Indianapolis Public Schools, *Eighteenth Annual Report of the Public Schools of the City of Indianapolis, for the School Year Ending June 30, 1879* (Indianapolis: Douglass and Carlon, 1879), p. 45. This report is more valuable than its title suggests. It is the first printed report issued since 1869 and contains a ten-year review of the school system, including the establishment of the public library.

[4] W. F. P. to C. E., ALS, June 29, 1872.

[5] This letter does not now exist but is referred to in W. F. P. to C. E., ALS, July 10, 1872.

Dr. Elliott, and Poole thought the doctor would conclude the negotiations before leaving Boston.

Excited about the possibilities of beginning a new venture, Evans
wrote Poole to ask if it would not be to his advantage to visit some
of the libraries in the Boston area and see their methods of operation. Since the Boston Public Library had been so successful, he
was especially interested in their administrative procedures and organization. Poole quickly poured cold water on this suggestion.[6] He
did not like the idea of Evans visiting the Boston Public Library as
a prospective librarian, though he had no objection to his going
there and looking around quietly. After all, the Indianapolis Public
Library intended to adopt Poole's system in its entirety, and the
master did not see much need for Evans wasting time looking at
other systems on the East Coast. However, as a matter of prudence,
he warned his protégé against mentioning the position to anyone
until he had been officially appointed.

As a matter of good judgment, Poole thought Evans ought to go
ahead and take his vacation in August, so that his vacation time
could come out of Boston Athenaeum funds. Charles need not worry
about his resignation; that could be submitted after the Indianapolis
board had formally appointed him librarian. Apprehensive about
the matter leaking out, Poole also warned Evans not to allow himself
to be kept in the Boston area by any offer of a salary equivalent to
that offered for the new position. In Indianapolis he could be independent, though near Poole if he should need help. If he were
to take a position in the Boston area, he would be forever under
the shadow of Cutter, Winsor, and Abbot, and he "would have to
conform to their ideas or his library board would think he didn't
know his business." [7] Just what the difference was in conforming
to Poole's ideas or conforming to the ideas of Cutter and the others
the Cincinnati librarian did not say, but presumably he thought
Evans liked Poole's methods better and would have more freedom
of movement in the Midwest.

When Poole took his vacation in mid-August, he undoubtedly
returned to his family in Brookline and took the opportunity to
talk with Evans personally about the prospective job.[8] It was his
impression that the position would be available about October 1,

---

[6] W. F. P. to C. E., ALS, July 24, 1872.
[7] W. F. P. to C. E., ALS, Aug. 4, 1872.
[8] Williamson, "William Frederick Poole," pp. 247–248.

1872, and after receiving a formal communication from the board in early August he clearly thought that the matter was settled.

A very significant step forward for the fledgling library was taken on September 1, 1872, when the Indianapolis Library Association offered to transfer its book collection to the new institution. After accepting the offer, the board of school commissioners appointed a library committee to administer the new institution. This committee consisted of four members of the school board plus an advisory committee of three citizens whose duty it was "to attend the stated meetings of the committee for consultation in regard to all matters affecting the interests of the library." [9] The first members of the citizens' advisory committee were John D. Howland, the Rev. Hanford A. Edson, and E. B. Martindale, all members of the Indianapolis Library Association and men who had been interested in the public library movement from the beginning.

September, 1872, continued to be an important month in the life of the new library as Poole submitted his first list of books. American and foreign acquisitions were arriving in quantity by late October. Poole informed Evans of every detail, probably to keep up his interest. By mid-October the young man was understandably impatient at the lack of official word from the board. He had been led to believe that he would be appointed librarian in August. Over three months had passed since the committee first approached him about the position and still no official action had been taken. Meanwhile, on Poole's advice, he had turned a deaf ear to other possibilities. The letter of early August reporting that the board wanted Mr. Evans and would offer him $1,200 per year was good news, but where was the official document stating that he had been named librarian? To Evans' queries Poole counseled patience while he privately continued to prod the board for official action.

---

[9] B. R. Sulgrove, *History of Indianapolis and Marion County, Indiana* (Philadelphia: L. H. Everts and Co., 1884), p. 434. The committee was appointed on September 6, 1872. Although the citizens' advisory committee had no legal status, the members could and did exert considerable influence at the monthly meetings of the library committee. It was common practice for the entire library committee to meet and consider library matters and then to pass recommendations on them to the full board of school commissioners. During the early years of the library, the recommendations were routinely accepted. This type of organization, while common, led to innumerable misunderstandings and dissensions in more than one library during the late nineteenth century, and had much to do with Evans' eventual dismissal in 1878. Williamson, "William Frederick Poole," pp. 239–240, 275–276.

The long-awaited letter finally came. Dr. Elliott wrote Charles Evans on November 16 that the board had met the previous evening and had elected him librarian of the Indianapolis Public Library at a salary of $1,200 per annum.[10] Elliott reported also that the library rooms were almost ready and the books were beginning to arrive. They had asked Poole to advise them about a date for Evans to begin work. Since it was the opinion of the board that the library could be opened to the public on January 1, 1873, would Evans be so good as to notify them when he could arrive in Indianapolis?

Poole gave the same advice he had given all along: the board needed Evans immediately and the quicker he could begin work the better.[11] Since the board had already agreed that it would be to their advantage to have Evans spend some time with Poole, their suggestion was that he stop in Cincinnati and then come to Indianapolis with the Cincinnati librarian. All of this information Poole communicated to Evans with enthusiasm. He wanted Evans to start west as soon as possible. As a plan of action, he suggested that Evans buy a ticket on the Baltimore and Ohio Railroad to Chicago, via Philadelphia, Baltimore, Washington, D.C., Cincinnati, and Indianapolis. The additional cost to Chicago would be only a dollar and eventually he could use that part of the ticket for a pleasure excursion. Professionally, despite his previous advice on visiting other libraries, he thought Evans should stop in Philadelphia to see the Library Company and the Mercantile Library. No letter of introduction was necessary; he had only to say to Mr. Smith and Mr. Edmands that he was one of Poole's protégés and they would see that he had a good visit. There was little to see in Baltimore except the city; however, he should stop in Washington and visit the Library of Congress, where he should check with the chief cataloger on their methods. Since this visit to Washington would be his first, he should see everything he could of the city itself. Then he should proceed to Cincinnati for instruction under Poole.

After completing this letter of interminable advice, Poole failed to mail it immediately and on November 29 added a postscript. In the meantime he had received Evans' letter telling him of Elliott's thought that the library would be open on January 1. His postscript

---

[10] T. B. Elliott to C. E., ALS, Nov. 16, 1872. See also confirmation of this letter, T. B. Elliott to C. E., ALS, Nov. 22, 1872.

[11] W. F. P. to C. E., ALS, Nov. 27, 1872, with postscript dated Nov. 29, 1872.

fairly bristled at the thought of opening the library so soon: "It is utterly absurd to think of opening the library of Ind. Jan. 1. Dr. E. did not write such nonsense to me." Although Evans thought he ought to give some notice to the Boston Athenaeum and clean things up before he left, Poole was impatient for Evans to come west immediately. "You must not stop two weeks in Boston after you send in your resignation. What do you care about fixing things up? Let them attend to that. You are wanted here. Kiss the young lady you are courting and leave town." [12]

Unknown to Poole, Evans had already submitted his resignation to the Athenaeum on November 25, to take effect at the earliest date convenient to the library committee.[13] Evans' friends therefore had to make haste to give him the reception mentioned previously. However, on Saturday evening, December 6, the self-appointed committee and Evans' friends gathered to present him with the gold watch, chain, and locket. The following day the Athenaeum library committee voted to employ Joseph Merrill to take Evans' place, and Charles Evans headed west.

If Evans thought that Poole's influence extended beyond the library committee in Indianapolis, he was headed for a shock. The midwestern distrust of easterners was deeply rooted, as Poole himself had previously noted when he had been unable to appoint Evans to a position in Cincinnati.[14] Indianapolis was a smaller city than Cincinnati and took an even more provincial view about bringing in an outsider to head the new city library. John H. Holliday, proprietor of the Indianapolis *Evening News* and later a good friend of Evans, wondered aloud why it was necessary to import someone from the Atlantic Coast to arrange a little library of a few thousand volumes. Could not a city of 65,000 inhabitants supply such a person? What Indianapolis needed was not "a Boston import" who did not understand the city and therefore could not select the kind of books its citizens needed.

If the librarian is to buy books suited to our preferences, he must be acquainted with us, and the "highly recommended" young man from Boston knows no more of our literary inclinations than he knows of the military drill of the Chinese. . . . Either in the arrangement of a library or the purchase of books for it, we need no better "experts" than we have

---

[12] *Ibid.*

[13] C. E. to the library committee, ALS, Nov. 25, 1872, in Boston Athenaeum, "Records of the Library Committee, 1859–1892," B. A. Archives.

[14] W. F. P. to C. E., ALS, July 3 and Aug. 14, 1871.

at home, and the city can well spare the unjust sarcasm on her poverty of literary cultivation implied in the act of sending to the Atlantic for a librarian to do it.[15]

Holliday's highly literate diatribe was merely a reflection of the common midwestern prejudice and would certainly have to be taken into account if Evans were going to succeed in the new job. Even the great Poole, when he left Cincinnati for the librarianship of the Chicago Public Library in 1874, wrote Evans that some of the newspapers had talked a little about the "foreigner" at first, but now everything was coming out all right.[16]

Several years later, in an article on organizing and managing public libraries, Poole called for experience as the chief qualification for a librarian.[17] He characterized the local prejudice against employing nonresidents as "absurd, and one which individual members of the board do not observe in conducting their own affairs." Moreover, he noted that normally the local applicants for new library positions were people who had failed in everything else. They were "broken down ministers, briefless lawyers, unsuccessful school teachers, and physicians without patients." To call upon such people and expect them to distinguish themselves in librarianship was a delusion: "The same energy, industry, and tact, to say nothing of experience, which insure success in other avocations are quite as requisite in a librarian as book knowledge. A mere bookworm in charge of a public library, who has not the qualities just named, is an incubus and a nuisance." [18] To Poole librarianship was a profession and Charles Evans had fitted himself for the profession by good training under an acknowledged master.

However valid Poole's observations, they helped Evans little during his first weeks in Indianapolis. The local newspapers kept up their comments on the "Boston import." In an obvious reference to Evans' youth and presumed susceptibility to feminine charms, the Indianapolis *Journal* noted: "The imported librarian finds the services of those six beautiful young ladies from the High School of great assistance. With an addition of six more assistants the library will probably be opened before the coming summer is over." [19]

---

[15] Indianapolis *Evening News,* Dec. 9, 1872, p. 2.

[16] W. F. P. to C. E., ALS, Jan. 9, 1874.

[17] W. F. Poole, "The Organization and Management of Public Libraries," in *Public Libraries in the U.S.,* 1876, pp. 476–504.

[18] *Ibid.,* p. 489.

[19] Newspaper clipping, Indianapolis *Journal,* Jan. 4, 1873, I. P. L., "Scrapbook."

The constant carping from the Indianapolis press could not have made the month of January a very pleasant one for the twenty-two-year-old librarian. A stranger among a hostile populace, Charles Evans must surely have wished many times that he had ignored Poole's advice and stayed in his comfortable haven at the Athenaeum.

Despite his critics, however, Evans continued to catalog books and to arrange them on the shelves in the library rooms of the high school building, where the board had allotted space for the new institution. As a result of his efforts, his first support came from an editorial in the *Sentinel* on February 6, 1873: "The library will open with over 12,000 books on the shelves, and a cursory examination of those already on hand will convince any one that the selections have been made by those who understand the needs of such an institution. Mr. Evans, the librarian, it is evident, thoroughly understands the requirements of his position, and the appearance of the library when opened to the public will testify to his ability." [20] This editorial gave Evans' morale a much needed boost and helped him to endure the continual brief barbs from the other newspapers. Moreover, the *Sentinel* had begun a program of support for Evans which continued throughout his tenure in Indianapolis.

As Evans quietly and conscientiously went about his work, the tone of the other newspapers began to change. Always at his best among highly cultured people, Evans' courteous and deferential attitude toward this group had the desired results. Holliday unbent enough by March 28 to say that "the Librarian Mr. Charles Evans is a young man of experience and acknowledged ability, and under whose direction the Library has been most admirably arranged." [21]

Preparations for opening the library to the public moved along steadily, and on March 21, 1873, the library committee issued an eight-page pamphlet giving the rules and regulations which were to govern the library.[22] The firm hand of William F. Poole can be seen in this pamphlet, for the librarian was given responsibility for strict enforcement, a policy which both the teacher and his younger pupil believed essential. The library was to be open daily from 9

---

[20] Newspaper clipping, Indianapolis *Sentinel*, Feb. 6, 1873, I. P. L., "Scrapbook."
[21] Newspaper clipping, Indianapolis *Evening News*, March 28, 1873, I. P. L., "Scrapbook."
[22] Indianapolis Public Library, *Rules and Regulations of the Public Library of Indianapolis Adopted by the Board of School Commissioners, March 21, 1873* (Indianapolis: Wright, Baker and Co., 1873).

A.M. to 9 P.M., though no circulation service would be given on Sunday. The use of tobacco, conversation, and other conduct inconsistent with the quiet and orderly use of the room was proscribed. Residents of the city could become registered borrowers either by presenting a bond signed by a responsible citizen or depositing the sum of three dollars. Both the *Sentinel* and the *Evening News* gave extensive coverage to this action and published the rules in their entirety.

The decision to keep the library open on Sunday for reading and reference drew strong editorial support from the *Evening News*. Although the leading American librarians agreed with Justin Winsor, who declared that "the hours that a library is open must correspond to the hours in which any considerable number of people will come to it—all night, if they will come all night, in the evening certainly, and on Sunday by all means," as late as 1889 the majority of American public libraries were not open on Sundays.[23] Of those which were open, Chicago, Cincinnati, St. Paul, and Indianapolis were among the larger libraries open both in the morning as well as in the afternoon. Evans felt that Sunday opening in Indianapolis had been an indispensable part of his work, and in his first report he justified it in the altruistic terms which were common to librarians during this period: the library provided a place of recreation and culture for those who would not go to church and would otherwise turn to the gin palaces.[24]

The extent of Evans' four months of work can be seen in his report of the status of the library in the rules pamphlet. Some 10,000 volumes would be ready for lending when the library opened. To help the public use the collection as efficiently as possible Evans had prepared a complete alphabetical catalog of the entire collection, plus an additional catalog of the 4,000 books donated by the Indianapolis Library Association. Several copies of the latter catalog were available for public use. As soon as the 2,500 books still on order were received, he intended to print a complete dictionary catalog for purchase by the library's patrons.

---

[23] The Winsor statement occurs in International Conference of Librarians, *Transactions and Proceedings of the Conference of Librarians Held in London October, 1877* (London: Printed at the Chiswick Press, 1878), p. 171. Cited hereafter as *Int. Lib. Conf.*, 1877. Mary S. Cutler, "Sunday Opening of Libraries," *Library Journal*, XIV (May–June, 1889), 176–190.

[24] Indianapolis Public Library, *The First Annual Report of the Public Library of Indianapolis, 1873–4* (Indianapolis: Printing and Publishing House, 1874), p. 14.

The Indianapolis Public Library had been placed in the south wing of the high school building located at the corner of Michigan and North Pennsylvania Streets, very near the center of the city. An old mansion that had been converted to public use, it stood some distance from the street and was surrounded by tall trees and ornamental shrubs. The library was placed to the left of the entrance hall in rooms that had once been used for double parlors and a dining room. In these rooms were the books for circulation, arranged in alphabetical order by the subject they treated: works of fiction under *A*, works of science under *B*, biography, *C*, and so forth. It was a pragmatic scheme, had been devised by Poole, and was later used with variations by Evans in a number of other libraries. On the second floor was a small reading room containing periodicals. Circulars had been printed and distributed throughout the city calling the attention of the citizens to the early opening of the library. Charles Evans had prepared well; now he waited to see the effect upon the public.

Claps of thunder and a downpour of rain greeted the citizens of Indianapolis when they came to the high school building on Tuesday, April 1, to register and receive their borrowers' cards. Despite the inclement weather, which one newspaper reported kept all at home "who were not driven out by dire necessity," 122 had registered as borrowers at the end of the first day. After a week of registration the library was ready for the formal opening exercises. No books had yet been circulated, but procedures had now been set up to give prompt service beginning April 9. Charles Evans and his crew of assistants were kept busy with the clerical chores required by the heavy registration.

The citizens of Indianapolis were proud of their new public library. The city could now take its place with other midwestern cities such as Cincinnati and St. Louis, both of which had flourishing public libraries. To celebrate the formal opening the library committee had prepared an elaborate program to be given in the high school hall on Tuesday evening, April 8. Despite another onslaught of rain the hall was filled to capacity well before the time for the program to begin. Although the great majority of the audience was composed of "the very best men and women of the Capital city—those who read, think, and have an interest in the public's welfare," all trades and professions were represented as well as a substantial number of youths.

All who should have been on the program for various reasons were duly recognized. The promoters of the public library idea were represented, as were those who presumably would now make the most use of the new institution. The single omission from the program is the name of Charles Evans, Librarian. Perhaps the young man was well content to see the occasion marked so auspiciously by the elocutionary talents of Judge Roache and Governor Hendricks. It was important for the public library to be launched with the good will of so many prominent citizens. Let others make the pretty speeches and assure the support from the right sources. Evans would assure the excellence of the daily work upon which the success of the library would eventually depend. Yet even the most self-effacing scholar must have felt some slight irritation that his name was not even mentioned in the accounts of the formal opening by the three leading newspapers in Indianapolis. Charles Evans was a young man, just past his twenty-second birthday. He could scarcely have been happy with this omission, even though he passed over the slight in silence.

Regardless of Evans' reaction to the opening exercises, the Indianapolis Public Library was off to a good start. The young librarian had more than enough work to keep him and his assistants busy. Almost immediately the attendance and circulation records indicated that the space allocated to the library would not hold enough people. The reading room had seating space for only twenty-four; on the first Sunday an average of fifteen persons used the reading room all day long. With considerable pride the Indianapolis *Journal* reported a total circulation of 1,386 books during the first four days. Such an enthusiastic beginning augured well for the library, but progress would certainly be hindered unless expanded quarters were provided.

The circulation of books rose steadily. Within sixty days of the opening, over 15,000 books had been withdrawn for home use. Almost 2,500 citizens had registered as borrowers, the chief users being, however, the well-to-do and children. The editor of the *Sentinel* deplored the fact that so few borrowers were found among the working classes.[25] He did not want to call the library a failure so soon after its establishment, but the library had been created primarily for the workingman who could not afford books. If the library were to achieve its original high-minded mission, serious efforts

---

[25] Newspaper clipping, Indianapolis *Sentinel,* May 1, 1873, I. P. L., "Scrapbook."

would have to be made to encourage more reading among the poorer classes. To this end the editor urged the librarian to pay special attention to applicants from this group and to make them feel at home in the library. It also seemed advisable for the board to advertise the library among their constituents so that books would be distributed where they would do the most good.

The one segment of the population best served by the library was generally acknowledged to be the youth, especially young men. From the very beginning Indianapolis youth flocked to the library. The normal view of this youthful passion for books was expressed in a letter to the editor of the *Journal*.[26] The writer thought the use of the public library by so many "clever little boys" one of the encouraging signs for the future of Indianapolis. The public library provided the boys with an opportunity to develop themselves to the limit of their capabilities, and there would undoubtedly come a day when these same boys would push the fortunes of Indianapolis to a new high. In view of such enthusiastic reception from the Indianapolis citizens, the only problem the writer could see to hinder this healthful development was a lack of books and space. The circulation of books had increased at such a dazzling pace that there were simply not enough books to go around.

Years later, recalling his first experience with the public library, one of the local Indianapolis historians, George S. Cottman, paid tribute to the early work of the library in these words:

> Strong impressions made on the youthful mind are lasting and I vividly remember the elation with which just fifty years ago I came from the country to Indianapolis. One evening I wandered into the reading room of the Indianapolis Public Library, which was then in the old high school building at Pennsylvania and Michigan Streets. The chance meeting on that occasion with Charles Evans, the Librarian, and the courtesy he extended to a mere country boy, went far toward making me realize that all the wealth of the ages collected there was, in a sense, mine. The precious books I carried off one by one to my den in some cheap boarding house for night consumption, and to this day Shakespeare, Dickens, and I know not how many English classics are associated in my mind with the smell of coal oil, the yellow glare of smoky lamps and aching eyes. But they were worth it. I have reason for feeling toward my library alma mater quite as kindly and grateful as any son of a college can feel toward his "fostering mother." [27]

---

[26] Newspaper clipping, Indianapolis *Journal*, Feb. 17, 1874, I. P. L., "Scrapbook."

[27] As quoted in Charles E. Rush, "Historical Account of the Indianapolis Public Library from 1873 to 1893," typewritten MS, Indianapolis, 1925, p. 10, I. P. L. Archives. See also newspaper clipping of Cottman's letter to the editor of the Indianapolis *News* in Eliot Evans, "Scrapbook."

The librarians of the late nineteenth century, who saw themselves and their libraries in the role of the great adult educators, would have been pleased by such a testimonial. Cottman's tribute, however, was specifically to Charles Evans, a young man not too much older than himself. Evans' readiness to help and encourage the local youths and his courteous attitude toward them did much to make the library a popular place for the young. He was pleased that the largest use of the reading room on Sunday was by this same group, and he thought it a tribute to the good work the library was doing.

But there were scoffers; not all rejoiced at the thought of youths reading so many books. Then, as now, some citizens regarded much reading as a dangerous thing. Mrs. Hetty A. Morrison in an article entitled "An Hour in the Public Library" wrote a chatty expression of the minority view.[28] While not attacking the institution as such —she later was a candidate for the position of librarian—she noted that there was a danger that the young were reading too much. One boy had openly confessed to her that for a long time he had been going to the library every other day! She admitted a "thrill of pleasure" when she saw two or three Negro boys asking for such books as *Bear and Forbear* and *Strive and Succeed,* for she knew that their great-great-grandfathers had possibly been priests of voodoo. Still, it was not a good thing, she thought, to trust to a child's instinct in the choice of books. Moreover, the books were not always sufficiently worthwhile to compensate for the time taken away from youthful play.

Mrs. Morrison's dissent definitely represented the minority viewpoint. The newspapers of Indianapolis regularly gave support to the library by printing whatever Evans provided and took pride in his release of circulation statistics. By comparing the steady growth of the Indianapolis Public Library with older and better supported libraries, Evans encouraged the citizens to believe that Indianapolis was a bookish city. In his first annual report he noted that in one short year Indianapolis had assumed fifth place in circulation among the public libraries of the country. His basis for assigning Indianapolis fifth place was a table of statistics he had found in the report of the Lawrence, Massachusetts, Public Library. While library statistics for the period are notoriously unreliable, it is probably true that Indianapolis ranked among the top ten in the country.[29] Some

---

[28] Newspaper clipping, Indianapolis *Sun,* Nov. 15, 1873, I. P. L., "Scrapbook."
[29] A comparison of circulation statistics in *Public Libraries in the U.S.,* 1876,

5,200 borrowers had withdrawn the 14,000 volumes 101,821 times for home use. Even the Cincinnati Public Library, then under the direction of the energetic Poole, had circulated only a little more than twice that number from a book stock over three times as large.

But delving below the impressive statistics, could one say that the library was really serving the needs of the people or was it merely providing light recreational material that had little substance? Evans was alive to any possible criticism that the circulation figures did not indicate substantial reading interests. Four pages of his report were devoted to an analysis of the circulation. He reported the same conclusions as other libraries: the library had circulated three times as many works of fiction as it did all other works combined. This seemed to be a universal law for public libraries: three-fourths of the people read for amusement and only about one-fourth for self-improvement. Anticipating the public reaction to such figures, Evans entered a vigorous justification for spending public funds for fiction. To lower the number of volumes of fiction or to discard them from the shelves entirely was not a satisfactory solution. Such a procedure would merely drive away those who might otherwise read and subsequently be enticed to read works of greater merit. The library already had a policy of excluding the positively vicious and immoral books. Lest his best customers misunderstand, he hastened to add that this policy did not exclude the class of works represented by Mrs. E. D. E. N. Southworth or Mrs. Mary J. Holmes, sentimental novelists whose works were very popular in the late nineteenth century.[30] Their works were not immoral but literarily weak, and they adequately met the needs of the class of readers for

---

indicates that Indianapolis stood thirteenth among all libraries in the country, though strangely enough the statistics for Indianapolis are not included in the printed report. However, Chicago, which is included, did not begin its great period of growth until Poole went there in 1874. Of the thirteen, only eight are tax-supported public libraries and Evans could claim with some justice that Indianapolis stood sixth among tax-supported public libraries in 1876. Since this group of eight included such large cities as Boston, Chicago, St. Louis, Cincinnati, and Cleveland, Evans could well be proud of the high ranking of his library in a short three-year period. His claim for 1874, too, has validity, if one limits his terms to tax-supported institutions.

[30] Mrs. E. D. E. N. Southworth was one of the most popular writers of the mid-nineteenth century. F. L. Mott lists three titles by Mrs. Southworth on the best-seller list in the period 1860–69, which means that each of the titles sold more than 300,000 copies. Mrs. Mary J. Holmes did not quite make the best-seller list, but three of her titles appear on the better-seller list for the same period. Frank L. Mott, *Golden Multitudes: The Story of Best Sellers in the United States* (New York: Macmillan, 1947), pp. 308–309, 320–321.

whom they were intended. No good purpose would be served by eliminating their works and such a policy would discriminate against a substantial number of citizens. With vigor Evans pursued his point even further. "The loud outcry against this class of reading does not come from those who by experience have learned the needs of the poorer classes of society." Yet it could not be said that even Mesdames Southworth and Holmes provided the majority of fiction titles read by the public. On the basis of a survey which Evans made on two different days in March, 1874, he discovered that the authors against whom the charge of sensationalism could be lodged accounted for only one-tenth of the total, while the works of Dickens, Cooper, and Scott were near the head of the list in circulation. After all, the deepest students often turned to the pages of a novelist for relaxation, and "there is a difference only in degree from the relaxation they experience in reading 'Middlemarch,' and the momentary forgetfulness of her cares of the sewing-girl losing herself in the pages of the 'Deserted Wife.' " [31] Reading of whatever type was worthwhile, he asserted, and Indianapolis ought to be proud of the reading record made by her citizens.

As busy as Evans was that first year in Indianapolis, helping readers find the books they wanted, promoting reading, and supervising the work of his circulation clerks, he had many other duties to perform. One of the early problems, closely allied to that of circulation, was to organize the book collections so that specific titles could be located with a minimum of effort. In 1873 dictionary card catalogs, used now in practically all American public libraries, were just beginning to make their appearance. The normal procedure for all librarians was to publish a book catalog or series of catalogs. Several of these would then be placed in the reading room for use by the patrons and a number of them would be sold. They were kept up to date by a series of supplements. After an interval of time when a number of supplements had been issued, the catalog would then be reprinted in its entirety by incorporating all the material from the supplements. Libraries also exchanged these catalogs among themselves so that the librarians could compare their collections. The publication of a useful catalog was one of the fundamental tasks of a good librarian of the 1870's.

Classification of books presented yet another problem. Most schemes for the classification of books were based on crude divisions

---

[31] I. P. L., *First Report, 1873–4*, p. 11.

determined by the local librarian, or adaptations of schemes used by larger libraries. Melvil Dewey's *Decimal Classification and Relativ Index* which would later become predominant among American public libraries did not appear until 1876. While there was much discussion among librarians as to what the best classification system should be, the normal pattern was to arrange the books by broad subject divisions and to number them as they stood on the shelves. At Indianapolis, Evans used a pragmatic scheme and system of notation devised by Poole.[32] Following Poole's broad subject classification, he used the letters of the alphabet to refer to the "department," that is, the subject or alcove in which the volume might be located, and arabic numerals to refer to the specific position of the individual volume in that alcove. Therefore Francis Parkman's *Pioneers of France in the New World* was located in department *D*, or the American history alcove, and was the one hundred and eighty-fifth book in that particular department. Parkman's *The Jesuits in North America* was given the number "186, *D*," indicating that it was the one hundred and eighty-sixth book in the department of American history.

Poole believed strongly in giving every book a specific place within its broad subject division.[33] The librarian could leave space for expansion by reserving certain blocks of numbers in the beginning. However, the time would come when all the reserved numbers would be used up. When that time arrived and one found books on the same subject widely separated by number, then the librarian would have to reclassify the entire collection. The flaw in this plan was the expense of reclassification every ten or twenty years. While Poole recognized this difficulty of the fixed location system, he remained until his death skeptical of the more flexible scheme de-

---

[32] Thomas V. Hull's statement in his "The Origin and Development of the Indianapolis Public Library, 1873–1899" (Unpublished Master's thesis, University of Kentucky, 1956), p. 41, that little information exists about the first classification scheme is inaccurate. In addition to the classification numbers in the Indianapolis Public Library, *Catalogue of the Public Library of Indianapolis* (Indianapolis: Press of Printing and Publishing House, 1873), another Indianapolis historian gives Poole the credit. See W. E. Henry, comp., *Municipal and Institutional Libraries in Indiana: History, Condition and Management* (Indianapolis: Under the direction of the Louisiana Purchase Commission of Indiana, 1904), p. 77. Henry stated that the books were classified according to a method recommended by Poole and that the system of notation also came from Poole. Even a cursory examination of the catalog leads to the conclusion that the scheme was one of Poole's pragmatic classifications.

[33] W. F. Poole, "The Organization and Management of Libraries," in *Public Libraries in the U.S.*, 1876, p. 494.

veloped by Dewey.[34] Again the disciple followed his master: Evans used variations of Poole's system at Indianapolis and other places. He always disliked the Dewey classification scheme.[35]

Evans had begun work on the classification and arrangement of books immediately after he came to Indianapolis. He wanted to publish a catalog as quickly as possible, but first it was necessary to classify all the books Poole had ordered, plus the collection of the Indianapolis Library Association. From Cincinnati Poole continued to exercise long range supervision of Evans' work and to help him with the catalog. By July, 1873, the manuscript was complete enough for the board to order it printed, and *The Catalogue of the Public Library of Indianapolis, 1873,* came from the press in early November.

Similar to the catalog of the Boston Mercantile Library which Poole had published in 1854, Evans' book was a title-a-line catalog with just enough information for the patron to recognize the book he wanted and to order it from the shelves. The Indianapolis catalog indexed 12,790 volumes by author, title, and subject word, with some cross references. For each entry Evans gave the name of the author, the title, place of publication, date and size, and beside each entry, the call number. Pseudonymous works were found under the real name of the author, where known, with reference from the pseudonym. Evans was very good at ferreting out the real name of popular authors who wrote under assumed names, and his old friends Mary A. Bean and Harriet H. Ames occasionally asked him to help them find such names.[36] He had a phenomenal memory which retained much of the material he had ever had occasion to handle.

Evans' catalog had 365 pages plus a historical introduction, a preface with explanations, and a list of periodicals for which the library subscribed. The volume was printed on toned paper in brevier type and was bound in brown cloth. Local newspapers reviewed the work favorably and one reviewer added his personal appreciation of the work of Charles Evans: "When Mr. Evans began

---

[34] William Stetson Merrill to W. L. Williamson, TLS, Oconomowoc, Wis., March 9, 1952. Letter in possession of Mr. Williamson; copy in possession of the author.

[35] C. E. to W. F. P., ALS, Nov. 11, 1891, Poole Papers, Newberry Library. Evans called the decimal classification "the detestable Dewey system of notation."

[36] M. A. B. and Harriet H. Ames to C. E., ALS, n.d., but probably 1871. Several other letters in the collection also indicate requests for information on authors and titles.

his work there was some feeling against the Board because they employed a man from the East to arrange and catalogue their library, in preference to one of our own citizens. This was quite natural, but if any trace of it now remains it is purely sectional and not personal to Mr. Evans, who has done his work in a very superior and thorough manner, both in his catalogue and the admirable arrangement of every detail of his office." [37]

Although the catalog was a good one for its day, Evans later regretted the time spent on this type of catalog and resolved never to print another one in the same manner.[38] Although he was unable to keep his resolution, he preferred small subject catalogs similar to those issued by the Boston Public Library. This first Indianapolis catalog was later supplemented by a list at the end of his first annual report plus two separate lists: one published in January, 1876, and another in January, 1878.

Pressed as he was to meet the demands for circulation of books already on hand, to classify the books already ordered, and to produce a good printed catalog, Charles Evans still found time to order additional books for the library. With such an enthusiastic response to the library, with the great number of people coming and going daily, and with the work which had to be done to get the catalog ready for publication, one can only be amazed that Evans still had time to collect books. However, the red-headed young man from Boston was well aware that book collecting is the fundamental reason that libraries exist and that without book resources to meet the recreational, informational, and research needs of the readers there would be no point in their coming to the library.

The books already acquired had been carefully selected. Evans himself stated that the volumes received from the Indianapolis Library Association had been chosen with discrimination.[39] Poole, with his twenty years of experience both in a private library and a large public library, had done well in naming the 8,000 basic works needed by a public library. The catalog which Evans published revealed a balanced selection of the literature of the day. Charles Darwin, one of the most controversial figures, was represented by six works and his friend T. H. Huxley by four. Henry Ward Beecher was listed with seven titles of which one title was an eight-volume

---

[37] Indianapolis *Evening News*, April 1, 1874, p. 4.
[38] Charles A. Cutter, "Library Catalogues," in *Public Libraries in the U.S.,* 1876, pp. 572, 574.
[39] I. P. L., *First Report, 1873–4,* p. 8.

set of his sermons. Bancroft's nine-volume history was included, as was C. F. Becker's twenty-volume *Weltgeschichte.* Von Ranke and Francis Lieber were both represented by several titles.

With almost 13,000 titles in the library at the end of the first year Indianapolis had made a good beginning. However, it was only a beginning and most of the items had been acquired before Evans arrived on the scene. What kind of materials did he think the library should add in substantial number? What were his goals for the public library of Indianapolis? The local citizens did not have to wait long for an answer. One of the earliest items to receive favorable publicity from the city newspapers was Evans' purchase of a rare pamphlet on the history of Vincennes, Indiana.[40] Not only intrinsically valuable for local historians but also an association item, the pamphlet had once belonged to General Winfield Scott. Stated the newspaper: "He has a great many such treasures there now, and manifests a genius for the collection of old prints which are of any value." Thus, very high among Evans' goals for the Indianapolis Public Library was a collection of source materials for the study of Indiana history. Doubtless this decision was an extension of his Athenaeum experience where he had learned to respect the source materials for historical research. All of Evans' actions during his first year as librarian bear out the fact that his intention was to make the library a depository for local history. On July 30, 1873, Charles Cox, local hardware dealer and book collector, gave the library 147 volumes, some dating as far back as 1740.[41] Included in the collection were fine editions of the British poets, essayists, and voyagers. However, more important for historical research were the first city directories of Indianapolis (1855) and Cincinnati (1819). The reporter quoted Evans as saying that he would welcome donations of books of any value from whatever source. He was especially interested in books or documents related to the city's history and encouraged other citizens to follow Cox's example. "A nucleus is now formed around which may be clustered a library of rare antique books which will eventually become of great value."

The second significant donation during the library's first year of operation came from the Reverend Elijah T. Fletcher and con-

---

[40] Newspaper clipping, from an unknown source but probably Indianapolis *Sentinel,* n.d., I. P. L., "Scrapbook."

[41] Newspaper clipping, Indianapolis *Sentinel,* July 30, 1873, I. P. L., "Scrapbook."

sisted of a variety of early Indianapolis and New York newspapers collected by his father. In commenting upon Fletcher's gift in his first annual report, Charles Evans again took the occasion to call public attention to the library's attempt to build a good local history collection: "I would like to mention, in this connection, the intention of the management to make the library the depository of everything in any way relating to the history of the city and the State, and would ask the cooperation of all friends of the library to assist them. No book or pamphlet, however trivial, can be of so little value as not to find a place in such a collection as it is our desire to make. At present there is no library in the State where the future historian can find his materials at hand." [42] The parallel between this statement of Evans and the statements of Poole on Civil War materials is striking. It shows that Evans had learned his historical lesson well and that he proceeded to put into practice Poole's ideas on historical collecting.

As an extension of his interest in building up a good collection of Indiana materials at the public library, Evans joined the Indiana Historical Society. This society had never been very active, and from its beginning in 1830 periodically some local citizen had to revive and reorganize the institution.[43] After a period of fourteen years of inactivity, the society was revived on October 8, 1873. Among the members attempting to reorganize the society and place it on a permanent footing was Judge A. L. Roache, a strong supporter of the library movement. At the second meeting held on November 26, 1873, Charles Evans stepped forward, signed the constitution, and became a member.

The society was more ambitious than realistic. After a few meetings the interest sagged and the organization again lay moribund until January 6, 1877. That Evans had not lost his interest in the meantime was demonstrated by his presence at the new meeting. On February 6, 1877, he was appointed a member of the executive committee whose function was to formulate a plan for promoting the society's interests. Apparently the executive committee could not overcome the inertia of the members, and, after a few meetings in 1877 and a meeting in 1879, the society again was inactive until its reorganization in 1886. Evans, therefore, did well to foster an in-

---

[42] I. P. L., *First Report, 1873–4*, p. 8; see also newspaper clipping, Indianapolis *Sentinel*, Feb. 27, 1874, I. P. L., "Scrapbook."

[43] Indiana Historical Society, *Publications*, no. 1: *Proceedings of the Indiana Historical Society, 1830–1886*, pp. 5–7.

terest in a center for source material on Indiana history at the public
library, for the Indiana Historical Society was incapable of achieving its high purposes during this period.

Yet the picture of Charles Evans as a librarian interested in historical matters must not be overdrawn, for he was well aware that
the majority of the citizens of Indianapolis cared little for scholarly
works. His vigorous defense of the purchase of fiction indicated
clearly his response to the public demand. However, he did try to
maintain a sense of proportion, always with the idea that if he could
only get the citizens to read anything they might later be enticed to
read more substantial works.

This balance which Evans tried to achieve in selecting library
materials can be clearly seen in the list of magazines for which the
library subscribed. During the first year the library received seventy-
one magazines regularly. Among these were journals to appeal to
all interests. For the professional men there were the *American
Chemist,* the *American Journal of Science,* and the *American Law
Review.* For the clergy and those religiously inclined the library
provided representative journals of the Baptists, Catholics, Metho-
dists, and Presbyterians. The high-brow literary magazines were
especially in evidence with such titles as the *Atlantic Monthly,
Blackwood's Magazine,* the *Edinburgh Review,* and the *North American Review.* For those with lighter tastes Evans provided *Frank
Leslie's Illustrated Paper, Godey's Lady's Book, Oliver Optic's Magazine, Punch,* and *St. Nicholas.*

The same kind of balance was sought in the purchase of new
books. During the infrequent meetings of the library committee,
Evans' list of books to be purchased were routinely approved. As
quickly as the new books were received, Evans processed them and
published their titles in the Indianapolis newspapers so that the
public would be informed. From architecture, with J. Fergusson's
history, to zoology, with the treatises of Agassiz, these lists of new
books revealed a good group of titles from all fields of learning.
Popular works included such titles as Jules Verne's *Twenty Thousand Leagues Under the Sea,* a best seller of the period, and T.
Gynne's *Nanette and Her Lover* and *The School for Dreamers.* For
the venturesome who really wanted to improve themselves the library provided F. M. Muller's *History of Ancient Sanskrit Literature!*

It was apparent from the further comment by the local newspapers that Evans' acquisition policy met with general approval. As a preface to one of the lists of books added in 1874, the editor remarked:

> Through the ceaseless watchfulness of Mr. Charles Evans, librarian of the public library, a copy of every valuable book is added to that admirable institution as soon as the volume issues from the press of the publisher. In this manner the patrons of the library have access to the very latest publications in the book line, and even the poorest may keep himself posted in passing events in the literary world, provided he have the time to read. The following comprises a list . . . of the latest additions to the library which will be found of value to those who patronize what is emphatically a popular institution.[44]

Further evidence of local newspaper approval of Evans' efforts during the first year occurred at the time of his first annual report. Both the *Sentinel* and the *Journal* printed the annual report in its entirety, except for the appendixes. In commenting upon the report, which covered the period from April 9, 1873, to April 9, 1874, the *Journal* noted that it showed a "thorough appreciation of the wants and scope of the library" on the part of Evans and presented a variety of facts in an interesting manner. Indianapolis could well be proud of her public library and her young librarian.

Evans' mentor, W. F. Poole, bestowed the real praise which warmed his heart. On May 19, 1874, Poole wrote Evans that he had just received a copy of his annual report. It was an excellent document which did him much credit. Evans had not only presented statistical data but had been suggestive and critical in his comments upon that data. Moreover, he had "treated some of the most controversial points in library management with good taste." Poole wanted Evans to be sure to send copies of the report to Dr. Hooper and F. E. Parker in Boston. When the former had been told that Evans was to become librarian at Indianapolis, he had looked up, almost under his spectacles, and asked Poole, "Do you think Charles is qualified to take charge of a library?" Upon Poole's prompt assurance that he was, Hooper stared at him in amazement and said, "I am very glad to know it." Both Hooper and Parker thought well of Evans, and they would be gratified to know that he had achieved so much. Poole closed with an accolade which would bring joy to any hard-working young man: "I congratulate you on your success."

Evans, the Boston import, could view his first year as librarian

---

[44] Newspaper clipping, Indianapolis *Sentinel*, March 14, 1874, I. P. L., "Scrapbook."

of the Indianapolis Public Library with great satisfaction. He had
made the library a very popular institution, as the number of registered borrowers and the circulation of books indicated. He had
cataloged and classified over 14,000 books and had published a
good catalog in order to make these volumes easily accessible to the
public. He had kept the public so well informed of the library's
activities that the tone of press opinion had slowly shifted in his
favor. For the future he had begun a collection of source materials
for the study of Indiana history. Just past his twenty-third birthday,
Charles Evans submitted to the board of school commissioners a
report in which many a senior librarian could have taken pride. The
ill winds of local prejudice had died down and the library had been
set on a proper course. With favorable currents to help him along,
Evans could guide the library into ever expanding horizons of usefulness.

Cheap Fiction and Conniving Politicians

4

In the 1870's Charles Evans was a handsome young man with tremendous energy and driving ambition. All the work of the first year or two in Indianapolis was not accomplished on an eight-hour day. As one of his Indianapolis friends later remarked, Evans always had "a poor appreciation of the necessity for sleep and other regular habits." [1] With the vigor of youth, however, Evans wanted to get on with the job.

Physically, Evans was tall, about five feet, eleven inches, in height. Of medium build he walked erect and not without a certain show of pride. He loved walking and his gait was brisk and sure. His outward manner was partly a conscious imitation of the New England men he so much admired and partly a concealment of an uncertain spirit which felt keenly the lack of proper family background and academic training. Sometimes his attempted reflection of the noble ideals of the Bostonians gave strangers the impression of arrogance and more than once was responsible for his serious trouble with the library's public.

The pictures of Evans during this period reveal him as serious, yet relaxed and at ease. His eyes were fixed and clear, but not in-

[1] The physical description of Evans came from a variety of sources. G. T. Porter to C. E., ALS, Dec. 3, 1910. Two photographs of Charles Evans at this period of his life exist. One, in Eliot Evans, "Scrapbook," and inscribed in Charles Evans' handwriting, "Nov. 1875," appears in this volume. The other is in the Evans Papers, has a Boston photographer's name on the back, and was probably made just before Evans left the Boston Athenaeum in 1872.

tense. On his daily walk to and from the public library he was observant of the various activities along his route. As he passed the Nicholson cottage on North Meridian Street, he sometimes saw small Meredith swinging on the wooden gate, from which position he gazed shyly at the passers-by. With a restraint which gave no hint that he saw the child, Evans walked on, but in later years, when both were members of the Indianapolis Literary Club, he recalled the scene vividly and in detail. Perhaps Evans saw a striking similarity between his own shyness and that of young Nicholson.

Charles Evans wore clothes typical of the period: a broad black neckcloth, with a low collar turned down over it, covered a white shirt with black studs. At other times he changed to a bow tie and wing-tip collars. His red hair, parted just slightly left of center, was combed back to both sides, a hair style he maintained throughout life. At least as late as November, 1875, he did not yet have the mustache which later would become the hallmark of the serious face of the scholar.

His manner, which ordinarily appeared distant to people whom he did not know, changed rapidly under the right conditions. For his friends there was always the quiet twinkle in his eyes, the good-natured anecdote to share, and the lively interest in their activities. Not that Charles Evans was ever essentially a gregarious person with a hearty slap on the back for anyone—his relations, even with those closest to him, often gave the appearance of restraint. Yet underneath ran the deep bond of understanding which made his Indianapolis companions friends for life. To those men who shared his interests in books and reading, he was an informative and helpful colleague.

The Farm and Trades School had instilled in Evans a love of the outdoors, and especially of boating. While there was little time for cultivating the outdoor life during his first years in Indianapolis, by the late 1870's his youthful vigor found expression in a weekly boating exercise with the Reverend Myron W. Reed, Pastor of the First Presbyterian Church and one of the most popular ministers in Indianapolis. They were sometimes accompanied by the latter's young sons. Reed's homely philosophy and knowledge of woodcraft appealed strongly to Evans. These outings with the parson and his boys usually ended with a picnic at a spot near Crown Hill where the young ladies of Henry Ward Beecher's church had once rolled their rotund pastor down its side. On such excursions the two men

Figure 1. Charles Evans at the age of sixty-eight.

Figure 2. The Boston Asylum and Farm School in 1858, from *Reports of the Superintendent and Teachers, January 12, 1958.*

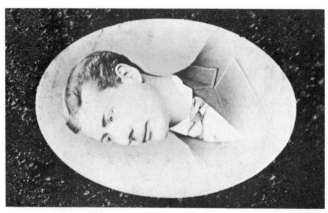

Figure 4. Charles Evans as a young man in Indianapolis, November, 1875.

Figure 3. The first building of the Indianapolis Public Library, 1873.

Figure 5. Family portrait made in Baltimore about 1888, including Mrs. Evans, Eliot Howland, Charles Evans, and Gertrude.

Figure 6. The Evans home at 1413 Pratt Boulevard, where Charles lived from August, 1898, until his death in 1935.

Figure 7. Samples of the halved three-by-five cards from which Charles Evans created his bibliography.

A PRIVATELY-PRINTED, SIGNED AND NUMBERED EDITION OF THE

AMERICAN BIBLIOGRAPHY

BY

CHARLES EVANS

A CHRONOLOGICAL DICTIONARY

OF ALL

BOOKS, PAMPHLETS and PERIODICAL PUBLICATIONS

PRINTED IN THE

UNITED STATES OF AMERICA

FROM THE GENESIS OF PRINTING IN 1639

DOWN TO AND INCLUDING THE YEAR 1820

WITH BIBLIOGRAPHICAL AND BIOGRAPHICAL NOTES

Volume I

1639 - 1740

* * * HERE'S THE BOOK I SOUGHT FOR SO.—SHAKESPEARE.

THE PUIR MAN THAT HAS PATIENCE TO MAK' A BUIK, HAS SOME CLAIM TO THE PATIENCE O' HIM WHA ONLY READS IT.—ELIOT WARBURTON.

PRINTED FOR THE AUTHOR

MDCCCCII

Figure 8. Title page of the prospectus announcing that volume one of the *American Bibliography* would soon appear.

Figure 9. The *American Bibliography* of Charles Evans, volume one open to page 1.

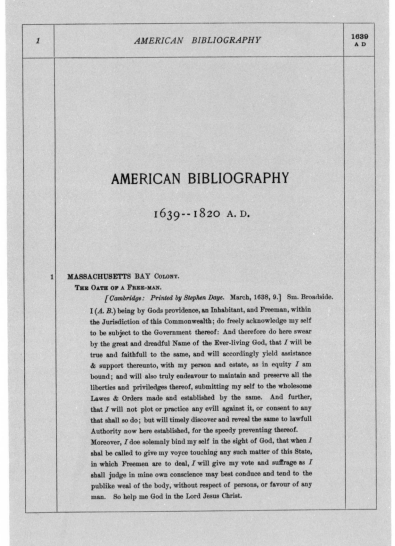

AMERICAN BIBLIOGRAPHY

1639--1820 A. D.

1   MASSACHUSETTS BAY COLONY.
     THE OATH OF A FREE-MAN.
        [Cambridge: Printed by Stephen Daye. March, 1638, 9.]   Sm. Broadside.

     I (*A. B.*) being by Gods providence, an Inhabitant, and Freeman, within the Jurisdiction of this Commonwealth; do freely acknowledge my self to be subject to the Government thereof: And therefore do here swear by the great and dreadful Name of the Ever-living God, that *I* will be true and faithfull to the same, and will accordingly yield assistance & support thereunto, with my person and estate, as in equity *I* am bound; and will also truly endeavour to maintain and preserve all the liberties and priviledges thereof, submitting my self to the wholesome Lawes & Orders made and established by the same. And further, that *I* will not plot or practice any evill against it, or consent to any that shall so do; but will timely discover and reveal the same to lawfull Authority now here established, for the speedy preventing thereof.

     Moreover, *I* doe solemnly bind my self in the sight of God, that when *I* shal be called to give my voyce touching any such matter of this State, in which Freemen are to deal, *I* will give my vote and suffrage as *I* shall judge in mine own conscience may best conduce and tend to the publike weal of the body, without respect of persons, or favour of any man. So help me God in the Lord Jesus Christ.

Figure 10. American Bibliography, volume one, page 1, showing the number
1 item in Americana, "The Oath of a Free-man."

threw off the restraints of pulpit and library and again became boys, each with a boy's enjoyment of the freedom of the rolling meadows and woods.

At least part of the time Evans roomed with a young clerk, Fred J. Shepard. The two were members of a young group of bachelors who frequently dined together and called themselves alternately the Idiot Club and the Centennial Etiquette Club of America.[2] The club was a democratic gathering, including not only Shepard, a college graduate, and Evans, the city's public librarian, but also a member of a fire engine company and an aspiring young painter whom the group called "The Viking" because of his marine paintings. Possibly it was with this group that Evans celebrated his twenty-fifth birthday in November, 1875. In honor of such a festive occasion, his friends had presented Charlie with a bottle of good wine, which, on the day following, left no headache but rather a feeling of exhilaration. While this birthday indulgence was not typical, it did indicate that Evans could occasionally relax and enjoy himself with young bloods of his own age.

The most pressing professional problem facing young Evans at the beginning of his second year in Indianapolis was the problem of space. From the first week it had been apparent that the library was inadequately housed, for reading-room space had never been equal to the demands placed upon it. While many citizens undoubtedly thought that this was a temporary problem which would vanish once the novelty of the institution had worn off, the pressure on the public library continued to grow. Perhaps no one could have foreseen the results of Evans' tremendous energy: the well-organized book collections, the steady stream of borrowers, and the increasing public interest. By the end of the first year the need for more space had become critical. Seeking ways to meet this need occupied the time and attention of the librarian and the library committee for the next eighteen months.

In an editorial in March, 1874, the *Sentinel*, Evans' early and consistent supporter, urged Indianapolis to do something about a new library building.[3] With Cincinnati's recent completion of a

---

[2] Fred J. Shepard to C. E., ALS, Feb. 7 and April 18, 1897; G. E. Channing to C. E., ALS, Dec. 14, 1875. Other descriptive material comes from Charles Evans, "Looking Backward," Indianapolis *News*, Jan. 15, 1927. The address was printed in full under the headline, "Fifty Years of Literary Club History Recalled by Founder," and separate copies were printed on good paper.

[3] Newspaper clipping, Indianapolis *Sentinel*, March 1, 1874, in I. P. L., "Scrapbook."

new edifice, all citizens ought to be made aware of their own library's deficiencies. It was common knowledge that the current library rooms were too small, ill heated, and poorly ventilated. The number of people using the library facilities had increased to such an extent that one frequently found every chair occupied and readers standing along the walls. If the library's usefulness were not to be circumscribed, then adequate quarters had to be provided.

The editorial brought forth a variety of proposals both for renting additional property and for building a new library. Some hoped that a wealthy and public-spirited citizen might be persuaded to donate funds for a "suitable hall that will be an ornament to the city." As the interest grew, a number of people with business property, private residences, and old church buildings for sale attempted to influence the board in the direction of their real estate. Thus began a struggle which grew increasingly bitter as personalities became emotionally involved and political groups took offense when their choices were slighted.

The wrangle over a site continued throughout the summer and early fall. Not until November did the library committee announce its choice: purchase of the Sentinel Building from the Indianapolis Hall Company for $125,000.[4]

The report of the library committee raised a storm of protest among many people. Heated debates took place in the meetings of the school board and the city council. Some of Evans' close friends entered strong protests against the action. John D. Howland, respected Federal Court clerk, wanted the city to build a new library building and not spend money on a dilapidated structure which had been "wretchedly built" in the beginning. Strong as Howland's comments were, they received warm approval while other citizens spoke out even more vehemently about this "unwise and inexpedient" use of tax funds. Before the fray ended, three of the five members of the citizens' advisory committee had gone on record publicly against the purchase.[5] Such an excitable atmosphere was scarcely conducive to a reasonable examination of library sites. Unwilling to complete the deal in the face of such opposition, the committee postponed action for another six months.

In July, 1875, the board of school commissioners again took up

---

[4] Newspaper clipping, Indianapolis *Sentinel,* Nov. 7, 1874, I. P. L., "Scrapbook." The entire report, dated November 2, 1874, is reproduced in this clipping.

[5] Newspaper clipping, Indianapolis *Sentinel,* Nov. 20, 1874, I. P. L., "Scrapbook."

the matter with a determination to settle it once and for all. This time neither the combined efforts of public opinion nor the voices of all the newspapers in the city could stay them from entering a lease agreement for the Sentinel Building. The taunts in the newspapers, one of which became almost hysterical over the proposal, would have wounded far less sensitive men than those who controlled the school board. While the charges that the commissioners had been motivated by pecuniary interests incensed them, they could not stop the continual attacks upon the decision as the most foolish the board could have made.

This acrimonious debate could not help having an unfavorable effect upon Evans' conduct of the library. Two of his earliest friends, doctors H. G. Carey and T. B. Elliott, had left the board of school commissioners in July, 1874, although Carey was immediately appointed a member of the citizens' advisory committee. The attack upon the school board by one of the city's most partisan newspapers, the *Journal,* was definitely not to the library's advantage. While it is not easy to connect Evans directly with the opposition of the *Journal,* it is certain that he opposed the selection of the Sentinel Building. He was in good company, for his position reflected the opposition of all the city's newspapers. This circumstance probably insured that there would be no publication of criticism of Evans' own views. However, the mere fact of opposition was not likely to endear him to a school board which had its back to the wall and still rejected the overwhelming opinion of the public. Evans was known to be a Republican, a fact in which he took considerable pride. While all the newspapers opposed the board's choice, the opposition had been led by the *Journal,* the leading Republican paper in the state. Any man who has been deeply hurt, rightly or wrongly, is apt to make an association of all those in the opposite camp, whatever their degree of opposition. There were strong political cross fires in Indianapolis in 1875. Years later Evans himself spoke of the high political feeling by saying that when children were born in Indianapolis they were brought up in the political belief of their parents as surely as they were nurtured in their parents' faith.[6] So evenly divided were the two groups that one could forecast the results of an election by noting which party had produced the most children twenty-one years before. The men who had been most vigorously attacked by the *Journal* were Democrats. Austin H.

---

[6] Charles Evans, "Looking Backward."

Brown, local Democratic chieftain, had come in for especially severe criticism. The political current in Indianapolis in the 1870's was no place for the politically unskilled. Whether or not Evans personally antagonized these men at the time is not clear, but it is worth noting that Austin H. Brown later led the movement for Evans' dismissal and was aided in his maneuver by others who had borne the brunt of the *Journal's* attacks.

The contract which the board had signed with the owner of the Sentinel Building called for occupancy of the building within eighty days. After promised improvements to the building proceeded more slowly than anyone had foreseen, the board of school commissioners expressed dissatisfaction with the contractor's failure to meet the deadline.[7] Since the building was already forty-five days behind schedule in early December, the board adopted a resolution to notify the owner that an abandonment of the lease was justifiable.

The board's resolution apparently spurred the owner to renewed activity, for the newspapers announced in late December that the public library rooms were nearly ready. Though some unhappiness over the location lingered in the minds of those controlling the newspapers, there was a tendency to be as generous as conditions permitted and to hail the opening of enlarged quarters. However, even the relatively dignified *Evening News,* which had not stooped to the invective of the other newspapers during July, could not resist referring to the new library rooms as "Cockroach Hall."

When the public library opened in its new quarters in early January, 1876, the *Sentinel,* an early and continuous supporter of Evans despite their political differences, used the occasion to write a history of the public library and to point out the even better service to be expected in the future. Of Evans' three years as chief administrator of the library the *Sentinel* reporter said: "The success of the library is largely due to the librarian, Mr. Evans, whose courtesy, patience, and kindness in assisting teachers, authors, reporters and others seeking information is unlimited, whose taste in selecting is discriminating and admirable, and whose management of everything pertaining to the library is most excellent. To him and his courteous assistants . . . the thanks of the public and of the writer are many times due."[8] Charles Evans was entering

---

[7] Indianapolis *Evening News,* Dec. 4, 1875, p. 2.
[8] Newspaper clipping, Indianapolis *Sentinel,* Jan. 2, 1876, I. P. L., "Scrapbook."

his fourth year as librarian of the Indianapolis Public Library with the general approval of the local citizens.

Whatever Evans' doubts about the wisdom of renting the Sentinel Building, he prepared to make full use of the expanded facilities which it afforded. During the two years in which a new location had been under consideration, he had continued to build upon the solid foundation he established the first year. Reports of the library committee indicate monthly purchases of American books with less frequent but substantial purchases of books published in England, France, and Germany. The acquisitions policy certainly did not slow down for lack of space nor lack of time on the part of the librarian during this period of planning.

As a part of his acquisitions policy, Evans was very conscious of the necessity for complete files of journals or newspapers. The committee had approved a purchase of a file of the Cincinnati *Commercial* in April, 1874, and just prior to the move, in October, 1875, had approved purchase of a file of the *North American Review*. Also before the move to the Sentinel Building the library had received a significant gift of newspapers. Mayor John Caven had given the library 264 volumes embracing nearly every daily and weekly newspaper published in the city. Interestingly enough, these volumes completed the file of newspapers which Fletcher had given earlier, so that the Indianapolis Public Library now had a complete collection of local newspapers.

While Evans was primarily interested in newspapers as a source of local history, he also promoted their acquisition for current reading. The expanded quarters provided space for a newspaper reading room, and subscriptions were entered for forty newspapers, both American and foreign. The newspaper reading room was opened on February 2, 1876, and continued for two years. For a variety of reasons it was closed in February, 1878, "much to the regret of its frequenters." [9] Some of the reasons for discontinuing this part of the library's activities are indicated by Evans in his second report covering the years 1874–78. Administration of the reading room had been difficult and its usefulness doubtful. Nearly all of the newspapers in great demand had been local newspapers, with few patrons reading either other American or European newspapers.

[9] Indianapolis *News*, Feb. 16, 1878, p. 3. The *Evening News* dropped "Evening" from its masthead on May 9, 1876, and became simply the Indianapolis *News*.

Theft and abuse were common since no user felt a responsibility for these papers as did the users of proprietary libraries which had large and well-supplied newspaper reading rooms. The tendency for such a room to become the daily resort of the idle and vicious raised serious questions, and Evans doubted the wisdom of establishing newspaper reading rooms in public libraries with limited incomes. Since legal counsel believed library funds could not be used in this instance, the committee thought that the money spent on the newspaper room could be more judiciously expended for additions to the general collection, and therefore ordered the room closed.

Evans' consistent program of acquisitions and solicitation of gifts resulted in expanded resources for the library. By April, 1876, the number of volumes in the library had grown to 27,290, plus 2,241 pamphlets. Evans was proud of his collection of local newspapers, city, state, and federal documents. From the first he had hounded the local Congressmen for copies of federal documents, especially the Patent Office Reports. To those who questioned the value of the latter he said:

> That the documentary literature of the country is now but seldom used, and by many considered of little value, does not, in the least, determine its worth in the future or furnish any criterion upon which to base an estimate of its importance to the student fifty or a hundred years hence. The degree of rarity to which this class of literature will attain in a few years, is a matter of astonishment to those who know how freely it has been distributed; and, perhaps, no better antidote could be given to those who are in the habit of turning over to . . . little ones an illustrated volume of the Patent Office Reports . . . than to bend their energies for a couple of years toward an attempt to secure an early volume of the same. It, therefore, becomes a matter of great importance that this fleeting literature should be carefully collected and preserved while it can be had.[10]

Such a clear and concise statement of the problem of collecting research materials would do credit to any acquisitions librarian in a modern university library—it is remarkable that it should have come at a time when many did not recognize the value of this type of publication and from a young man of twenty-eight who had not known the discipline of research training. Yet here again, as in the case of the local historical materials, Evans had learned valuable lessons in the Athenaeum. Both from the records of items added to the library and the occasional newspaper publicity on a rare gift,

---

[10] Indianapolis Public Library, *The Second Report of the Public Library of Indianapolis, 1874–8* (Indianapolis: Issued by the Library, 1878), pp. 3–4.

Evans' excellent job in collecting materials which would be of use to the future scholar is revealed.

Meanwhile the circulation continued to expand. Each year saw a higher total circulation than the year before. Not only did the total go up, but the quality also increased. The 1878 report showed that the percentage of circulation in the humanities and social sciences had doubled during the four-year period.[11] Though this increase in percentage was cause enough for praise, Evans was even more interested in calling attention to the injustice of ignoring the meaning of the total circulation. He had frequently been taken to task by some irate citizen who complained of the trashy novels in the library, but Evans always maintained that he did not buy trashy novels. He did add weak ones which served the purpose for which they were intended. Nor was Evans alone in his defense of fiction purchases; the editor of the leading newspaper in the city, the *Evening News,* twice printed lengthy editorials in defense of fiction reading.[12] However, Evans' statistics for 1874–78 provided additional ammunition to fire at his critics. It was a matter of congratulation that over 8,000 volumes in the department of arts and sciences, over 5,000 volumes of travel, and over 12,000 volumes of historical and biographical works had been taken into homes and read in the year 1877–78 alone! How many of these titles would even have been known to the citizens if the public library had not been in existence? To Evans the meaning was obvious: whatever its faults, the public library provided for Indianapolis citizens an opportunity for intellectual growth which would not be provided by any other agency.

Administering the collection in line with what he believed to be the best practice for all, Evans ran into difficulty during the early months of occupancy of the new building. He tightened up the rules for the reading room, making a special attempt to reduce the noise. Moreover, all magazines and books had thenceforth to be requested by means of call slips which provided space for the number and letter of books and the applicant's name and residence. They had been designed to lessen the labor of the attendants, who were often asked to recommend some good book, and also to educate the applicants in the proper use of the catalog. Evans hoped that those who consulted the catalog would be surprised and

---

[11] *Ibid.,* p. 9.
[12] Indianapolis *Evening News,* Feb. 16, 1876, p. 2; Indianapolis *News,* July 7, 1877, p. 2.

delighted to find that there were other authors than Mrs. South-worth and Mrs. Holmes. The rules had been framed simply and he anticipated no difficulty in their administration.

The change, however, provided many users an opportunity to vent their indignation at a variety of abuses both real and imagined. The necessity for using the catalog, though it had been in existence for over two years, called forth comments on the "enigmatical Bostonian catalogue," while the call slips themselves were noted as "red tape in the library" where one had to give a personal history to secure a book. One enterprising gentleman even composed a poem on "How to Get a Book from the Public Librari." [13] The poorer class of novels received their full share of criticism at this time. Moreover, the attendants, previously models of courtesy, had reportedly become uncooperative and inattentive to the wishes of the patrons. Such criticisms flowed freely during the first six months of 1876. Even the *Journal* called the new regulations "too ponderous." There must have been times when Evans wondered if the library had not been more comfortable in the crowded little rooms in the high school building.

However, if Evans' policies had their critics, they also had their defenders. Several of Evans' friends pointed out the inefficiency of the previous mode of calling for books when patrons "were obliged to stand four or five deep waiting for each other to draw books." The new system saved time for the patron and was the proper way of administering a library.

One of his pseudonymous defenders thought that the lower class of fiction neither vitiated the taste of the reader nor barred him forever from enjoying better literature. His own experience, he noted, had been just the opposite, and comparable to that of nearly all of his school companions who had dropped their earlier reading of fiction for more solid material as they grew older. "Nearly all of us, I know, used to be fascinated with such books as Oliver Optic's, and at the time they used to be a great delight to us, but now we hardly so much as glance at the titles of his works. Pardon the egotism, but though we have delighted in these works once, and I am sorry to say even reveled in dime novels occasionally, I do not think our tastes are now 'vitiated.' " [14]

---

[13] Newspaper clippings, Indianapolis *Sentinel*, probably about April 2, 1876; Indianapolis *Journal*, probably June 27 or 28, 1876; I. P. L., "Scrapbook."

[14] Newspaper clipping, Indianapolis *Journal*, June 30, 1876. This letter answered "Is the Public Library a Public Benefit?" which appeared in the

This statement was merely a repetition of Evans' contention: those who read works of fiction now would subsequently be led to read more solid material. This was a part of the function of the public library. Baldly stated, the public library drew the populace through the provision of weak, though harmless, fiction and hoped that once the patron began reading novels he would come into contact with other forms of literature and be challenged to develop himself on a higher level. After the people became accustomed to the new rules, the criticisms died down, and only an occasional letter expressed unhappiness over the way the library was managed.

As an administrator Charles Evans did his best to provide competent service at the lowest possible cost. In the document submitting Evans' four-year report to the board of school commissioners, the library committee included a table showing the comparative cost of circulation per volume. Though the table included cost of service in the reading and periodical room as well as in book use, the cost per volume was computed only on those which circulated for home use. As the circulation figures rose during the four-year period, the cost per volume decreased. In 1874–75 the cost had been $3.43, whereas in 1877–78 it had been reduced to $2.42. In providing service at this low cost, Evans was well aware that the competence of experienced staff members made this efficiency possible, and consequently he urged the rewarding of good work by salary increases.[15] In 1874 he had succeeded in having the salaries of his day assistants raised to $500 per year.[16] One year later the salaries of his three chief assistants were raised to $600 per year. With a program of gradual increases and a relatively stable staff Evans was working toward the kind of personnel situation which could eventually be highly beneficial to the library. He had managed to equate the salaries of his assistants roughly with those of public school teachers. Unfortunately for Evans and for his library, America had entered a period of recession in November, 1873. Although Indianapolis did not begin to feel the financial pinch until 1875, city officials, with the exception of the school board, had been resorting for several years to deficit financing. By the spring of 1876 drastic economies had become an absolute neces-

---

Indianapolis *Journal*, probably June 27 or 28, 1876. Both clippings are in I. P. L., "Scrapbook."

[15] I. P. L., *Second Report, 1874–8*, p. 18.

[16] I. P. L., "Library Reports," I, entry for July 13, 1874, and August 10, 1875, I. P. L. Archives.

sity. Although the tax levy had remained the same, property assessments had dropped; and in May the school board in a general program of retrenchment recommended that the library committee reduce salaries according to the following schedule: [17]

Librarian	$1,200
1st Assistant	550
2nd Assistant	500
3rd Assistant	500
4th Assistant	500
Attendant	400

Since Evans had been raised to $1,500 per year only the previous year, he was not happy about the proposed reduction. At the time the library committee recommended a raise in pay, in May, 1875, six of the members had signed a letter testifying to his good work as librarian: "We bear testimony to the superior qualifications, great industry and careful attention to duty of that officer, and believe the present compensation entirely disproportionate to the services rendered the public and that the proposed salary as compared with that in other cities, is not high." [18] On June 29, 1876, the question of the proposed reduction came before the library committee. Evans not only requested that his salary not be reduced but also presented no recommendations for other reductions for the staff. At about the same time John Holliday, editor of the *Evening News* and a man who had continually fought deficit financing schemes, came to Evans' defense.[19] In an editorial which pointed out that cutting a salary is not always an economy, Holliday noted that Charles Evans had performed his work in an admirable manner and ought to be made to feel that he had a future in Indianapolis. The board of school commissioners should remember that reading people regarded Evans as "one of the most valuable public agents connected with the interests of education in this city." Rather than

---

[17] Indianapolis Board of School Commissioners, "Minute Record Book," entry for May 5, 1876. Microfilm copy in I. P. L. Cited hereafter as Indianapolis School Board, "Minutes."

[18] *Ibid.*, entry for May 21, 1875. The letter was presented at this meeting and the recommendation that Evans' salary be raised to $1,500 per year to date from January 1, 1875, was adopted.

[19] Holliday's editorial must have sounded strange to his readers. Here was an editor inflamed with a passion for reduction of city expenditures, yet recommending an increase in a city salary. The key to Holliday's position is found in the opening sentence of his editorial "cutting down a salary is not always economy. With regard to the librarian of the city library we think this is notably true." Indianapolis *News*, June 2, 1876, p. 2.

giving a decrease, the board ought to see to it that Evans received an increase at the earliest possible moment.

Holliday's plea and that of Evans were of little avail. The school board cut the salaries, though the library committee was not content that Evans' own salary should stay at the $1,200 mark. Less than six months later, at the urging of the committee, the school board increased Evans' salary to $1,350 beginning January 1, 1877.

Evans' second report gave full credit for much of the success of the library to the intelligent and faithful service of the assistants. He had managed to keep his first assistant from the beginning to April 5, 1877, when she submitted her resignation. In accepting her resignation, Evans made special mention of her conscientious attention to duty during her employment. He noted that all the assistants had responded with cheerful alacrity to the many demands made upon them, and all merited and deserved recognition from the board in the form of an increase in the small salaries they were then receiving.

Although not all citizens agreed on the alacrity and cheerfulness with which the assistants performed their duties, there seems little reason to question Evans' general evaluation. There will always be patrons who take offense at something, and no assistant always performs at the peak of his or her efficiency. On the whole Evans had a devoted group of assistants who worked hard to help make the Indianapolis Public Library a success. As a good administrator, he had trained them carefully, and by his efforts to provide adequate compensation for their work he instilled in them a strong personal loyalty. Upon his dismissal from the librarianship in 1878, his assistants wrote a very warm letter of appreciation for his efforts in their behalf.

Evans' concept of public relations was largely limited to familiarizing the public through the local newspapers with what was in the library. Much of the information which Evans released to the newspapers could also be found in the catalog and the supplements which he issued. However, Evans recognized the limitations on these latter sources, and he therefore published his acquisitions lists regularly. In January, 1877, he began a new program through the courtesy of the *Journal*. He proposed occasionally to give brief notes of the library holdings in the areas of history, biographies, and any other topics which might be suggested by correspondents. Such notes would enable parents and teachers to direct their children's reading properly and to "obtain for themselves the full benefit of the 'People's College.' " Using as a basis the catalogs of other libraries, especially those of the Boston Public Library, Evans' first list grouped English history by chronological period, and in narrative essay fashion he commented upon the various titles of interest.

As a matter of general interest to their readers, all newspapers occasionally published articles on the Indianapolis Public Library, plus the usual letters to the editor either praising or damning its management. Evans was the subject of a number of interviews, and he was never hesitant about giving his views on library problems or reading in general. Typical of his comments to reporters was the one about a copy of Maurice Thompson's *Hoosier Mosaics,* which the reporter saw on the shelves. With complete candor Evans pronounced it sickly trash and agreed with the author in regretting that it had ever been published. However, it had been placed in the library as a "frightful example to all ambitious book makers endowed with more zeal than genius." [20] Always, though, Evans pointed with considerable pride to the consistent trend toward better reading during his six years in Indianapolis. The general tone of most articles was favorable, and if the reporter could not resist an occasional dig at some minor error, after all he was looking for material which would prick the interest of the reader. On the whole, Evans had every right to be pleased with his treatment by the city's newspapers.

Evans had an opportunity to become very well acquainted with several of the local journalists and newspaper editors after the establishment of the Indianapolis Literary Club in January, 1877. The object of this club, soon to become the most prestigious in Indianapolis, was to promote "social, literary, and aesthetic culture." As the third such organization in the Midwest, it followed a pattern established first by the Literary Club of Cincinnati and later followed by the Chicago Literary Club. In the founding of this institution Poole's influence on Evans was again pronounced. Evans had visited Poole in Cincinnati and had been impressed by a meeting of the Literary Club in that city. "The distinguished company . . . the delightful informality, and good fellowship; the ability of the essayist, and the interesting discussion, all made of it a memorable

---

[20] Newspaper clipping, probably Indianapolis *Journal,* Jan., 1876, I. P. L., "Scrapbook."

evening." [21] After Poole had moved to Chicago in 1874 to become the librarian of the Chicago Public Library, he had promoted a club there patterned after the one in Cincinnati. The Chicago club was an immediate success, and Evans, viewing Poole's efforts from a distance, wanted to organize a similar venture in Indianapolis. As early as November 16, 1874, he wrote to Poole about his thought of promoting a literary club. Would Poole be so kind as to send him a copy of the Cincinnati constitution? Poole heartily approved of Evans' idea and told him he would write to Cincinnati for a copy. He wished Evans every success in his Indianapolis efforts.

For some reason Evans' plans did not come to immediate fruition. Another three years passed before the Indianapolis Literary Club was organized. In either late December, 1876, or early January, 1877, Evans talked with his good friend John D. Howland about a literary club for Indianapolis. Howland was enthusiastic about the plan and urged Evans to contact about a dozen other men who might be interested in such an organization. Invitations were promptly dispatched and on January 10, 1877, six men met in the library of the Howland home to consider the formation of the Indianapolis Literary Club. Charles Evans, remembering the event fifty years later, recalled that all had been captivated by the idea and its promise. There had been much pleasant raillery when the six discussed who would be their Dr. Johnson, their Goldsmith, Burke, Reynolds, and other literary counterparts. On one point all were agreed: Charles Evans would be their Boswell, "the little tin can tied to the big dog's tail." He was promptly designated the first secretary of the new organization.

These six men invited eleven others to join them as charter members. On January 20, 1877, they met to draw up a constitution and plan a schedule of exercises. There was general agreement that club

---

[21] Charles Evans, "Looking Backward," states that the Indianapolis Literary Club and the Indianapolis Public Library were the second of the three great literary institutions established in the West. Evans apparently did not remember very well the dates of the literary clubs. The Literary Club of Cincinnati was organized October 29, 1849, and the Chicago Literary Club, March 4, 1874. Technically Evans was also incorrect on the dates of the public libraries: Cincinnati Public Library opened to the public in July, 1856, Chicago Public Library opened to the public on January 1, 1873, and Indianapolis Public Library opened to the public on April 9, 1873. While it is true that the Chicago Public Library did not achieve prominence until Poole went there January 2, 1874, it still predates Indianapolis. Therefore both literary club and public library in Indianapolis must be placed third in any mention with the previous two.

business was to be kept to a minimum so that the informality of the gathering would be maintained. Meeting every Saturday, the club quickly settled into a routine whereby a member would read a paper, deliver a talk, or lead a conversation on something that he had read recently. After the member had finished his remarks, the president would then invite comment from the other members. The comments would continue for another hour, after which the president would declare the meeting "informal," whereupon the discussion might continue indefinitely into the night.

Duties of the secretary were not onerous. Although required to keep a record of attendance, he performed this duty as unobtrusively as possible. When the club voted to admit new members, the secretary had to collect the ballots. While he was given the pleasant duty of informing new members of their election, he was spared the embarrassment of notifying those who were not elected, this chore being given to some other club member. Another duty was keeping the minutes, and Evans' records were models of neatness and accuracy. The secretary was also supposed to keep members informed of their appointments—"to bring them to the club willing or not, and when the case was hopeless, to find a substitute." Evans' zeal in keeping the members informed was so great during the early days that he was known as "the postal card fiend." [22]

Another responsibility of the secretary was to procure cigars for the club's meetings. In order to facilitate the informality of the weekly assembly, the club had provided for the cigars to be paid for out of the club treasury. One of Evans' successors, T. L. Sewall, reported that Evans himself had been a "slave to that kind of immorality known as the tobacco habit; the single blemish on an otherwise fair character." [23] However, his lot in selecting cigars for the fastidious tastes of the club members was "not a happy one." One week he would be damned by those whose "depraved appetites demanded strength," while the following week he would receive the curses of those who clamored for mildness.

While Evans had been the major force behind the club's organization, he was content to let others enjoy the limelight. Not one of the most voluble members, he nonetheless thoroughly enjoyed

[22] Theodore L. Sewall, *The Club's Secretaries. Toast Delivered on the Tenth Anniversary of the Club, Monday Evening, January 10, 1887* (Indianapolis: Indianapolis Literary Club, 1887), gives a complete description of the duties and performance of the club's secretaries.

[23] *Ibid.*, p. 3.

the club's meetings. In later years he compared other social gatherings which he attended as a visitor either favorably or unfavorably to the pleasant meetings of the Indianapolis Literary Club. Always interested in the club and its activities, he addressed both the twenty-eighth and fiftieth anniversary celebrations. On the latter occasion he spoke with great pleasure of the early meetings of the club, noting that they had been carefully planned and well attended. With particular relish he recalled one meeting when a violent storm had reduced the attendance to the secretary and the essayist for the evening. Over their cigars they discussed the situation. The essayist felt strongly that his paper should be delivered since he had devoted considerable time to its preparation and the meeting had been well advertised. Therefore he called upon the secretary as the only officer present to open the meeting. The secretary, not in the mood for a lengthy speech, suggested that the reading be deferred to another evening. Upon the essayist's insistence the secretary arose and addressed the empty chairs with a motion "that an emergency having arisen in which the peace of mind, if not the life even of the Secretary was in danger, that leave be given the essayist to print his paper at his own expense; and declared the motion unanimously carried—the Essayist not voting." [24] Since the meeting was officially still open the essayist took the floor and, in order that the records would show him present, moved that a vote of thanks be tended the secretary for attending the meeting. The essayist's motion was also unanimously carried with the secretary modestly not voting. After this parliamentary maneuver the secretary moved that the club adjourn; this motion also carried unanimously with both essayist and secretary voting. "And the entire Club, arm in arm, went out in the storm to their homes, mutually pleased with themselves and each other."

Evans also recalled with pleasure his association with other prominent men of Indianapolis who had contributed much to state and national life: Addison C. Harris, brilliant lawyer and later "ambassador to the proudest court in Europe"; Albert G. Porter, "governor, statesman, diplomat"; Walter Q. Gresham, "brilliant soldier, jurist, statesman"; and William P. Fishback, "a man of wide reading and culture, with a singularly active and retentive mind, who could always be depended upon to enliven the discussions with interesting comments from his fund of knowledge." Their con-

[24] Charles Evans, "Looking Backward."

tributions to the interesting and beneficial companionship of the club had reflected the brilliant talents which they had so generously given to public life.

In remembering his friend Walter Q. Gresham, Evans noted that it was customary at the conclusion of the regular club exercises for the members to draw up their chairs in congenial groups. Over their cigars they would then relax into a mood generating many good stories and fond reminiscences. At the end of the evening, when the secretary took a last look around the room before turning out the lights, he could always tell which chair Judge Gresham had occupied because it had the largest circle of chairs around it.

Charles Evans, then, found in the club interesting companionship with the leading Indianapolis citizens. How much he participated in the other social life of Indianapolis before the formation of the club is unknown, although his association with the group of young bachelors undoubtedly occurred much earlier. From the photographs of young ladies of Indianapolis in the Evans family papers, he apparently did not lack feminine companionship. What other social life he enjoyed is not revealed, but there were occasional invitations to a military ball, a musical event, or pleasant evenings with men like the Reverend Mr. Edson. However, all earlier social events were overshadowed by the Indianapolis Literary Club, and that organization gave him his fondest memories of the city.

During the first two years of the club's life Evans read the following papers: "Manners in Literature," "The Cincinnati Literary Club," and "An Evening with Dr. Johnson," in addition to which he also lead conversation on "Fasting and Visions." Only the manuscript of "An Evening with Dr. Johnson" survives in the family papers. The essay is a well-prepared discussion of the individuals who comprised the literary club which met in Sir Joshua Reynolds' back parlor in the middle of the eighteenth century. In his introduction Evans stated that if he could personally have chosen the time, place, and persons, he would have chosen to be one of this company rather than of any other about which he had read in literature. His paper recreated the eighteenth-century scene in vivid fashion and indicated considerable knowledge of the period.

Charles Evans' efforts to put the Indianapolis Public Library on the map had not gone unnoticed on the national scene. Again Poole's interest and encouragement accounted for the reputation

Evans gained nationally. However, Poole was not solely responsible. Dissemination of Evans' library reports and the catalog called attention to the good work he was doing in Indianapolis, and there were always his old friends in Boston to keep his name alive in that area. In the early spring, 1876, when the twenty-eight librarians issued a formal printed call for a national conference of librarians, Charles Evans' name was on the list. Before the call had been issued, when Frederick Leypoldt of the *Publishers' Weekly* had written to Evans about the idea, Evans had responded enthusiastically in a telegram which read, "Excellent idea. Add my name and depend upon my attendance." [25]

Melvil Dewey, chief figure behind the move for the Philadelphia conference, was in communication with many librarians, who were urged to contact him directly. Never bashful about making suggestions via letter, Evans proposed on June 24, 1876, that the committee on arrangements should be composed of Justin Winsor, Librarian of the Boston Public Library; William F. Poole, Librarian of the Chicago Public Library; and Lloyd P. Smith, Librarian of the Library Company of Philadelphia. Of Smith he noted, "the latter is jolly, companionable, and at *home.*" The other two librarians he suggested for the obvious reasons that their names would carry weight among librarians throughout the country. Although his mentor Poole was at first reluctant to accept because he was so far removed from the scene of preparations, he eventually yielded and the committee suggested by Evans was appointed.

Poole in turn urged Evans to read a paper at the conference, a suggestion which Dewey seconded. Upon Evans' return from an eastern vacation he wrote Dewey that he would lead a discussion on the subject, "The Sizes of Printed Books." To modern readers, who almost totally ignore the note on the catalog card which indicates the size, the subject appears trivial. However, in 1876 the problem of how to indicate the sizes of books was a subject of much interest to librarians. Standard library practice consisted in ascertaining the binder's fold of the sheet and counting the number of leaves from signature to signature to determine whether the volume was a quarto, folio, or octavo. In the interest of speed and economy in cataloging, many believed that this time-consuming practice should be abandoned. It might still be necessary to de-

---

[25] C. E. to F. Leypoldt, telegram, May 18, 1876, in "1876 Scrapbook," A. L. A. Archives.

scribe incunabula and rarities in minute detail, but the time had come to adopt a more practical method for dealing with the flood of books coming from American presses. In his paper Evans traced the earlier ideas of Charles C. Jewett on the problem, pointing out two reasons which he had given for showing the size of books: to enable a person to distinguish between different editions of the same book and to convey the idea of the size of a book to a person who had not seen a copy. Evans dispensed with the first reason by saying that librarians now designated all books by edition with the exception of the first. If the second reason were to have any real meaning to the patron, the logical thing to do was to measure the book by its outside covers.

Evans' paper, delivered in the hall of the Historical Society of Pennsylvania on October 4, 1876, was provocative and resulted in the appointment of a committee to consider the matter. On the committee was the irrepressible Dewey, who insisted that the measurement be made in terms of the metric system in harmony with the French and German custom. According to Dewey it would only be a matter of time until the entire world adopted the metric system; hence librarians would do well to anticipate this happy state of affairs. While some of the members of the committee were out smoking, Dewey rammed his proposals through and the conference adopted the centimeter as the unit for measuring books, and the library profession has been plagued with the decision ever since.[26] The metric system certainly did not meet the second requirement stated by Jewett: that the size would be known to a person who had not seen the book. However, the general principle enunciated by Evans—that detailed bibliographical description was a luxury which librarians could no longer afford—has been amply demonstrated.

The conference concluded with the formal organization of the American Library Association. Justin Winsor was elected president; A. R. Spofford, W. F. Poole, and Henry A. Homes, vice-presidents; and Melvil Dewey, secretary. Originally the association had intended to have a combined secretary-treasurer, but Dewey found it impossible to perform both offices, and the following April the *Library Journal* announced that Charles Evans had been added to the executive board of the American Library Association as its first treasurer. Evans' activities in the new association had been

---

[26] "The Proceedings," *American Library Journal*, I (Nov. 30, 1876), 141.

noted with approval by an Indianapolis newspaper, and the library committee continued his pay during his attendance at the conference.

In addition to the article on the sizes of books, Evans wrote three reviews for the *Library Journal*. All are thorough, judicious, and well written. The longest reviewed the catalog of the Mercantile Library of Brooklyn and well demonstrated Evans' critical faculties. Stephen B. Noyes, the librarian at Brooklyn, had departed from the dictionary catalog and had produced a new style—the alphabetico-classed catalog. After an appreciation of the excellent reference value of the catalog, Evans then criticized the approach of Noyes, doubting its value for the users of the Mercantile Library.

A more revealing review, which sparkles with his quiet humor, analyzed the catalog of the Fletcher Free Library of Burlington, Vermont. This catalog had been compiled by Evans' old Boston Athenaeum colleague, Harriet H. Ames, and he gave her volume a glowing recommendation. The fact that in a careful examination of 300 of the 600 pages of the catalog the reviewer had been unable to find even a typographical error was evidence of the painstaking manner in which the work had been performed. In addition to the marvelous accuracy of the proofreading, Evans also commended the careful indexing of series, the systematic use of cross references, and the intelligent use of notes for readers. After the critical notes Evans then ended in a humorous vein:

> It is for these reasons that we must confess to a feeling of disappointment in our examination of the volume under notice. When a reviewer can no longer impale errors "Thick as autumnal leaves, that strew the books in Vallombrosa," on the point of his pen; when he can no longer gloat over them as does a miser his gold and magnify the smallest into a heinous offense; then, like Othello, he finds his occupation gone, and there is nothing left for him but to give that praise which generations of his race have kept the essence only, in vials carefully labelled, "Faint praise, to be used only in damning." [27]

That Evans had been chosen by C. A. Cutter, editor of the section on bibliography of the *Library Journal,* to review three important catalogs is a measure of the prominence he had achieved

---

[27] Charles Evans, "Review of *Fletcher Free Library of Burlington (Vt.) Catalogue,*" *Library Journal,* III (April, 1878), 70; "Review of *Catalogue of the Mercantile Library of Brooklyn,*" pt. I, A–C, *American Library Journal,* I (May 31, 1877), 330–331; and "Review of *Catalogue of Books in the Roxbury Branch Library of the Boston Public Library,*" 2nd ed., *American Library Journal,* I (Sept. 30, 1876), 21.

by 1878. Perhaps even more indicative is the first review Evans wrote for the journal—a review of the catalog of the Roxbury branch of the Boston Public Library, which appeared in the first number of this periodical. In that review Evans indicated his knowledge of the earlier system of Jewett for cataloging the books of the Boston Public Library and noted his appreciation for Winsor's later efforts, which had been not so much catalogs as manuals of what and how to read. Having gone through the trouble of printing a catalog, Evans was always careful to commend full indexing and typographical accuracy. In speaking of the 300 pages it took to index 11,000 volumes, Evans recalled a remark of Henry Stevens: "If you are troubled with a pride of accuracy, and would have it completely taken out of you, print a catalogue."

The following year, British librarians, viewing the efforts of their American cousins to advance the profession, decided to establish a library association for the United Kingdom. Their idea to precede the organizational meeting of their group with an international conference of librarians was enthusiastically received by Dewey, who urged American librarians to attend the conference and learn what librarians in other countries were accomplishing. The Anchor Line would provide transportation direct from New York to London and back for $90. The trip would take about eleven and one-half days; thus there would be about twelve days to visit British libraries before the conference began in London on October 2, 1877. Dewey's efforts resulted in a party of sixteen, including most of the officers of the American Library Association; the party sailed from New York for Glasgow on the "Devonia" immediately after the annual conference of the American Library Association, which was held in New York September 4–6, 1877. In mid-Atlantic the executive board of the American Library Association held a meeting which Dewey later reported fully in the *Library Journal.* A Scotch lassie, returning to her home on board the same ship, was reported to have brought out the paternal instincts of three of the elderly librarians—Winsor, Poole, and Smith—who vied with each other in seeing to her every need. Samuel Swett Green remembered distinctly the picture of the dignified and distinguished Mr. Smith "coiled in a heap on the floor of the saloon while his adopted daughter ornamented his face with patches of moistened paper, the rest of us standing around in a state of positive hilarity." This young lady was undoubtedly Janette C. Mascrip, who had relatives in Indianapolis and in whom Evans manifested some romantic interest during his visit abroad.[28] The party stopped at Glasgow, visited the lake country, and saw some of the libraries in Edinburgh. Miss Mascrip apparently accompanied the party through Scotland and saw much of Charles Evans. As is often the fashion of young people not likely to meet again, Charlie probably promised more of friendship than he intended. At any rate, Janette remembered the occasion romantically the following year. Noting her pique at his failure to write, she still wanted his picture, if he had any, and expressed anxiety to know about his future, if he cared to let her know.

The party proceeded from Scotland to Leeds, Birmingham, Manchester, Liverpool, and Oxford, where they received a royal welcome from their British colleagues. It was an exhilarating but exhausting trip, and the American librarians arrived in London in the afternoon of the day just before the opening of the conference.

The conference opened at 10 A.M. on October 2, 1877, in the lecture theater of the London Institution, Finsbury Circus, with Mr. Robert Harrison, Librarian of the London Library, in the chair. At the organizational meeting Mr. John Winter Jones, Principal Librarian of the British Museum, was elected president. Three American librarians, W. F. Poole, Lloyd P. Smith, and Justin Winsor, were elected vice-presidents along with several other English and European librarians, and six other American librarians, including Charles Evans, were elected members of the council. No American read a paper during the four-day conference; but Dewey, Cutter, Poole, and Winsor frequently made comments upon the papers and contributed much to the discussion. However, there is no indication that Charles Evans made any contributions, but then this was a typical Evans pattern. While he enjoyed these early conventions, he was not a flashy member of any gathering. What he accomplished was done quietly, through contact with individual members rather than through public discussion. Yet, in his own way he made a very favorable impression upon the British librarians.

The American members of the conference visited many of the London libraries, including the British Museum, the Athenaeum

---

[28] Janette C. Mascrip to C. E., ALS, Aug. 2, 1878. This letter leaves little doubt that Miss Mascrip, who described herself as "a dignified housekeeper of 23 summers," was the lassie mentioned by Samuel Swett Green in *The Public Library Movement in the United States, 1853–1893* (Boston: The Boston Book Company, 1913), p. 57. She talks of making "poor Mr. Smith so ridiculous," and of Poole and Winsor.

Club, and the Library of the Corporation of London. Evans enjoyed all the visits and attempted to make the most of his trip. The principal social function for the librarians was a dinner given by the Lord Mayor of London. At this banquet, Evans was introduced to Matthew Arnold.[29] The Greek termination of the name Indianapolis caught Arnold's ear, and he asked Evans to tell him about the city and its people. In the course of their conversation Evans mentioned two things: the public library and the Indianapolis Literary Club. With a degree of pride he told Arnold that with a comparatively small collection of books the public library ranked fifth among all the libraries of the United States in circulation. As evidence of the culture of the people, Evans noted that both the prose and poetic works of Arnold circulated widely. He used the same device in describing the Literary Club, noting that Arnold's works had been the subject of an interesting evening at the club and that his opinions were frequently quoted by members both in their essays and in the subsequent discussion.

After the London conference several of the American librarians, including Charles Evans, paid a visit to the great libraries in Paris. They returned to London to sail for the United States on October 20, 1877. Such a trip had been tremendously stimulating for Evans, and it appeared that all had gone well during his more than two months' absence from Indianapolis. In early December the library committee voted to continue Evans' salary during his October absence.

However, all was not so well in Indianapolis as it looked on the surface. Even before Evans' departure Austin H. Brown had been busy. In late July he had proposed an amendment to the rules of the school board on the selection of the city librarian.[30] Heretofore the librarian had been appointed by the library committee with mere ratification by the school board, but Brown proposed that the librarian be elected at the second regular meeting of the school board in August of each year. Brown's proposal was laid over until the next meeting, and that meeting also passed without action. The proposal was finally reported on August 18, 1877, with the recommendation that the library committee nominate the librarian at the

---

[29] Green, *Public Library Movement*, pp. 69–71, gives an excellent description of the dinner. The Evans Papers contain Charles Evans' copy of the menu for the occasion. Charles Evans, "Looking Backward," describes his meeting with Matthew Arnold.

[30] Indianapolis *News*, July 21, 1877, p. 3.

first meeting in July each year. The board would then concur in the nomination or reject it. Although such action was not calculated to make Charles Evans feel very secure on the eve of his departure for Europe, still the board had not yet adopted the measure, and two letters from irate citizens had appeared in the *Journal* with strong statements about the perniciousness of Mr. Brown's action.

However, Brown was not one to be disturbed by opposition to his plan. He was in no hurry, but he intended to get rid of Evans. On September 21, 1877, during Evans' absence, the board decided that it had the full power in the appointment of the librarian.[31] There was yet no alarm among Evans' friends, for Evans could not be replaced without cause until the following summer, and they did not know that this step was merely the preparation for his eventual replacement.

Upon Evans' return the library was in good condition. The German books which he had ordered in the late summer had arrived, and November circulation was 40 per cent above that for the previous year, additional evidence of the library's steady growth under Evans' management. However, on December 5, 1877, Evans and the library suffered a depressing blow in the death of John D. Howland. Having been a member of the citizens' advisory library committee from the beginning, Howland had been one of the foremost advocates of a public library and a staunch friend of Evans. His loss came at a critical time for the Indianapolis librarian. With the general respect which Indianapolis citizens had for Howland's judgment, it would have been difficult for the board to force Evans' removal as librarian.

To add to his difficulties, Evans chose at this time to begin a new registration of the borrowers. He felt very strongly that no certificate of guarantee should be binding for more than three years since it was necessary to weed out dead registration cards, notify those who were surety for delinquent fines and losses, and check on the guarantees which might be fraudulent.[32] Moreover, since most book losses could be traced to the removal of patrons from the city, this new registration would increase the safeguards on the city's property.

In the first four months, although the new list totaled 3,500, with an additional 200 to 300 being added each month thereafter, some

---

[31] Indianapolis *News*, Sept. 22, 1877, p. 3.

[32] I. P. L., *Second Report, 1874–8*, p. 5.

unhappiness arose from this reregistration. There were still borrowers who objected to the requirement that a guarantor must be a person of property, and a number of people were irritated by the necessity for reregistration. Evans had once before been accused of "neglect of duty, insolence of manner and making an insinuating, insulting remark to a patron of the library." [33] Undoubtedly the extra work required of the library staff in the reregistration and the truculence of some of the patrons operated to Evans' disadvantage during the early months of 1878. Evans would have been more than human if he had not occasionally snapped at a patron.

However, the report for the year 1877–78 was cause for optimism and demonstrated the success of Evans' administration. In June, 1878, the library committee unanimously renominated Charles Evans for reelection to the post of librarian and at the same time announced that a scheme for the reorganization of the library was in preparation. All seemed to be going well, but in late June there were rumors in Indianapolis that Evans would not be reelected. By July 1, 1878, John H. Holliday felt compelled to take notice of these rumors on the editorial page of the *News*. Commenting upon the "rare fitness of Mr. Evans for the place" and the petty intrigues that were involved in an attempt to replace him, Holliday strongly defended Evans' retention as city librarian. Through hard work Charles Evans had raised himself to the first rank among American librarians and had placed the public library of Indianapolis among the first rank of American libraries. No citizen of Indianapolis should be misled about the qualifications for a public librarian.

> The proper management of libraries has come to be a profession. . . . There is as much difference between a library and a collection of books as there is between a pile of bricks and a house; and that our library shall not become a storeroom of ink and paper in bindings made expensive and unwieldy by hap-hazard selection, it is necessary that a trained librarian preside over it. Of course there are some who find fault with his management, but no man in such a place can please everybody, and if Mr. Evans is displaced because somebody don't like him, and not because his work is not meritorious, it will be a matter for lasting regret.[34]

---

[33] That Judge Hines felt it necessary to explain the rule on property qualifications to the school board is a partial indication of the unpopularity of this new registration. Indianapolis *News*, Jan. 19, 1878, p. 3, April 24, 1877, p. 3, and May 5, 1877, p. 3. J. S. Spaulding had complained bitterly of Evans' conduct in a letter to the board. Apparently Evans had denied him a new registration card because he had lost the old one.

[34] Indianapolis *News*, July 1, 1878, p. 2.

Holliday had come a long way since the editorial on the Boston import in December, 1872; Evans himself could not have written a better defense of his own work nor could he have made a better plea for his retention in the position.

Although the school commissioners were supposed to elect a librarian on July 1, they postponed the election until the second regular meeting in August. Meanwhile, on July 6, the school board was reorganized for the year, and Evans received additional bad news. His good friends H. A. Edson, W. P. Fishback, and A. C. Harris were not reappointed to the citizens' advisory library committee. Despite the appointment of two fellow members of the Indianapolis Literary Club, O. C. McCulloch and Myron W. Reed, it was clear that Evans would not have the deep and loyal support he had enjoyed in the past. As several local candidates for the job began to be mentioned by the local newspapers, it appeared doubtful that Evans could be reelected.

On August 16, 1878, at a regular meeting of the board, the first order of business was selection of the city librarian. All board members were present except one. A motion was made to concur in the June report of the library committee recommending the reappointment of Charles Evans. That report had been signed by all four of the school board members: C. C. Hines, H. G. Carey, J. J. Bingham, and Robert Browning. However, Browning secured the floor and explained that he had recommended Evans' reappointment in good faith. Since that time he had become convinced that he had made a mistake, and Evans ought to be replaced for he had made himself objectionable to a great many patrons of the library. Judge Hines rose to answer Browning and eulogized Evans very highly. Clemens Vonnegut, a former member of the library committee, also spoke favorably of Evans' work. Austin H. Brown, however, stated that it was not a question of Evans' efficiency; the commissioners owed it to the public not to appoint a librarian who would be a standing insult to a great many patrons. Evans had needlessly offended many people, and therefore should be replaced. At this point even Dr. Carey wavered. These were serious charges made in complete candor by his fellow commissioners. He would personally vote to confirm the report of the committee with the understanding that there would be a change in Mr. Evans' deportment if he were retained. The board then voted on the motion and rejected the report by a tie vote: 5 to 5.[35] One newspaper reported that a different result would have been obtained had the other board member, George Merritt, been present. The library committee then retired and nominated Albert Yohn, a local bookseller, who was promptly elected librarian.

Thus did Indianapolis reject its first librarian. As the board rejected Charles Evans for personal and political spite, it turned its back on six years of almost phenomenal library progress. He had built good research collections for the student and the scholar. He had made these resources available to an ever increasing public. He had contributed much to the intellectual life of the city through the formation of a distinguished literary club. Despite his debt to Poole, Charles Evans had achieved much of this on his own. From a highly promising, even brilliant career, Evans was cut off, and at the early age of twenty-eight! It was a blow from which he never fully recovered.

The charges against Charles Evans were serious, but they ought to be understood within the context of the times. Civil service, though talked about, had not yet become a reality and most governmental jobs went to individuals with some political connection. Only the year before, Justin Winsor had been forced to leave his position as head of the most successful public library in the country because of petty political considerations. Moreover, there were candidates enough for Evans' position, for, after all, $1,350 was a good salary for 1878. It was easy enough for a few malcontents to bring serious charges against Evans and force their consideration by the board. Indianapolis was a highly tense, politically oriented city, and it should not be too surprising that some of Evans' supporters wavered in the face of political pressure. Worst of all, Evans had displeased the leading Democratic spokesman, Austin H. Brown.

Librarian-board relationships were very difficult in the latter part of the nineteenth century, and, as Williamson has remarked, "years had to pass, librarians had to resign or be fired, libraries had to fall into decay and confusion for lack of effective executive action . . . before librarian-board relationships could be improved." [36] There are all too many instances of librarians who lost their positions from political interference for Evans' case to have been an isolated one.

---

[35] For retention of Evans: W. A. Bell, H. G. Carey, John Coburn, C. C. Hines, and Clemens Vonnegut. Against Evans: J. J. Bingham, Austin H. Brown, Robert Browning, William F. Reasner, and Peter Routier.

[36] Williamson, "William Frederick Poole," pp. 239–240.

The division of authority and responsibility between the board of school commissioners and the library committee created an almost impossible administrative situation. The board of school commissioners was composed of elected officials and entrusted with the final authority, and as Schlesinger has pointed out in his *Rise of the City,* most men of culture and education avoided politics at this period.[37]

Yet were the charges against Evans true? Was he really a "standing insult to a great many patrons of the library" as Brown contended? That Evans had served most of the public well has already been indicated. Cottman, the small boy from the country, testified to Evans' interest in the struggling youth.[38] Moreover, Evans' annual reports and his continual battle for fiction purchases indicate keen sympathy with the poorer classes of readers and an appreciation for their needs. While it is true that Evans was not a jovial person, the evidence of his pleasing the general public is convincing. There is no reason to believe that his lack of gregariousness was misinterpreted for haughtiness by a majority of the library's patrons. The newspaper support for Evans, both in editorials and through favorable letters to the editor, is clear on this point. That Evans had given Indianapolis an excellent, working library, too, is beyond dispute.

The point on which Evans was most vulnerable was the criticism that he enforced the library's rules too rigidly. Evans was not a flexible man. The rules had been formulated by competent people who had the best interests of the public in mind and Charles Evans intended to see that they were enforced. Although some citizens regarded such an attitude as a public virtue, Evans displeased some politically prominent individuals by his actions. His refusal to grant a new library card to a man who had to seek redress from the school board itself is a case in point. A few vocal individuals could well magnify this weakness into a major administrative fault. The clearest indication of Evans' rigidity and its effects can be seen in the actions of his successor, Albert B. Yohn. When he assumed the librarianship, Yohn continued almost every policy and every proposal of Evans with one notable exception: he relaxed the rules and devoted himself to creating a more favorable public image of the library. By publicizing his willingness to make exceptions and to permit some leeway in interpretation of the rules, Yohn enjoyed

---

[37] Arthur M. Schlesinger, *The Rise of the City, 1878–1898* (New York: Macmillan, 1933), chap. XII, "Political Factors and Forces," pp. 387–420, is an excellent description of the political situation in this period.

[38] See chap. 3.

some of the favor with the public which Evans lacked. Perhaps if Evans' friends or even the library committee had pointed out the virtue of yielding a minor point to gain a major library victory, changes could have been made which would have enabled Evans to continue in office.

Evans remained in his position until August 31, 1878. During this period he wrote to Cutter, Winsor, and, of course, Poole. Despite a deep sense of depression which had brought him as close to "utter wretchedness as can be," he attempted to cover up his hurt by writing humorously to these three that he had been "decapitated." Cutter responded in similar vein, stating that he wished he could "put a head" on Evans, but not in the usual sense of that term. Winsor was not so kind. He wrote a brisk, businesslike letter asking what the trouble was: "I was sorry indeed to find your note here. What is the meaning of it? What new drift of events that has brought it about? . . . P. S. I am inquisitive because if I recommend you, I shall at once be asked, why was he turned out at Indianapolis?" [39] Though Winsor later wrote that he thought conditions in Indianapolis were not conducive to good government, he offered little in the way of concrete aid to Evans.

The "unkindest cut of all" came from Evans' personal friend, Mary A. Bean, Librarian of the Brookline Public Library, who found the situation completely incomprehensible. While trying to be helpful, "Little Beanie" probed deeply into Evans' past and asked if it were not possible that he had been guilty of offending the public or the board of trustees without realizing it.[40] She mentioned the old moods and the little notes which resulted from them in the Athenaeum days. Was it possible that Evans had let his earlier faults gain the ascendency and had given the appearance of cold reserve and hauteur? Beanie advised him to analyze the matter thoroughly and get to the root of the trouble. It was for his own good to place himself aright in the eyes of his friends and the public. Although she could not believe that Charlie deserved such treatment, she thought he ought to look for an explanation that would please everybody. He must pocket his pride and fight for his place, since he could not afford to lose his present high standing in the profession.

Even though Beanie spoke from the best of motives, her letter

---

[39] Justin Winsor to C. E., ALS, Aug. 20, 1878. See also Justin Winsor to C. E., ALS, Aug. 27, 1878.

[40] M. A. B. to C. E., ALS, Aug. 20, 1878.

was not designed to lift the spirits of Charles Evans. His despondency
had begun in late July, when it appeared that he would have difficulty being reelected. That fear had been realized and he was already beginning to feel that he had disgraced himself and the profession. Now his best friend, in good Shakespearean fashion, had
suggested that the fault was not in his stars but in himself. If
Beanie did not, indeed could not, understand the politically charged
atmosphere of Indianapolis, how could any other librarian who
did not know him nearly so well? Her keen analysis had come too
close to the truth and hence could but add to his depression. He had
been too inflexible with some of the patrons. There were those who
felt "personally aggrieved at imaginary slights or seeming coldness
and condescension" on the part of Evans. In pointing her moral
Beanie noted that if one stroked the fur the smooth way, the cat
would purr. However, go the wrong way and the claw would come
out sharply on the hand, even though the hand accidentally or un-
wittingly did the deed. In Beanie's fable the cat was the public, but
the trouble with her advice was that it came too late. The claw had
already descended and the scratch was already infected. A new librarian had been elected, and Charles Evans' service at Indianapolis
ended on August 31, 1878.

William F. Poole was not helpful either. Although Poole had
immediately written both Lloyd P. Smith and Justin Winsor that
Evans' nonelection stemmed wholly from personal and political
causes, he expressed less interest in Evans' plight in Indianapolis
than their old relationship warranted. However, he did want to
call Evans' attention to the fact that whatever was reported in the
Library Journal about his dismissal ought to be done discreetly,
and he thought the best person to do the job was Winsor. While
Poole thought there must be a position for Evans somewhere, he
could not suggest one at the moment. His complete lack of appreciation for Evans' position was revealed at the end of his letter on
August 24, when he asked if the young librarian had done anything
about indexing *Cornhill* and *Temple Bar,* for, wrote Poole, "you
will now perforce have the time." [41]

As the time approached when Evans would have to surrender the
keys to Albert Yohn, his prospects seemed gloomier than ever.
Poole had written Winsor a long letter explaining the Indianapolis

---

[41] W. F. P. to C. E., ALS, Aug. 24, Oct. 4 and 16, 1878. Beanie later wrote that
Poole thought Evans was not entirely blameless in the matter. M. A. B. to C. E.,
ALS, Jan. 1, 1885.

problem and had asked him to write the paragraph for the *Library Journal*. The latter had written a brief note deploring the circumstances. Both Winsor and Poole hoped that Lloyd P. Smith might find something for Evans in Philadelphia. However, such words gave little comfort to Evans as the last of August approached without a single concrete job proposal. The prospect of no more salary checks could only have added to Evans' misery. While in this state of depression, he gave serious thought to the prospect of going West to write for newspapers.[42] He felt himself not only without a job, but without friends and wholly without incentive for living. In the West he could start life anew.

The last day arrived, and Evans was still without prospects. At 10 A.M. on Saturday, August 31, Albert Yohn became the librarian and Charles Evans stepped down. The library which had been his very life for six years was entrusted to the hands of another. Into this library he had poured his energy, his devotion, all the sense of care which other men might give to a family and home. Charles Evans left the Indianapolis Public Library that warm and humid Saturday morning with a feeling of impending doom. He had forfeited his position as one of the leading American librarians, and he had disappointed his friends who had believed in him.

---

[42] M. A. B. to C. E., ALS, Aug. 20, 1878.

Newspapers, Radicals, and
the Right Woman

5

Charles Evans' world was really not so hopeless as he thought on August 31, 1878. Some of his friends were interested in his future and had already made inquiries about another position for him. On September 3 Charles A. Cutter wrote from Boston that there was a cataloging vacancy at Johns Hopkins University.[1] The only drawback was the university's insistence that their cataloger have some knowledge of German, and Cutter doubted that Evans had the language facility.

Cutter's letter was followed by a friendly communication from F. W. Clarke, Professor of Chemistry at the University of Cincinnati.[2] Clarke had known Evans in the old Athenaeum days and had been favorably impressed with his performance there. He had seen a notice of the school board action in the Cincinnati papers and informed Evans of the vacancy in the librarianship of the Cincinnati Mercantile Library. Since the death of the librarian the preceding spring, a committee had been searching for a successor. While Clarke himself was not connected with the Mercantile Library, he thought Evans would be a good man for the position and would be happy to recommend him to the board. Quite apart from the importance of the position, the compensation was $2,000 per year.

---

[1] C. A. Cutter to C. E., ALS, Sept. 3, 1878.
[2] F. W. Clarke to C. E., ALS, Sept. 5, 1878.

There were, then, reasons why Evans' spirits should have lifted
a little. Two weeks, after all, is a relatively short time when one is
looking for a job. However, this period can seem an unbearably
long time to a young person who is out of work and who deems himself a failure. While he knew his friends were trying to be helpful,
they were not making much headway.

At the same time of Evans' dismissal at Indianapolis, another
event occurred which was to affect his future. A yellow fever epidemic had broken out in the lower Mississippi Valley.[3] Though
sympathetic toward all the victims of this disaster, Indianapolis
citizens were especially touched by the appeals from Memphis, where
the death rate was rising steadily. By late August a relief committee
had been formed to raise funds for the stricken city and on August
27, Dr. J. G. E. Renner, one of Charles Evans' closest friends, announced his intention to go to Memphis. Just Evans' age, Renner
was a popular young doctor with a keen interest in his profession.
He had earned a good reputation in Indianapolis, especially for
his work among the city's poor, and many of his friends tried to
dissuade him from a course which involved so much personal risk.
Daily reports from Memphis told of additional hundreds who had
been stricken and the death toll was unbelievably high. Despite the
remonstrances of his friends, August 29 found Renner in Memphis,
rendering what aid he could. For the next two weeks he regularly
received money and supplies from the Indianapolis relief committee. In his grateful acknowledgment of these gifts Renner wrote
poignant dispatches about the people of Memphis. The fever was
malarial in its most intensified form, and there was an urgent need
for additional doctors and nurses.[4]

On September 11, when word reached Indianapolis that Renner
was down with the fever, Charles Evans immediately determined
to go to Memphis to aid the young doctor. According to his friends,
he had become increasingly despondent over his disgrace and welcomed this opportunity not only to make Renner's last days more
comfortable but perhaps even to find his own quietus in one last

---

[3] The most complete record of this epidemic is J. M. Keating, *A History of the
Yellow Fever: The Yellow Fever Epidemic of 1878, in Memphis, Tenn.* (Memphis:
Printed for the Howard Association, 1879). From August 15 to October 1, 1878,
the Indianapolis *News* carried dispatches from the lower South almost daily.
Description of Renner is from Thurman B. Rice, "The Hoosier Health Officer,"
Monthly Bulletin Indiana State Board of Health, XLIV (May, 1941), 114.

[4] Indianapolis *News*, Sept. 2, 1878, p. 1, and Sept. 3, 1878, p. 4. By September 5
the death toll in Memphis had reached 768, Indianapolis *News*, Sept. 5, 1878, p. 1.

heroic struggle.[5] It was a noble impulse to risk his life to help suffer-
ing humanity, and this move would partially compensate for his
recent disgrace.

Under any circumstances Evans' journey would have been fool-
hardy. He had no medical ability, no practical nurses' training, and
no knowledge of how to exist in an epidemic-ridden city. During
the early days of the epidemic nine out of ten who were stricken
with the fever died. According to the final report 5,150 of the 19,600
persons who remained in Memphis during the siege died.[6] Doctors
themselves were not exempt from the disease. Neither Evans' own
strong body nor his will would be sufficient to spare him. Any
thought of his going to Memphis could only carry the additional
news that he probably would not return. Knowing all this, on Thursday, September 12, Charles Evans boarded the train for Memphis.

Describing his ride from Louisville to Memphis for the *News,*
Evans gave the journey a certain dramatic flair.[7] He thought all the
country had a hushed air, as if the people in the little towns feared
that the fever might any day reach them. As the train drew nearer
Memphis, the towns were depopulated. Stores and houses were
closed and only a few Negroes were about. "At nearly every station
piles of pine boxes of a suspicious length, were awaiting transportation, and at Badett, the station before reaching Memphis, a Negro,
afflicted with the disease was put on the forward car."

Evans arrived in Memphis on Saturday evening. The shops were
all closed and few people were visible. He went immediately to Renner's hotel, but no one seemed to know anything about his friend.
The doctor's room was in disorder with clothing and other items
scattered about. After an attempt to bring some order into the room,
Evans proceeded to the medical department of the Howard Association where he learned that Renner had taken the fever on Septem-

---

[5] Indianapolis *Journal,* Sept. 18, 1878, p. 8. "It is hinted by his friends that he
went south in the desperate hope of meeting his quietus, his removal from the
librarianship having 'cut him up' terribly, that he felt himself disgraced to a
certain extent, and did not care much what befell him." There seems little
reason to question this statement despite the Indianapolis *News* assertion that it
was wicked and absurd. For letters indicating Evans' state of mind during this
entire period see Janette C. Mascrip to C. E., ALS, Aug. 2, 1878; M. A. B. to
C. E., ALS, June 11 and Aug. 25, 1883.

[6] Keating, *A History of the Yellow Fever,* p. 116.

[7] Charles Evans to the Editor, Indianapolis *News,* Sept. 18, 1878, p. 1, and
Sept. 19, 1878, p. 1. Holliday printed Evans' letters in their entirety. They provide vivid and detailed accounts of Evans' actions and impressions of Memphis,
and the description of Evans in Memphis is drawn heavily from these accounts.

ber 11 and had been taken to the Court Street Hospital. Unable to do more that evening, Evans went back to the Peabody Hotel to spend the night.

Early Sunday morning with considerable anxiety Evans approached the old hospital building. Renner had written only twelve days before that the disease was fatal to almost everyone who had it and that all treatments so far had failed. These words could not have been far from the mind of Evans as he entered the old schoolhouse which had been converted into a hospital. Within the building he found additional cause for alarm. Renner was occupying a room with three other sick physicians. All four doctors were regarded as hopeless cases. The physician attending Renner told Evans that the crisis of the disease normally came during the third day. Renner was already in his fifth day and rapidly growing worse. Death seemed only a matter of hours away.

When Evans entered the room, Renner recognized him at once and seemed glad to see him, though he was too weak to talk much. Covering his own fear by characteristic activity, Charles Evans began to make his friend more comfortable. At Renner's request he walked to the east part of the city to find an especially skilled nurse. Then he and an old German gave Renner a sponge bath and changed the mattress and bed clothes. After this work had been accomplished, Renner talked with Evans a short while, telling him of the work he had done. On the day he had come down with the fever he had seen over 100 patients. This confirmed what Evans had already learned from others—that Dr. Renner, a man of prodigious energy, had probably killed himself by overwork.

During the afternoon Renner became delirious but quieted down in the evening. When Evans left him, he appeared no worse than he had been in the morning. However, about midnight he again became delirious and had to be held on the bed. Reverting to his native German, the doctor's anguished cries so disturbed the other patients that he was removed to a small building attached to the hospital where the dying were kept. When Evans arrived on the scene early Monday morning, he found Renner unconscious. Sitting by his bedside throughout the morning as life ebbed, Charles Evans reflected on the unselfishness of this friend who had devoted himself first to the poor of Indianapolis and now to these strangers in the South. Renner was the embodiment of that impelling call to duty which Evans had learned to respect at the Farm School. As the doctor died quietly at 11:30 A.M., Evans commented, "a noble life, well ended."

Evans aroused himself from his mood of contemplation and sadness to attend to the burial details. He wanted to move quickly to accomplish his last work for his friend. However, in circumstances where Renner's sickness and death constituted only one out of many, Evans was frustrated at every turn. He could not find any of the doctor's clothes except the ones he had worn when he became sick. From his own wardrobe he then supplied the appropriate burial garments, and the Howard Association provided the casket.

Overwork at the undertakers necessitated postponement of interment until the following day. On Tuesday morning, September 17, Charles Evans accompanied Renner's body to its final resting place in Elmwood Cemetery. One of the doctor's patients had sent him a bouquet of flowers on Sunday morning and this "simple offering" Evans placed at the head of his grave. Then the young man turned and walked slowly away. He had done what had to be done.

Back in his room in the Peabody Hotel, Evans wrote a lengthy dispatch for the Indianapolis *News* in which he described the circumstances of Renner's death and burial. With characteristic thoroughness he gave the exact location of Renner's lot in the cemetery and listed all the unopened letters that he found in the hotel room. He requested instructions and then spent the remainder of the day trying to locate Renner's other personal possessions without success.

Evans' dispatches from Memphis genuinely alarmed both his friends and his enemies. The *News* called him a second hero and expressed the greatest solicitude for his health.[8] Charles Evans was a strong man but so was Renner, and the fever appeared to spare the strong no more than the weak. By his action in going South to nurse his friend Charles Evans had excited great sympathy among the populace. In commenting sarcastically upon the concern of some, the *Journal* noted that the very people with whom Evans had been most unpopular as librarian now showed the liveliest interest in him. Agreeable to a general wish that Evans be urged to return, the relief committee, composed of Thomas H. Sharpe, John Love, J. J. Bingham, H. Bamberger, and A. H. Brown, sent Evans the following telegram on September 17: "In behalf of your friends the relief

---

[8] Indianapolis *News*, Sept. 17, 1878, p. 1.

committee request your immediate return. In the name of humanity, come back. If you are short of funds draw on us for $50." [9] Lack
of an immediate reply from Evans led some to speculate that he too
had gone to his death; however, the following morning Evans sent
a short dispatch to Holliday: "More dangerous to leave than stay,
but accept advice. Return by Louisville and Cincinnati." [10]

This dispatch was received early enough to include in the evening
News, in which Holliday again took the opportunity to praise Evans.
The editor noted that Evans "considerately takes the long route
instead of coming direct to Indianapolis." However, if he had the
seeds of the disease in his system, his friends would be better pleased
if he came by direct route so that they could help him out if he
became ill. Disdaining a morning story of the *Journal* that Evans
had gone away with suicidal intent, Holliday noted that "this dispatch fully answers the wicked and absurd assertion in the *Journal*
this morning." Holliday was determined to make Evans a hero, and
if he had to do so by crushing the report of his old enemy the *Journal,* so much the better.

Actually, Evans had a much more pragmatic reason for returning
to Indianapolis via Cincinnati. Having done his duty toward Renner and having purged himself through his noble deed, he wanted
to have a look at the Cincinnati Mercantile job which Clarke had
written about. Before he left Indianapolis, Evans had contacted
Poole about the Mercantile position and hoped that he could secure
it.[11] If not, then perhaps his friend Thomas Vickers would hire him
for a cataloging position in the Cincinnati Public Library.

After spending a couple of days in Cincinnati, Evans arrived in
Indianapolis about midnight on September 22. His had been a long
and harrowing undertaking but he had the feeling of a mission
accomplished. Still he felt uneasy. Having seen the desperate
need for doctors and nurses in Memphis, he wrote his friend "Little
Beanie" that he felt that he had turned his back on a solemn duty.[12]
Though he had not the skill of some, he could possibly have helped
with the administrative duties at the Howard Association headquarters. Yet it was good to be back among his friends. He had left
in disgrace and had returned a hero.

[9] Indianapolis *Journal,* Sept. 18, 1878, p. 8.
[10] Indianapolis *News,* Sept. 18, 1878, p. 4.
[11] W. F. P. to C. E., ALS, Oct. 4 and 16, 1878.
[12] M. A. B. to C. E., ALS, Sept. 27, 1878.

From Cincinnati, Evans had sent post cards to both Poole and Bean. "Papa" Poole was very unhappy that Evans had undertaken "so rash a scheme as going to Memphis." [13] In an earlier letter to Poole, Evans had stated that he knew that his mentor would not approve of his trip to Memphis, and Poole confirmed Evans' judgment on that point. The Chicago papers had carried several telegrams about Evans, and every day Poole had expected to read that he was down with the fever. He hoped Evans would not again so try the sympathies of his friends; however, he had not written just to scold Evans. The future was what was important. What were his plans? Did he have a position? The Mercantile job had already been filled but how else could he be of help? He asked that Evans keep him posted on his activities.

Beanie had more sympathy than Poole.[14] Her religious nature strongly approved the motive which had led Evans to Memphis. She was proud of his unselfish devotion to his friend and sympathized with him in his loss under such terrible circumstances. When she received the copies of the dispatches Evans had written to the *News,* she was even more horrified at the thought of her "brave Charlie" in that situation. Evans always wrote well and had vividly portrayed the death and desolation of the city of Memphis. With Beanie's horror also came an even greater appreciation of the heroism of "our boy Charlie—who could so far forget self—as to take his life in his hand—and face almost certain death—with such fortitude and strength of purpose." Still she was thankful that he was out of Memphis and thought he had done enough. She thought his disappointment and trials could now be seen more in perspective and that his professional life would be richer for this experience.

To return to Indianapolis with so many favorable comments about his brave deed was encouraging. Even Poole's little lecture did not seem so severe when everyone in the city spoke highly of his action. Holliday suggested a memorial "for his noble heroism in taking his life in his own hand in going to Memphis to nurse and attempt to save the life of Dr. Renner." [15] He thought many would be willing to contribute to this worthy purpose. Such comments partially redeemed the bitterness and despair of July, August, and early September.

[13] W. F. P. to C. E., ALS, Oct. 4, 1878.
[14] M. A. B. to C. E., ALS, Sept. 25 and 27, 1878.
[15] Indianapolis *News,* Oct. 21, 1878, p. 4.

However, as week succeeded week and month succeeded month without any opportunity to return to professional life, Evans again became despondent. Poole urged him to write Winsor, Cutter, and Dewey to see if they could not find something for him in the East. "There is an opening for you somewhere. So keep up good spirits and find it, and use your friends to help you." [16] This was excellent advice if one could afford to heed it. When Evans received the letter from Poole, he had already been out of work over six weeks and had spent some of his funds in his journey South.

As the months passed, Evans undoubtedly took a temporary job in Indianapolis. What he did is not known. Perhaps he worked for Holliday on the *News*. He certainly wrote well enough, and his ability to keep books would have made him an asset in the business department of the newspaper.

During this period, he continued his activities in the Indianapolis Literary Club. On November 16 he read his paper on Dr. Johnson and on March 1 led the discussion of "Fastings and Visions." He also enjoyed the third annual dinner of the club at Becker's on Monday evening, February 24, 1879. As the expense of these famous dinners was borne out of the treasury, no member felt embarrassed by lack of funds. These early dinners were later reported to have been delightful in direct proportion to their wetness.[17] Although Charles Evans himself indulged only occasionally, Louis Howland recalled many grave and substantial citizens and church members who were "supposed to have had no knowledge of alcohol except as applied externally" making a beeline for the beverage table. Yet despite the wine which flowed freely and the cigar smoke which rose abundantly, the annual dinners were not bacchanalian festivals. They were typically Victorian evenings where everything was done discreetly, decently, and in order. As the club member relaxed after the feast, he could nod assent to the various toasts to literature, science, the bar, the pulpit, and the press by such dignitaries as Governor T. A. Hendricks, the Reverend W. A. Bartlett, and Benjamin Harrison. With its food, its Roman punch, and its speeches, the third annual dinner was a "full" one in every sense of that term and helped to establish the subsequent reputation of these occasions.

Shortly after the third annual dinner, the spirit of Evans and his friends again became hopeful. A. B. Yohn, who was acknowledged

---

[16] W. F. P. to C. E., ALS, Oct. 16, 1878.

[17] Louis Howland, *Club Reminiscences, Read to the Indianapolis Literary Club, April 4, 1932*, pp. 6–7.

to have done a good job as a librarian, submitted his resignation in early March, for reasons of poor health. The library committee, while fully appreciating Yohn's reasons for resigning, had been too pleased with his performance as city librarian to let him go without some effort. They therefore suggested that he take a vacation of from three to six months and then reconsider his decision.

Interestingly enough, Yohn had followed almost every policy Evans had suggested for the development of the library. His only difference, and it was a significant one, was that he created a more favorable public image than his predecessor. As early as October 26, 1878, the *Journal* and the *Herald* agreed that the public library was a credit to the city and "the young lady attendants models of politeness, attention, patience, and accomplishment." This change in tone brought a cynical comment from the *News:* "So great a change in such a little while?" Since Yohn had continued Evans' attendants in their positions, the *News* had reason to doubt that the same individuals had been made over by the new man.

However, Yohn continued to build on this image. He provided a new book shelf for those who wanted to browse, he issued Harper's special list of interesting juvenile books for young readers, he compiled reading lists on specific topics for the reading and literary clubs of the city. Many citizens were surprised at the richness of the library, especially with respect to art, literature, and history of races, which the *News* thought reflected just credit on Evans' selection policies. Yohn also publicized the fact that he would buy any book which a patron could not find in the library unless there were some good reason to prevent his doing so. The library committee obviously did not want to part with a man who combined the book knowledge of Evans with a sound public relations approach.

Following the advice of the committee, Yohn took a two weeks' vacation and then came back to the library on a part-time basis. Meanwhile he reconsidered his decision to resign. However, by the first of May it became apparent that his continued ill health would force him to do so. He agreed to remain as librarian until the end of his term but his office work would have to be done by an assistant. At the time this announcement was made, a note appeared in the *News* stating that "Charles Evans, formerly city librarian, expects to return to Boston in a few days." [18]

---

[18] Indianapolis *News*, May 7, 1879, p. 4.

This had been the opportunity for which Evans' supporters had waited. On May 10, 1879, the *News* published a letter from James I. Gurly, who wanted to know why Evans could not be appointed since Yohn was to resign.[19] Going over familiar ground, Gurly noted that good librarians were difficult to find. Indianapolis had been fortunate in its first two, but it was unlikely that the third appointee would do as well. Charles Evans had one fault—he did not try to conciliate all types of people. However, Evans was young and had probably learned his lesson. Moreover, he had one great characteristic—"he took raw boys and girls and made them efficient library officials." What did the public care if Evans was a "complying man" or not? What they wanted was a well-managed library, and Charles Evans had given them that.

Other citizens also spoke up in Evans' behalf. One supported him on the basis of his heroism during the yellow fever epidemic, an old and often politically effective appeal. Though he did not know Evans personally, he had told many of his friends that such "fearless and noble conduct" should be rewarded.[20] Another thought it was "very strange that we must make believe to look everywhere for a librarian when the man who naturally belongs to the position is at hand." [21]

Unfortunately the efforts of the Evans' partisans did little to move the school board. Again Evans went through the tortures of the damned as there first seemed to be hope, then less hope, and finally none as the library committee turned its gaze elsewhere for a city librarian. Introspective by nature, Evans remembered the circumstances of August, 1878, when his hopes had been dashed almost beyond repair. The public was fickle and friendship vain. His only recourse was to leave Indianapolis. Perhaps in another locality he could become a wealthy man and then be free of the petty conniving of politicians.[22] The lesson of his past was plain; if a man wanted to enjoy and cultivate the pleasures of the mind, he must have money to do so. Did not that distinguished coterie at the Athenaeum prove the importance of money for the pursuit of leisure? Were not his own friends in the Indianapolis Literary Club largely free of

[19] Indianapolis *News,* May 10, 1879, p. 2.
[20] Indianapolis *News,* May 12, 1879, p. 3.
[21] Indianapolis *News,* May 29, 1879, p. 3.
[22] Varina Vollmer to C. E., ALS, June 4, 1879. This letter reveals very well Evans' attitude. The suggestion that he was thinking about sheep raising in the Southwest is strong presumptive evidence that Evans left in June, 1879, for Texas.

that financial uncertainty from which public officials have always suffered? The only thing which counted was money—money to afford one's own books and the leisure of men like Eliot, Emerson, and Blake. He must devote himself to the making of money.

In this depressing state of mind Evans turned to the newspapers and read of enormous fortunes to be made in Texas. This vast area was now burgeoning with immigrants who were quickly bringing law and order to its towns. One could make his own way in the new country, could become wealthy, and then retire to some cultural center like Boston and enjoy the luxuries of its Athenaeum. He had been told that sheep raising offered an opportunity to turn a quick profit. Why not try it? He was young and vigorous. He might even find other wealth that he sought—the loving woman of "perfect face, and soft-black hair."

On May 31, 1879, Charles Evans submitted his resignation as secretary of the Indianapolis Literary Club. His resignation came on the night of the one hundredth meeting of that organization. With regret Evans took leave of his "many pleasant associations" in the city and especially "the Halcyon nights I have spent with you." [23]

Shortly after this, Charles Evans left the city. Whether he went immediately to Texas as this letter to his friend Varina Vollmer indicated he would or whether he returned first to Boston is not known. No records remain to tell of his life between May 31, 1879, and May 13, 1881, when he appeared in Fort Worth, Texas, as a sales representative of the paper and stationery firm of C. E. Vreeland of Dallas.[24] He may have attempted sheep raising in the southwest part of Texas, but whatever he did, there is evidence that these were difficult and troubled years for Charles Evans. He completely separated himself from his friends, and his one relative, his brother, during this period. Crushed with his sense of guilt, Charles Evans felt that all his friends, even as Poole, blamed him for the unfortunate turn of affairs at Indianapolis, and he fled from them.[25]

Nothing in Charles Evans' life had prepared him for Texas. His

---

[23] C. E. to the Indianapolis Literary Club, ALS, May 31, 1879, in the club archives, quoted in F. H. Insley to the author, Feb. 14, 1960.

[24] Fort Worth *Daily Democrat*, May 13, 1881, p. 4.

[25] M. A. B. to C. E., ALS, Jan. 1, 1885, states that Poole "felt you were not entirely blameless in the old trouble." Bean told him that he had mistaken his friends, but the fact that they were unable to find him some job in a nine-month period Charles Evans probably took as an indication of their attitude.

background, his training, his thoughts were not concerned with business affairs. He had neither the shrewd, calculating manner nor the knowledge of this part of the country to turn its opportunities to his advantage. Texas was indeed a state where a man could make a fortune overnight, but he could also lose it as quickly. Evans' lack of understanding of people and his retiring nature served him even more poorly in the business world than it did in the library profession. His poor business judgment actually resulted in a loss of the small amount of funds he had accumulated during this time.

As a salesman for Vreeland, Evans impressed B. B. Paddock, editor and publisher of the Fort Worth *Democrat*. By July 2, 1881, he had moved to Fort Worth and was apparently working for Paddock. On that date he met with thirteen other young men to form a literary club called the Fort Worth Lyceum, and avowed purpose of which was the collection of a good library. As Fort Worth had no public library, the Fort Worth *Democrat* thought the necessity for some collection of books laudatory and suggested that citizens not only encourage but also aid the young men in their endeavor.

Evans worked for the *Democrat* for almost a year, joining the staff in the summer of 1881 and continuing until the newspaper suspended publication in June, 1882. Although his chief duties were to look after the business affairs of the paper, he probably did some writing. As a struggling western paper, the publication consisted largely of local news, advertisements, and many reprints of stories from metropolitan newspapers in the East and Midwest. The presence of a variety of reprints from Indiana and Boston suggest some selection by Evans, and although the evidence is far from conclusive, several articles give evidence of Evans' style of writing, especially an editorial on "Ralph Waldo Emerson" and one entitled "Celebrated Men of Humble Origin." It is certain that he wrote the short note on the death of Jules Fly on September 24, 1881, and likely that he wrote some of the reports on the W. C. Young family, in one of whose members he was soon to take a decided interest.

As a newspaper employee, Evans gave great satisfaction to the owner, Captain Paddock, who publicly expressed his approval of Evans' work as business manager in April, 1882.[26] That Paddock could also express his appreciation in more tangible form is clear from the entries in Evans' bank book for the first four months of 1882. Whether Evans remained in Paddock's employ after the news-

---

[26] Fort Worth *Democrat-Advance*, April 16, 1882, p. 4.

paper failed is not clear. When Evans left Texas in 1884, Paddock stated that most of the time Evans had been in Texas he had worked for him.[27] Paddock subsequently became editor of the *Gazette,* which was formed by combining the *Democrat-Advance* with the *Livestock Journal* in August, 1882, and it is possible that Evans worked for the *Gazette* during the remainder of 1882. Although the nature of his work is uncertain, he continued to have a good income.

Sometime in 1883, probably in the fall, Charles Evans joined the firm of Max Elser as bookkeeper. The company sold books, pianos, wallpaper, and organs, and managed the Fort Worth opera house. Since competence in technical detail had always been his strong point, Evans was a satisfactory employee for Elser and apparently popular with the public.

During the time that Evans was working for the Fort Worth newspapers he had met Lena Young, daughter of Colonel William Crawford Young, a wealthy cattleman and hardware dealer.[28] Lena, a graduate of Mansfield Male and Female College, with her two sisters, Annie and Lora, was very active in literary societies and the other social life which Fort Worth of the 1880's provided. Charles Evans may well have been the young reporter who described the meeting of a literary society at the Young residence on January 6, 1882. Certainly in a frontier town of 7,000 people Evans had ample opportunity to meet Lena during the six months following her graduation from Mansfield in June, 1881. If, however, he missed such an opportunity, an occasion to remedy misfortune awaited him. In March, 1882, Lena actively supported a movement by the W. C. T. U. to provide a general reading room for the citizens of the town.[29] Since there were no other library facilities in the town, the W. C. T. U. reading room was designed to serve all interests. In addition to the standard temperance titles, the group raised a considerable sum

---

[27] B. B. Paddock to "To Whom It May Concern," ALS, Dec. 9, 1884. Paddock does seem to be stretching the truth in order to get Charlie off to a good start in Baltimore. It is difficult to see how Evans could have worked for Paddock more than two years at most out of the three and a half years he spent in Fort Worth, and this does not include all of the time Evans spent in Texas.

[28] Lena Young Evans to Eliot Evans, MS history of her family prepared for the trial of *Lena Young Evans et al.* vs. *Lizzie Young et al.,* 1912. See also *Abstract of Record, Reply Brief and Argument for the Complainants and the Joint and Several Answer of Lizzie Young, Lora Young Lofton, and John T. Lofton,* General No. 603, in the District Court of the United States, Northern District of Texas, all in possession of Eliot H. Evans.

[29] Fort Worth *Democrat-Advance,* March 19, 1882, p. 4, lists Lena Young as one of the monthly subscribers to the library fund.

of money with which to buy histories, novels, and travels, and to keep the reading room open from 9 A.M. to 10 P.M. every day except Sunday. Outright donations were supplemented by proceeds from musical and literary entertainments to which the organization charged twenty-five cents admission. A person as interested in books and reading as Charles Evans could scarcely have missed this opportunity. If he had not met Lena before this time, their mutual interest could well have brought them together now. It is likely that Charlie had already begun accompanying her to the various ice cream parties, lectures, and musicals which the W. C. T. U. sponsored.

Whatever the circumstances under which they met, by the early spring of 1883 Lena Young had consented to become Mrs. Charles Evans.[30] Evans' joy knew no bounds and his letter to "Little Beanie," the first in five years, reflected his new-found happiness. Though he had had many girl friends before he met Lena, only once before, in 1874, had he been seriously enough interested in a woman to consider matrimony.[31] Almost ten years had passed and Evans was now thirty-three. It was beginning to appear that he was to live the life of a bachelor, but the prophecy of Mrs. Vollmer had been correct: in the great country to the south he had found the right woman.

With Lena's willingness to become Mrs. Evans fortune again seemed to smile upon Charlie. In late winter, 1883, he was approached about a possible return to his old position in Indianapolis.[32] Early spring saw a renewal of his correspondence with his friends W. F. Poole and Mary A. Bean, the latter rejoicing with him that "sunlight again shines upon your path."

Another event occurred at this time which seemed to augur well for Evans. In April, 1883, Judge Walter Q. Gresham, one of his Indianapolis friends, was appointed Postmaster General. Charles Evans, sensing the opportunity to use his stalwart Republicanism and his friendship with Gresham, immediately wrote the Postmaster General and asked for the postmastership at Fort Worth.[33] With

---

[30] M. A. B. to C. E., ALS, June 11, 1883.

[31] W. F. P. to C. E., June 14 and 22, 1874. Poole had heard a rumor that Evans was married but denied it since he did not believe Evans would do such a thing and not notify him. That he wrote a second letter about Evans' domestic affairs indicates his concern. Though the name of the woman is not revealed, she could have been the same one Evans was courting when he left Boston in December, 1872.

[32] W. F. P. to C. E., ALS, March 15, 1883; M. A. B. to C. E., ALS, March 9, 1883.

[33] F. N. Bassett to C E., ALS, April 12, 1883, acknowledges receipt of Evans' letter of April 7.

additional responsibilities in the near future Charles Evans could use the annual $2,800 salary. Gresham's chief clerk responded that Evans' name would be given careful consideration when the Fort Worth appointment came up, though nothing more was done until the fall, when Evans had other Indianapolis friends write in support of his nomination.[34]

On January 11, 1884, Evans' nomination as postmaster of Fort Worth was sent to Congress.[35] However, if he thought he could secure the position without a fight, he was in for a rude awakening. The postmistress at the time was Mrs. Belle M. Burchill, a competent woman and the wife of one of the prominent Republicans of Fort Worth. Hearing rumors that there was a move afoot to unseat her, she went to Washington the day before Evans was nominated. As it turned out, she arrived just in time to apply political pressure on her own behalf.

Evans' nomination precipitated a serious internal wrangle among the local Republicans.[36] With the weakening hold of the Republicans after Reconstruction, some in the local party wanted to dispense with Negro support. Evans' nomination had landed him squarely in the middle of this fight. Shortly after Evans' nomination went to Congress, the local Republicans met to consider the situation. A bitter verbal battle ensued with one local party member calling Evans a "sneak thief" and with others decidedly unhappy because the local members had not been consulted about the appointment. Some complained that Evans was not known and others even questioned his Republicanism. Only strong pressure from one of Evans' supporters kept the group from endorsing Mrs. Burchill. The *Gazette,* a Democratic newspaper, could not have been more pleased over the dissension in the Republican ranks. Moreover, it came strongly to the support of Mrs. Burchill and wondered why President Arthur should oust a woman who had given satisfaction to the business community to further a "miserable political scheme."

At the height of the furor Evans went to Washington with some other state Republican leaders and talked personally with Gresham. He accomplished nothing. In a confidential letter to Evans, Gresham mentioned that the incumbent and her friends persisted in their

---

[34] A. C. Harris to C. E., ALS, Sept. 3 and 11, 1883; W. A. Bartlett to C. E., ALS, Oct. 13, 1883.

[35] Fort Worth *Gazette,* Jan. 11, 1884, p. 3.

[36] Fort Worth *Gazette,* Jan. 17, 19, and 31, Feb. 10 and 28, 1884.

efforts to make it appear that injustice had been done.[37] While assuring Evans of his friendship and continued support, Gresham noted that the appointment was a presidential one and that he could only recommend. In short, Gresham and Arthur had to back down in the face of political pressure. With the backing of the local newspaper and some local Republicans who had managed to deliver the vote in the past Mrs. Burchill returned in triumph to Fort Worth.

Failure to obtain the post office appointment was a deep disappointment to Evans. His Republicanism was beyond question, but to seek even quietly to overturn a fellow party member who had given good service was not in accord with his highest ideals. Although the Republican party in Texas seldom pulled together and quite often let elections go by default, the injection of a scheme to turn one party member out for another could hardly help the party.

During the fight Evans could give little attention to marriage preparations, and the wedding which had been planned for early January had to be postponed. Another unfortunate event had occurred which also led to a longer engagement than probably had been anticipated. In April, 1882, Lora Young had been seriously injured in a skating accident. Since her mother was dead, the burden of caring for her fell to the two sisters. Lena Young felt a strong responsibility toward her younger sister and served as her personal nurse until the time of her marriage. The illness was critical during most of 1882 and 1883, and Lena was almost confined by her nursing duties. In the summer of 1883, Colonel Young sent his daughters to Hot Springs for two months in the hope that Lora would recover. Because the trip did seem to help, Colonel Young took her to Hot Springs again in early December for a short stay. They were, therefore, away from Fort Worth during the time that the Republican quarrel took place, though they probably read the unfavorable articles in the *Gazette*. Young, a Confederate colonel and an ardent Democrat, never cared for Evans, who was not only a "damn Yankee" but a Republican too.[38] His unhappiness over the prospect of his daughter marrying this northern man could only have been intensified by the postmaster fracas.

---

[37] Walter Q. Gresham to C. E., ALS, Feb. 5 and March 5, 1884; C. W. Walker to C. E., ALS, Feb. 6, 1884.

[38] Interview with Eliot Evans, Jan. 29, 1959.

Despite the setback to Evans' hopes, early in the year 1884 Lena Young and Charles Evans were married.[39] John Collier, founder and President of Mansfield College, officiated at the ceremony, which took place in the fine new home on Lamar Street which Colonel Young had built the year before. Reporting the happy occasion, the *Gazette* noted that "both the contracting parties are popular members of Fort Worth society, and their host of friends wish them a long and happy wedded life."

Charles Evans entered his marital relationship with more than the usual expectations. He was now thirty-three and, as Beanie had correctly observed, had never known the blessings of home life. He hoped that his future employment would enable him to provide well for his wife and to make her feel proud of him. Though the future might have been brighter with the post office appointment, he had a good job, and perhaps something even better would be forthcoming. At last he could share his life and could depend upon Lena to give him the comfort and understanding which he had never received and to which his sensitive nature would respond. While meditating upon the warmth and affection which he felt for Lena, he had written to "Little Beanie" of his faith in the future. Beanie, too, rejoiced with her "Charley Boy," but she felt compelled to give him some "sisterly advice," which turned out to be a short sermon.[40] The gist of Beanie's preachment was that Evans should be very careful not to hurt his new wife as he had often hurt his friends in the old Athenaeum days. His moodiness was his only fault, but it was a fault he would have to watch. "Home rightly founded and cherished, is nearest heaven in joy and peace; carelessly or thoughtlessly established and soon neglected, it becomes worse than *Dante's Inferno*." Perceptive words from a maiden lady of forty-four!

How well Evans took this advice is hard to determine, but in his selection of Lena Young as his wife Charles Evans chose more wisely than he knew. A petite young lady and socially graceful, Lena was also talented and intelligent. She had taken full advantage of the formal education which was available, even if the facilities had often been poor. Her early education at a parochial school in Nauvoo, Illinois, had given her a good background in languages, and she read and wrote well in Latin, French, and German. Familiar

---

[39] Marriage license and certificate.
[40] M. A. B. to C. E., ALS, Jan. 9, 1884.

with most of the English and American classics, she also had a flair for creative writing. Always sensitive to his needs, she created for Charles Evans a home where he could be secure from the world, and she became a faithful and devoted companion who underwent a great amount of hardship for her husband. In later years when Evans was away on long research trips he always expressed ardent longing to return to home and Lena. Typical of these letters is one written from Annapolis in 1906: "I got your good letter yesterday. It gave me much pleasure; and I believe every word that speaks your love, and return them with the same warmth and affection that I did twenty years ago. We are so much one in thought and life that we do not realize how much we are dependent upon each other until we are parted from each other. I shall count the days until we are once more in each other's arms, my dear one." [41] The devotion of Lena to Charlie became the mainstay and prop to his life.

Soon after his marriage Evans was again involved in politics. At the Republican meeting in January he had proposed that the state convention be invited to meet in Fort Worth. This proposal had carried and preparations had to be made for that assembly. When the Tarrant County Republicans met to select their delegates, Charles Evans had gained a following among the local party group, and he was named secretary of the committee on permanent organization. However, the entire meeting was unfortunate for the Republicans. First, they could not agree on whether or not to support the national candidate to be chosen at Chicago. Then there was a wrangle over how many delegates to send to the state convention. In the struggle that followed, J. W. Wray said that it was clear that the colored people intended to have their way, and if so, he asked all respectable white Republicans who had any respect for themselves and their party to retire. Wray's speech created a great stir among the group, and the bolters left amidst a chorus of jeers from the Negroes. The local Republican Negro leader, the Reverend A. L. Dotson, noted that these Republicans were the kind that threw their arms around the Negroes before the election but would not speak to them the week following.

Since the bolters included all the officers of the convention, they proceeded to the courtroom to elect delegates. Evans was elected secretary unanimously and also asked to serve as treasurer of the

---

[41] C. E. to L. E., ALS, Sept. 23, 1906.

paltry $16 collected to defray expenses. A new slate of delegates, including Evans, was selected; however, when the convention met again in Fort Worth on April 28, the credentials committee refused to seat the bolters. This action led them to perfect a new organization with the avowed aim of making the organization a white man's party. The *Gazette* could hardly contain itself and headlined its report of the meeting, "Lily-White Rads." [42]

Evans' interest in the Republican party of Tarrant County continued during the summer. After the national convention nominated Blaine and Logan, Evans was one of forty local Republicans who met to form a Blaine and Logan Club. Moreover, with the pressure for party unity after the Chicago convention, the local dissension abated, and in a rare demonstration of unity, they unanimously selected local officers and convention delegates for the second state convention. Charles Evans was chosen as local secretary and also as one of the delegates. Though the delegates headed for Houston with enthusiasm, the tide was running against the Republicans that year. While Cleveland's popular majority was less than 100,000 votes, the Democrats carried every state in the South and the northern states of Connecticut, Indiana, New York, and New Jersey. It was just as well for Evans; he would never have been a successful politician. Never again did he participate actively in the work of the party, although he always supported the Republican candidates at the polls and never hesitated to express his views vigorously to the party's officeholders. On the other hand, Lena shared her father's politics, and after the passage of the Nineteenth Amendment, she trudged dutifully to the polls at each election to cancel Charlie's vote.[43]

As the election approached, so did another event in Evans' life: late in the year his first child was born, a girl who was named Gertrude. The baby added to Charlie's sense of responsibility and he was delighted a month later when he had an opportunity to return to professional life. The Enoch Pratt Free Library, gift of a local merchant to the city of Baltimore, was just being organized. As chairman of the library committee of the new institution, John W. McCoy had visited the major public libraries in the United

---

[42] Fort Worth *Gazette*, May 4, 1884, p. 8.

[43] Eliot Evans frequently told his parents that they should not even bother to vote since they cancelled each other's ballots. According to his son, Charles Evans was as staunch a Republican as he has ever known, while Lena Evans always voted the straight Democratic ticket. Interview with Eliot Evans, Jan. 29, 1959.

States. During his tour he had been particularly impressed with Poole's methods of library administration at Chicago.[44] Upon being asked if there were anyone familiar with his methods of library work who could become assistant librarian in Baltimore, Poole had promptly nominated Evans. Poole's recommendation of Evans apparently impressed McCoy as much as his library methods. Even before he left Chicago, McCoy wrote Evans and invited him to come to Baltimore for an interview. The board would pay the full cost of his trip to Baltimore whether or not Evans took the position. Poole urged Evans to go to Baltimore; he was confident he could have the place and he would be the only man on the premises who knew anything. It was a good opportunity to get back into the profession, and the salary would be as good or better than he could get elsewhere.

Evans wasted no time after receiving the two letters. With the Republican defeat his chances for a political plum were dead. Texas had already been disappointment enough, and he was willing to get back into his old harness. On December 14 he arrived in Baltimore, where McCoy showed him every attention. At a meeting of the board of trustees on December 16, Evans was unanimously elected assistant librarian at a salary of $1,800 per year, the appointment to be effective on January 1, 1885.

Returning to Fort Worth, Charles Evans made hurried arrangements to wind up his affairs. He was jubilant over the prospects in Baltimore and was eager to leave Texas. In his anxiety to move to Baltimore, though, he was careless about his finances. On December 27 he sold his furniture to W. W. Hayward, proprietor of Hayward's News Bureau.[45] While he seemed to make a profit of $100 on this transaction, he actually lost the entire sum, for Hayward never paid a cent of the promised $350. Time, however, was short and the family needed to be on their way. Using the notes signed by Hayward as security, Evans borrowed $300 from his friend Paddock to take care of his moving expense. In late December with Mrs. Evans and Gertrude, Evans boarded the train for Baltimore.

---

[44] W. F. P. to C. E., ALS, Dec. 2, 1884; John W. McCoy to C. E., ALS, Dec. 3, 1884.

[45] Four notes of W. W. Hayward to Charles Evans in the amount of $87.50 each, Dec. 27, 1884. B. B. Paddock to C. E., ALS, Feb. 1 and 21, March 11, April 5 and 16, May 10, Aug. 8, Sept. 18 and 21, Oct. 10, 1885. Also W. W. Hayward to C. E., ALS, Jan. 17, Feb. 19, April 10, and Charles Emery to C. E., ALS, Feb. 19, 1885.

While Evans knew little about Dr. Lewis H. Steiner, the librarian at Baltimore, he had the virtual assurance of Poole and McCoy that the actual administration of the library would be in his hands.[46] With a minimum income of $50,000 per year and a new building and four branches already completed, the Enoch Pratt Free Library would offer Evans another opportunity to make his mark in the library profession. As Evans' train left Fort Worth for Baltimore, the prospects for the year 1885 were happy indeed.

[46] W. F. P. to C. E., ALS, Dec. 2 and 31, 1884; John W. McCoy to C. E., ALS, Dec. 3, 1884.

The Clash of Red-headed Welsh
and Pennsylvania Dutch

6

Arriving in the city of Baltimore on January 4, 1885, Evans took his family to the Howard House, a good hotel in the main business district.[1] Ever mindful that his $1,800 salary might not stretch very far in Baltimore, he soon located a boarding house where all three could live for $15 per week until he had time to rent a house. Having settled his family in their temporary home, he began library work in earnest.

Evans' first month at Baltimore was an enjoyable one. There were numerous advantages to his position. For the first time he had an opportunity to work in a potentially large public library system. Moreover, the building was new and adequate, despite its architectural limitations. The new assistant librarian could not help agreeing with his friend Poole's judgment on the latter score.[2] Typical of public buildings of the Victorian era, it was a two-story structure with a central tower, Romanesque in design. In keeping with Enoch Pratt's frugal character the façade had been constructed of Baltimore County white marble and granite, which gave it a rich appearance, but the rest of the building, not visible from the front, had been constructed of brick. The center doors were of heavy, carved oak,

---

[1] C. E. to L. E., ALS, Sept. 25, 1906; L. E. to Eliot Evans, ALS, Feb. 14, 1911.

[2] B. B. Paddock to C. E., ALS, Feb. 1, 1885; C. E. to Joseph Wheeler, MS draft of a letter probably mid-April, 1933. W. F. Poole, "The Progress of Library Architecture," *Library Journal,* VII (July–Aug., 1882), 135–136.

and the vestibule and stairway were decorated with a variety of marble and other stones, giving an appearance of massiveness.

The first floor of Pratt's building contained the delivery room for books and a smaller room for the registration of borrowers and for book returns. To the rear of both was the stack area. The second floor rear, reached by an impressive stairway, was devoted to a reading room with a seating capacity for 250 readers. The rest of the second floor was devoted to offices, workroom, and a room for the board of trustees. With all of its flaws the building provided working space and reading space as good as could be found in most nineteenth-century libraries. An additional feature often overlooked in library planning of this period was the provision of space for expansion of the book collection to 250,000 volumes. For a library which had not yet cataloged its first title, this was an encouraging sign. Even if his knowledge of aesthetics was limited, Pratt had planned wisely for the future of his library. As Poole had not let his criticism of the building prevent his recommendation of Evans to McCoy, so Evans did not allow his own personal thoughts about the building to interfere with his work. He was pragmatic enough to use the opportunity provided. As long as he had adequate resources to do the work he loved and freedom to organize the system as he wished, he could be happy.

Freedom in one's work appeared to be a great virtue of the Enoch Pratt. Unlike Indianapolis, there would be no political interference here. When Enoch Pratt had given the building he had stipulated that the board would be selected by him and would be self-perpetuating. No member could be "appointed or removed on religious or political grounds."[3] In accepting Pratt's $833,333.33 the city had agreed to a $50,000 per year annuity for operating expenses. Since a capricious taxing body could not tamper with the library's annual income, Evans thought surely this was an opportunity to build a great public library. Some of this enthusiasm he undoubtedly communicated to Paddock, for the latter wrote Evans in February that he was "delighted that everything presents such a roseate hue."[4] Evans immediately settled down to his task of preparing the initial list of 10,000 books to be ordered for the library and to

---

[3] "Letter of Enoch Pratt to the Mayor and City Council of Baltimore," in *The Enoch Pratt Free Library of Baltimore; Letters and Documents Relating to Its Foundation and Organization* (Baltimore: Press of Isaac Friedenwald, 1886). Cited hereafter as Enoch Pratt Free Library, *Documents.*

[4] B. B. Paddock to C. E., ALS, Feb. 1, 1885.

setting up a classification scheme for the 200,000 volumes the library eventually hoped to have.[5]

While the enthusiasm for his work continued, his optimism was short-lived. The freedom from politics did not mean *ipso facto* that Evans would be allowed to promote his own ideas without interference. The first restraint came from the head librarian, Dr. Lewis H. Steiner, whom the board had appointed the previous November.[6] Fifty-eight years of age when he assumed the direction of the Enoch Pratt Free Library, Steiner had had a varied career, including the practice of medicine, politics, journalism, and education. Pratt thought that such a distinguished individual, though without practical library experience, would give prestige to the new venture. Evans could do the technical work while Steiner gave the over-all supervision, dealt with the public, and formulated policy. To help Steiner become familiar with other library systems the board had sent him on a tour of important public libraries about the same time that McCoy made his trip, though the two did not go together. Both Steiner and McCoy had been impressed with the methods of library administration at Chicago, much to the annoyance of Boston librarians and to Poole's delight.[7] Therefore, both Evans and Poole thought that Steiner would give Evans a free hand in administering the day-to-day operations and the technical side of the library's work. Such, however, was not to be the case. Perhaps there was not enough policy-making to keep Steiner busy after the original code of regulations had been drawn up in early 1885. In March, after Evans had been at work for two months, he wrote to Poole that Steiner was not the man they had thought him to be, by which he meant to indicate that the latter was not permitting Evans to have his way about everything.[8] So far the head librarian had distinguished himself primarily as an obstructionist. Just what obstructions Steiner placed in Evans' way is unknown, but it is significant that early in his work at Enoch Pratt, Evans was having difficulty with his immediate superior.

Almost equally annoying, but forgivable, was the direct inter-

---

[5] Baltimore *Sun*, Nov. 4, 1886, p. 4. C. E. to W. F. P., ALS, April 8, 1888, Poole Papers, Newberry Library.

[6] Hart, *Enoch Pratt, the Story of a Plain Man* (Baltimore: Enoch Pratt Free Library, 1935), pp. 57–58. James H. Phalen, "Lewis H. Steiner," in *Dictionary of American Biography*, XVII, 562–563.

[7] W. F. P. to C. E., ALS, March 13, 1885.

[8] *Ibid.*

ference of Pratt. For years Enoch Pratt had supervised the most minute detail of his own business. Despite his statement to the board in 1884: "I leave it [the library] to you with confidence," [9] he had no intention of leaving administrative matters solely in their hands nor in the hands of the board's appointees. Having decided to give away over a million dollars, Pratt felt a great sense of responsibility for launching his enterprise in the right way. No procedure was too small for his attention, and the hiring of the staff became his personal concern. Before anyone was hired, Pratt and the board personally interviewed each applicant.[10] Although the old man's manner was brusque, he tried to show his kindness to the staff, and Charles and Lena Evans were at least occasional guests at dinner at the Pratt residence. That his invitations to dinner frequently took the tone of a summons rather than a friendly outstretched hand was merely a reflection of his personality. He was accustomed to send his employees notes which said things imperiously. While Evans' sensitive nature sometimes took offense when the intent was kind, he was willing to overlook these annoyances, for he had a keen appreciation of Pratt's generosity toward the public library. Charles Evans seriously intended to stay in the position of assistant librarian at the Enoch Pratt Free Library until a better opportunity came along.

So despite the obstruction of Steiner and the occasional interference of Pratt, Evans worked diligently throughout his first year. Again, as at Indianapolis, he used Poole's classification system. Although the scheme itself was an inflexible one, it could be made expansible by the addition of a decimal zero to each of the original numbers, and Evans believed he had prepared adequately in his detailed outline for a library of 200,000 volumes. While he used the Poole scheme for the basic collection, he found a system which John Edmands had devised very useful for those parts of the collection—such as English prose fiction, juveniles, essays, and periodicals—where an alphabetical arrangement by authors or titles was more feasible.[11] Edmands' work seems to have been similar to the Cutter alphabetical tables, a system of author marks combining the first letter of the author's last name with a series of three

[9] "Letter of Enoch Pratt, Formally Transferring the Management of the Library to the Board of Trustees," in Enoch Pratt Free Library, *Documents*, p. 49.
[10] Hart, *Enoch Pratt*, pp. 60–61.
[11] C. E. to W. F. P., ALS, April 8, 1888, Poole Papers, Newberry Library; "Plans for Numbering, with Especial Reference to Fiction: A Library Symposium," *Library Journal*, IV (Feb., 1879), 38–40.

numerals for easy arrangement of books upon the shelves. Where the letters of the alphabet in Poole's classification stood for various subjects and the combinations were more complicated, the letters and numbers in the Edmands scheme represented the authors' last names.

As an example of Evans' industry that first year in Baltimore, one can examine the statistics of the book collection at the time the central building was dedicated. On January 4, 1886, the Enoch Pratt Free Library contained 20,000 fully cataloged volumes, all added during the preceding year.[12] An additional 12,000 volumes had been purchased and cataloged for the branches. When one remembers that Evans not only had to prepare the lists of books to be purchased, but to order them, to make a classification scheme, and then to train his assistants to use it, while doing a significant part of the work himself, one can only marvel at the amount of energy expended by the man. McCoy, always his good friend and admirer, later wrote that he had never, in forty years of association with libraries, met Evans' superior in rapid and accurate work.[13] Evans' work and his standards had suffered no diminution during his absence from the profession.

Evans' friends in the profession had been glad to see him return to the fold. W. DeM. Hooper, then librarian of the Indianapolis Public Library, sent warm greetings of the staff there along with the copies of various library forms which Evans had requested.[14] Beanie felt "like singing songs of praise—Jubilate and all the rest of it." Tempering her joy with some words of advice, she urged Charlie not to let this golden opportunity slip through his grasp by a repetition of any of the mistakes of his first experience. She was glad that he had returned to the profession, and she had no fears for her "Charlie Boy" unless he became so absorbed in his work that he forgot to cultivate his social qualities. On June 20, James L. Whitney, Assistant Librarian of the Boston Public Library and Treasurer of the American Library Association, wrote his con-

[12] "Address of Dr. Lewis H. Steiner, Librarian," in Enoch Pratt Free Library, *Documents*, p. 107. Enoch Pratt Free Library of Baltimore City, *Report of Librarian to the Board of Trustees, January 1, 1887* (Baltimore: Press of Isaac Friedenwald, 1887), p. 6. Cited hereafter as Enoch Pratt Free Library, *Report, 1887*

[13] John W. McCoy to C. E., ALS, n.d., but probably Dec., 1886.

[14] W. DeM. Hooper to C. E., ALS, Dec. 21, 1884; M. A. B. to C. E., ALS, Jan. 1, 1885; J. L. Whitney to C. E., ALS, June 20, 1885.

gratulations. According to Whitney, "You stand no. 2 in Mr. Dewey's American Library Association list and no. 1 in the affection of many librarians." As proof that he was really back in the fold, he should send two dollars for his 1885 association dues. Possibly because he was short of funds at the time, Evans did not report immediately, but at the end of the summer he sent Whitney payment for membership fees for 1885 and 1886. Whatever the trials of the Enoch Pratt Free Library, it was good to be back in the profession and to have such cordial comments from his fellow practitioners.

Irritated as he was by certain conditions at the library, Charlie tried hard to follow Beanie's advice. With Lena at his side he found it easier to make social contacts and to enjoy the hospitality of some prominent Baltimore residents. They came to know well the Edward Stablers and John W. McCoys. Lena was adept at the kind of conversation which makes an invitation to dinner a pleasant visit, and Charlie felt more comfortable in her presence.[15] She relieved some of the necessity for his conversational efforts. On his salary they were also able to afford a colored nurse and even occasionally to make side trips to Annapolis and Washington, D.C. They made some lasting friends among the Enoch Pratt Free Library staff, and Evans even became a good friend of Daniel Coit Gilman, President of Johns Hopkins University.

As Evans continued his work in Baltimore, he could not help being impressed with one favorable aspect of Pratt's character. Though he had certain faults, Pratt never embarked on an enterprise without sound preliminary preparation. He had built the building, presented it to the city, appointed the board of trustees, and then hired a staff. Not content to open until everything should be in readiness, he allowed the staff an entire year in which to secure books and organize them for use. To celebrate the opening of his library, an imposing dedication program had been planned. The formal ceremonies took place at the Academy of Music at noon on January 4, 1886.

Pratt's speech, while the shortest of the group, told the citizens exactly what they could expect from the library.[16] Expressing gratitude that his plans had been completed, he bluntly stated the mean-

---

[15] That Charles Evans felt his wife was a better conversationalist is seen in C. E. to L. E., ALS, Oct. 24, 1921. Gertrude Evans Jones to the author, Nov. 14, 1960.

[16] "Address of Enoch Pratt," Enoch Pratt Free Library, *Documents*, pp. 68–69.

ing of a free circulating library. By the word "free" he did not mean
to imply freedom to keep books at will but freedom from charge
for their use. The board had provided for the protection of the
library by the adoption of sound rules gathered from the experiences
of public libraries in other cities. With the wish that Baltimore
would protect the library and increase its usefulness, Enoch Pratt
closed: "My work is finished. I am satisfied."

Completing the exercises was Dr. Steiner, who expressed the hope
that he would be able to perform his duties in a manner to secure
"the greatest good to the greatest number in the community." [17]
Tracing the history of ideas through the printed page, Steiner allied
democracy with learning. The public library was a continuation
of the public schools—a people's university—and he urged the people to use it wisely. Nothing in his speech was particularly new to
his audience. The role of the public library as an institution of
continuing education was an accepted one. With the conclusion of
Steiner's speech, the formal ceremonies ended and the dignitaries
proceeded to Pratt's home for dinner.

The following day the library was opened for use without restriction on race, color, or creed. It was popular from the beginning
and both registration of borrowers and circulation were large the
first year. In the twelve-month period total registration was 25,693,
and total circulation from the central building, 287,319.[18] When
the circulation of the four branches, opened in February and March,
was added to the latter total, the Enoch Pratt Free Library had
circulated a total of 410,319 volumes, or an average of fifteen books
for each registered borrower. Classification of the circulation followed roughly the same form Evans had used at Indianapolis. For
the central building the proportion of fiction and juvenile books
to the rest of the circulation was 68 per cent, confirming Evans'
earlier estimate that about three-fourths of the users of a public
library read for amusement and only one-fourth for improvement.
Average daily circulation from the central library was 942, or about
one-third more than the average at the Indianapolis Public Library
during Evans' last year there.

To acquaint the patrons with the book collection Evans had prepared finding lists which were sold at twenty cents per copy. The

---

[17] "Address of Dr. Lewis H. Steiner," Enoch Pratt Free Library, *Documents*,
pp. 101–107.

[18] Enoch Pratt Free Library, *Report*, 1887, pp. 5–7, 10.

collection was very strong in the areas of history, religion, and English literature. A later librarian of the Enoch Pratt Free Library stated that Evans' extraordinary ability in evaluating books had resulted in a collection of such high quality that fifty years later some of them were still in daily use, whereas others were so rare and valuable that they were continually requested for interlibrary loan.[19] The total number of volumes in the system at the end of 1886 was 45,109. With continuing high expenditures for books and periodicals and the added work of processing and circulating them the library had a busy year, but the statistics offered abundant evidence of the value of the library to the citizens of Baltimore.

With such high circulation and such rapid increases in book acquisitions Evans and his staff worked hard to keep up. Always a strong believer in the importance of good, cheap finding lists, Evans had to struggle to keep up with the demand. In late February he published the second edition of the *Finding List,* a book of 153 pages. A twelve-page supplement followed in May and a twenty-three-page supplement in November. In addition to these lists of books, the branch libraries also published a joint finding list. Though the actual work on the latter list was probably done by the branch librarians, it is likely that Evans supervised their work. There was truth in Pratt's remark, "I don't think there is a more thoroughly organized Library than mine & Mr. E. was very successful in it." [20]

In line with his practice, Pratt continued to keep a close eye on the new enterprise. His biographer mentions his constant surveillance. "He haunted the Library at all hours. On business days he usually came to the central building after dinner, which he took between three and four o'clock, and stayed several hours. There was no detail too slight, no expenditure too trivial to escape his scrutiny." [21] This continual meddling in legitimate administrative affairs bothered Evans and no doubt accentuated his continuing difficulties with Steiner. After all, he was not a newcomer to the library business. He had conducted another library with almost as many books and had led it to eminence among the country's public libraries. Attention to detail was one of his strong points, and he

[19] Joseph L. Wheeler as quoted in Baltimore *Evening Sun,* Feb. 9, 1935, in Eliot Evans, "Scrapbook."
[20] Enoch Pratt to [George W.] Childs, ALS, probably Dec. 11, 1886.
[21] Hart, *Enoch Pratt,* p. 64.

was irked by Pratt's examinations and questions on his procedures. However, he could endure Pratt; respect for the man's wealth and position assured that. In fact, Evans probably secretly admired the old man. His humorous references to Pratt's stinginess and his anecdotes of his business ability reveal strong if subtle admiration. There is no real bitterness for Pratt in Evans' letters.

However, if he could and had to endure Pratt, Evans felt no such compunction about Steiner. He blamed his superior, incorrectly perhaps, for much of Pratt's interference. What he could not say to Pratt he did not hesitate to say to Steiner. Shortly after the formal opening of the library, the dogmatism of Evans and the equally obstinate behavior of Steiner met in a head-on clash. First to take cognizance of this matter was the library committee, composed of three members of the board and headed by John W. McCoy, the man who had been instrumental in bringing Evans to Baltimore. In the disputes on library matters Steiner's typical behavior was to take the matter to Pratt.[22] It is not unlikely that Evans reciprocated by taking his side of the question to McCoy. At a meeting on February 15, 1886, the committee reported that "there is not sufficient cooperation and sympathy between the Librarian and the Assistant Librarian." [23] Upon receipt of this report, the board of trustees ordered the library committee to bring this matter to the attention of both individuals and request that a more harmonious working relationship be established. This should have been, and perhaps was, a familiar danger signal to Evans. Apparently a temporary truce was declared, for no further official action on the matter was taken until the following fall.

Evans needed the temporary truce. He had a personal reason for submitting to Steiner's direction and for continuing his work. On February 27, 1886, his first son was born, and he more than ever needed the salary his present position afforded. He had repaid Paddock in full by September, 1885, at what was undoubtedly a considerable drain on his finances.[24] With another child to support he had good reason to remember Beanie's advice to "pocket his pride deep down."

The Evanses named their boy Eliot Howland, taking the name

[22] C. E. to W. F. P., ALS, July 28, 1887, Poole Papers, Newberry Library.

[23] Arthur H. Parsons, Jr., to the author, Dec. 16, 1958, summarizes all the data on the Evans-Steiner trouble from the minutes of the board of trustees.

[24] B. B. Paddock to C. E., ALS, Sept. 9, 1885.

from Charlie's Boston guardian and his old friend in Indianapolis. The birth of a son gave renewed hope to Evans, and he wrote Samuel Eliot a "long and interesting letter" about his family and his work in Baltimore.[25] If he was aware that storm clouds were gathering, he gave no indication of them to Dr. Eliot. The latter wanted to be kept informed about Charlie's family and sent a Faneuil Hall spoon for his namesake.

Despite the long letter to Eliot about his good fortune in Baltimore, Evans' relationship with Steiner deteriorated during the summer. The trouble was obvious to the staff, and one member later remarked that the trustees ought to have known that a red-headed Welshman and a Pennsylvania Dutchman could not work together.[26] By early fall Pratt asked for Evans' resignation, which was duly submitted, to take effect on November 1.[27] In his letter of resignation Evans defended his two years of "faithful and laborious service" and disclaimed any responsibility for the state of affairs which existed in the library. He thanked Pratt personally for his "many acts of kindness, and expressions of kindly feeling and sympathy toward me in the trying and delicate position which you have frequently admitted has fallen to my lot in this Institution."

When the board received Evans' letter, they resolved to refer it to a special committee to determine what had caused the state of affairs mentioned by Evans. After careful interviews with Steiner, Evans, and other members of the library staff, they asked Evans if he thought he could continue as assistant librarian in view of his animosity toward Steiner. With complete candor Evans replied that he could not. If Steiner remained, he would have to go, for such a bad relationship between the two was injurious to the best interests of the library. Evans was not a discreet man. When something displeased him, he said so in frank and forthright language, even if it cost him his job.

In fairness to Evans the committee held seven sessions to try to determine the best course of action for the board. Reporting on October 30 to the full board, the committee stated that "the unfortunate state of affairs referred to by Mr. Evans arises from a

---

[25] Samuel Eliot to C. E., ALS, June 5, [1886?].

[26] This is what Anna Doerkson told Lawrence C. Wroth when he joined the staff of the Enoch Pratt Free Library in the early part of the twentieth century. Interview with Lawrence C. Wroth, May 15, 1958.

[27] C. E. to Enoch Pratt, ALS, Oct. 4, 1886, as quoted in Arthur H. Parsons, Jr., to the author, Dec. 16, 1958.

complete alienation of feeling between that gentleman and the Librarian which has steadily grown during Mr. Evans' term of service." While the committee was reluctant to fix blame, they believed that both parties had been guilty of regrettable and unfortunate conduct. It is clear that both Evans and Steiner were strong-willed and outspoken men, and they did not keep their differences of opinion hidden from their subordinates. While the committee did not say much about Evans in view of his scheduled departure, they did point out Steiner's administrative failings. His chief fault was his censure of Evans in the presence of other employees, using "contumelious epithets" and criticism "which was destructive of all discipline and unworthy of one who is expected to set all his subordinates an example of unvarying dignity and courtesy." He also failed to give sufficient consideration to the suggestions of these subordinates. The committee called Steiner's attention to the fact that these difficulties ought to have been communicated to the board.

In concluding its report, which the board accepted, the committee made the following recommendations:

1. Evans' resignation be accepted as of December 1, 1886.
2. Applications be accepted for the position of assistant librarian.
3. The librarian be given a copy of the committee report and the trustees consider the report confidential.
4. The records of the committee's meeting be preserved until otherwise determined by the board.

After a year, the board ordered records of this special committee destroyed.

It would be easy enough to justify Evans' dismissal from Baltimore in terms of the poor administrative behavior of Steiner. The head librarian had created a situation in which no assistant could continue to function very effectively. Before his staff Steiner had ripped Evans' ego to shreds with his outbursts and frequent criticism of his assistant's alleged shortcomings. Such a position was not only impossible from an administrative point of view but positively harmful for Evans. The latter had apparently submitted as long as he could. He even postponed his resignation for several weeks after Pratt requested it in the hope that something could be worked out. Moreover, the letters of Pratt and McCoy testify to Evans' capability as an internal administrator. In reporting Evans' resignation the Baltimore *Sun* commented that "his pleasant manners and obliging disposition have made him many friends in Baltimore, who will be sorry that he is going away." [28] The library staff in a formal letter testified to his kindness, courtesy, justice, and encouragement.

However, the board had noted that not all the fault lay with Steiner. Evans had been guilty of some undefined actions which had provoked Steiner's ire. It was too bad that his "obliging disposition" and "pleasant manners" did not apply to Steiner as well as to the general public. Pratt, fully appreciative of Evans' talents as an organizer of libraries, commented that he had one fault: "his temperament don't brook serving under a master." [29] Poole, too, was apparently not pleased with Evans' action in the situation, for Evans still felt he had to justify his action to Poole as much as nine months later.[30] There seems little reason to doubt Pratt's blunt but perceptive evaluation. Evans had his own way of doing things and he insisted on doing them in just that way. A prodigious worker, he could not stand interference from people who slowed up his program. While there is good reason to believe that he was a courteous and sympathetic boss, he simply could not abide the criticism of the man at the top. If Steiner shouted at Evans, the latter almost certainly shouted back. In spite of his personal feelings Evans would have done well to remember that Steiner was the head librarian.

The board had accepted the recommendation that Evans' resignation be accepted as of December 1, 1886. It is probable that he remained in the library and completed various projects on which he had been working, including seeing the second supplement to the finding list through the press. There is some evidence that his salary was continued until January 1, 1887, although he did not work in the library during December.[31] Meanwhile, he had to look for a new position, for now he had to support a family of four.

In early December, Evans asked Pratt and McCoy for letters of recommendation to George W. Childs of Philadelphia. Childs was the editor of the Philadelphia *Public Ledger* and a prominent figure in a variety of literary enterprises. Just what position Evans hoped to obtain through Childs is not definitely known, but the major reason for seeing him must have been the Library Company of Philadelphia, where the position of librarian had been vacant

---

[28] Baltimore *Sun*, Nov. 4, 1886, p. 4.
[29] Enoch Pratt to [George W.] Childs, ALS, probably Dec. 11, 1886.
[30] C. E. to W. F. P., July 28, 1887, Poole Papers, Newberry Library.
[31] Jean-Barry Molz to the author, TLS, April 9, 1958.

since the death of Evans' friend Lloyd P. Smith on July 2, 1886. Although Childs was not a member of the board of trustees of that library, Evans may have thought he could introduce him to some of the influential members of the board. During this period Evans was definitely considered for the position, but the trustees eventually turned elsewhere and for the first three months of 1887 he was out of work.[32]

Again Evans turned to Poole and asked for help. Poole by this time was the leading librarian in the Midwest and was frequently consulted about candidates for library positions.[33] He put Evans in touch with Jessie Allan, Librarian of the Omaha Public Library, who wanted someone to classify the library and make a card catalog. Evans offered to do the work at a rate of $2,000 per year on a monthly basis.[34] Moving his family to Springhaven, a boarding house at the summer resort town of Owings Mills, a small village a few miles north and west of Baltimore, he departed for Omaha and began his work there on April 18, 1887. As much as Charlie disliked the thought of being away from Lena and the children, he would take any library job which would provide for their support.

When Evans took the Omaha position, he thought it would not last very long, but after he settled down to work, he realized that the reclassification of the book collection would take several months. Evans' justification of his work had been communicated to the trustees before he arrived and was such a good defense that the president of the board used his statement as a part of the annual report. The first two paragraphs are important, not only because they show Evans' familiarity with the thinking of his own time, but also because almost any guide to a library, from Evans' day to the present, has stated the justification of the card catalog in almost identical terms:

A good card-catalogue of a library is of the same importance as a good index to a book.

Its aim and purpose is to be an index of the contents of the library. In its use it is a time-saver. It shows at a glance what the library possesses.

[32] Information on this point is confusing, but see C. E. to L. E., ALS, Feb. 12, 1908. "By the way Barnwell who was the Librarian chosen when I asked to come here [Library Company of Philadelphia] you remember has dropped out of his position since last summer in a way that reflects upon his mentality."

[33] Williamson, "William Frederick Poole," p. 306, notes that in his later years Poole became virtually a one-man placement bureau.

[34] Extract from the minutes of the Omaha Public Library Board as quoted in Arthur H. Parsons, Jr., to the author, TLS, Omaha, July 16, 1956.

It is a necessity for a safe administration of the library to guard against duplication. It answers, as in no other manner can be answered, the oft repeated questions: What books by any particular author are there in the library? Have you a book of a particular title in the library, whose author's name I have forgotten? What books and monographs has the library upon any particular subject? It furnishes a complete and ready reference to every book in the library; and, as it contains the latest accessions to the library, it is a manuscript ready for the printer whenever it is found necessary to issue a printed catalogue.[35]

In addition to making a card catalog Evans had been authorized by the board to reclassify the books, make a shelf list, and to prepare a finding list for the printers. All of this work was to be accomplished for a library of nearly 20,000 volumes without closing the library a single day. Even when classification and cataloging were less complicated than they are today, such an undertaking was formidable.

Using the Poole classification system and the alphabetical numbering scheme of Edmands as he had done at Baltimore, Evans worked diligently throughout the summer. In July he paused long enough to write a letter congratulating Poole, who had just been appointed librarian of the Newberry Library.[36] With the financial resources at the command of the Newberry board of trustees and the opportunity to build a great research library, Poole was in a good position to make this librarianship the fitting crown to his life's work, and Evans was delighted for him.

Evans had intended to complete his Omaha finding list by October, but when fall came he was still busily engaged in classifying and shelf-listing books. In December he wrote to Poole that his experience at Omaha had convinced him that a new library could be formed in half the time that an old one could be altered.[37] In the same letter he noted that he had arranged and numbered 3,300 volumes and had made catalog cards for 2,430 of that number during the previous month. The other 870 volumes represented the only help he had received in the past four months. However, he did not complain about the work load, for he believed that this was the best and most systematic work he had ever done. In addition to his cataloging work he had also helped with the plans for new

---

[35] Omaha Public Library, *The Tenth Annual Report of the Board of Directors of the Omaha Public Library for the Year Ending May 31st 1887* (Omaha: F. A. Manger, 1887), pp. 10–11.

[36] C. E. to W. F. P., ALS, July 28, 1887, Poole Papers, Newberry Library.

[37] C. E. to W. F. P., ALS, Dec. 30, 1887, Poole Papers, Newberry Library.

quarters for the library. Since the library would move into this new space soon after the first of the year, he thought it would take on new life from that time. He now hoped to be through by February 1.

During the winter there were problems at Owings Mills. Eliot Howland, always sickly as a baby, became seriously ill and had to have constant attention from his mother.[38] With Charlie a thousand miles away in Omaha, Lena had a difficult time with the family responsibilities. Fortunately she had friends who cared for Gertrude and helped her in other ways, but this was scarcely an adequate substitute for the head of the house. Evans was concerned about his family, and the baby's illness strengthened his desire to find a permanent position. That he had had to spend the Christmas season away from his family only added to his unhappiness.

When he could, Evans stilled the natural desire to be with his family by hard work. Though his work schedule was exhausting, he did find time to keep up his professional reading. The *Library Journal* was a regular part of his program. He was especially pleased with the issue containing the proceedings of the American Library Association convention, held at Round Island in 1887. Poole, as president of the association, had delivered an address on public libraries which Evans thought added a glowing leaf to Poole's biography. Moreover, two of the participants in the conference had quoted from one of his annual reports at Indianapolis, and another had favorably mentioned his 1877 paper on the sizes of printed books. With deference toward his mentor, Evans remarked that these notices reminded him of Poole's advice of many years before: "Get an idea into the world in connection with your name."[39]

Evans also read *Library Notes,* a magazine published by the Library Bureau. Noting Poole's defense of wooden shelving in a recent issue, he called it "a gem set in a mess of hare-brained ideas and bad spelling," an obvious reference to Melvil Dewey's use of simplified spelling in the journal's articles. With less charity toward Dewey's publication than it probably deserved, Evans added superciliously, "The only other item in it worth remembering was an advertisement of a patent ink stand at the end."

---

[38] L. E. to Eliot Evans, typed copy of a letter, March 2, 1929, in possession of Eliot Evans.

[39] C. E. to W. F. P., ALS, Dec. 30, 1887, and April 8, 1888, Poole Papers, Newberry Library.

Omaha also provided an opportunity for him to continue his literary reading. Dipping into the *Atlantic Monthly* for January, 1888, he was delighted with an article on "The History of Children's Books," by Caroline Hewins. In earlier days she had been a member of the Athenaeum staff and Evans was pleased that she had retained her same dry humor. Another example of connecting one's name to an idea, he noted to Poole. Another magazine which he enjoyed was the *Dial* for which Poole wrote regularly.

When the time came, Evans helped with the removal of the library to its new quarters, and this move slowed the work on his finding list. During the late winter serious differences of opinion began to develop between Evans and the board.[40] Perhaps the board found the time necessary to rearrange the library greater than they had planned. The annual report indicates that they were determined that this task would not last beyond the year. "An expert cataloguer was employed for a year in putting this system into operation; but now our own librarian can carry on the work, and add to the catalogue from time to time such accessions as are made to the library." While appreciating Evans' services in setting up such "a simple and admirable system," the board voted to dispense with his activities at the end of his year's term on April 15, 1888.[41]

Despite the strain existing between Evans and the board, by April 8, 1888, Evans had sent 230 pages of the finding list through the printers and fully expected to see the job completed before he left. As finally published, the list contained 252 pages and listed about 20,000 volumes. Though it had been a difficult year, Evans could leave Omaha with the satisfaction of a job well done. All of his work of rearranging, reclassifying, and cataloging had been accomplished without closing the library a single day. The planning and thought which Evans had devoted to the program before he began had resulted in a very efficient operation. He had designed

---

[40] According to Parsons, "one of the legends in this library is to the effect that there was a serious difference of opinion between Mr. Evans and the board toward the end of the time he was employed here in Omaha," Arthur H. Parsons, Jr., to the author, TLS, July 16, 1956.

[41] Omaha Public Library, *Eleventh Annual Report of the Board of Directors of the Omaha Public Library for the Year Ending May 31st 1888* (Omaha: Rees Printing Company, 1888), p. 10; extract from minutes of the Omaha Public Library Board as quoted in Arthur H. Parsons, Jr., to the author, TLS, July 16, 1956.

the classification scheme for a library of 100,000 volumes, and by the addition of a decimal zero the capacity of the library could be doubled without disturbing the arrangement.

In addition to his satisfaction in completing the Omaha project Evans thought he could look forward to another job. During his year in Omaha there had been offers of other positions, but he had not felt that he could take them. In the summer of 1887, A. R. Spofford, Librarian of Congress, had offered to secure a cataloging position for him in the California State Library. More importantly, a group of Baltimore citizens had raised funds to revive the Mercantile Library, and President Daniel C. Gilman, of Johns Hopkins University, who had seen him in operation at the Enoch Pratt, asked Evans to come back to Baltimore to reorganize the collection. Since the invitation to Baltimore came near the completion of Evans' work in Omaha, it is difficult to understand why he refused it. He fully appreciated the offer but recommended one of his former assistants at the Pratt Library. Though Gilman accepted Evans' recommendation, he commented that he would have felt "more certain of success" if he could have obtained Evans' services. This commendation from a former librarian pleased Evans, and he wrote Poole that he cared more for these words of Gilman than for all the combined opinions of a Steiner or a Pratt.[42] With such individuals as President Gilman and the Librarian of Congress looking out for him surely something good would turn up.

Upon his return from Omaha, Evans found his family well and happy.[43] Lena was especially grateful to Poole, who had been so helpful in their trying circumstances. In May, Evans took his wife to Washington, D.C., for a visit, and while he was there, he saw Spofford. The latter told him that Professor G. Stanley Hall, who was to head the new Clark University in Worcester, had visited him two weeks before. Spofford had recommended Evans to Hall as the librarian for the new institution. There was also a vacancy in the Howard Library at Tulane, and he had been in correspondence with the people in New Orleans. Since Poole wanted him at the Newberry and the East Saginaw, Michigan, Public Library wanted their collection cataloged, it appeared that Evans could have his choice of jobs. However, such was not to be. Hall intended to tour the

---

[42] C. E. to W. F. P., ALS, Dec. 30, 1887, Poole Papers, Newberry Library.

[43] C. E. to W. F. P., ALS, May 21 and June 9, 1888, Poole Papers, Newberry Library.

world before he made any decisions about Worcester, Poole's board would not let him pay what Evans thought he needed to support a family, and the East Saginaw job never materialized.

There were other positions open, but none of them resulted in Evans' employment. H. J. Carr, Librarian of the Grand Rapids Public Library, wanted to have his library cataloged but doubted that he could get the board to consent to having it done. There was also a position in Memphis that might have been promising. Certainly it was not lack of job possibilities that kept Evans unoccupied. Since most of the positions wanted someone to do cataloging, he asked Poole if he thought it would be a good idea to branch out into this type of library work. He could develop a corps of assistants, and they could set themselves up as library experts in the organization of libraries. Poole himself had done this with Mary A. Bean and Harriet Ames in 1869–70.[44] The only question in Evans' mind was whether or not there was enough work to warrant asking such assistants to give up permanent employment for an uncertainty.

Summer and early fall passed without any concrete job offer, and Evans' hope that he would not be forced into another period of idleness had been disappointed. Upon his return to the Baltimore area he joined his family at Owings Mills, and they all boarded there during the time Evans was out of work from April, 1888, to March 18, 1889. How he sustained his family during this period is a mystery, although it is possible that Mrs. Evans received $500 as her share of some property from her mother's estate, a cushion which would have helped considerably. Whatever the source of funds, Evans' family seemed to fare well despite his lack of employment. In early October he sent Poole a photograph of the family which had been made by one of the summer boarders.[45] Although Evans did not think the photograph did Mrs. Evans justice, he hoped Poole would like it well enough to give it a place among his children and grandchildren.

In late fall a movement began among Evans' friends to have him return to Indianapolis. This was not the first time he had been asked to consider a return. A. C. Harris and Austin H. Brown, now repentant, had both been interested in him in 1883.[46] However,

---

[44] Williamson, "William Frederick Poole," pp. 229, 602.

[45] C. E. to W. F. P., ALS, Oct. 8, 1888, Poole Papers, Newberry Library.

[46] A. C. Harris to C. E., ALS, May 4, 1883; W. F. P. to C. E., ALS, March 15, 1883. C. E. to W. F. P., ALS, March 11, 1889, Poole Papers, Newberry Library.

Evans at that time had responded that he would not return unless the vote of the board was unanimous. Since the vote had lacked two votes of being unanimous, Evans had rejected the offer. This time, however, Evans very much wanted to return and promised Poole that if he secured the position he would not again let it slip from his grasp. Because of his unbusinesslike conduct of the library, the librarian, W. DeM. Hooper, had been extremely displeasing to the board. They even refused to accept his resignation and insisted upon dismissing him. Indianapolis was therefore without a librarian in September, 1888. The chairman of the board, J. H. Greenstreet, wrote to Poole and asked for Evans' address.[47] Poole immediately wrote to Evans, suggesting that he write his confidential friends and find out the facts. If he should have the opportunity to return to Indianapolis, he hoped he would do so "and *not make conditions,* as I have understood you did on a previous occasion. It is a good place as the world goes, and no body can fill it so well as yourself."

Evans could not bring himself to take all of Poole's advice. Much as he was interested in securing the position, he wanted to be certain of support and of a decent salary. Poole felt called upon to emphasize his advice in an additional letter in late November.[48] He hoped that Evans would not let the matter of salary stand in his way. Poole's theory had always been that when an individual saw the place he wanted, he should get it and leave the matter of salary to adjust itself when it should be found what he was worth. Thinking that Evans had already closed the matter with Greenstreet, Poole advised him to reopen negotiations and let his friends know that he was flexible on this point. But Evans insisted upon $2,000, as little enough for himself and his family. Yet he kept his friends working throughout the winter in the hope that he would be recalled to his old position. The composition of the board had changed almost completely in the intervening period and the new members did not move quickly. As he wrote to Poole, "It is weary work waiting on Committees."

Not until March 11, 1889, could he write to Poole that he had won the appointment. Greenstreet had written him that after personally canvassing the board members, he could now assure Evans'

---

[47] W. F. P. to C. E., ALS, Oct. 10, 1888.

[48] W. F. P. to C. E., ALS, Nov. 27, 1888. For Evans' insistence on a decent salary, see C. E. to W. F. P., ALS, Nov. 23, 1888, and March 11, 1889, Poole Papers, Newberry Library; and A. C. Harris to C. E., ALS, Dec. 1, 1888.

election to the position. Out of eleven members, seven were heartily in favor, one would not object, and three were out of the city. At their meeting on March 15 the board confirmed Greenstreet's recommendation to elect Evans as librarian at a salary of $2,000 per year. The legislature had raised the permissible library tax rate from two to four mills, which would give the library about $20,000 per year and assure its financial future. In the quiet contentment of that hour Evans wrote Poole: "Altogether the outlook is brighter than it ever has been and I shall work hard to place the Library in the rank to which it is entitled. Of one thing be assured. I shall not let go of this opportunity, if I can help it, until I have a call to go up higher. I have been such a trouble to you, that my first thought after reading Mr. G.'s letter was, now I can remove one thorn from his side—take away one worry—and perhaps give him pleasure, certainly relief." [49] His resolution was a noble one, for Charles Evans had met with so many difficulties that he very much needed a long period of success in his professional work. On the surface Indianapolis would seem to be the right place. He had begun the library, he knew the people, and he would have strong support from prominent friends. Just past his thirty-eighth birthday, he stood at a crucial point in his career. How he utilized the opportunities in Indianapolis would determine his future in librarianship.

---

[49] C. E. to W. F. P., ALS, March 11, 1889, Poole Papers, Newberry Library.

Deep Water in Indianapolis

7

Of all the jobs Charles Evans had held, none had really given him more genuine pleasure than the librarianship of Indianapolis. Immediately after receiving Greenstreet's telegram that he had been elected librarian, Evans left for the Midwest and reported for duty on Monday, March 18, 1889. Because of the low state of his finances he did not take Mrs. Evans and the children with him but left them in Owings Mills until he could find suitable accommodations. He had managed to do this by mid-April, and, borrowing $75 from his brother John, he sent for them in early May. But the early weeks of his return to Indianapolis belonged to Evans alone, and they were pleasant ones. He was overjoyed by the reaction of the local newspapers, which spoke highly of his previous good work and looked forward to great things from him again. So busy was he receiving good wishes the first two weeks that he began to wonder if he would ever get any work done. Writing Poole, he chuckled that the citizens had "become so accustomed to congratulating while President Harrison was here that they had to keep it up and taper off on me." [1]

The climax to this very satisfying welcome home came at a Literary Club dinner honoring former Governor Porter just prior to his departure to assume his new post as minister to Italy. A charter member of the club, Porter was one of Evans' most loyal

---

[1] C. E. to W. F. P., ALS, April 20, 1889, Poole Papers, Newberry Library. For the newspaper reaction see clippings in Eliot Evans, "Scrapbook."

friends. In an "eloquent and kindly" speech after the dinner, the new minister made lengthy reference to Evans' association with the club and noted that in recalling Evans to the librarianship Indianapolis citizens did themselves honor and Charles Evans justice. Taking their cue from Porter, the other guests extolled Evans' virtues in a similar manner, and the dinner became more of a welcome home to Evans than a farewell to Porter. Always sensitive to the good will of cultured people, Evans was deeply moved by the obvious sincerity of his old friends. With such praises ringing in his ears he felt that he could at last settle down to a long period of competent library work.

This belief was reinforced by the members of the board of school commissioners, who assured him that they were through experimenting with librarians and would give him their best support in building up the library. Evans thought the board was a good one and the outlook altogether bright.

While he was still enjoying the "welcome back" from his friends, Charlie's brother, John Evans, now a very successful businessman in East Weymouth, Massachusetts, gave him some sage advice on his relations with the public. He was glad that his "little brother" had found such a warm welcome in Indianapolis, but he felt compelled to add these words: "Don't be too distant & formal with the patrons of the library; show yourself once in a while & not leave all the *chinning* to be done by subordinates, common people want to see the head sometimes." [2] No one has ever received better advice than Charles Evans, and few have paid as little attention to it. John Evans was reiterating warnings which Beanie had given many times. Coming from a person who had been as successful in business as his brother, Charles should have weighed this counsel well. That he did not is apparent from his early actions in the library.

Hooper had left the library in a complete state of chaos.[3] The book collection had been allowed to degenerate, the old books had worn out without either being rebound or replaced, and the classification system had broken down because Evans' successors had not followed his original plan. Moreover, no catalog or finding list had been published since 1885. The library's housekeeping needed im-

---

[2] John Evans to C. E., ALS, April 29, 1889.

[3] This is apparent from Evans' monthly reports to the library committee. The charges against Hooper are given in I. P. L., "Library Reports," II, Sept., 1888, I. P. L. Archives. See also W. F. P. to C. E., ALS, Oct. 10, 1888. C. E. to W. F. P., ALS, April 20, 1889, Poole Papers, Newberry Library.

mediate attention. Since the technical aspects of library work were always Evans' chief stock in trade, he proceeded to do what needed to be done. Almost from the beginning his time was occupied with the social activities of his friends and the technical details of library administration. Even the former were reduced to a minimum so that the latter would progress more rapidly. There simply was no time left to cultivate either the patrons or the board members.

However, as an internal administrator Evans was very good indeed. When he arrived in Indianapolis, there was decided unhappiness among the staff. Eliza G. Browning, an assistant librarian, had been acting librarian from September, 1888, to March, 1889. A native of Indianapolis and a staff member for almost ten years, she had a reasonable expectation of succeeding Hooper. Two other staff members had also been applicants for the position, so Evans had to try to overcome this feeling of jealousy at the outset. This he did by endorsing a personnel classification and pay plan which had been prepared earlier by Morris Ross, an editor of the *News* and a member of the citizens' library advisory committee. Using this plan as his basis, Evans called attention to the excellent work of the assistants and suggested general salary raises for all employees.[4] The salaries were based on both position and the length of service of each individual. Under this program, shown in Table 1, Evans promoted Mrs. Isabella McElhennen to the post of assistant librarian on the basis of his previous knowledge of her good work and her thirteen years of experience. While he demoted Miss Browning to the position of librarian's assistant, he provided the soothing balm of a recommended $100 increase in salary.

Since Evans himself was receiving a salary of $2,000, $500 more than his predecessor, the total recommended increases, excluding the library page, came to $1,507. This does not seem unreasonable in view of an anticipated $20,000 annual budget. Evans also made provision for yearly increases of $25 each in the professional ranks. The library committee accepted Evans' recommendations and by mid-April Evans reported to Poole that his staff was working smoothly. He continued to work on his administrative structure

---

[4] I. P. L., "Library Reports," II, March, 1889, I. P. L. Archives. Evans prepared the March report that was read at the April meeting. "At the first meeting of the Committee I presented a scheme for the reclassification of the force based on length of service . . . ," C. E. to W. F. P., ALS, April 20, 1889, Poole Papers, Newberry Library. Hull, "Indianapolis Public Library," p. 64, gives Browning credit for the first personnel plan in 1892. This is obviously an error.

during the summer months, refining his program and improving the evening staff, which consisted of male attendants, usually students from one of the local colleges. He also introduced a merit schedule for these night attendants with rates ranging from forty cents to sixty cents per night. Under his program the staff turnover was heavy; some resigned and some were let go without regret, but Evans was determined to improve the quality of the night service.[5]

TABLE 1

Classification and Pay Plan Recommended by Evans, April, 1889

Name	Position	Time of Service	Salary Recommended	Present Salary
Mrs. McElhennen	Assistant Librarian	13 years	$700	$500
Miss Browning	Librarian's Assistant	9 years	600	500
Miss Schonacker	1st R. R. Attendant	9 years	600	500
Miss Marsee	2nd R. R. Attendant	6 years	550	450
Miss Adams	1st Lib. Attendant	6 years	550	450
Miss Newcomb	2nd Lib. Attendant	1 year	400	313
Miss Morris	3rd Lib. Attendant	1 year	400	240
Miss Kelley	4th Lib. Attendant	1 year	400	240
Alfred Navin	Library Page	—	$1.00 per day	240

Evans had found considerable slackness in the staff regulations and he insisted upon tightening up the situation. The rules called for one hour for dinner, but the staff had been taking longer periods. Whereas the library was scheduled to be open twelve hours per day, it had actually been opened twelve and one-half hours. Moreover, the stipulation that the staff should have only two weeks of vacation with pay had never been observed; everyone had been taking three weeks. Such loose administrative practice galled Evans, and he was determined to have none of it. Upon his recommendation the library committee in September accepted his codification of the regulations and recommended that the school board adopt it. In his "Regulations for the Government of Officers and Employees" Evans defined the functions of the library committee, all the officers of the library, and the conditions under which each should work.

The description of the duties of the librarian seems especially pertinent since it gives Evans' view of his own job. Recognizing

---

[5] I. P. L., "Library Reports," II, April, May, June, July, and Sept., 1889, I. P. L. Archives.

his responsibility to the board, the librarian was to have charge of the library and all the public property in it. "He is responsible for the safety of such books and property, and for the preservation of order in these departments." The rules called for the librarian to deposit with the treasurer money received during the month and to report to the board at its first regular meeting each month. The meat of the description is found in paragraph three: "The Librarian shall be responsible to the Library Committee for the proper management of the internal economy of the Library. He shall, under their direction, have control of, supervise, and direct the working force, and, so far as practicable, assist in the detail work of the several departments. He shall nominate an Assistant Librarian and other employees annually on the Thursday before the first Friday in September, subject to the approval of the Committee." [6] Written into his description was the statement that promotion for the staff would be in terms of length of service and efficiency in the lower grades.

Under Evans' program the assistant librarian assumed major responsibility for the circulation department. Duties of other attendants were carefully explained, and the total picture represented a more exacting staff picture.

No one could deny that Evans' personnel plan and his codification of the rules represented a decided improvement over the chaotic state of affairs under Hooper; not only that, but his program was ahead of its day in library administration. As one of Evans' later successors remarked in an excellent evaluation of his program for the Indianapolis Public Library: "No one needs to be told that his ideas and ideals were instrumental in shaping policies and laying foundations which would challenge the best of modern professional standards." [7] Not only had this been true for Evans' first period in Indianapolis but it was even more true of his second. The requirements for the staff were fair and the increased salaries compensated for the loss of some privileges. No one could ever accuse Charles Evans of being uninterested in his staff nor of lacking vigor in pushing policies which would result in their economic advancement.

---

[6] "Regulations for the Government of Officers and Employees," in Indianapolis Public Schools, *Manual of the Public Schools of the City of Indianapolis . . . 1890–91* (Indianapolis: Sentinel Printing Company, 1890), pp. 178–183.

[7] Amy Winslow, "Ten Years of the Indianapolis Public Library," *Library Journal*, LIII (May 1, 1928), 395.

Although Evans indicated to Poole that his reclassification of the staff had placed the library in good working order, the staff was probably less happy than Evans believed. Few people enjoy giving up free and easy ways for a stricter schedule, even when there is a concession such as a salary increase to make the schedule more palatable. The rules presented explicitly the responsibilities of the staff under the new management: "Each attendant will sign the Attendance Register in the order of their arrival in the building. They will also report to the Assistant Librarian at the time when leaving or returning during the day. It is expected of the attendants that they arrive in season to give their uninterrupted time to their work from the hour of working." [8] Such a rigid program must have been especially vexing to Miss Browning, who had known some of the freedom of a person in command. Professional people from Evans' day to this have regarded a certain freedom of movement as one of the virtues of their status. However, any complaints the staff made apparently did not reach Evans.

Had Evans taken over a good working library, he might have been able to devote more time to the public. As previously indicated, Hooper's neglect was everywhere evident. Immediately, in monthly reports to the library committee, Evans began to suggest changes. Each of his reports reveals rational, well-designed plans to improve the library's service. Since personnel policy was crucial to the improvement of the service, he had begun with his classification and pay plan and then proceeded to the other deficiencies. Foremost in his thinking, after the staff arrangements, was the confusion in book classification. If his original plan had been followed, this would not have happened. Since it had not, Evans decided that the only thing to do was to reclassify the entire library of some 40,000 volumes. He thought the fact that the last finding list issued had contained the names of from 5,000 to 6,000 volumes not in the library in 1889 made this work imperative. Neither the staff nor the patrons could find the books they wanted. In line with the work he had finished a year earlier at Omaha, he began work on the reclassification. However, the pace was necessarily slow, since he had to devote some of his time to other pressing matters.

Another program which had to be started soon was a good binding plan. To repair the damage to the old books and to save as many as he could Evans set up a binding scheme which called for some

---

[8] Indianapolis Public Schools, *Manual, 1890–91,* p. 181.

commercial binding and some binding by the library staff. The
extent of the needed work can be seen from the monthly reports,
where the number of volumes reported to have been repaired by
the staff sometimes ran as high as 2,000. This program also provided the opportunity to do some necessary weeding, and in three
months during the summer of 1890, a total of 2,690 volumes were
condemned and sold as waste paper.

Evans knew very well that he could not take books out of circulation for reclassification and binding and discard others without
adding many new volumes. The acquisition of new items had
slipped far behind the needs of the library. Along with the new
personnel plan Evans had submitted a plea for the library committee to authorize the librarian to spend $500 per month on book
acquisitions to be divided equally between old and new titles.[9] The
committee responded by giving Evans $5,000 to spend on books
during the year. Within the first month Evans placed with local
booksellers orders for 2,000 books which had been published during
the preceding three years. During 1889–90 there followed heavy
monthly purchases of American and English books.

All of these activities, worthy in themselves and essential for the
growth of the library, took time, valuable time, and placed an
almost unbearable load on Evans. Working day and night, he did
not have time for the ordinary social "chinning" of which the public
was so fond. The results of his prodigious energy, however, became
clear when he published his first finding list the following year.
Rejecting the idea of a complete catalog, he had decided to issue
subject lists similar to those of the Boston Public Library. The 1890
finding list was a work of ninety-eight pages, covering the subjects
of biography, history, and travels, which were among the most
heavily used books in the collection. Containing biographical references to about 35,000 individuals, the list was both economical and
useful. Poole's encomium that it was a "sensible and excellent work"
pleased him.[10]

Evans had also sent a copy of his list to Beanie and received the
reply that Beanie herself, after an eighteen-year tenure at Brookline,
was having trustee difficulty. She asked Charlie to come East for
the American Library Association convention, which was to be held

---

[9] I. P. L., "Library Reports," II, April, 1889, I. P. L. Archives; C. E. to W. F. P.,
ALS, April 20, 1889, Poole Papers, Newberry Library.
[10] W. F. P. to C. E., ALS, July 29, 1890.

in the nearby White Mountains. He could come by Brookline for a few days afterwards and she would have an opportunity to talk with him about her problems. In this trying time she needed her friends who knew what real library work was and were not just "Dewey-worshippers." [11] With appreciation for his gift of the finding list and joy at his reinstatement, she closed with the hope that he would come for the convention.

Poole also encouraged Evans to go East for the convention,[12] and it would probably have been good for Evans and for Indianapolis if he had gone. After seventeen months during which he had not failed to be at his desk in the library a single day, Charles Evans was tired. He needed a vacation and he needed to get away from the library, although he frankly saw no prospect of doing so.

Rejecting Poole's invitation, Evans gave three reasons for not going: work, the expense, and a new baby.[13] This third addition to the family had been named Charles Sumner after his father and his father's friend of Boston Athenaeum days. Although Charlie and Lena had rejected a thought to call the baby "junior," later, as a young man, the middle name "Sumner" was dropped, and he became known as Charles Evans, Jr. In this respect he followed the example of his father who had dropped the "Theodore" from his own name in the early 1870's and henceforth was known simply as "Charles Evans."

The baby not only prevented Evans from going to the American Library Association conference but also seriously disrupted life at the Evans home on Pennsylvania Street. In a mood of depression the father wrote to Poole that the baby was well formed, healthy, and everyone was proud of him.

Nonetheless, when his devoted father thinks of the additional pairs of shoes, frocks, dresses, and gimcracks generally, there are moments of deep financial depression out of which he rises a confirmed disciple of Malthus. Gone are the days when I could pack my valise and go where my fancy led me. Gone, and in place of this freedom I find only—napkins! Napkins everywhere. I trip over them on the floor. Dripping from the bath I grab them, in place of the towel, from the towel-rack. They wave from every clothes line in the back-yard, and the green of the turf is hid by them. My table-napkin goes untouched, its name condemns it, and when at night I lay my weary head upon the pillow it rests upon the moist lump of a forgotten napkin. Everywhere I find these reminders that I am no longer

[11] M. A. B. to C. E., ALS, Aug. 10, 1890. ,
[12] W. F. P. to C. E., ALS, July 29, 1890.
[13] C. E. to W. F. P., ALS, Aug. 2, 1890, Poole Papers, Newberry Library.

master of my own time, or "boss of the household ranche." I don't know why I trouble you with this tale of woe, unless it is because at home I get no sympathy. The gentle creature upon whose sympathy and comfort I could always count listens to me with a patient smile, and so I come to you—not exactly the author of all my woes—but my earliest, truest friend, and—one who knows how it is himself.[14]

No marriage counselor had told Evans that with three small children demanding her attention, Lena could not give him the comforting attention he needed. Charlie was going through the same indifference to his existence that occurs in most households when a new baby arrives. It was unfortunate for him that this new baby came at this particular time. The nominal head of the family very much needed the companionship of his wife in order to withstand the blows from outside.

The first year with the board of school commissioners had been a honeymoon. Almost routinely the library committee accepted Evans recommendations and the board approved them. After that, criticism from the public began to mount, and Evans, already under heavy strain at the library and at home, began to feel the force of these complaints. The board was only too willing to listen to anyone who had a complaint either real or imagined, and while the exact nature of the complaints is unknown, they were probably similar to those Evans had encountered during his first period in Indianapolis. With the addition of a new baby to his responsibilities, Charles Evans felt that he had reached the limit in Indianapolis. Never had he been anywhere where there were "so many people who knew just how a library should be conducted, or who were so fertile in expedients for running it in the ground." [15] Their most pressing need was for a new building which might give them a new lease on life. In this despondent frame of mind he said to Poole, "All of which is only preliminary to saying that if Mr. Poole learns of any call to come up higher I hope he will give me the opportunity." Charlie could scarcely have known it or even expected it at the time, but things in Indianapolis were going to get a great deal worse instead of better. His looking around for a new position would be his undoing.

The one bright spot in Evans' existence continued to be association with the Literary Club. As previously noted, he had been

---

[14] *Ibid.*
[15] *Ibid.*

welcomed back into the organization with genuine warmth. This was the only social pleasure and obligation which Charlie did not shirk. As regularly as clockwork, Monday evenings found him in that brilliant assembly of the local literati, which now included such figures as James Whitcomb Riley, the Hoosier poet; Benjamin Harrison, United States President; and Theodore C. Steele, one of the portrait painters in the "Hoosier Group." Also, during the first year of his return to the club, they had elected to membership Meredith Nicholson, rising young author on the editorial staff of the *News.* Moreover, Evans' good friends W. P. Fishback, Addison C. Harris, Hanford A. Edson, and John H. Holliday were still active members. Perhaps his despair during the summer was partly due to the fact that this stimulating group did not meet in the months of June, July, August, and September.

The club was not content to let Evans attend without making some contribution. On February 3, 1890, Charlie read a lengthy paper on the historian John Lothrop Motley. He had originally been scheduled to talk on two historians: Motley and Francis Parkman, both of whom he had known in his Athenaeum days. However, he found his paper on Motley growing to such proportions that he limited himself to the one man. Evans' paper was a fifty-eight-page treatise, handwritten on legal-sized paper. Evans began with a recollection of his first encounter with Motley: "Perhaps the boyish reverence for one so famous pleased him—for what in life is there so pleasing as the frank flattery of the young—at any rate the admiration was returned by a courtesy and kindness which has remained as a pleasant memory of one of the greatest names in American literature." [16]

After the personal relation he proceeded to the biographical data and to Motley's works themselves. Much of what he said was based upon a two-volume edition of Motley's correspondence published in 1889, but he had also read extensively in *The Rise of the Dutch Republic, The History of the United Netherlands,* Holmes's biographical memoir of Motley, and numerous Motley articles in the *North American Review.* His treatment of the historian is as exhaustive as an essay could be. It reveals wide reading and is brilliantly written. Evans emphasized chiefly the historical persons treated by Motley and read long descriptive sketches of each.

---

[16] Charles Evans, "John Lothrop Motley," MS. Almost all of the data that follow can be gleaned from Evans' manuscript itself.

Throughout the essay he editorialized on his theory of history, on his favorite historical figures, and on his personal prejudices.

One of the unusual features of Evans' discourse came after he read a letter that Bismarck had written to Motley. Both men had been fellow students at a German university, and Motley had taught Bismarck an old New England song, "In Good Old Colony Times." The Indianapolis Literary Club and their guests were undoubtedly amused when Charlie broke into a stanza of this bit of New England doggerel, indeed the same stanza that Bismarck had roared into Edison's phonograph only a few months before.

Evans' essay on Motley was a good historical document and revealed qualities which would become pronounced in his later work: competence with his subject matter, good writing, and logical exposition with a trace of humor. Its great deficiency was its length which, near the end, warned Evans that he was "trespassing too much upon the patience of the club."

The following year, when Theodore L. Sewall moved up to the presidency of the club, Evans was elected secretary, a position he held until he left Indianapolis in July, 1892. On April 27, 1891, he again read a paper, though a shorter one than that of the previous year. Perhaps the members had admonished Charlie for his lengthy effort the year before. For his discourse Evans this time chose the German poet Gotthold Ephraim Lessing. To this address he gave the title: "The Bible of an Infidel: A Review of Lessing's 'Nathan the Wise.' "[17] Evans had first become seriously interested in Lessing upon reading *The Old Faiths and the New; a Confession,* by the German writer David F. Strauss. This little book had been very popular in America and one sentence of Strauss had particularly caught Evans' attention: "As every religion has its traditionally sacred books, thus the sacred book of the religion of humanity and morality which we profess, is no other than the Nathan of Lessing." This statement had intrigued Evans into reading *Nathan the Wise* more carefully, and after several years' meditation on the subject, he had decided to share his thoughts with his fellow club members. Again Evans prepared thoroughly and contributed a thoughtful and informative paper. Surprisingly, his paper shows remarkable familiarity with German literature. In view of his lack of facility with the German language, it is difficult to account for this interest.

---

[17] Charles Evans, "The Bible of an Infidel: A Review of Lessing's 'Nathan the Wise,' " MS.

However, the books in his personal library included titles of Goethe, Lessing, and Heine,[18] and his paper on Lessing revealed a good grasp of their contents.

As in his paper on Motley, Evans began with a brief biographical sketch of his author and followed this with a critical analysis of his works. In his devotion to religious tolerance, Lessing found a sympathetic reader in Evans. There is little doubt that Charles Evans subscribed to the main theme of *Nathan the Wise:* "to show that names and forms and confessions are of no importance compared with the spirit—the moral grace—which constitutes the sole criterion of a true religion." In tracing the difficulties into which such a religious position put Lessing, Evans trod carefully the doctrinal ground which might have stirred up the club, but the weight of his argumentation was always with Lessing. As the body of his paper he used the story of the three rings with which Nathan answered the Sultan's question, "What is the true religion?" Then Evans noted the enthusiastic reception of the play, which Lessing, incidentally, did not live to see. After tracing the religious bigotry which pursued Lessing even beyond his bier, Evans concluded with the statement: "Let us be grateful that we live in an age when it is not only possible, but easy, and with sensible people habitual, to distinguish between character and opinion."

These were the two papers, then, that Evans read before the club during his second stay in Indianapolis. They were in keeping with the broad-ranging nature of the club's essays. An examination of the program for the year 1890–91 reveals that there were essays on Tolstoi and Ibsen and a comparative study of Tennyson and Theocritus. Of special interest to the local members was the first essay of the year by James Whitcomb Riley, "Dialect in Literature." Such a feast of literary delights gave Evans rest from a weary week.

If August, 1890, had provided a time for moody reflection, the fall gave little more occasion for hope. Evans continued to lose good staff members and had to allow some positions to go unfilled in order to save money.[19] This increased the work load on those staff mem-

---

[18] Typewritten list of books in the library of Charles Evans, 1935. Though it would be difficult to discover the dates when Evans acquired these specific titles, they all have imprint dates before 1880.

[19] I. P. L., "Library Reports," II, Jan.–Dec., 1890, I. P. L. Archives. Staff turnover in 1890 was high. The most serious loss occurred when I. C. Schonacker, First Reading Room Attendant, resigned after "an exceptionally faithful service of ten years."

bers who were still with him and naturally put an even greater burden on the librarian himself. Despite his momentary happiness over an impressive gain in the number of volumes in the library in September, the following months revealed that Evans was still having difficulty with some board members.[20] He asked Poole if he had heard anything about the new Carnegie Library in Pittsburgh. Since it seemed to offer an opening for a good man to make his mark, he hoped that Poole would keep him in mind if the Pittsburgh board asked for a nomination.

As the end of the year approached, Evans lost a battle to extend borrowing privileges. In late December he asked the library committee to permit the professors of Butler University, just outside the city, to borrow books, a request which the committee flatly rejected.[21] Since the committee was going to be obstinate with the professors, Evans felt compelled to call their attention to the fact that a number of people living outside the city had been using the library already, although legally not entitled to do so. Was he to interpret the committee's action to mean a tightening up in the enforcement of the rules? There was strong political pressure for serving residents just outside the city, and Evans thought the committee ought to be aware of this pressure. However, his arguments did not persuade the committee, and there was nothing to do but continue to try to enforce the restrictions against those outside the city limits.

While the committee had been inflexible on borrowing privileges, they had loosened administrative control in early December when they gave Evans discretionary authority in placing subscriptions for magazines.[22] Since this was an obvious need and fairly routine, Evans had not gained much. The year 1890 had been one of mixed blessings, and Charles Evans said goodbye to it with a feeling of relief.

With the approach of the new year there was a glimmer of light. For some time the library committee had been active in efforts to secure a new building. With the backing of a number of leading citizens the need for a building specifically designed for library purposes had been pointed out. Indeed this had been the contention of John H. Holliday since 1875.[23] In the state legislature on January

---

[20] C. E. to W. F. P., ALS, Oct. 14, 1890, Poole Papers, Newberry Library.
[21] I. P. L., "Library Reports," II, Dec. 31, 1890, I. P. L. Archives.
[22] I. P. L., "Library Reports," II, Dec. 4, 1890, I. P. L. Archives.
[23] Indianapolis *News,* July 26, 1875, p. 2.

19, 1891, Frederick J. Mack, by request, introduced a bill to authorize the school board to issue bonds for a building.[24] The bill passed both houses without difficulty and was signed by the Governor on February 26. Passage of this bill provided a renewal of hope for Evans. Here was a real opportunity to put into practice some of Poole's advanced ideas on library architecture. About $100,000 would be available for the building itself, since the lot had already been purchased with other funds, and the furnishings would also be bought from different resources. With optimism tempered with reality Evans wrote Poole that he and perhaps a member of the board would visit several recently constructed buildings.[25] In order to be prepared to talk intelligently, he asked Poole's advice on new buildings and for a bibliography on library architecture. Noting that he probably would not be consulted too much, he still was in a position to "do some tall kicking if I find them going too far astray."

Poole was delighted with the prospect for Indianapolis and was only too happy to respond with a detailed bibliography and considerable advice.[26] Poole's chief point, a good one, was that a library should be planned from the inside out. All too often the architect sacrificed the interior for the external effect. At Cincinnati the investigators would see all the bad features of the eastern buildings and at Dayton some of the principles which Poole recommended. He especially suggested that Indianapolis "make a building for use as a library, and not a show building." He was pleased for Charlie and thought this was an opportunity to erect a "good and sensible building."

Thus with the coming of spring, things were looking up in Indianapolis. In February, Holliday enriched the library with 200 pamphlets and 225 magazines. By late March the second catalog, *Finding-List of Books in the Classes of Poetry and the Drama, Literature and Polygraphy*, came from the press. The catalog analyzed by author and title all dramas and dramatic poems in the library and also essays found in collected works. Representing an enormous amount of work, the list indicated that the reclassification was proceeding surely, if somewhat slowly.

In April, 1891, the library committee renominated Evans for his

---

[24] Indiana, House of Representatives, *Journal*, 57th Session, 1891, pp. 205–206, 1079.

[25] C. E. to W. F. P., ALS, Feb. 28, 1891, Poole Papers, Newberry Library.

[26] W. F. P. to C. E., ALS, March 6, 1891.

third year as librarian. The school board accepted the recommendation, and Evans wrote Poole that his annual agony was over and that he was a fixture in Indianapolis for another year.[27] However, he was far from pleased with the way things were going. Especially distressing were the plans for the library building. The board had employed W. R. Ware of New York, "a library expert," as consulting architect, and they were paying little attention to Evans' suggestions. Slashing away at the choice of Ware, Evans showed the board Poole's letter of advice and told them that Poole was the only library building expert he knew. Evans' remonstrance scarcely touched the committee.

> With wise foresight it has been determined to build a library capable of containing 75,000!!! volumes—we have nearly 50,000 volumes now and are adding at the rate of from 4 to 6,000 yearly. Good God! it does seem to me sometimes that the most perfect recipe for making an Ass of a sensible man is to make him a member of a Library Committee. But what can one do. They think that a Librarian doesn't know anything; and he is perfectly certain that they don't. So there is nothing for me to do but to keep quiet, and "saw wood." [28]

No one could possibly have given Evans better advice than to "keep quiet and saw wood," and it is unfortunate that he did not do just that. The library committee had already determined to make the library building an ornament to the city, and the very best for which Evans could hope was some consideration on minor changes that he might propose for the interior. He would have done well to express his opinion firmly but politely. Then, when it was apparent that the library committee did not intend to take his advice, he could have desisted and saved his position. Such, however, was not his nature. He had no doubt that he was right in his contentions. The library building plans were "an abortion, born of ignorance and prejudice, and fostered, in the person of the architect, by stupidity." [29] Since he lost his friend and the library's best friend in June, when Greenstreet was not reelected to the board, there was

---

[27] C. E. to W. F. P., ALS, April 18, 1891, Poole Papers, Newberry Library.
[28] *Ibid.*
[29] C. E. to W. F. P., ALS, June 15, 1891, Poole Papers, Newberry Library. Evans was obviously trying to emulate the master on the matter of library buildings. The previous autumn Poole had attacked the Boston Public Library as a Venetian Palace and Evans heartily approved of his attack. C. E. to W. F. P., ALS, Oct. 14, 1890, Poole Papers, Newberry Library. The only difficulty, as Williamson, "William Frederick Poole," p. 694, has pointed out, was that "Evans' official life was at stake."

more reason than ever for him to have toned down his opposition. Yet he was by this time so emotionally involved that to keep quiet was unthinkable. With a pen dipped in vitriol, Evans wrote to Poole about the design Ware had accepted:

Ware, the so-called Library expert!—(God save the mark!) sent five plans out of the thirteen he received as the best in his judgment to select from. These differed in uniform badness, in some considering we wanted a club-house, and the others that we wanted a barn. He also sent a sixth plan, as he expressed it, to show the Commissioners how bad the five were that he kept. This sixth plan was the only one in which the architect had the faintest conception of the interior arrangement of a Library.[30]

Evans vigorously pointed this fact out to the commissioners and attempted to show them how easily the sixth plan could be modified to meet the specific needs of the Indianapolis Public Library. To his complete and utter disgust, the commissioners ignored his advice. Instead of the sensible plan, they chose one done by a Dayton architect in which the interior was so poorly arranged that the library assistants would be forced to walk hundreds of unnecessary miles every year. To get to the patent room, a patron would have to walk through the private office of one of the officers of the board, who had no connection with the library. Said Evans, "The thing is a botch from beginning to end . . . I am so heartily sick of it that I do not want to remain here to see it carried out, and hope you will notify me of any Library where there is an opportunity for me to get a position." [31]

Poole had written to Evans that the plans represented the same old mistakes, "sacrificing the interior, where people live and work, to an outside, which is supposed to please architects, but does, in fact, please nobody." [32] He concluded that he was amazed that such things were going on in Indianapolis, a place he once knew as having unusually sensible people. Taking this letter as his cue, Evans told Poole he was going to compel every one of the commissioners to hear it read with full emphasis, "whether they like their medicine or not." [33] He was tempted to expose the incompetency of the architect in the local press, even at the cost of his position. Such intemperate language and such outbursts were scarcely designed to endear Evans to men with whom he had to work constantly. It was manly,

---

[30] C. E. to W. F. P., ALS, June 15, 1891, Poole Papers, Newberry Library.
[31] *Ibid.*
[32] W. F. P. to C. E., ALS, June 3, 1891.
[33] C. E. to W. F. P., ALS, June 15, 1891, Poole Papers, Newberry Library.

perhaps even noble under the circumstances, to talk about sacrificing his position, but Evans had a wife and three small children to
support, and he was already pinched financially. Moreover, even
the most favorable Evans advocate could not look kindly upon his
interference with what he undoubtedly regarded as a primary function of the board. He could talk, express his views with deference,
and attempt to persuade gently, but when he forced the commissioners to listen to Poole's letters and cast aspersions upon their
judgment, he was going much too far. His own sense of righteousness and his deep sense of indignation were too much for the board.

Whatever the unhappiness over the building and Evans' general
dislike of his own position at this time, the annual report of the
librarian indicated steady library progress.[34] Obviously the disagreement had not significantly affected the work of the library, despite
its injury to Evans personally. Evans himself, in his report to the
library committee in June, 1891, called the year a successful one
in the library's history. Book use had been heavy, the prospective
building gave hope of greater usefulness, one-third of the reclassification had been completed, and two finding lists had been published. Moreover, the library had managed to keep abreast of the
best current American literature. Added to the energetic program
of weeding and replacement of worn-out books, these new books
gave a better appearance for the entire collection. The library now
contained 47,600 volumes, registration had reached 13,273, and total
circulation, including home, reading room, and periodical use, had
been 269,542. Evans' annual report gave no reason for discontent.
In a little over two years he had taken the chaotic mess left by
Hooper and had developed a sound program. By any standards the
annual report was one with which citizens of Indianapolis should
have been highly pleased.

Further progress lay just ahead. In September, Judge Cyrus C.
Hines, an early member of the Indianapolis Literary Club and a
former member of the library committee, gave the library copies
of the second and fourth Shakespeare folios. He also signified his
intention of presenting a copy of the Howard Staunton facsimile
of the first folio as soon as one could be found. Evans' joy in this
gift was unbounded. He reported to the library committee that there
were but thirty-six copies of the second folio in America and only
twenty-four of the fourth folio. The former had a market value of

---

[34] I. P. L., "Library Reports," II, June, 1891, I. P. L. Archives.

from $200 to $750 and the latter one, $100 to $200. Said Evans, "The generous gift of these literary treasures, unaccompanied as it was by any condition other than the necessary one, that the volumes should be used only in the Library, is the most valuable gift that the Library has thus far received, and seems to me worthy of special mention, and special thanks from the Library Committee." [35]

During the fall the French and German books which Evans had ordered the previous spring began to arrive, and Evans was pleased to publicize this fact for the benefit of Indianapolis' large German population. More important, in December there was promise of another valuable gift: Henry D. Pierce, a good friend of Evans, offered the library thirty original drawings from the Darley Gallery of Shakesperian Illustration.[36] Pierce stipulated that they were presented in memory of his father and requested that each bear a small label indicating that fact. He personally would defray the cost of having each drawing framed and wanted them to be placed at eye level in the new building. The library committee accepted this gift and ordered Evans to draft a suitable letter expressing their thanks. Evans assured Pierce in a formal letter that the committee did appreciate his gift and the spirit which prompted it and would follow his instructions for its preservation. Unfortunately, the school board rejected the gift. One member J. P. Frenzel "insulted the generous donor and outraged decency by asserting, in substance, that Mr. Pierce desired to make an ostentatious display." [37] This drew the retort from Pierce that he was merely following custom since every pamphlet received in the library worth more than twenty-five cents was designated by a book plate. He had not asked for a large amount of wall space for a pretentious tablet to advertise himself but a simple label to indicate in whose memory the gift was made. Coming to the defense of the library committee, the *Sun* castigated the school board in blistering terms for its "bad form and dense ignorance." The editorial warned that if the library committee could not give the final word on receiving a gift, then other citi-

---

[35] I. P. L., "Library Reports," II, Sept., 1891, I. P. L. Archives.

[36] Henry D. Pierce to C. E., ALS, Dec. 29, 1891, in I. P. L., "Library Reports," II, Dec., 1891, I. P. L. Archives. The gift was accepted and Evans was asked to acknowledge the committee's thanks at the meeting on January 7, 1892. See also the two-column newspaper clipping, "Enriching the Library," from Indianapolis *Journal*, Jan. 3, 1892, in I. P. L., "Library Reports," II, Jan., 1892, I. P. L. Archives.

[37] Newspaper clipping, Indianapolis *Sun*, March 21, 1892, in Eliot Evans, "Scrapbook."

zens would think twice before offering one. The editor could not understand why board member J. B. Conner had used this as an excuse to attack Evans for accepting the gift inasmuch as he had been present when the committee met and had endorsed Evans' letter. Concluded the *Sun:* "Mr. Pierce would be justified in withdrawing his gift and presenting it to some institution that is managed by men that have the brains and refinement sufficient to know how to act and talk on such occasions." It is difficult to see how the proferred gift could have been interpreted other than in a favorable light; the would-be donor was following a normal nineteenth-century pattern, and his gift would have been a worthy addition to the resources for the new building. Evans undoubtedly encouraged the gift, as he did all others made to the public library. His conception of a library was broad enough to include not only the building of good collections for research and study but also paintings and artistic drawings which would attract people to the library. By this time the board may well have been irritated by Evans' continual criticisms of the building and, accordingly, could have viewed this as an unwarranted attempt to dictate part of the interior decoration. The storm clouds were definitely darkening, and, despite Evans' support in the local papers, he would have done well to take warning.

In November, 1891, a niece of President Harrison wrote Evans from Minneapolis that Herbert Putnam had resigned as public librarian.[38] His reasons were purely personal: his wife wanted to be near her people in the East. Both Charlie and Lena felt that they would not let something as minor as relatives stand in their way of going to Minneapolis, especially since the salary was $3,000 per year. In fact, Evans felt like the late Artemus Ward: he would be willing to sacrifice all his relatives to obtain it.[39] He immediately wrote to Poole that he would appreciate a recommendation from him.[40] Indianapolis was unlikely ever to go beyond the $2,000 he was then getting, and he was extremely "sore over the Library Building Matter." While he thought his relations with the board were still good, he wanted to get away. There was one feature of Minneapolis

---

[38] Elizabeth Irwin Morris to C. E., ALS, Nov. 7, 1891. Evans conveyed the wrong impression about Mrs. Putnam's desires to be in the East. Her aged mother was ill and she needed to be near enough to take care of her.

[39] Artemus Ward, "To the Prince of Wales," as quoted in John Bartlett, *Familiar Quotations*, 13th ed. (Boston: Little, Brown, 1955), p. 664.

[40] C. E. to W. F. P., ALS, Nov. 11, 1891, Poole Papers, Newberry Library.

that disturbed him—"the detestable Dewey system of notation"—
but he would "even be willing to submit to that for the sake of the
additional salary."

There was good reason for Evans to be interested in the Minneapolis position. Poole called the public librarianship of that city
the best in the Midwest outside Chicago.[41] "The salary, the climate,
the people, and their new and beautiful building are the attrac-
tions." Minneapolis had an elective library board of six members
with two elected every other year, plus the mayor of the city, the
president of the board of education, and the president of the University of Minnesota as ex-officio members. Therefore, the political
interference would be far less than it was at Indianapolis, where
the library was a stepchild of the school board. Not only did the
Minneapolis Public Library have a spacious new building that had
been erected at a cost of $250,000, but room had been provided
in the new structure for the book collection of the Minneapolis
Athenaeum, an art school and art gallery, and a museum. Branch
libraries had been opened, and, significantly, the Minneapolis library was the first public library in the country to open its shelves
freely to the patrons.[42] With an operational budget in 1891 of
$38,775.68 and with the immediate prospect of increasing this to
about $50,000 per year, it was in a far better situation than Indian-
apolis. Furthermore, in 1892 the public library was believed to rank
sixth in the country in terms of annual circulation. There were, of
course, problems at Minneapolis, mostly allied to the making of
a good card catalog and the issuance of a new finding list, but these
were matters in which Evans was an acknowledged expert. No position could have appeared to be more challenging, more professionally rewarding, nor more financially profitable to Evans than did
this one. As quickly as possible, he set the wheels in motion to secure it.

The prospect for Evans looked very promising. President Harrison's niece, Elizabeth Irwin Morris, had worked for Evans at the
Indianapolis Public Library just after his return in 1889. When he
notified her that he would be interested, she immediately brought
pressure on the board members with whom her family was ac-

[41] W. F. P. to C. E., ALS, Dec. 7, 1891.
[42] "Text of Act Creating Library Board, 1885," in Minneapolis Public Library,
Second Annual Report, December 31, 1891 (Minneapolis: Harrison and Smith,
1892), pp. 20–22; "Editorial," *Library Journal*, XVII (March, 1892), 84.

quainted.[43] The board turned to Poole for advice and the latter wrote a glowing recommendation for Evans. Meanwhile, Evans urged his supporters in Minneapolis to keep his name out of the papers. He did not want to injure his case at home by advertising the fact that he was looking for a new job.

The board was so well pleased with Evans' qualifications that they urged him to come to Minneapolis at once to talk with them. Evans made the trip in mid-December, favorably impressed the board, and thought surely he would be elected. The only person unimpressed by Evans was an ex-officio member, President Cyrus Northrop of the University of Minnesota, a man whose judgment was highly respected. Although several assured Evans that if a vote had been taken immediately after his visit, he would have been elected, delay was fatal to his chances. Apparently upon Northrop's recommendation the board chose Dr. James K. Hosmer, a professor of English and German literature at Washington University, St. Louis.

Evans was deeply disappointed in the election of Hosmer. Though he had tried to keep his activities secret, his attempt to secure the new position in Minneapolis could not be kept out of the local newspapers. When it appeared as if Evans might be successful in his Minneapolis application, the local clamor for his Indianapolis post became a din. Writing to Poole on February 6, he expressed serious doubts that he could be reelected and asked his old friend to keep "a weather eye to windward" for him.[44] His opponents had just the weapon they now needed. Evans had opposed the new building plans, he had been obstinate in his opposition, and now he wanted to leave. His opponents were only too happy to speed his departure.

The shape of things to come was clearly indicated at a meeting of the library committee on March 3, 1892. According to the regulations which Evans himself had drawn up, the committee had to nominate a librarian for the coming year at their meeting immediately preceding the school board's first meeting in April. If the school board should concur in the nomination, the appointment would become effective. Otherwise, "at the same or next regular meeting of the Board," the committee should make other nomina-

---

[43] Elizabeth Irwin Morris to C. E., ALS, Nov. 20 and Dec. 2, 1891; Frank C. Nickels to C. E., TLS, Dec. 4, 1891, telegram, Dec. 9, 1891, ALS, Dec. 16 and 30, 1891, and TLS, Feb. 9, 1892.

[44] C. E. to W. F. P., ALS, Feb. 6, 1892, Poole Papers, Newberry Library.

tions, one of which would become effective if concurred in at the regular meeting following the nomination. At the March 3 meeting the advisory members and Evans were asked to withdraw, and the members from the school board appointed a subcommittee on expenditures for furnishing the new building. Apparently the board members intended to see to it that Evans had no voice in the choice of equipment for the new library. One of the local newspapers reported that charges of inefficiency had also been brought against Evans in this secret caucus.[45] These charges had three parts: (1) Evans allowed his young lady attendants to receive visits from friends during working hours, (2) Evans was too cold and reserved in manner toward patrons who needed reference help, and (3) Evans neglected other duties while making a very complete and exhaustive catalog. According to the newspaper, "nothing could be said against him as a librarian nor against his executive ability, but upon the charges noted, it is said, two members of the board are trying to oust him." The nomination was postponed until a special meeting on March 17.

At the special meeting, J. W. Loeper, seconded by William Scott, nominated Evans.[46] Again the matter was deferred until the following day, when Clemens Vonnegut moved Evans' nomination and was seconded by Loeper. The nomination carried by three votes, but Dr. J. J. Garver and J. B. Conner abstained. Then, in a move supposedly designed to insure Evans' reelection, Conner moved that the assistant librarian be made superintendent of the library. The assistant librarian would have charge of all library forces, the attendants, the management of the books and reading rooms, and would report to the librarian. However conceived, this was a slap in the face to Evans. What he was being called upon to accept was the position of figurehead. This resolution, concurred in by the members, would have stripped him of all authority in administrative matters.

To add insult to injury, the committee passed another crippling resolution asking that the superintendent of schools appoint a committee of four to select library books for school use. This committee would recommend books to the librarian, and, while he might add to the list, he could not delete titles therefrom. Moreover, all book

[45] I. P. L., "Library Reports," II, March 3, 1892, I. P. L. Archives; newspaper clipping, "Librarian Evans," Eliot Evans, "Scrapbook."

[46] I. P. L., "Library Reports," II, March 17 and 18, 1892, I. P. L. Archives.

purchases would have to be authorized by this committee henceforth. No one who knew Evans even slightly could seriously believe
that he would accept such restrictions upon his administrative authority. Board member Conner knew this too, and undoubtedly
hoped to make Evans' position so untenable that he would resign
rather than submit to such humiliating conditions.

When the action of the library committee became known, all the
Indianapolis newspapers rushed to Evans' defense. In a lengthy
editorial one newspaper charged that two board members had devised these conditions purely for personal spite. One was reported
offended at Evans' opposition to the building plans and another
because of Evans' refusal to replace one lady attendant with one
of his own lady friends. The editorial quoted from two prominent
citizens who strongly defended Evans as a librarian. It concluded
with a quotation from an outstanding lawyer who said: "No one
has gone to Mr. Evans in vain for information, and to place in his
stead a man with no experience and poor executive ability would
be a calamity to the city. The public library should be taken out
of the hands of the school board and the public given a chance to
vote for librarian, then no such outrage could be perpetrated upon
the people." [47] The *News* thought that the librarian had been
changed so often that people had come to believe something wrong
with the board—"they do not want a man who has manhood enough
to try to do his work thoroughly and without favoritism." [48] The
editor did not believe that the public would be satisfied to let so
competent a person as Charles Evans be dismissed.

When the school board met to pass on the resolution, President
Baker ruled Conner's motion on creating a superintendent out of
order. Conner insisted strongly on this portion of the report and
went to the heart of the matter: "The adoption of some such resolution as this is pertinent, as the chair well knows, to Mr. Evans retention as librarian. I for one will not vote for Mr. Evans unless this
or a rule containing similar provisions is adopted. Unless his services, in which he is very efficient, can be had without injuring the
library by his poor administrative ability, I am not in favor of
continuing him in his position." [49] Again the newspapers came to
Evans' defense, rejected Conner's contention that he was inefficient,

[47] Newspaper clipping, "Librarian Evans," Eliot Evans, "Scrapbook."

[48] Newspaper clipping, Indianapolis *News*, March 19, 1892, Eliot Evans, "Scrapbook."

[49] Newspaper clipping, "A Restriction of Duties," Eliot Evans, "Scrapbook."

and argued for his retention. And again they attributed the opposition to Evans to personal spite. The *Sentinel* reported, "Without question he is the best librarian the city has ever had. . . . The people of Indianapolis have been foolish enough to elect people to control their school interests, and incidentally their library interests, who are not fitted by nature, by acquirements, nor by aspirations, for business intrusted to them. It is a gratifying fact that the democrats on the board are opposed to this latest folly." [50] This circumstance was gratifying but strange, since Evans himself was a good Republican. The *Journal*, while joining the *Sentinel*'s plea for Evans' retention, rejected the idea that the board was shot with politics. At no time during the entire controversy did the newspapers of Indianapolis support the school board. Even more vigorously than in 1878, they urged the merits of Evans' case and refused to accept all statements concerning inefficiency or incompetence.

As the first week in April approached, the battle over Evans intensified. In view of Conner's statement at the meeting of March 17, Vonnegut, one of Evans' good friends, asked him if it would not be wise to assure Conner that the librarian would voluntarily delegate authority to his assistant librarian.[51] This might possibly take some of the steam out of Conner's attack. On April 3, Pierce, who had tried unsuccessfully to donate his pictures to the library, suggested that he would form a committee of distinguished citizens, raise a $100 fund to press the matter through the newspapers, and get every church, literary society, newspaper, and influential group of any kind to protest Evans' dismissal. He noted that even the Republican *Journal* called it spite work, and Evans' friends were not content to see him lose the position. That Evans was in constant communication with his friends and supporters is evident. However, Evans' friends and supporters were not politicians, and they did not have the necessary pressure to force one or two commissioners to change their minds. Evans had much underestimated the power of his opposition.

Evans went down in defeat at the board meeting held on April 1, 1892. The motion to concur in the report of the library committee was lost by tie vote of 5 to 5—the same as in 1878.[52] One board

---

[50] Newspaper clipping, Indianapolis *Sentinel*, March 23, 1892, Eliot Evans, "Scrapbook."

[51] Clemens Vonnegut to C. E., ALS, March 19, 1892; Henry D. Pierce to C. E., April 3, 1892.

[52] Newspaper clippings, Eliot Evans, "Scrapbook."

member had been absent, but since he was thought to be opposed to Evans, the result would not have been different. However, the matter was not yet settled, for it was necessary for the board to elect a successor before Evans relinquished the position. On April 15, when the board met again, William Scott moved to reconsider the vote of April 1, but this motion was lost. Dr. Garver then introduced a resolution to declare the office vacant and give the position to Eliza G. Browning, but this was withdrawn as a courtesy to two of Evans' supporters who were absent. It is clear from the newspaper accounts of this meeting that Dr. Garver had determined to have Evans removed and to have Miss Browning elected his successor. All of the wrangle continued to be played up by the press, which was unanimously favorable to Evans' retention. At length, on May 6, the matter finally came before the board directly, the other votes having been largely parliamentary maneuvering. Evans' nomination this time was defeated by a 5 to 4 vote. Thereupon Garver "steam-rollered" the nomination of Miss Browning, contrary to the rules which stated that the library committee would make the recommendation. However, President Baker sustained the nomination with a highly dubious bit of legal reasoning that the motion came from Dr. Garver, chairman of the library committee. In view of the statement of Vonnegut that not a member of the committee had been notified of Garver's intention, Baker's reasoning was farcical. Albeit, the anti-Evans forces were in control and determined to have their way. At the following meeting on May 21, Miss Browning was elected librarian after a verbal battle which showed how bitter the fight had become. Loeper even refused to vote because he thought the whole thing was illegal anyway. Thus did Charles Evans lose a second time at Indianapolis. Either to soften the blow or to salve their own consciences, the members of the board voted him an extra month's salary. It was a questionable end to a sorry political scheme.

Public sentiment and every newspaper in Indianapolis, both German and English, supported Evans, indicative of his ability,[53] and

---

[53] C. E. to W. F. P., ALS, May 7, 1892, Poole Papers, Newberry Library. The clippings in Eliot Evans, "Scrapbook," confirm Evans' statement that "what has been done has been against the entire press of the city, English and German." The Indianapolis *News,* June 4, 1892, p. 4, also states that Evans was endorsed by the local press as a unit. J. P. Dunn in his *Greater Indianapolis,* I, 512, noted that the imported librarians "did not get along with the school board, which

the fact that the board was vicious and that board members who cast votes against Evans did so for spite is equally beyond dispute. The facts do not bear out Evans' inefficiency, and the other charges were so trivial as to be virtually meaningless. Dr. J. J. Garver, his bitterest opponent, made wild and inexcusably ignorant statements about Evans' conduct in the library. It is easy enough to document Evans' contention that his dismissal was due to personal dislike.

Poole, who thought Evans was not entirely blameless in the first Indianapolis fray, backed him completely this time.[54] When informed that Evans was in "deep water in Indianapolis," he wrote that "there are no more vindictive people in the world than library directors whose personal pride and interests have been crossed." After his return from the American Library Association convention in May, Poole wrote that there was deep respect for Evans among the leading librarians and a feeling that he had been greatly wronged in Indianapolis. Moreover, he had seen Edward Stabler, Jr., one of the trustees of the Enoch Pratt Free Library, and President Gilman of Johns Hopkins. Both wanted to help and offered to do anything they could. All of Evans' friends thought he had a much stronger case in 1892 than he had had in 1878. Perhaps the profession had seen too many good librarians lose their positions because of the maliciousness of politically dominated boards.

Not all the blame, of course, should be placed on the board, although there is little doubt that most of Evans' friends saw it this way. Early in January a member of the library committee, perhaps Conner, had written Evans anonymously to warn him about his conduct of the library.[55] This anonymous member stated that he was personally friendly to Evans, but if this were so, he chose a queer way of expressing his views. Among other things of which he accused Evans was lack of common sense as evidenced by not producing a good catalog in a reasonable time. This statement was not only unfair to Evans but absolutely untrue. No one could have

---

was usually the fault of the school board." Dunn's comment on the school system, I, 277, also indicates some undercurrents probably operating in Evans' case: "The school law of 1871 was effective for taking the schools out of ordinary politics, but as the system developed, there grew up a system of public school politics, which was at bottom a contest of banks for the custody of the school funds, and which was as objectionable as party politics. It became a prominent feature of controversy in the nineties."

[54] W. F. P. to C. E., ALS, April 11, TLS, May 12, and ALS, May 26, 1892.

[55] A member of library committee to C. E., ALS, Jan. 1, 1892.

worked more diligently with more to show for his time than had Evans. However, the warning should have been sufficient to make Evans more conciliatory toward the board. He had admitted to Poole upon his return to Indianapolis that he knew only one board member as a holdover from his first period in Indianapolis. He should have used his first few months to strengthen his ties with the board. By this time he had had enough bitter experience to have learned that in a power struggle the board made the final decision.

Another letter, much more serious in its implications, had come from Albert E. Newton, a former Indianapolis citizen and friend of Evans who was residing in Los Angeles.[56] On March 4 he wrote Evans that he had heard of the friction between the librarian and the school board, especially in regard to the new building. His advice was "Diplomacy, my Dear, Diplomacy; be of all things diplomatic." As he saw the matter, Evans thought he was right; on the other hand, the board thought they were right. Newton advised Evans to control his impatience "at their ignorance, bull-headedness and conceit that they know it all." While Charlie was appreciated and esteemed by the best people, he ought to remember that he had the *experience* but the board had the *power*. His friends were concerned lest he lose his post, and they begged him "to be wise, to be politic, to be diplomatic, and to bear disappointment if arrangements do not go your way." Drawing a moral from his own situation in the banking business, Newton remarked, "My bread and butter is here & I must be politic & know the bounds of my authority & suggestions." Here was an excellent letter from a genuine friend. His advice was only a reinforcement of what Beanie had told Evans often and of what his brother John had said upon his return to Indianapolis. No city librarian could possibly hope to hold his position unless he got along with his board. Evans had deeply antagonized the board—far more than he realized. Even though he wrote Poole that his objections had been firmly and courteously expressed, he admitted that one opponent felt so violently about the matter that he swore Evans would never set foot in the new building.[57] One of Evans' functions as librarian certainly was to keep his board informed, to keep the communication lines open, and, if possible, to maintain favor on his side of any question. Barring this, he would have done well to accept with what grace he could the determination

---

[56] Albert E. Newton to C. E., ALS, March 4, 1892.
[57] C. E. to W. F. P., ALS, April 10, 1892, Poole Papers, Newberry Library.

of the board to go contrary to his wishes. This was a serious administrative failing, however impressive Evans' achievements as an internal administrator, however great his following among the local populace, and however high his reputation in the profession.

Bread and Butter for the Children

8

Despite the righteousness with which Charlie and his friends viewed his cause in Indianapolis, the dismissal posed serious problems for the Evans family. Charles Evans had never been a prosperous librarian, and, though he was a frugal man, his salary in Indianapolis barely covered the family's living expenses. Upon coming to Indianapolis he had rented a comfortable house in a superior residential section of the city, rent for this property taking about one-fourth of his salary each month. When it became apparent in late April that he could not be reelected librarian, Evans made arrangements to rent a small cottage on the outskirts of the city in order to cut his rent in half, intending to move the family to this new home in early June. Meanwhile the family had to exercise the closest scrutiny of expenditures in order to save some of their meager resources for the lean months ahead.

In writing of his dismissal to Poole on May 7, Evans also entered an urgent plea for his mentor to find him another job quickly: "If it were not for my family I should be glad to be out of it. I have never been a forehanded man in money matters, and now it is very necessary that I do not remain idle. I would be under the greatest obligations to you if you could put me in the way of doing something soon. . . . I would like to continue in Library work, but any work which promises bread and butter and clothes for the children would be accepted. I have no wish or disposition to remain idle." [1]

---

[1] C. E. to W. F. P., ALS, May 7, 1892, Poole Papers, Newberry Library.

Writing this letter gave Evans considerable pain. After all, he had promised Poole that a return to Indianapolis would not only lift one burden from his shoulders but that he would not let this opportunity slip from his grasp until he was called to a more responsible position.[2] Now, scarcely three years later, he was forced to write again in the most despairing tones of his loss of a job. As each new failure was added to Evans' record, he placed himself more and more beyond the pale for many top library administrators. Even the most favorable interpretation of his professional history clearly revealed that there was much to be desired.

Poole answered Evans' letter on the eve of his departure for the annual convention of the American Library Association.[3] Among other possibilities, Evans had asked Poole about the Milwaukee Public Library, where K. A. Linderfelt had just been dismissed for embezzling library fines. Poole responded that there was no prospect of a replacement for Linderfelt before autumn, but he would see what he could do for Evans at the convention. Meanwhile Evans prepared to turn over the library to Eliza G. Browning, who seemed certain of confirmation as librarian. On May 21 he relinquished the reins at Indianapolis for the second time and began an intensive search for another job. The additional month's salary granted by the board would give the family sufficient income until the first of July, after which Charles Evans somehow had to secure another position.

Upon Poole's return from the East, he wrote Evans an encouraging letter.[4] Perhaps feeling some personal responsibility for having encouraged his protégé's inflexibility in the library building matter, he tried to cheer him by reporting that there was deep respect for Evans among the convention librarians. A number had offered to help find him a new job. The most promising position at hand was the post of chief assistant in charge of circulation at Columbia College. Poole had contacted George H. Baker, the librarian, and had pressed him to give the job to Evans. Baker demurred that he wanted time to think the matter over. To insure favorable consideration for his recommendation Poole privately asked both Cutter and Fletcher to speak to Baker in Evans' behalf. Both men agreed to do

[2] C. E. to W. F. P., ALS, March 11, 1889, Poole Papers, Newberry Library.
[3] W. F. P. to C. E., ALS, May 12, 1892. C. E. to W. F. P., ALS, May 7, 1892, Poole Papers, Newberry Library.
[4] W. F. P. to C. E., ALS, May 26, 1892.

so, and Poole advised Evans to make direct application for the job.[5]

Believing the time had come to talk with Poole personally, Evans went to Chicago in late June to discuss job prospects with the master. Two additional positions had come to Poole's attention since the convention. The first, the librarianship of the United States State Department, seemed the better. Since Evans was a personal friend of President Harrison, Poole thought he should apply directly to the President. Evans followed this advice only to learn that the position had already been filled.[6]

The second position was the librarianship of the Portland, Oregon, Library Association, an expanding institution with good prospects for the future. Although Evans thought the proposed salary insufficient, he contacted the board to see what could be done.[7]

The first of July passed without any definite offer. Evans was bitter about Baker, who had not written and presumably was still "winding up the Waterbury watch of his deliberation."[8] Even more discouraging was a publisher's rejection of the manuscript of a little story of about 5,000 words which he and Lena had translated from the French. He felt partially vindicated by the defeat of two of his enemies in the Indianapolis school board elections, but he could scarcely be recalled to his old position without an arbitrary action of the new board in removing Browning.

On July 12 he received a letter from Poole asking him to accept an appointment as a temporary replacement for Dr. William K. Williams, Head of Classification and Reference, at the Newberry.[9] On the instructions of his physician Williams had taken a long leave of absence in late June. Although the Newberry trustees would

---

[5] C. A. Cutter to W. F. P., ALS, May 26, 1892, Poole Papers, Newberry Library. Cutter told Poole that he had spoken to Baker "about Charlie" and had mentioned the gold watch presentation at the Athenaeum. "I think that shows his qualifications for such positions,—that he can satisfy the public in his intercourse with them."

[6] C. E. to W. F. P., ALS, July 12, 1892, Poole Papers, Newberry Library; E. W. Halford to C. E., TLS, June 27, 1892. Halford was private secretary to President Harrison and also a native of Indianapolis.

[7] W. M. Ladd to C. E., ALS, July 8, 1892, and TLS, Sept. 1, 1892; C. E. to W. M. Ladd, MS draft, n.d., but in reply to letter of Sept. 1, 1892, Evans rejected Ladd's offer primarily on the basis of salary. He asked for $2,500, which Ladd's association could not pay.

[8] C. E. to W. F. P., ALS, July 12, 1892, Poole Papers, Newberry Library.

[9] *Ibid.* W. F. P. to E. W. Blatchford, TDS, June 30, 1892, Blatchford Papers; Newberry Library, Committee on Administration, "Minutes," July 11, 1892, and W. K. Williams to W. F. P., ALS, Sept. 2, 1892, Newberry Library.

pay only $1,200, all too little for a man with three children, Evans accepted the post thankfully with the hope that something permanent would be forthcoming. Temporarily he would leave his family in Indianapolis, and, after winding up some personal affairs, would report for duty on Monday, July 18, 1892.

Arriving in Chicago on Sunday, Evans spent the day sight-seeing,[10] thus establishing a pattern which he was to follow in his research trips in later years. Riding the cable cars and viewing the sights provided an escape mechanism for his lonely hours. On this occasion he first took a street car to the North Side Park, which took him by the Newberry Library and enabled him to see how that part of the city looked. Impressed with Lincoln Park, the miles of nicely kept grass, the trees and flowers, he could not help thinking how the children would have enjoyed the menageries and the sheer beauty of the park if they could have been with him. After a good dinner and cigar, Charlie took a car for Hyde Park to see the southern part of Chicago. He wandered about the grounds of the Columbian Exposition and was so impressed with its beauty that he determined on the spot that Lena should also see this display. He thought it far outstripped the 1876 exposition in Philadelphia.

After a good night's sleep he reported the following morning for work at the Newberry Library. He found it a flourishing institution. In the five years since Poole's appointment the book collection had grown rapidly, and in 1892 the total stood at 78,179 books plus some 28,000 pamphlets.[11] More impressive than the statistics themselves was the quality of the books. Poole, in his attempt to build a great reference library in the few remaining years left to him, had purchased entire collections rich in incunabula, fine bindings, and illuminated manuscripts. Impressed with the high quality of the acquisitions, Charlie wrote Lena that "the cost of the book does not seem to cut any figure, if the book is wanted it is purchased. They have many richly illustrated works whose value runs up into the thousands, and rare books of nearly equal value from their scarcity." [12]

However, there were some other problems that bothered Evans. Although he found the lack of system and the general confusion

---

[10] C. E. to L. E., ALS, July 19, 1892.

[11] Newberry Library, *Proceedings of the Trustees of the Newberry Library for the Year Ending January 5, 1892* (Chicago: Knight, Leonard and Company, 1892), p. 12. Williamson, "William Frederick Poole," pp. 623, 674–675.

[12] C. E. to L. E., ALS, July 27, 1892.

in administration personally disturbing, his basic complaint was the lack of decent salaries.[13] This was a grievance which Evans shared with other staff members and one which had been a continual bone of contention between his predecessor and the trustees. The Newberry was a rather typical case of a private library where the two top administrators were the only staff members who made any money. Poole, as chief librarian, had a salary of $5,000, while his assistant librarian, C. A. Nelson, received $3,000.[14] However, the median salary for the library was $720, and some staff members were forced to make extra money by working overtime at night.

Under the assistant librarian were four departments: order and accession, cataloging, classification and reference, and medical. Evans was first a temporary and then a permanent replacement for Williams, who had been head of the classification and reference department. His department was responsible for assigning call numbers, for the physical processing of the new books, and for reading-room service. Evans supervised the work of two other classifiers, J. C. M. Hanson and Frederick P. Noble; two processing and shelving clerks; and three reading-room assistants. The total staff of the library at the time numbered about thirty, but almost half were on vacation when Evans began work.

Charlie wrote Lena that the staff had received him courteously and that he had little difficulty fitting into the situation.[15] True, when one of the classifiers returned from his vacation, he expressed some annoyance to find Evans in charge, and Williams is reported to have resigned when he learned of Evans' appointment. Yet Evans, mindful of the nature of his appointment, treaded carefully for the first few months. The rare courtesy of which he was capable came to the fore. William Stetson Merrill, then head of the order and accession department, noted that "in social intercourse with others he was cordial in manner and polite in the old-fashioned mode of bowing low when greeting someone." [16] His earnest efforts to please Poole met with considerable success. When C. A. Nelson went on his vacation in August, he asked Evans to take his place in relieving Poole of some of the minor details.[17] Later Evans learned that this had been done at Poole's request, and he reported to his wife that

---

[13] C. E. to L. E., ALS, Aug. 17, 1892.
[14] Williamson, "William Frederick Poole," pp. 692–697.
[15] C. E. to L. E., ALS, July 22 and Aug. 2, 1892.
[16] Merrill, "Early Days at the Newberry Library," p. 23.
[17] C. E. to L. E., ALS, Aug. 17, 1892.

he intended to make little use of the authority the position conferred.

The Newberry Library had used Poole's classification system from the beginning, but by the time Evans arrived there was a definite need for expansion.[18] Drawing upon his previous experience with Poole's scheme, Evans proposed adding a zero to each old number. In this way the library could gain nine new numbers between each old number. These additional digits could be treated as decimals in arranging the books on the shelves. Thus, an old number H1522 would become H15220 and the number next to it H15230. The intervening nine digits were then available without reclassifying the entire collection. These were the radical yet simple improvements in the system which Evans proposed to Poole, Nelson, and Blatchford, one of the trustees, in late July. Approval of the proposal was immediate, and, in line with Poole's custom, Evans was left free to work out the details by himself. Although the library itself could have used more direct supervision by the chief, Evans liked this freedom and found it one of the enjoyable aspects of working for Poole.

As head of the department, Evans also did a part of the actual classification. He assumed responsibility for books in the fields of archaeology, customs, education, fine arts, language, and natural science. Noble and Hanson classified works in other subject areas. With the rapid increase in acquisitions, there was plenty of work to keep all three classifiers busy. Before Evans learned that Williams would not return, he had spoken to Poole with some apprehension about the future of his job.[19] His mentor assured him that there was nothing to worry about, for the Newberry had plenty of work and indicated that he could stay as long as he desired. Upon receipt of Williams' resignation in early September, Evans was assured of a permanent position in the library.

While this news was encouraging for Evans, he did not like the prospect of living alone in Chicago. Nelson had made arrangements for Evans to board at a house across the street from the site where the new library building was being erected. The other boarders were interesting people; the food was good and the accommodations

---

[18] Merrill, "Early Days at the Newberry Library," pp. 23–24, discusses Evans' changes in the Poole classification thoroughly. See also Merrill to W. L. Williamson, TLS, Oconomowoc, Wis., March 9, 1952, copy in possession of the author.

[19] C E. to L. E., ALS, Aug. 31, 1892.

adequate. Since other staff members often took their noon meals there, Evans had an opportunity to discuss professional matters under pleasant conditions. If Evans' descriptions of the meals are typical, he fared well.[20] Breakfast consisted of steak, potatoes, muffins, cakes, and coffee; lunch of chipped beef, potatoes, bread, iced tea, blueberries and cake; and dinner of a roast, potatoes, tomatoes, cucumbers, watermelon, peaches, and a small cup of coffee.

Despite his pleasant quarters, Evans hated the life of "forced celibacy" and missed the children so much that he was tempted to pick up a smudgy-faced child in the park and hug him.

Yet Evans was torn among a variety of considerations. He wanted another job which would pay more and did not want to be faced with the problem of moving twice. Chicago rents seemed prohibitive on his present salary, and neither he nor Lena viewed the possibility of living in a flat with any degree of enthusiasm. Still, living apart was expensive, too. Basic cost for room and board for Evans was $32 per month. When he added $20 per month for the rent of the cottage in Indianapolis and $40 per month for food and incidentals for the family, he had only eight dollars left for other items, far too little for a safe margin. Despite all this, he insisted that his family eat well and that Lena have help with the laundry and ironing.[21] It should not have taken an economist to point out to Evans that this was virtually impossible on $100 per month. How Evans could have rationalized not moving the family to Chicago, thereby stopping the drain on his slender reserves, is difficult to understand. Steadily he was forced to withdraw money from his account in the Merchants National Bank, and by late November the balance was so low that Lena had to use the children's money to buy a much needed new gas stove.[22]

Still Evans kept protesting all through the fall that it was much too costly to move the family to Chicago. As late as November, he foresaw nothing but a continuation of their separate existence and even considered bringing one of the children to Chicago to spend the winter with him as a partial relief to Lena. Finally, however, the financial drain of maintaining two households had to stop when the bank account was reduced almost to nothing.

---

[20] C. E. to L. E., ALS, July 27 and Oct. 10, 1892.

[21] C. E. to L. E., ALS, July 27, Aug. 2, and Sept. 1, 1892.

[22] C. E. to L. E., ALS, Nov. 28, 1892. He thanked the children for loaning Lena the money and promised to pay it back the next time he wrote.

In Indianapolis, Lena and the children made out as best they could. In mid-August Charlie joined them for a weekend, the only trip home that he made in the second half of 1892. Shortly thereafter trouble multiplied when Eliot's dog bit a boy, and the boy's parents threatened a suit for damages.[23] The thought of the court costs and of this miserable scheme which "shyster attornies" were trying to force upon him was so upsetting that Evans could scarcely do his work. In the midst of his depression over the incident he thought seriously of very quietly moving the family to Chicago and forgetting everything in Indianapolis. He was quite willing to pay the doctor's bills, but he would not pay one cent of tribute to a shyster lawyer. For some reason Lena did not want to move and managed to calm Charlie down; perhaps she still hoped that circumstances would occur to reunite them in Indianapolis. As cold weather approached, Charlie worried about the children's clothes, their schools, and the spread of diphtheria in the neighborhood.

To give Lena a little rest and perhaps to boost his own morale, Charlie urged his wife to join him in Chicago in mid-October for the dedication exercises of the Columbian Exposition. They had received complimentary tickets from an Indianapolis friend, and the Newberry Board had decided to close the library on October 20 and 21 so that the staff could attend the ceremonies. Yielding to Charlie's insistent letter, Lena came to Chicago on Wednesday and stayed until Sunday.

However, during her absence things had not gone well in Indianapolis. Eliot had misbehaved and then had become ill. The nurse was upset and displeased that she had not been able to manage the children. Poor Lena had to administer discipline to Eliot and try to restore the household to its former good order. As Charlie noted on another occasion, "Men *are* useful and handy things to have around." [24]

Another problem arose in November when John Evans and his wife came West.[25] Although they were very anxious to visit Lena and the children in Indianapolis, Lena did not feel she could receive them in their present circumstances. The house was inadequate, she did not have the proper china, and they could not really afford the extra food. However, when John and Helen came to Chicago,

[23] C. E. to L. E., ALS, Aug. 17, 24, 31, and Sept. 1, 1892.

[24] C. E. to L. E., ALS, Aug. 2, 1892.

[25] C. E. to L. E., ALS, Nov. 4, 11, 14, and 24, 1892.

they absolutely insisted to Charlie that they were going back East via St. Louis and Indianapolis so they could see the children. While in Chicago, they treated Charlie to the theater and sight-seeing. When Charlie casually mentioned his approaching birthday to his brother, John gave him $25 for a present. Charles sent $15 to Lena to entertain John and Helen and to purchase candy and toys for the children.

Charlie had enjoyed John's week-long visit, but the aftermath was deeply depressing. When his forty-second birthday arrived on the following Sunday, there was little about which to rejoice. He missed his family, it cost too much for him to go to Indianapolis either for Thanksgiving or for John's visit there, and their slender resources were almost gone. He wrote to Lena, "My succeeding birthdays always seem occasions for fits of the blues, and yesterday was a day of deepest disgust to me." [26] He was frustrated by his failure to provide for his family adequately and to give them the things that he saw his peers provide.

Despite his unhappiness over the continual separation from the family, Evans had known moments of enjoyment in Chicago in addition to Lena's and John's visits. In September, when Poole gave a lecture on old books to a class of young ladies from Evanston, Mrs. Poole came to the Newberry. She was delighted to see Evans, called him "Charlie" repeatedly, and spoke in glowing terms of the good old days. Moreover, she insisted that he come out and spend some time with them in Evanston. It pleased Evans that Mrs. Poole still remembered him so affectionately and that she regarded him as favorably as she had in the days of his young manhood.

Lacking anything better to do, he twice departed from his usual practice and attended church services. Evans, a religious liberal, was not a churchman.[27] The first preacher he went to hear was Dr. Hiram W. Thomas, one of the two most liberal pastors in Chicago. While the full house and the singing led by a cornet impressed Charlie, he thought Thomas preached a very weak liberalism. His fellow club member, Dr. H. A. Cleaveland, Pastor of the Meridian Street Methodist Church in Indianapolis, was twice as radical and "four times more able to express the faith within him."

---

[26] C. E. to L. E., ALS, Nov. 14, 1892.

[27] His son, Eliot Evans, does not remember that his father ever attended church. Neither he nor Lena attended, nor did they encourage the children to do so. Interview with Eliot H. Evans, Chicago, May 20, 1960. C. E. to L. E., ALS, Oct. 10 and 27, 1892.

Having heard Thomas, he thought he might as well hear the other notable liberal preacher. After he put Lena on the train for Indianapolis early on Sunday morning, October 23, he went to hear Dr. David Swing, described by one admirer as "the Emerson of the American pulpit." Evans was much more interested in Swing than he had been in Thomas, although there is no evidence that he found the good doctor stimulating enough to hear regularly.

October was a busy social period. To bring the month to a fitting close for Evans, Poole invited him to go to a Chicago Literary Club meeting. In keeping with the spirit of the exposition, Poole led a discussion on Columbus. Evans enjoyed the evening but could not help comparing this group adversely to the one he had founded. He noted to his wife that there were just a few more members present than they ordinarily had in Indianapolis.[28] Moreover, he quite frankly found their after-meeting luncheon without cigars a shade under the Indianapolis program.

Then there was the boardinghouse gang, who could always talk him into a quiet game of whist. Evans enjoyed cards and several years later could still be lured back to the boardinghouse occasionally for whist with his old friends. However, except for the special occasions, his life quickly settled down to a routine: awake at 6:30, breakfast at 7:30, to the library by 8:45, lunch at 1:00, back to the library by 2:00, dinner at 6:30, then a walk, a smoke, and reading or writing in the library until 9:00 or 10:00, and then to bed.[29]

Evans' indecision about moving his family to Chicago probably would have ended in late November in any case. His bank account was perilously low and his cash on hand was nil; hence, drastic action had to be taken in early December. As if financial troubles were not enough, the people who owned the house returned to Indianapolis sooner than they had expected and wanted immediate possession. Having now been pushed to take action, Charlie was exasperated in the extreme. While he recognized the necessity for moving eventually, he did think that the decision might have come at a better time. In early December he wrote Lena, "What a nuisance it all is anyway, this thing of living." [30]

Again he began his discouraging search for an adequate place to

---

[28] C. E. to L. E., ALS, Oct. 27, 1892.
[29] C. E. to L. E., ALS, July 27, 1892.
[30] C. E. to L. E., ALS, Dec. 13, 1892.

live. He haunted the real estate offices and found nothing that he
either desired or could afford.[31] As a basis for his calculations he set
a rental maximum of $35 per month in the city and $25 in the
suburbs. Despite his best efforts he was forced to write Lena on
January 5 that he had no results. He had spent every minute he
could spare from work looking at undesirable houses and flats and
was so heartily sick of it all that he had determined to take whatever was offered. He was especially irritated by the Indianapolis
property owners who wanted to move right in. Vexing his indignation to Lena, he wrote that there was "too much of the disposition
to override one in Indianapolis. I shall be heartily glad when the
dust of that detestable hole is off our feet for ever." [32]

Finally in mid-January he found a third story flat on Oak Street
at $30, although renting it involved buying some of the furniture
too. They could take it until May 1 and then look around for something permanent. Although he had not seen the place, one of his
fellow boarders vouched for it, and Evans decided that the family
could make it do temporarily. They could sell part of their own
furniture and not have to move it. He wrote to Lena that he would
take this flat if nothing else were offered. Just before the time for
the move, however, he did find a flat on the poor end of Cedar Street
—the first floor of a house which faced a brewery.

In order to have more free time to make the final arrangements
in Indianapolis, Lena sent Eliot and Gertrude ahead to stay with
their father, who met them at the station.[33] Fascinated by the train
station in a big city, Eliot wandered off, much to the irritation of
his father, who had problems enough without adding a lost child
to the medley. Gertrude and Eliot boarded at the house on Washington Square with Evans for about two weeks, attending the neighborhood school during the day while their father worked. Then
Lena and little Charlie came to Chicago in early February and the
family settled down to life in the big city. By this time the senior
Evans was glad to put up with almost any inconvenience in order
to have the family together.

Added to Evans' other worries late in the year 1892 was the situation at the Newberry. Whatever his failure to face reality in other
situations, he was well aware that his professional life now depended

[31] C. E. to L. E., ALS, Dec. 17, 20, and 21, 1892, and Jan. 5, 1893.
[32] C. E. to L. E., ALS, Jan. 9, 1893.
[33] Interview with Eliot Evans, Chicago, May 20, 1960.

upon Poole. Though a robust man, Poole was now seventy-one and under terrific pressure both within the library and outside it. Just before the November election, he suffered a serious fall which dislocated his right shoulder and broke his right arm.[34] Evans was deeply concerned about Poole's accident and wrote his wife that he thought the fall would have killed an ordinary man, and "if we lost him dear, we would lose our mainstay in life, sure." A week later he reported that he thought Poole would "pull through all right and live to see the completion of his magnum opus." However, as weeks passed, it must have been apparent to Evans as it was to the other staff members that Poole was far from well. With Poole's health obviously declining, Evans undoubtedly experienced great anxiety about his future.

There were other features at the Newberry which disturbed Evans. The trustees had become very unhappy over what they thought were Poole's administrative failings.[35] The work was not properly supervised and the cataloging was not proceeding as rapidly as they wished. Moreover, they were not pleased about the expenditure of such large sums on books. Repeatedly they asked Poole to develop sound acquisitions policies which would enable them both to stop the drain of book funds and also to cut down on the staff.

Administratively, the situation had some similarity to the Enoch Pratt Free Library. The trustees continually interfered with the staff and listened to all complaints. Encouraged by such receptive ears, the staff were not reluctant to discuss their problems with the trustees; the assistants at the Newberry were not the first nor the last to think that they knew how to run a library better than the librarian. One of the most loyal staff members, William Stetson Merrill, wrote to a former colleague that "the Newberry has always had the reputation among its staff of having something always wrong with it." [36] Reflecting the annoyance of working with a difficult group, Nelson, after leaving the Newberry, wrote humorously to Poole: "Present my love to all the *good* boys and girls on the *staff*, the *bad* ones will not care for it." [37]

---

[34] Williamson, "William Frederick Poole," p. 706. Chapter 15 of this work, "Years of Satisfaction and Stress, 1892–1894," is an excellent summary of the deterioration of librarian-trustee relations during Poole's last two years. C. E. to L. E., ALS, Nov. 11 and 14, 1892.

[35] Williamson, "William Frederick Poole," pp. 708–724.

[36] W. S. Merrill to G. W. Cole, ALS, June 15, 1892, as quoted in Williamson, "William Frederick Poole," p. 720.

[37] C. A. Nelson to W. F. P., ALS, July 7, 1893, Poole Papers, Newberry Library.

Not all of the difficulty lay with trustee interference, though one can be sure that Evans, out of his fierce loyalty to Poole, placed most of the blame on the trustees. The head librarian was much too involved in his job as chairman of the World's Literary Congresses, which were to be held in conjunction with the Columbian Exposition. Yet he could do little when the trustees did interfere. One of his stated principles was to conform to the wishes of the trustees. With declining health, heavy outside responsibilities, and trustee interference, Poole had a very difficult year. Under the circumstances staff morale deteriorated even further in 1893.

Poole's relationship with the trustees received a serious blow in May, 1893, when the board voted to abolish the position of assistant librarian.[38] By this means the trustees apparently hoped to force Poole to take a more active role in supervising the staff. Whatever the motive, the move was a mistake. Poole simply did not have time to devote to day-to-day library operations.

After Nelson's post was abolished, Evans was more directly affected by the dissatisfaction of one of his own staff members. J. C. M. Hanson, a long-suffering classifier, lost all patience in late May and wrote a lengthy letter to Poole expressing his unhappiness over the situation in the classification and reference department.[39] Most of his work for the year past had been the drudgery of copying cards by the thousands, with no suitable opportunity for the more intellectually challenging tasks for which he had been trained. However, he had not previously complained but had spent all his spare time working on a detailed classification of music, in which he had a great interest. This scheme he had finally proposed to Poole, who had encouraged him by saying that he would trust his judgment in the matter of classifying the music collection. Now Evans had taken the matter out of Hanson's hands and was working on a scheme of his own. If Evans, who knew nothing about music, was to have charge of the new classification for music, then Hanson wanted to be transferred to cataloging. In an obvious dig at Evans' lack of formal training, Hanson spoke of his own "knowledge of thirteen languages, a knowledge extending farther than reading a title page by aid of a dictionary." Noting that this was the first time he had ever "taken the liberty to toot my own horn in your pres-

[38] Newberry Library, Committee on Administration, "Minutes," May 9, 1893, Newberry Library.

[39] J. C. M. Hanson to W. F. P., ALS, May 25, 1893, Poole Papers, Newberry Library.

ence," he hoped that Poole would give his request serious consideration.

What Evans' reaction to this letter was is not known, but can certainly be inferred. There is no evidence that Poole acted favorably upon Hanson's request, and in late July the latter resigned to accept a position at the University of Wisconsin.[40]

July also saw the resignation of another staff member, Mary I. Crandall, after only a month as head of the cataloging department. In a pleasant letter to Poole she stated that she resigned to accept a more agreeable position at Cornell University. However, about a week after her resignation became effective, she wrote a blistering letter to E. W. Blatchford, President of the Board of Trustees, about the "absolutely false statement which one of the staff has made concerning me." [41] With an attack upon the discord among the staff as a chief reason for her accepting another position, she noted that there had been "carping, hostile and jealous criticism." She felt intensely wounded at these covert attacks upon the character of her work and personality and wanted to set the record straight before she left. Such was the state of morale at the Newberry in summer, 1893.

Also in July, Poole asked the committee on administration to grant time off for staff members who wanted to attend the World's Library Congress.[42] The committee granted this request for those members of the staff who were also members of the American Library Association. Since Poole was to be given time to attend both the Congress of Librarians and the Congress of Historians, the committee directed him to put Evans in charge of the library during his absences. Why Evans did not go to the congress is a mystery. He had not attended an American Library Association meeting since 1877, and this would have been an excellent opportunity not only to renew acquaintances but to make contacts for a better job. Perhaps he hoped that the trustees would revive the position of assistant librarian, and by doing a good job during Poole's absence he would be in a position to qualify for the appointment.

[40] Newberry Library, Committee on Administration, "Minutes," July 25, 1893, Newberry Library. Hanson's resignation was dated July 24, 1893, and the committee accepted it to take effect on August 15.

[41] Mary I. Crandall to W. F. P., ALS, July 23, 1893, Poole Papers, Newberry Library; Mary I. Crandall to E. W. Blatchford, ALS, July 31, 1893, Blatchford Papers, Newberry Library.

[42] Newberry Library, Committee on Administration, "Minutes," July 12, 1893, Newberry Library.

Another episode of trustee interference transpired in August when the "unseemly bickering" between Florence Brooks and Mabel McIlvaine came to a head.[43] Since Miss McIlvaine was a niece of a member of the committee on administration, that committee held a formal inquiry to determine the facts. Neither Evans, as head of the department, nor Poole was asked to testify. All through the fall this personality clash continued until the trustees finally asked Poole to transfer both McIlvaine and Brooks to other positions in the library and nominate someone else to take charge of the reading room.

A crisis in the relationship between Poole and his trustees came in early December, 1893, when the board told him of their decision to make him "consulting librarian" at half his present salary and bring in another man as "director" to supervise the work of the staff. Such an action was a blow to Poole and Evans. Other distinguished librarians had lost their positions, but surely this could not happen to Poole! The blow stunned Poole as it did also his faithful lieutenant. While no appointment had yet been made, it was apparent that the trustees would move rapidly in that direction.

Poole, in poor health and overworked during 1893, saw his strength ebb under the impact of this psychological blow. While he continued to work on a variety of enterprises in early 1894, he was obviously becoming weaker. In February he suffered a couple of falls and a brief illness from which he did not recover. He died on March 1, 1894.[44]

In the death of Poole, Charles Evans had lost his best friend. He could only wonder what would happen to him now that "Papa" Poole could no longer look after him. The funeral on March 3 was a moving emotional experience for Evans. With two other assistants at the Newberry and three assistants from the Chicago Public Library, he served as an active pallbearer. Certainly for Charles Evans this was the end of an era. There was no longer anyone upon whom he could depend, no one individual who would see to it that he had a job and that he received favorable recommendations. Charles Evans owed much to William Frederick Poole, and it was a debt that he did not take lightly.

After a suitable interval, when the Newberry committee on ad-

---

[43] Williamson, "William Frederick Poole," pp. 722–724; Newberry Library, Committee on Administration, "Minutes," Aug. 18, 1893, Newberry Library.
[44] Williamson, "William Frederick Poole," pp. 735–737.

ministration began its search for a new librarian, Evans wrote to Justin Winsor at Harvard and asked for a recommendation for the position.[45] According to a public statement by the committee, the new librarian must be a "man who is what Dr. Poole was thirty years ago." In Evans' opinion there was no one in the library profession who fit that description better than he himself. After all, Poole had been his first instructor, his constant correspondent, and his closest professional friend. Moreover, Evans had adopted most of Poole's methods in all the libraries in which he had worked. In addition, he had a good knowledge of the Newberry situation which he thought would enable him to "carry on the work without friction." On May 1 the Harvard librarian responded that he had seen George E. Adams, the chairman of the Newberry committee, and learned that the committee had decided not to advance anyone presently on the staff.

The trustees did not proceed rapidly to the selection of a new chief, and affairs at the library continued to worsen. For nine months there was no executive head. In June a Chicago newspaper printed a lengthy report on the Newberry in which it called attention to the lack of harmony among the trustees, the poor salary scale for employees, the lack of authority for the head librarian, and the petty rules for the staff.[46] Three ranking librarians were reported to have refused the job. Someone on the board or on the staff had been talking out of school.

Finally, on October 22, 1894, the board elected John Vance Cheney, then librarian of the San Francisco Public Library, to succeed Poole. Cheney assumed his duties in December, 1894, and brought with him Alexander J. Rudolph, who had been his assistant librarian at San Francisco.[47] Cheney, a literary man, was accustomed to leaving the technical details to Rudolph. The new assistant librarian of the Newberry had many ideas of his own and was determined to place them into practice, including the use of the Rudolph Indexer for the preparation of the catalog and shelf list. Using a firm hand in a lax situation, Rudolph assigned duties and gave specific instructions. By late December, he had decided to

---

[45] C. E. to Justin Winson, ALS, April 27, 1894, Harvard Archives. Justin Winsor to C. E., ALS, May 1, 1894.

[46] Newspaper clipping, in Eliot Evans, "Scrapbook."

[47] Merrill, "Early Days at the Newberry Library," p. 25. Merrill provides an interesting account of Rudolph's arrival and the subsequent staff reaction to his policies.

reclassify the collection by the Dewey Decimal scheme. Announcement of this decision triggered a quick flash of Evans' temper, and in his own emphatic way, Evans told Rudolph such a proposal was absurd.

Rudolph merely walked calmly over to Merrill's desk and told him that he would take charge of the classification. Upon Merrill's protestation that classification was Evans' job, Rudolph said, "There will be some changes made." On January 7, Evans and three other staff members received letters from Blatchford, dismissing them from their posts and granting them thirty days' leave of absence with pay.[48]

Out of work again, Evans this time had no friendly teacher to help him find a job. His salary had remained the same throughout his period of service at the Newberry, and, though the depression beginning in early 1893 undoubtedly increased his buying power, he was still pinched to provide proper support for his family. According to the notification from Blatchford, he would be granted thirty-days terminal leave with his dismissal to take effect at the end of that time, February 9, 1895. One of the most desirable positions then open was the new Carnegie Library of Pittsburgh. In addition to the lure of $4,000 annual salary, the board could offer a new million dollar building and several new branch libraries. Naturally the board did not lack applicants for this position. On January 10, Evans wrote to Justin Winsor for a letter of recommendation to the Pittsburgh board.[49] He also asked Spofford of the Library of Congress and President Gilman of Johns Hopkins University to do the same. Both Gilman and Winsor wrote letters for Evans, though Winsor's was somewhat restrained. The board was impressed with Evans' letters from two such distinguished individuals and the chairman of the selection committee, George A. Macbeth, came to Chicago early in February to interview him. After a favorable talk with Evans, Macbeth invited him to come to Pittsburgh to meet the other trustees. Though the interview in Pittsburgh was equally favorable, other factors finally worked against Evans' appointment. The chief factor against him was the committee's desire for a librarian with

---

[48] E. W. Blatchford to C. E., ALS, Jan. 7, 1895; Newberry Library, Committee on Administration, "Minutes," Dec. 31, 1894, Newberry Library.

[49] C. E. to Justin Winsor, ALS, Jan. 10, 1895, Harvard Archives. A. R. Spofford to C. E., ALS, Jan. 14, 1895; D. C. Gilman to the trustees of the Carnegie Library, Pittsburgh, ALS, Jan. 31, 1895; Justin Winsor to the trustees of the Carnegie Free Library of Pittsburgh, ALS, Jan. 14, 1895.

a knowledge of their population or a similar population. In March
he learned to his regret that Edwin H. Anderson of Braddock,
Pennsylvania, had won the post.[50]

Evans had tried to leave the Newberry before he was forced out
by Rudolph, but the Pittsburgh position was the most promising of
any that he considered. He had also applied for the position of
librarian of the new John Crerar Library through Blatchford.[51]
Again using Gilman for support, he was disappointed. Though
Gilman noted that Evans possessed in a high degree "acquaintance
with the technicalities of library administration," he thought the
board would prefer a man of broad views, varied acquisitions, and
a hearty sympathy with popular education.[52] Once they chose such
a man they could then supplement his services with several library
experts. Certainly Evans was seeking too high a position in view
of his failures at other libraries. The openings at both the Newberry and the John Crerar—and even the one at the Carnegie Library of Pittsburgh—were positions legitimately beyond his aspirations. They might not have been if Evans had known an unusually
successful period elsewhere, but despite "twenty-three years . . . of
practical Library work," [53] Evans had not been administratively
successful since his first period in Indianapolis, some twenty years
before. All three positions were among the top positions in terms
of financial support and librarians' salaries. The very best that Evans
could hope under such circumstances would be for an assistant
librarian's position, somewhat comparable to the position Nelson
had held at the Newberry.

One other position was tentatively proposed to Evans in late Janu-
ary, 1895. Edward G. Mason, President of the Chicago Historical
Society, approached him about organizing the society's materials.[54]
The society had under construction a new building and wanted to

---

[50] W. N. Frew to D. C. Gilman, TLS, Feb. 2, 1895; George A. Macbeth to C. E.,
ALS, Feb. 2, 1895; George Macbeth to C. E., telegram, Feb. 14, 1895; George A.
Macbeth to C. E., TLS, Feb. 20, March 4 and 22, 1895; W. N. Frew to C. E., TLS,
March 11, 1895; "Anderson the Chief," newspaper clipping.

[51] C. E. to E. W. Blatchford, MS draft of a letter, n.d. (probably late 1894).

[52] D. C. Gilman to Messrs. Jackson, Blatchford, and Keith, Feb. 26, 1895, in
J. C. Bay, *The John Crerar Library* (Chicago: [Directors of the John Crerar
Library], 1945), pp. 35–36.

[53] The term comes from C. E. to D. C. Gilman, ALS, Jan. 23, 1895. All the
Pittsburgh correspondence was returned to Evans and Gilman had included
this letter with his original recommendation. Evans outlines in this letter what
he believes to be his qualifications.

[54] Edward G. Mason to C. E., TLS, Jan. 30, Feb. 20, and March 28, 1895.

have everything in readiness when the edifice was formally opened. Mason wanted to know what Evans would charge for this work which he estimated would take two or three months. Whatever the sum mentioned in Evans' response, it was more than the society felt it could pay at the time, and Mason reported that nothing further would be done about the matter before the fall. Well over a year later, Mason would again approach Evans about the Chicago Historical Society with a quite different result.

In early April the search for a new position was further complicated when Charlie was stricken with typhoid pneumonia. So seriously ill did he become that the doctors gave up all hope.[55] At this point Lena, with courage and determination, dismissed the doctors. With the help of an Irish male nurse named Curran, she devotedly nursed Charlie night and day. For days the issue was in doubt, and John Evans came to Chicago when he was told that his brother probably would not recover. Even after the worst was over, Charlie was so weak that he could not go to work until August.

During this period the expenses mounted. In late 1894 the family had moved to Lake View, a better residential section, into an apartment on Roscoe Street. While John Evans helped out with the medical expenses, and Lena's stepmother, Elizabeth Young, gave them some financial aid, the Evanses were in desperate financial straits.

In this period of crises the Poole family came to the rescue. Evans had maintained his contact with Mrs. W. F. Poole and others of the family who lived in Chicago. When the situation looked hopeless, Lena wrote to one of Poole's daughters, Mrs. C. C. Poole, and told her the entire story.[56] Early in May, Evans had written to Mrs. Cyrus H. McCormick to ask about the librarianship of the McCormick Theological Seminary. Since Mrs. McCormick had given the seminary a new library building, now nearing completion, he thought the collection might need to be reclassified and hoped that he could have the job. Mrs. McCormick's secretary had written that the matter had not been decided, but the librarian would probably be appointed from the faculty. The outlook was therefore not promising when Mrs. C. C. Poole intervened. She went to see Mrs. Mc-

---

[55] Interview with Eliot Evans, Chicago, May 20, 1960. *Abstract of Record,* Gen. No. 603 in the District Court of the United States, Northern District of Texas, p. 86.

[56] Mrs. C. C. Poole to C. E., ALS, May 25, 1895; H. O. Edmonds to C. E., ALS, May 21 and July 24, 1895.

Cormick personally and told her of "Papa's high regard for Charlie," urging her to appoint him to the seminary librarianship.

Nothing came of the matter immediately, possibly because of the lengthy convalescence; however, in midsummer Cyrus H. McCormick, Jr., asked Evans to have lunch with him so that they could discuss the seminary librarianship. Result of the lunch with McCormick was Evans' appointment, for he began reclassification of the seminary library in August, 1895.[57]

It must have been a relief to Evans to know that he had a job again. Already desperately poor, he had become steeped in debts that had accumulated rapidly during his illness. Although his brother had paid Dr. Gregory for the home calls, the office calls had yet to be paid. The extent of Evans' illness can be seen in the fact that he had to make twenty-nine office calls in the period from July 13 to September 13, 1895. Gratitude was certainly in order when McCormick offered him the seminary post.

The Virginia Library at McCormick Theological Seminary was, in some ways, a strange place for Evans to work. Not a religious man in the conventional sense, he was certainly a fish out of water at such an institution. As a religious liberal, he could scarcely subscribe to the constitution of the seminary which called for all professors to be members in full communion of the Presbyterian church and to subscribe to a confession of faith based upon Presbyterian dogma.[58] However, Evans was first of all a librarian in a day when academic librarians did not enjoy faculty status. As a librarian, he had a definite job to do. The library had grown to 20,000 volumes with very little in the way of arrangement. According to the report of a local newspaper in late December, Evans was arranging the collection "after the most approved modern methods, and when

---

[57] Seminary records for this period are very incomplete. Cyrus McCormick and his mother were at this time paying most of the deficits of the seminary and it is possible that he hired Evans and paid him out of his own funds. It is certain that Evans began work late in the summer, for he is listed in the fall catalog. McCormick Theological Seminary, *Annual Catalogue of the Officers and Students of the McCormick Theological Seminary of the Presbyterian Church, Chicago, 1895–96* (Chicago: Rogerson Company, 1895), p. 5. This catalog was certainly issued before September 26, 1895, which is listed as the opening day of the fall term. Erroneously the catalog records "Charles Evans, A.M. [*sic*], Librarian."

[58] "Constitution of the Presbyterian Theological Seminary of the Northwest . . . 1872," Appendix F, in Leroy J. Halsey, *A History of the McCormick Theological Seminary of the Presbyterian Church* (Chicago: Published by the Seminary, 1893), p. 534.

all is complete the moment a book is called for it can definitely be stated whether the library contains it. . . ." [59] While the subject matter might be slightly different from other collections with which he had worked, the job of classifying the materials made use of the same techniques. As Evans proceeded with his usual methodical approach to accomplish his task, he enjoyed very pleasant relations with the faculty and students. The faculty later testified to his good work in reorganizing the Virginia Library, and one of his successors found Evans very interested in discussing the problems and prospects of their book collection. [60]

Yet Evans was aware that his position at the seminary was probably a temporary one. The faculty might be willing to accept him as a library expert and even be pleasant to him until they had their library in good working order, but it would be too much to hope that they would continue him indefinitely in a post that normally called for a faculty member trained in theology. With these thoughts in mind he was very receptive to any suggestion of a library position with more permanent status.

In March, 1896, Edward G. Mason approached Evans again about the Chicago Historical Society. [61] Mason had a keen appreciation for Evans' organizational abilities and recognized the society's need for such a man. He felt sure that the McCormicks, having secured the services of one so competent, would be unwilling to give him up easily. However, Mason wondered if Evans would be willing to act as a consultant to the trustees on the arrangement of the society's collections. It was their intention to move into the new building in May. If Evans could devote some of his evenings to arranging for the cataloging, the maps, the circulation system, and anything else he thought desirable, the trustees would gladly pay for his services.

This was the opportunity for which Evans had been waiting. For some years he had been interested in historical work, and this would give him a definite opportunity to proceed rapidly with a project

[59] "Her Christmas Gift," newspaper clipping, dated Dec. 21, 1895, and clipping from the *Inter-ocean*, dated April 26, 1896.

[60] C. E. to Cyrus H. McCormick, Jr., ALS, June 8, 1896; John F. Lyons to Charles Evans, Jr., TLS, Feb. 9, 1935; Andrew Zeros to Charles Evans, Jr., TLS, Feb. 9, 1935; John Timothy Stone to Charles Evans, Jr., TLS, Feb. 9, 1935.

[61] Edward G. Mason to C. E., TLS, April 16, 1896; C. E. to Edward G. Mason, MS draft, April 17 and 20, 1896.

on which he had been working.[62] If he could do a good job for
Mason, perhaps the society would somehow be able to raise the sum
required for a permanent librarian. Mason had already approached
him privately with an offer, which though insufficient, might lead
to better things.

Therefore he responded affirmatively to the invitation to become
a consultant to the society in mid-April, 1896. He thought the society's collections could be put in presentable shape by the May 20
deadline so that the materials might be used freely by the members.
Meanwhile, the actual cataloging could wait to be done gradually
in the future.

As for Mason's proposal on the librarianship, he could not see
his way clear to drop the seminary work as long as McCormick
wanted him to continue. After all, McCormick had helped him out
when he most needed help, and he wanted to carry his blessing with
him when he left the seminary. At the earliest, he did not see how
he could be through with the reclassification there before September
1. After that date, if he were free, he would like to take up the work
at the society and carry it to a successful completion. Meanwhile
he worked at both positions during the spring of 1896.

For some reason the opening of the new building of the Chicago
Historical Society was delayed until fall, and no further response
came from Mason until June 5. At that time he wrote Evans to ask
him formally if he could become librarian of the society and at what
salary.[63] Evans, mindful of the importance of McCormick's good
will, wrote the latter about Mason's offer. Since he had not been able
to talk with McCormick about his plans for the seminary library,
he did not know what the prospects were in his present position;
however, he was inclined to think that it might be best for all
concerned if he accepted Mason's offer. While the cataloging was
about five months from completion, he thought that he could
gather up the loose ends by the first of July. If agreeable to Mc-
Cormick, he would work in an advisory capacity at the seminary
after that time. With genuine longing Evans spoke of the per-

---

[62] The conception of the *American Bibliography* is discussed in chapter 9.
The historical society position would enable him to push the first volume toward completion.

[63] Edward G. Mason to C. E., TLS, June 5, 1896; C. E. to Cyrus H. McCormick,
Jr., ALS, June 8, 1896; Cyrus H. McCormick, Jr., to C. E., telegram, June 12,
1896, and dictated letter, June 13, 1896.

manency of the society position, a permanency which he doubted the seminary would provide. Charles Evans was weary of jobs that changed every year, or every three years, and wished to settle in a library that promised stability, even if it meant less salary initially.

McCormick was in Erie, Pennsylvania, when he received Evans' letter, but he wired Evans to accept the society's offer. Upon returning to Chicago, he wrote Evans that the new position was "a very excellent one" and that he thought he had made the right decision. The seminary then appointed Professor Huizinga librarian, and McCormick asked Evans to contact the professor as early as possible to orient him to his new duties.

Upon receipt of this favorable information, Mason secured approval of the trustees to appoint Evans librarian of the Chicago Historical Society commencing July 1, 1896, at a salary of $1,800 per year.[64] After the trying years since Indianapolis, the Chicago Historical Society seemed just the place to complete his life's work.

---

[64] Edward G. Mason to C. E., ALS, June 20, 26, and 30, 1896.

From Trustees to Creditors

9

When Charles Evans accepted the job as librarian and secretary of the Chicago Historical Society, he had behind him an impressive list of previous positions, though his performance as an administrator left much to be desired. Moving from an assistantship in a large proprietary library, he had been head librarian of a second-ranking public library twice; assistant librarian of a first-ranking public library; and cataloging and classification "expert" at a small public library, a private research library, and a theological seminary. By background and training he had accumulated a depth of knowledge about books and some capability in internal library administration. In view of his past difficulties, he should have assumed his new position at the historical society with good resolutions about the future.

Evans had always been interested in American history, but not since his Athenaeum days had he been brought into such direct and daily contact with the actual source materials of that history. While the Newberry had collected heavily in this area, it was not one of the subjects Evans was responsible for classifying. Too, in assuming the position at the society, he was leaving the general public for a relatively small and homogeneous clientele. Again, he had not served such a group since his apprenticeship in Boston. While the Newberry was a scholarly library, it was open to all and in fact served as a major public reference library for many students in the Chicago area. Therefore his return to a small group of patrons with broad knowledge and keen interest in historical matters represented a situation somewhat analogous to that of twenty-four years before. With the absence of the tremendous work pressures of the public library and of the political factors which had brought about his downfall previously, Charles Evans could only hope for a rich, productive period of scholarly work. In his new position the courtly Evans manner and the deference to the famous could shine brightly. For Charles Evans, at the age of forty-six, the historical society seemed the perfect position in which to serve until his retirement.

For the second time in his life Evans was also to begin operations in a new building. Under the energetic leadership of President Mason the society had erected a large and spacious home on the corner of Dearborn Avenue and Ontario Street.[1] Still incomplete in July, 1896, the new quarters for the society had a romanesque hideousness which must have made the Enoch Pratt seem a marble palace. Yet the building was fireproof—a prime consideration for a society that had twice lost its collections by fire—and was considered a worthy home for such famous resources as the James Madison papers. The Gilpin Library, over which Evans was to preside, was located at the rear of the building. To insure the safety of its treasures the building committee had provided for sliding iron doors to shut the library off from the rest of the building and for iron book cases with marble shelves.

At the beginning of Evans' period of service, the society estimated its library collections at 20,000 books and 50,000 pamphlets.[2] The new librarian's first task was to arrange these materials in some order which would permit the members to have ready access to them. Evans had already made some suggestions toward this end in his capacity as adviser to Mason in the spring of 1896; however, there was still much work to be done, and Mason was especially interested in having everything in readiness for the formal opening, which had now been postponed until December. The society neither needed nor could it afford a thorough job of cataloging and classification in

---

[1] Paul Angle, *The Chicago Historical Society, 1856–1956, an Unconventional Chronicle* (Chicago: Rand McNally, 1956), pp. 133–147. Caroline M. McIlvaine, "Chicago Historical Society Library," in *Libraries of the City of Chicago* (Chicago Library Club, 1905), pp. 27–36, provides an excellent sketch of the library shortly after Evans left it.

[2] U.S. Bureau of Education, *Statistics of Libraries and Library Legislation in the United States*, chapter from the Report of the Commissioner of Education for 1895–96 (Washington: Government Printing Office, 1897), pp. 388–389.

a brief six-month period, but the members did want a serviceable arrangement of the materials which would permit ready access. Evans had already assured them that this was not an unreasonable request.

With typical Evans energy and self-confidence, he set about his task. By mid-November, President Mason could tell the annual meeting that the library had been arranged satisfactorily and also announce formally Evans' appointment as librarian.[3] This news apparently had not been widely publicized, for E. W. Blatchford, a life member of the society and president of the Newberry trustees, wrote Evans a congratulatory letter in early December. Blatchford was not the only society member with whom Evans had had previous contact. Most of the Newberry trustees were also members of the Chicago Historical Society, and three held society offices.[4]

Formal dedication of the society's new building took place on December 15, 1896. In keeping with the importance of the occasion the Chicago *Tribune* gave it front-page space.[5] For three hours in the evening almost 500 guests enjoyed the society's hospitality. As the society members congratulated themselves on their new quarters, the new librarian could take pleasure in the prophetic utterance of former Congressman Adams: "We might wish, and we do earnestly wish, for a larger collection. We hope the collection of books and valuable papers will grow to fill the utmost capacity of the present building. . . . But that is not all . . . we want the administration of this collection to be such that it shall be useful as well as interesting. We want it to be to the very largest extent accessible to the public. . . ." [6] To such hopes the energetic Evans gave his heartiest approval.

With the opening of new quarters the society did see a period of increased activity. In the rules adopted by the executive committee, the building was to be open to the general public on Mondays and Thursdays, while members would have exclusive right of access on

---

[3] Chicago Historical Society, *Report of the Annual Meeting*, Nov. 17, 1896. Except where otherwise noted, references are to the printed reports of the society, with consecutive page numberings, and usually bound together as Chicago Historical Society, *Report of Meetings*, vol. I. Cited hereafter as either C. H. S., *Report of Quarterly Meeting*, or C. H. S., *Report of Annual Meeting*. E. W. Blatchford to C. E., TLS, Dec. 12, 1896.

[4] Of the thirteen men who had been trustees of the Newberry Library in 1894, eleven were members of the Chicago Historical Society in 1896, when Evans became librarian.

[5] Chicago *Tribune*, Dec. 16, 1896, pp. 1, 5.

[6] Angle, *Chicago Historical Society*, p. 145.

the other secular days. The general attendance surprised both Evans and the committee. For the first two months the attendance was over 100 on public days and even reached the 500 mark on one occasion. Yet Evans, careful of any possible criticism against the large number, called attention to the circumspection of the public and thought the general interest in historical matters augured well for the society.

Gifts, too, increased after the formal opening. Among the significant new donations were fifty volumes of old Chicago newspapers from Moses J. Wentworth and the manuscript copy of Lincoln's speech before the first Republican state convention, May 29, 1856. Evans himself devoted his efforts to a thesis he had first hammered home at Indianapolis: the value of government documents for research. To build a good documents collection he cultivated exchange relationships with other historical societies and with state libraries. Locally, he was able to secure complete sets of the annual reports of the Chicago Board of Trade, 1871–95, and one of the two complete sets of the *School Reports and Proceedings* of the Chicago Board of Education, 1854–97. His efforts with state libraries resulted in significant acquisitions of Pennsylvania and Vermont state documents early in 1897.[7]

In his opinion the library was fortunate to be a depository for United States documents, and he reported completion of the chronological and numerical arrangement of the depository set in his second quarterly report. At that time the Superintendent of Public Documents, F. A. Crandall, was pushing for reform in the distribution of public documents, and in his annual report for 1896 he cited Evans as one of the librarians supporting his reform proposals: "Years of experience with the hit-or-miss methods formerly prevailing have led me to admire the efficiency and business methods now in use for the proper distribution of public documents."[8] Later Evans would express his admiration for Crandall's efforts as superintendent of documents in a more vigorous way, when he joined a number of other librarians in protesting his removal from the post at the beginning of the McKinley administration.[9]

Working together, Evans and Mason sought all the gifts they

[7] C. H. S., *Report of Quarterly Meeting*, April 20, 1897.

[8] U.S. Superintendent of Documents, *Second Annual Report* (Washington, D.C.: Government Printing Office, 1897), p. 39.

[9] W. E. Mason to C. E., TLS, April 16, 1897; F. A. Crandall to C. E., TLS, April 23, May 10 and 19, Nov. 29, and Dec. 20, 1897.

could possibly obtain. Nothing went unacknowledged and Evans estimated that the society could probably count on gifts of some 2,000 books and pamphlets per year.[10] Not only did the society receive an increased number of books but, in addition, photographs, portraits, and memorabilia of every kind. One gift elicited special mention—the saddle used by General U. S. Grant during the Civil War found its way to the society's new home.

With such materials flowing rapidly into the collection, Charles Evans was a busy librarian. In addition to soliciting new members, securing new gifts, and publishing the regular and special reports, Evans in early 1897 began reclassification of the materials. He reported that the old system had been so bad it was absolutely essential to do the job over. However, with the press of all these duties he began to feel the burden. In his April, 1897, report, he noted: "The labor of systematically arranging the books, manuscripts, maps, etc., belonging to the Society is progressing slowly as the work is necessarily carried on in connection with the other duties amid constant interruptions, and, at present, without any assistance." [11] The last phrase was undoubtedly intended to call the attention of the society to the fact that one man could not do everything. Although in September, 1896, the society had employed two assistants to help Evans, they had dropped one of them in early January and the other in early April.[12] Perhaps the conservative members of the executive committee thought too much money was being spent for salaries. At any rate they did not heed Evans' polite suggestion, and not until 1900 did he again have an assistant, who then worked for only two weeks. Meanwhile the society's collections and services were expanding. As secretary, Evans was also expected to attend the various special meetings when distinguished speakers discoursed on historical matters. Attending meetings, listening to historical lectures, and corresponding with other societies were pleasant duties, involving as they did contact with such men as Reuben G. Thwaites, John Fiske, Charles Francis Adams, and the former Vice-President Adlai E. Stevenson; but they also involved work for the secretary, who had to collect the papers, prepare them for the printer, submit proofs, and then have them printed and distributed to the members.

[10] C. H. S., *Report of Quarterly Meeting*, April 20, 1897.

[11] *Ibid.*

[12] C. H. S., *Report of Annual Meeting*, Nov. 17, 1896, and Nov. 16, 1897.

As the years rolled on the collections grew so fast that Evans simply could not keep up with the cataloging. As a compromise measure to facilitate use, he arranged the materials in a rough order by type. The first floor was devoted to purely historical works; the second to federal legislative documents and reports of institutions; and the third to newspapers, periodicals, and United States documents. In reporting on the backlog of work in the 1902 report, Evans' successor, Caroline McIlvaine, implied severe criticism of Evans' pragmatic ways.[13] Noting that a large amount of shelf room on the first floor was occupied by unclassified acquisitions since 1897, she implied that Evans had been inexcusably lax in not classifying these items. Her inference might have had more weight if it had taken into consideration the rapidity of acquisitions during these years; but Miss McIlvaine, like many librarians, tended to blame most of the chaos on her predecessor. During Evans' tenure numerous documents, pamphlets, newspapers, magazines, and manuscripts came to the society, including the Stickney collection of 2,204 volumes, fifty-seven pamphlets, and 409 periodicals. Except for the two-week period in 1900 and midsummer, 1901, Evans had to do everything except the janitorial work by himself. As Evans' successor, McIlvaine not only was relieved from the duties of secretary, but she also had a stenographer, clerk, and messenger to help her.[14]

Evans had been at the Chicago Historical Society only six months when he sensed the opportunity for another position. There had been considerable unhappiness over Spofford's direction of the Library of Congress. As the national library was about to move into its new quarters with increased responsibilities and services, a number of librarians expressed concern, and there were rumblings that an administrative change was long overdue.[15] Since a change seemed likely, Evans solicited the position of Librarian of Congress; and when this position was given to John Russell Young, he brought pressure to bear upon Young for the position of chief assistant librarian. While not wanting to take the position away from Spofford,

---

[13] C. H. S., *Report of Annual Meeting*, Nov. 18, 1902.

[14] C. H. S., "Minutes of the Executive Committee," Dec. 3, 1901, MS in C. H. S. Archives.

[15] "Editorial," *Library Journal*, XXII (Jan., 1897), 3–4. During 1897 the *Library Journal* made frequent, if subtle, comments on Spofford's administration. A sympathetic evaluation of Spofford can be found in David C. Mearns, *The Story Up to Now: The Library of Congress, 1800–1946* (Washington, D.C.: The Library of Congress, 1947), pp. 137–138. The story of the investigation of the library and the testimony of librarians is told by Mearns on pp. 126–130.

he thought the latter's age and natural disappointment in not continuing as the executive head of the library might make him reject the secondary position. If so, he wanted to be considered for the position. Writing to Senator Fairbanks, an Indiana friend of many years, Evans spoke with confidence of his qualifications for the job and noted that his appointment would be a good political gesture toward the West.[16] Since he was a librarian by profession, there could be little criticism by other librarians. Tossing in the names of many of the prominent individuals with whom he was acquainted, Evans asked Fairbanks for help in obtaining the position. He also wrote Young a similar letter. However, Evans was to be suprised. Spofford was indeed willing to accept second place and served with distinction as chief assistant librarian.

Whatever the political circumstances of the Library of Congress, Evans' aspiration for the post either of Librarian of Congress or chief assistant librarian revealed an egotism that was incredible in its naïveté. There could be little doubt that he had been a leader in the formation of the American Library Association, but he had not been active in the professional association for almost twenty years. In fact he had even passed up the opportunity to attend the convention when it met in Chicago in 1893. Moreover, his work with a variety of libraries could scarcely be interpreted favorably in the light of his inability to please his superiors. The head of the Library of Congress needed tact of the most diplomatic kind to steer the library on new and uncharted waters. There were many men in the library profession who not only had had more experience than Evans in large library systems but who had also been more active professionally in recent years. If a librarian were to be selected for the post, there were a variety of men such as F. M. Crunden of St. Louis, Herbert Putnam of Boston, B. C. Steiner of Baltimore, or even W. E. Foster of Providence, although Evans considered the latter "below me in library work." [17] In the names of the librarians whom the joint committee consulted about the reorganization of

---

[16] There are three MS drafts of letters to Senator C. W. Fairbanks, dated August 9, 10, and 11, 1897, in the Evans Papers. The draft of August 10 described the political virtues of appointing Evans.

[17] C. E. to L. E., ALS, Nov. 24, 1892. Evans had heard that Foster had turned down the offer of librarian of the University of Chicago, a position reported to pay $7,000 per year. He then noted that "it may be conceit, but I have always considered F. below me in Library work." Certainly a man who had been offered the position at the University of Chicago would have had consideration over Evans.

the Library of Congress were such men as Melvil Dewey, George H. Baker of Columbia University, and W. I. Fletcher of Amherst.[18] Surely these men would receive favorable consideration before Charles Evans. They had been active in the American Library Association, managed good libraries, and were recognized leaders in the field. Evans, too, had once been a leader, but 1897 was not 1876, and the profession had passed him by.

Yet incredibly enough the disappointment of the attempt in 1897 did not dampen Evans' spirits. When Young died two years later, after a brilliant, if short, tenure, Evans again put the wheels in motion to secure the position.[19] His efforts, however, were no more successful than they had been previously.

Between his attempts to secure the librarianship of Congress, Evans looked longingly toward Boston. After Justin Winsor's death, W. C. Lane, librarian of the Boston Athenaeum, was appointed librarian of Harvard University. Hoping to take advantage of the fact that his old guardian was now chairman of the board of trustees, Evans wrote Dr. Eliot asking for the place. Although Eliot tried to let him down as gently as he could, the implication of his response was that Evans did not have a chance.[20] After the committee appointed C. K. Bolton from Brookline, he wrote Evans that he had presented his name, but there had been several candidates of high merit, and "one cannot be surprised at the result." In a quiet "aside" he suggested that it might be better for Charlie to stay where he was than to meet the difficulties inseparable from a change of community. Yet Evans was undaunted. When he learned that Bolton would move from the Brookline Public Library to the Athenaeum, he investigated that position, also without success.[21]

Evans' aim was too high. There were far too many more prominent candidates available in all these positions. That he aspired to such heights is a reflection on his judgment and shows how much out of touch with library matters he had become. Yet, there is no evidence that Evans was ever able to evaluate himself and his work

[18] Mearns, *The Story Up to Now*, p. 132.

[19] There are so many letters on the subject in the Evans Papers that it is impossible to cite them all. Worth noting is a petition to President McKinley from nine of Evans' friends in Indianapolis urging the appointment. A copy of this document in the Evans Papers is dated January 19, 1899, only two days after Young's death! Among the other writers were David Starr Jordan, John Clark Ridpath, Daniel Goodwin, and a host of Indianapolis friends.

[20] Samuel Eliot to C. E., ALS, Feb. 21, [1898].

[21] Will A. Morse to C. E., ALS, Feb. 26 and March 2, 1898.

objectively. Merrill, his friend at the Newberry, noted that Evans was resentful of personal criticism and supremely confident of his own ability.[22] Even if he had had close professional friends in 1897–98, they would have had great difficulty in pointing out to him the obstacles in securing one of these positions. His self-confidence and stubbornness would admit no capability less than that of the leading librarians in the country.

There was one factor, however, which Evans had hoped would work in his favor for the Library of Congress positions. In a draft of a letter to John Young he noted: "I would only add that for the past ten years I have been engaged in the preparation of a Bibliography of all the publications issued in the United States for the first two hundred years; and this labor, happily approaching completion, has necessarily given a special knowledge of an important, but little known, period of American literature, not heretofore available to the Student and Collector." [23] This was the first semi-public announcement of the bibliographic enterprise which was to bring Evans lasting fame. When he had decided to undertake this project or even when the idea germinated is shrouded in mystery. On the basis of his dedication in the second volume of the *American Bibliography*, where he acknowledged his debt to the Boston Athenaeum as the "alma mater of my bibliographical life," two bibliographers have reached the conclusion that the idea germinated there at the time Evans was just beginning library work.[24] Undoubtedly Evans did pick up some bibliographical techniques at the Athenaeum. Poole was one of the first to apply a knowledge of printing techniques to historical criticism and was deeply interested in historical matters.[25] While Evans did follow his teacher's bibliographical as well as his administrative techniques, it is difficult to believe that a project as massive as the *American Bibliography* was conceived in his teens. For years Evans used his bibliographical

---

[22] W. S. Merrill, "Early Days at the Newberry Library," p. 23.

[23] C. E. to John R. Young, MS draft, n.d., but probably early Aug., 1897.

[24] C. S. Brigham, "Charles Evans," A. A. S. *Proceedings*, n.s., XXXV (April, 1935), 16; C. S. Brigham, "Charles Evans," *Dictionary of American Biography*, ed. Harris E. Starr (New York: Scribner's, 1944), XXI, p. 290; J. C. Bay, "Charles Evans, 1850–1935," A. L. A. *Bulletin*, XXIX (March, 1935), 163; interview with J. C. Bay, Elmhurst, Ill., March 20, 1958. If Evans had ever talked with anyone about the origin of the bibliography, it would surely have been one of these two bibliographers whom he knew well and with whom he was associated for many years.

[25] Williamson, "William Frederick Poole," pp. 189, 741.

knowledge in compiling catalogs and finding lists for public libraries. During that period he published no bibliographical essay or any other contribution which revealed strong interests in early American printing. In view of this lack of interest, the dedication to volume two should be interpreted much more strictly.

Although Dr. J. C. Bay, who lived near Evans in Chicago and knew him well, gave the Athenaeum credit for the inspiration and initiative for the bibliography, he has admitted that Evans never talked with him about the origin of the idea. The same has been reported by other bibliographical friends of Evans with whom he was associated for many years.[26] Despite Evans' interest in collecting historical materials in Indianapolis, there is no evidence of an active concern for American bibliography during the years 1872–79; Texas offered neither the resources nor the stimulus for bibliographic activity. In spite of the dedication of volume two, there is no positive evidence of either the existence of the idea or any actual work on the idea before 1885, when Evans returned to the profession as assistant librarian of the Enoch Pratt Free Library.

In his printed circular announcing the imminent appearance of the first volume of the *American Bibliography,* January, 1902, Evans stated that he had begun work on the compilation of the material "more than sixteen years ago," which should mean the year 1886.[27] An excellent opportunity for doing some spadework on the bibliography came during the sixteen months he was out of work in 1887–88. Baltimore had a number of private libraries with good bibliographical collections which Evans could have used. However, the lack of evidence that Evans used this material again raises serious doubts. Although "sixteen years" is a very specific term, it seems unlikely that it should be taken literally. The length of time given by Evans could well have been used for its impressive effect upon potential subscribers.

Omaha, because of its size and remoteness from the major collections of Americana, was not a good place in which to pursue bibliographic endeavors, even if the work load had not been heavy.

---

[26] Interview with C. S. Brigham, Worcester, May 6 and 12, 1958; interview with L. C. Wroth, Providence, May 19, 1958; interview with C. K. Shipton, Worcester, May 12, 1958; C. K. Shipton, *The American Bibliography of Charles Evans* (Worcester: American Antiquarian Society, 1955), XIII, v, states that Evans had this bibliographical project in mind at least as early as 1880, but Shipton does not remember on what he based this particular date.

[27] Charles Evans, *American Bibliography, Circular,* Jan., 1902. Cited hereafter as *A. B., Circular.*

The same could be said for Indianapolis, 1889–92, except for the good collection of published catalogs in the public library. However, it seems doubtful that Evans worked on the bibliography in Indianapolis. He was much too busy and much too involved with library affairs to do additional bibliographical work on the side. A man who had not failed to be at his desk a single day in over a year did not have time to pursue other projects. Besides, when he had an opportunity to talk about New England and its patriarchs to the Indianapolis Literary Club, he chose rather to talk about John Lothrop Motley and Gotthold Ephraim Lessing. Although there were later rumors that he did begin his *American Bibliography* during his second period in Indianapolis, at least one person, who should have known about his project, did not learn about it until the publication of the circular in 1902.[28]

The Newberry Library was, of course, different. A scholar's workshop with rich collections of early Americana, that library provided an excellent opportunity for bibliographical work. Moreover, Evans had the time for beginning such a project, since he was separated from his family for a six-month period. His duties were confined to the working day, and he could devote many of his evenings to work on the bibliography. At least one staff member knew that he was working on the *American Bibliography* at this time.[29]

Added to these favorable conditions was the aid and encouragement of William Frederick Poole. The latter's own interest in Americana had resulted in the Newberry's acquisition of "local history, early travel, controversial pamphlets, Fast Day, Thanksgiving Day, and Election Day sermons, and other early and contemporary historical material." [30] It has been estimated that Poole's efforts added over 4,000 Americana items to the library. Always more

---

[28] Hull, "History of the Indianapolis Public Library," p. 31, states, "It is reported that he began compilation of his great work *The American Bibliography* while in Indianapolis." However, he cites no source for his information. The quotation occurs at the end of Hull's description of Evans' first period of service, 1872–78, but the rumor probably refers to the second period, 1889–92. May Wright Sewall, wife of Evans' good friend, Theodore L. Sewall, was surprised at the announcement of volume one soon to be published. May Wright Sewall to C. E., TLS, Aug. 25, 1902. Mention of Evans' work on the bibliography in correspondence from other Indianapolis friends is also lacking.

[29] W. S. Merrill, "Early Days at the Newberry Library," p. 23. If Merrill knew that Evans was working on such a bibliography at the time, it is unlikely that the project was a secret from Poole.

[30] George B. Utley, "Source Material for the Study of American History in the Libraries of Chicago," Bibliographical Society of America *Papers*, XVI (pt. I, 1922), 19.

interested in the librarian as bibliographer than as technician, Poole had also collected a vast number of printed bibliographies and library catalogs. While the Newberry librarian was a very busy man in 1892–93 and Evans saw little of him, it would have been strange indeed for Evans not to have spoken to him about the advisability of such a project and received Poole's encouragement.

Therefore, while it may be true that Evans had been mulling over the idea for the "sixteen years" mentioned previously, the evidence points to a later date for the beginning of actual compilation. Moreover, in his second circular, November, 1903, Evans stated that he had undertaken the laborious compilation of the data because of the "constant daily need for such a work in his practical experience as a librarian for thirty years." [31] One can surmise from this statement that the conception of the bibliography simply evolved over a long period of years out of his experience in library work. Just when it received its final form, Evans himself probably did not know. By the time he reached the Newberry Library, however, the idea of compiling a record of early American printing was fairly well fixed. Under these circumstances, Evans probably approached Poole and asked his advice. As was his custom, the Newberry librarian was enthusiastic, gave Evans much advice about the proper approach, and told him to use the resources of the library freely. In view of Evans' protestation that he had been at work "for the past ten years" (1887) and "sixteen years ago" (1886), one can only say that his memory of the time the idea germinated became confused with the time he actually began work. On the basis of the evidence now available, the earliest date for active work on compiling the *American Bibliography* must be given as 1892, and the place, the Newberry Library of Chicago.

Confirmation of the work on the bibliography at the Newberry Library came in the form of a letter which Evans wrote his guardian when he went to the McCormick Theological Seminary three years later. Dr. Eliot, pleased to hear about the plan, wrote an encouraging letter to the aspiring bibliographer. If Evans had been at work on the bibliography for a long period of time, he had not revealed it to Dr. Eliot, for the latter's words indicate a relatively recent beginning: "Your letter interests me very much, and excited wishes in me that you may continue to do good work, and especially to bring your *magnum opus* to a victorious conclusion. That is a large plan,

---

[31] *A. B., Circular,* Nov., 1903.

but not too large, and I know from experience how it helps one to plan large things, even should they never be wholly executed as one might desire. But I think you have life, and strength, and high purpose, and will succeed." [32] Samuel Eliot's words were more prophetic than he could possibly have known. Evans would not achieve his original goal nor execute it exactly as he wished, but he would succeed in a manner that exceeded all expectations.

About this time, bibliographical interest in Americana was beginning to stir. In January, 1894, the *Library Journal* had published an article by George Watson Cole, rising young librarian, who, after tracing the history of American bibliography with an occasional side glance at what the English were doing, suggested that it was the right time for the compilation of a series of local bibliographies which could eventually become the basis for a comprehensive American bibliography.[33] In this paper he followed up a suggestion which R. R. Bowker had made in the preface to *The American Catalogue, 1884–1890*. Bowker had been interested in a bibliography of nineteenth-century American publications as early as the 1880's and was already at work on a bibliography of state publications.[34] Most of the librarians thinking about the subject believed in the value of a cooperative bibliography. The task of listing all the books published in America since 1639 seemed totally beyond the ability of one individual. Therefore Cole had suggested a means of putting local librarians to work and covering small geographic areas. This would give the individual librarians a sense of professional satisfaction and at the same time contribute toward a needed national bibliography. The idea of a cooperative enterprise was enunciated most clearly by Bowker at the second international conference and by the early founders of the Bibliographical Society of America during the next decade.[35] The absence of Evans' project from the various discussions

---

[32] Samuel Eliot to C. E., ALS, March 11 and 24, 1896.

[33] George Watson Cole, "American Bibliography, General and Local," *Library Journal*, XIX (Jan., 1894), 5–9.

[34] *The American Catalogue 1876–1884*, ed. R. R. Bowker (New York: Publishers Weekly, 1885), p. viii; and *The American Catalogue, 1884–1890*, ed. R. R. Bowker (New York: Publishers' Weekly, 1891), p. vi.

[35] R. R. Bowker, "Bibliographical Endeavors in America," *Transactions and Proceedings of the Second International Library Conference Held in London, July 13–16, 1897*, pp. 150–153. Cited hereafter as *Sec. Int. Lib. Conf.*, 1897. The Bibliographical Society of America grew out of the Chicago Bibliographical Society, begun in 1899. See Azariah Root, "The Scope of an American Bibliographical Society," Bibliographical Society of Chicago *Year-book* (1901–02), pp. 41–52; and William Coolidge Lane, "President's Address," Bibliographical So-

indicated an unfamiliarity with his undertaking on the part of the library fraternity. Most librarians received their first information about the project from Evans' circular announcing the publication of volume one.[36] Although Merrill and possibly other members knew about Evans' work, there is no mention of his efforts in the yearbooks of the Bibliographical Society of Chicago until after the appearance of the circular. This was the way Evans had planned. He wanted no widespread publicity until the work was almost completed.

The organization of the Bibliographical Society of Chicago in 1899 served to bring together those librarians and bookmen who had an interest in American bibliography. Why Evans chose not to associate himself with other bibliographers in the society is not clear. Always a scholar who worked alone, he was not naturally drawn to such organizations; but the society's reputation with Evans could not have been enhanced by the fact that one of its members was Alexander J. Rudolph, the man responsible for his dismissal at the Newberry Library. Another reason Evans may have had for not joining this group was lack of money with which to pay dues. Money was never in plentiful supply at Evans' house and by this time he had given up both his cigars and his occasional drink, probably for financial reasons.[37] Whatever the reasons, Evans joined neither the Bibliographical Society of Chicago, nor its successor, the Bibliographical Society of America. In some ways this was unfortunate, for the bibliographers in the societies could have given him much help.

Later, Evans had an additional reason for not joining the Bibliographical Society of America. When this organization was about to come into existence, Azariah S. Root, Librarian of Oberlin College and then President of the Bibliographical Society of Chicago, referred to Evans' circular of 1902 in these words: "Until we see the first volume we cannot tell with what painstaking energy Mr.

---

ciety of America *Papers and Proceedings,* I (1904–05), 43–49. Although Lane did not suggest that the Bibliographical Society of America undertake large cooperative projects, he did note with approval those which were under way.

[36] The Evans Papers contain numerous inquiries which Evans received from librarians all over the country after publication of the circular. The one notable librarian who did know what Evans was trying to do was his friend W. I. Fletcher at Amherst. W. I. Fletcher to C. E., ALS, April 6, 1899.

[37] Interview with Eliot Evans, Chicago, Feb. 1, 1961. Mr. Evans does not remember a time when his father either smoked or drank. By the middle of the 1890's, he had definitely developed abstemious habits.

Charles Evans has wrought out his proposed bibliography of books published in America from 1637–1820, but it is perfectly safe to say in advance that the book will not be a complete list." [38] Root then suggested that the society form a committee to interest librarians in compiling a supplement to Evans with the idea of obtaining a final definitive list. While the Oberlin librarian's proposal was not meant to be unkind—his library was one of the earliest subscribers—Evans found his suggestion a deep affront. His volume was not even off the press and here was a man with the audacity to suggest its inadequacies! Evans' reaction was swift and bitter: he would never have anything to do with this group. How deeply Root's statement wounded Evans' sensitive nature and professional pride can be seen years later when he wrote to his wife that the Bibliographical Society of America was a "small society with a big name, who have, intentionally, and purposely, ignored me and my work ever since the society was founded." [39]

The Chicago Historical Society provided Evans with further opportunities to come into contact with a good collection of Americana. Despite its name, the library's interests were not provincial. Though not so rich in Americana as the Newberry, the historical society during Evans' period as librarian rapidly added files of early New England newspapers, magazines, and documents. All of these materials provided good source material for his bibliography.[40] With the normal sympathetic interest of such a society Evans should have been able to push his project during this five-year period.

However, there were ways in which the society slowed him down. First, there was the lack of help and then the natural attention to expanding the society's services, a project in which Evans was as interested as the most ardent board member. Keenly aware that the society had a responsibility to make its resources known, Evans pushed several publishing projects. In his annual report for 1899 he suggested that the society could render a real service to scholarship by the publication of the Madison Papers, which had been presented to it by Marshall Field in 1893, and also by the publication of its own history. He followed this suggestion the next year by noting the increasing interest in historical study. How to aid

---

[38] Root, "The Scope of an Am. Bib. Soc.," p. 50.
[39] C. E. to L. E., ALS, Oct. 24, 1921.
[40] The valuable gift of New England newspapers reported in C. H. S., *Report of Quarterly Meeting*, April 20, 1897, must have been especially useful to Evans.

and encourage this awakened spirit should be a serious concern of the society. Again he expressed his opinion that the society could "best fulfill its mission" to make its resources available by publication and this time suggested a quarterly magazine which "could become the medium for publishing the manuscript material now in its possession for the benefit of all historical students, as well as become the voice for the expression of historical investigation in the West." [41] He thought the expense of such a publication would not be great, and it might well be made self-supporting. In publishing such a journal the Chicago society would be following the excellent example of other similar groups.

Another work of first importance for the local community would be the compilation of a list of deceased residents of the city prior to the great fire of 1871. Evans was continually made aware of the lack of such a list, and he thought that it could be compiled from the files of newspapers belonging to the society, the Public Library, and the Newberry Library. The only problem involved was expense which the society's general fund could not bear.

During his period as librarian of the Chicago Historical Society, Evans was in contact with many other society librarians. He was greatly interested in the relationship of the historical society to scholarship as a whole and to the work of other societies in particular. On October 24, 1900, Charles Francis Adams, President of the Massachusetts Historical Society, addressed the Chicago Historical Society on the subject "History Is Past Politics and Politics Are Present History." In the course of his lecture Adams noted that the geographical position of the Chicago Historical Society gave it an excellent opportunity for leadership in historical work. To this statement Evans gave a hearty "amen" and used it to reinforce his argument on the need for a publication program.

By the end of 1900 the Chicago Historical Society had expanded with much ambition. The lectures were well attended, the gifts and bequests to the collection were increasing, and the membership was the largest in its history. Annual membership stood at 179, while honorary, life, and corresponding members brought the total to 299. Much of the increase was due to a circular letter which Evans had sent inviting membership in the society. A total of two life members and fifty annual members joined the society—the largest enrollment in the group's history. Since life membership cost $500 and annual

[41] C. H. S., *Report of Annual Meeting*, Nov. 20, 1900.

membership $25, the new memberships added $2,250 to the society's treasury.

However, Evans was not content to rest on his laurels. He encouraged the organization's friends to be even more generous. Drawing an analogy that combined a serious note with a sense of humor, Evans said in his annual report:

In Boston they have a saying that no true Bostonian ever thinks of dying until he has done something for the Public Library, or for the Museum of Fine Arts. Then he *knows* that his hope of Heaven is well founded. This saying after all is only an expression of that debt of gratitude which every successful citizen should feel towards the institutions of the city which has helped to make him prosperous. There have been a number of true Chicagoans, and the work of this society has benefited by their generosity in the past, but its needs demand that the hopes of others of its friends shall be well founded in the Boston belief.[42]

The report of 1900 was on the whole an optimistic one, and the promise for the following year very good. Charles Francis Adams, who had delivered an address at the society in October, 1900, wrote to Evans in early December about a place for the 1902 meeting of the American Historical Association.[43] Adams was a vice-president of the association and would become president in 1902. He wanted the association to meet in Chicago that year so that he could expand the remarks that he had made before the society. If the Chicago Historical Society would extend an invitation to the American Historical Association to hold the convention in Chicago in 1902, Adams would be very pleased.

Adams had also placed himself in communication with Vice-President Franklin Head of the Chicago Historical Society and with other prominent individuals throughout the country who could effect his plan. In a letter to Head he suggested that the meeting could probably be arranged with the cooperation of the University of Chicago and the Chicago Historical Society. At the same time he paid a nice tribute to Evans: "I can think of no one better than Mr. Evans to manage the matter. I am sure he would take a lively interest in having the meeting in Chicago, and would spare no effort to make it a success." [44] He urged the society to send Evans to Detroit to the annual meeting of the American Historical Association at the end of December, 1900.

---

[42] *Ibid.*
[43] Charles Francis Adams to C. E., TLS, Dec. 8, 1900.
[44] Charles Francis Adams to Franklin H. Head, TLS, Dec. 17, 1900.

The executive committee unanimously adopted a resolution offering the use of the building and voted to provide funds for Evans' trip. Afterwards when Evans reported that the rules of the association stated that it would not meet in a western city more than once every three years the executive committee asked him to renew the invitation for 1903.[45]

However promising Evans' work at the Chicago Historical Society, in retrospect the 1890's had been rough years. Not only had there been professional dismissals at Indianapolis and at the Newberry Library, but the family too had known its trials. Evans' own serious illness in 1895, the poor health of Lena and baby Charlie, the inadequate housing in Chicago, and the small salaries all had their effect upon the family.[46]

Yet there were some brighter aspects to the picture. By 1898 the financial affairs of the family had definitely improved. Lena, very unhappy over the second floor apartment in Lake View, had been determined to move her growing family to a house farther out.[47] By checking the advertisements and tirelessly looking, she finally found a two story, seven room house at 1413 Pratt Avenue in Rogers Park. The dwelling was located in a good middle-class neighborhood with professional people and small businessmen predominating. The family rented the house and moved into it in August, 1898. The athletically inclined children could exercise in the vacant lots in the area, and the master of the house could work uninterruptedly in the large library on the first floor.

The following year, in May, 1899, Charles and Lena Evans were able to buy the house in Rogers Park, paying $1,150 down and assuming a mortgage for the remaining $3,000.[48] Although one can only wonder at the frugal habits of Evans which had enabled him

---

[45] C. H. S., "Records and Minutes of the Executive Committee," Dec. 21, 1900, and Jan. 3, 1901, C. H. S. Archives.

[46] Both Lena and little Charlie were seriously ill in December, 1897, and little Charlie suffered a broken leg in January, 1899. According to Eliot Evans, "Mother was a frail woman who did not enjoy good health as far back as I can remember." Eliot H. Evans to Gifford Ernest, TLS, Nov. 21, 1951; T. J. Evans to C. E., ALS, Dec. 29, 1897; Louis Howland to C. E., TLS, Jan. 28, 1899.

[47] Interview with Eliot H. Evans, Oct. 21, 1960. Charles Evans, Jr., *Chick Evans' Golf Book; the Story of the Sporting Battles of the Greatest of All Amateur Golfers* (Chicago: Thomas E. Wilson and Company, 1921), p. 22. Cited hereafter as Charles Evans, Jr., *Chick Evans' Golf Book.*

[48] MS draft of receipt for $3,050.00 for house in Lot 3, Block 2, in Carlson and Holmes subdivision, Rogers Park, Chicago, dated Oct. 27, 1899.

to save over a thousand dollars on the Historical Society salary, apparently the new position was beginning to remove the financial clouds.

The children too were growing up and presenting problems of their own. To the distress of Charles and Lena Evans none of the three was very good in school. All three enjoyed athletics, and young Eliot displayed the normal teen-age male interest in football. At Christmas, 1899, Charlie gave his youngest son a present destined to have an effect on the entire family: a golf club, which he bought for seventy-five cents at the Fair Store. Gertrude, the oldest child, also enjoyed outdoor life, with tennis a favorite. However, with the encouragement of her mother, she had written a story which was printed in the Chicago *Record*. It was this effort which had drawn warm praise from both her father and from Dr. Eliot.

Unfortunately, the family unit was in for more serious difficulties in the next four years. Constance Evans, the baby daughter born on August 29, 1899, died the following year in late October. Her death accentuated for Evans the number of close personal and professional friends he had lost by death in the 1890's. First, in September, 1893, there had been Mary Abbie Bean, the "little sister" who had given him good advice which he seldom took. His strongest supporter, William Frederick Poole, had died the following year. In September, 1898, Dr. Samuel Eliot passed from the scene to be followed within three months by Evans' last staunch supporter in the Chicago Historical Society, Edward G. Mason. As these props were taken away from Evans, he soon fell. Having cut himself off from the library profession and failing to cultivate other close friends in Chicago, he was soon placed in a difficult position. Charles Evans needed support, even to sustain him in the Chicago Historical Society, and, as usual, he did not develop support from the people with the power.

Under Mason, who guided the affairs of the society during the mid-1890's, Evans had been permitted to manage the library as he wished, but such a condition did not extend to Mason's successors. Although Evans continued to manage the society his own way during the one-year interim presidency of General Alexander C. McClurg, a new day dawned with John N. Jewett's election as McClurg's successor in November, 1899. Executive committee meetings were more frequent, and the members began to take an increasing interest in all aspects of the library's internal affairs.[49] According to Jewett, there was constantly increasing friction between Evans and the executive committee, but the first serious trouble came to light in January, 1901, when a subcommittee was appointed to examine and report on a system of cataloging for the library.[50] Dr. Otto L. Schmidt, a prominent physician and annual member since 1894, was apparently the instigator of the examination, although E. E. Ayer had made the original motion. By June the subcommittee presented a report urging the reclassification of the library according to the Cutter classification scheme. Evans, with some twenty-five years of experience, most of it in cataloging and classifying libraries, did not take kindly to the committee's interference in this matter. Although the committee recognized the necessity for some additional help to accomplish the new task, they were trying to dictate to him on a matter in which they had absolutely no competence. There is every reason to believe that Evans defended his methods with all the vigor and frankness of which he was capable. An uneasy truce was declared and the employment of a clerk did speed up the cataloging. By late September, Evans could report that 8,641 books and pamphlets had been entered in the accession catalog and about 1,200 cards had been written for the general card catalog. In order to move more rapidly upon the completion of the card catalog, Evans recommended that two or more assistants be added to the staff.

But cataloging was not the only matter which made it increasingly difficult for Evans to work with the executive committee. He had finally completed and had seen through the press a fifty-eight-page booklet giving the constitution, bylaws, membership, and certain historical information about the society.[51] Working from records which were not always accurate, Evans had done the best he could, but he asked at the end of the pamphlet that any corrections to the list be sent to him. Apparently Evans issued this pamphlet as a

---

[49] The following year Evans noted that "the meetings of the Executive Committee have been frequent, averaging fortnightly meetings throughout the year, and have been well attended." C. H. S., *Report of Annual Meeting*, Nov. 20, 1900.

[50] C. H. S., "Records and Minutes of the Executive Committee," Jan. 29, 1901, C. H. S. Archives.

[51] C. H. S., *Charter, Constitution, By-laws, Roll of Membership, MDCCCLVI–MDCCCCI; List of Officers and Members, MDCCCCI* (Chicago: Printed for the Society, 1901).

preliminary list until a more comprehensive edition could be prepared.

Because of certain omissions and certain incorrect addresses, the executive committee was highly displeased at the appearance of this publication. At its June 25 meeting, the committee passed a resolution, introduced by Dr. Schmidt, that Evans recall all the booklets he had mailed. He was to say to the members that a corrected copy would be sent soon. Evans was also to enclose return envelopes, properly stamped, and was ordered not to send out any more pamphlets.

Despite the severe condemnation of the group, Evans did not yield to their resolution. Perhaps, with a new clerk and the pressure to get the cataloging done, he did not have time to give to a matter that he regarded as trivial anyway. At least three months later he had not acted upon the committee's recommendation, and they voted to rescind the June action "whereas any damage which the errors and mistakes in said Book might do to the society has already been wrought." [52]

Relations between Evans and the committee continued to deteriorate during the fall, following an all too familiar pattern. Evans was given the opportunity to resign at the end of the current year or to be fired.[53] Determined to hold on to his position at all costs, he solicited proxies from a number of members which he intended to use to force his retention. At the November annual meeting President Jewett refused to recognize Evans' twenty-eight proxies and shortly afterward the committee unanimously voted to dismiss him.

As a result of this dismissal, one member, Delavan Smith of Indianapolis, resigned his membership. Jewett wrote a lengthy letter to Smith explaining the reason for dismissing Evans. The chief point with the committee was that they intended to manage the society, but Evans in his obstinacy wanted to exercise absolute control. Men accustomed to having their way in their private businesses did not intend for a mere librarian to stand in the way. Jewett's

---

[52] C. H. S., "Records and Minutes of the Executive Committee," Sept. 24, 1901, C. H. S. Archives.

[53] While biased, Jewett's letter to Delavan Smith contains a fairly good account of the events leading to Evans' dismissal. John N. Jewett to Delavan Smith, Dec. 11, 1901, ordered spread upon the records, C. H. S., "Records and Minutes of the Executive Committee," Dec. 26, 1901, C. H. S. Archives.

letter was a slashing attack upon Evans, the gist of which was contained in the following paragraph:

> For the two years that I have been president of the Society there has been a constantly increasing friction amounting at last to positive disagreement between the Executive Committee and Mr. Evans as Secy. as to the management of the Society and the work in the Library. The Committee has been composed of men of business methods earnest in their work in behalf of the Society and gentlemen with whom no reasonable man could have a quarrel. Mr. Evans apparently wanted the absolute management, and his obstinacy of disposition led him to disregard in many things the specific directions of the Committee and to offensively insist upon his own judgment and methods. I, several times, warned him that his course would inevitably lead to an open rupture; but he seemed absolutely incapable of yielding to warnings or advice. Every suggestion he affected to regard as a personal attack upon himself and in his office as Secretary he became insufferable.[54]

Jewett also accused Evans of lax administrative methods, duplicity, lack of good sense, and lack of regard for the opinions of other men. These were strong words; yet, despite Jewett's self-righteous attitude that no man could possibly quarrel with such capable businessmen, he closed on a note that was closer to the truth than Evans could possibly have realized: "He has learned nothing from experience, and probably never will." Similar words had been spoken by other trustees under whom Evans had served.

Thus ended Evans' career as a librarian, a career that had had certain elements of success but which had been marred by far too many evidences of failure. While Jewett's attack may have been more bitter than was warranted, he was undoubtedly right in his basic evaluation of Evans. The latter was determined to have things his own way administratively, and he would brook no opposition. That he was right in many instances cannot mitigate his obstinate and irrational behavior in working with men who had policy-making power. Indeed, if Evans had taken more time to cultivate what Beanie called "the social qualities," he might well have won the battles that he had lost. Charles Evans was capable of rare kindliness and geniality, as many besides Beanie noted, but he never strove to apply these charms to board members. This was a serious oversight and it made his career as a librarian a failure.

---

[54] *Ibid.*

The Old Bookseller's Bible: Genesis

10

Immediately after his dismissal from the librarianship of the Chicago Historical Society, Evans decided not to seek another position but rather to devote his entire time to completion of the bibliographical project already under way. What prompted this decision is not known, but one does not have to look far for good reasons. Poole was dead and so was Mason. No longer did Evans have influential friends in the library profession. In a search for a new job, there would certainly have been no likelihood of obtaining a favorable recommendation from the board of the Chicago Historical Society. The decision of that group had been unanimous and their attitude unmistakable. Indeed a comparable new library position must have seemed quite out of the question. Since Evans believed he could support his family through his bibliographic enterprise, his decision to devote all his time to completing the manuscript for the first volume must be viewed as his first realistic action in a long time.[1]

In less than two months after his departure from the society, early in January, 1902, the literary world was startled and amused by the

---

[1] It is clear from a number of sources that Evans intended to make money from the bibliography, and, by implication, from most of the correspondence with John H. Holliday. His *A. B. Circular,* Jan., 1902, p. 2, stated that he was issuing the work privately, for no publisher could print it except "upon such terms as would make the labor of years a labor of love, wholly without profit." L. E. to C. E., ALS, July 2, 1904, urged him to secure all the ready cash for volume one that he could; profit could come on the second volume.

appearance of an eight-page circular announcing the imminent
appearance of the *American Bibliography,* volume one. Printed on
quarto sheets, the circular was designed in the same manner and
with the same type faces Evans proposed to use in his magnum opus.
In keeping with the dignity and scope of his subject, Evans gave
his announcement a title as verbose as those of the old New England
printed books the completed work would attempt to describe:

A PRIVATELY-PRINTED, SIGNED AND NUMBERED EDITION
OF THE AMERICAN BIBLIOGRAPHY / BY CHARLES EVANS /
A CHRONOLOGICAL DICTIONARY / OF ALL / BOOKS, PAM-
PHLETS and PERIODICAL PUBLICATIONS / PRINTED IN THE /
UNITED STATES OF AMERICA / FROM THE GENESIS OF PRINT-
ING IN 1639 / DOWN TO AND INCLUDING THE YEAR 1820 /
WITH BIBLIOGRAPHICAL AND BIOGRAPHICAL NOTES / Volume
1 / 1639–1740 / *** HERE'S THE BOOK I SOUGHT FOR SO—
SHAKESPEARE / THE PUIR MAN THAT HAS PATIENCE TO MAK'
A BUIK, HAS SOME CLAIM / TO THE PATIENCE O' HIM WHA
ONLY READS IT. –ELIOT WARBURTON / PRINTED FOR THE
AUTHOR / MDCCCCII

As a project of scholarship, the *American Bibliography* was
greeted with considerable skepticism. Librarians, anxious for such
a listing of early American printing, did not know whether to hope
or to scoff. The organizations primarily concerned about the non-
existence of a record of the early American press had been talking
in terms of a cooperative effort to bring it about. Now, here was
a fellow member of the library fraternity, either ambitious or fool-
hardy, who announced that he not only proposed to accomplish
the task singlehandedly, but that the first volume was soon to appear! Furthermore, the work was a product of Chicago, a city far
removed from the major sources of early American printed books.
Up to this point Evans had never produced a bibliography nor was
he noted for publications in the field of colonial history. It was
preposterous to imagine that a man of Evans' limited background
and age could give the world either a good bibliography covering
a large number of years or a monumental one in view of the brevity
of human life. Was Evans aware of the difficulties which beset Joseph
Sabin, whose bibliography of works relating to America had not yet
been completed? Indeed did he have any conception of the mammoth task he was undertaking?

Evans anticipated such questioning, and to it he responded affirmatively in his circular. It was not as though he had started the bibliography only yesterday. He was aware of the misfortunes of previous devotees of American bibliography such as Sabin, Orville A. Roorbach, and Frederick Leypoldt, and therefore had determined not to bring his work to the attention of others until it was almost completed. Now, after sixteen years of diligent effort "under conditions which has necessitated that the work should be performed separate and apart from my professional duties as a Librarian, which has been my means of livelihood for a period of thirty years," Charles Evans was ready to tell the bibliographical world of its impending good fortune. Without any encouragement from individuals, institutions, or learned bodies, he had pursued his task while others only talked of the need for such a work. With a cocksureness which baffled and irritated other bibliographers, Evans boasted that he was ready to give the public a complete record of colonial imprints. Under such conditions it was not surprising that skepticism ran high.

When completed, Evans thought, his bibliography would contain about 70,000 titles, and, although he did not estimate the number of volumes to be published, he set the price of each volume at $15, which he thought little enough compensation for his diligent efforts. After all, the librarian who bought his bibliography could check it for titles possessed by his library and thereby save himself the cost of cataloging. In view of the high cost of making a local catalog of early printed books, the $15 seemed a small price indeed. As soon as Evans should receive assurance of 300 subscriptions, he planned to undertake publication.

Evans hoped to win librarians and book dealers to his plan, not only by reasoned argument but also by an appeal to their pride. With a touch of humor rare in such advertisements, Evans addressed the professionals in these terms:

> It isn't much that is asked of you. A few novels less in a year, and the name of your Library and its Librarian will be enrolled upon the published list of those who have aided in the publication of a work of first importance to your Library, yourself, and the Community you serve. And think of the joy which will fill your breast from saving even one mind from the incipient paresis which comes from reading a copy of the three hundred and sixty-fifth edition of a novel published the day before. It may be that the purchase of the extra-expurgated edition of the Plays of William Shakespeare, in words of one syllable, which children under six have shown no crying demand for, will also have to be dropped; but Shake-

speare can stand it. And in its place, your Library will possess a work which contains the full titles of the finest Collection of Sermons—but that is a subject upon which I am disposed to wax eloquent, so, as they say at the play, for further particulars see small bills enclosed.[2]

With similar wit did Evans appeal to the booksellers by suggesting that they let him become their Moses and lead them to the promised land. With mock piety and rapier thrusts, he exhorted the old book dealers to become alive to their past neglect of the national literature, to arrange their valuable wares in a good chronological manner, and then to let the ducats flow into their coffers. As the coins clinked in the cash box, the wise bookseller who had subscribed would find himself "stroking the sides of my book of books and fondly calling it the Old Bookseller's Bible." [3]

The reaction to Evans' circular was varied. Those book editors who reviewed it for newspapers were enthusiastic, not especially about the work itself but about Evans' facility with the English language.[4] They were particularly taken with Evans' description of old book dealers, and more than one newspaper quoted that page of the circular in full. Noting that bibliographies were supposed to be the driest of all books and bibliographers, by implication, the dullest of all professionals, the reviewer for the Cleveland *Plain Dealer* praised Evans' humorous bent of mind. Closely allied to this comment was that of a book dealer in New York who wrote Evans that "We are inclined to think that you would make more money writing humorous books than you will getting out this Bibliography. As a matter of fact page five of your circular is about the best humor we have seen in many a day." [5] In a similar vein the Chicago *Tribune* said, "His prospectus is so good that if he makes nothing out of the work itself he will still have the fun of writing these words." [6]

Back in Indianapolis, his friend, J. P. Dunn, editor of the Indianapolis *Sentinel,* gave a full column and a half to the circular.[7] He called attention to Evans' relationship to Indianapolis and his

---

[2] *A. B., Circular,* Jan., 1902, p. 4. The "small bills enclosed" were order blanks for the *American Bibliography.*

[3] *Ibid.,* p. 5.

[4] Newspaper clippings, Cleveland *Plain Dealer,* Feb. 23, 1902; Indianapolis *Sunday Sentinel,* Jan. 19, 1902; Chicago *Record-Herald,* Feb. 17, 1902; Chicago *Tribune,* Feb. 17, 1902.

[5] Charles L. Bowman to C. E., TLS, Jan. 11, 1902.

[6] Newspaper clipping, Chicago *Tribune,* Feb. 17, 1902.

[7] Newspaper clipping, J. P. Dunn, "A Great Work," Indianapolis *Sunday Sentinel,* Jan. 19, 1902; J. P. Dunn to C. E., ALS, Jan. 20, 1902.

good work in the public library in years past. Perhaps Dunn was too strong in suggesting that "he might have been here yet but for our historically idiotic school board"; but then Dunn was, without apology, an Evans partisan. While his review of the prospectus was highly favorable, he privately chided Evans for advising old book dealers on how to sell books when he freely admitted that he had not had a photograph taken in twenty-five years. Dunn thought that had there been a portrait to go with his review, just twice as many people would have read the article. So he advised Evans to "have yourself took," advice which Evans just as politely ignored.

If newspaper reviewers tended to be impressed, book dealers themselves and librarians tended to be suspicious. While 165 individuals and institutions expressed interest in Evans' project immediately, only thirty-one of these demonstrated that interest with subscriptions. The others thought they might want to subscribe, but not before they had more information than Evans had given in the circular. Answering specific inquiries of these institutions, the possible backbone of the subscription list, occupied much of Evans' time in 1902 and 1903. There were a number of librarians who doubted that Evans could produce such a work, though few expressed their doubts to Evans personally. Encouragement did come from a few, such as his old professional colleagues, S. S. Green, C. A. Cutter, and W. I. Fletcher.[8] And even Azariah Root, who had expressed his doubts to the Bibliographical Society of Chicago, indicated a willingness to support Evans' work. However, it was Fletcher, a friend of Athenaeum days, in a letter of January 20, 1902, who spoke frankly about the doubts of some librarians. In noting that he had received a letter from a lady librarian in the West asking for an opinion of Evans' work, Fletcher came directly to the point in his second paragraph:

> For several days I have been on the point of writing to you a letter of which the above is suggestive. It seems to me you are not going to work quite the right way. Take my own case. I must assure our Library Committee that the book is well done before they will subscribe. To be perfectly frank I must say I don't know about that. What you ought to do is to let two or three men in whom we all confide see your MS (or a part of it) and give us their opinion. Such men are Dr. Green, Barton of Worcester, Jameson of the Univ. of Chicago, Winship of the Carter Brown Library. I don't see how you can get many subscribers until you have sent out a circular with the backing of some such men. I have every con-

---

[8] S. S. Green to C. E., ALS, Jan. 8, 1902; C. A. Cutter to C. E., ALS, Jan. 13, 1902; W. I. Fletcher to C. E., postcard, Jan. 7, 1902.

fidence in you and your work, but I cannot impart that confidence to others without traversing by far the proper ethics of endorsement. I should distrust my own ability to judge of your work, even if I had an opportunity of inspecting it, and would depend upon the judgment of specialists. For the earliest part of the work Winship is perhaps the best critic. Do you know him pretty well? I would take pleasure in commending you to him, if you wish.[9]

This candid letter of Fletcher certainly summed up the attitude of many librarians, and it was good advice. Perhaps to soften the blow to an ego he knew would not take this advice kindly, Fletcher added a postscript which said, "If you are actually getting the subscriptions of such men as the above-named that is *their* endorsement, and pretty nearly a sufficient one."

Fletcher's latter statement cannot, of course, be taken at face value. Many a library which specialized in early Americana believed that they had to have Evans' work, even if it were a less desirable bibliography than they wanted. While Winship did submit a subscription immediately for the John Carter Brown Library, he was apparently fully as dubious as the others. Much later, after the appearance of volume one, when Evans asked him for an endorsement, Winship replied that a cursory examination of the volume led him to think that the bibliography was "quite as satisfactory as a work compiled at a distance from the principal collections could be"; but he doubted that Evans could continue the work as satisfactorily without ransacking the chief pamphlet collections.[10] In view of this backhanded compliment, it would have been strange indeed if Winship had not confessed his honest doubts to those librarians who wrote to him. Judging by the number of letters received by Fletcher asking for a recommendation, Winship must have been approached frequently after the appearance of the January, 1902, circular. In a day when the average novel was listed at $1.50 (and often sold for much less than list price), few librarians were willing to commit themselves to such an expensive set without being thoroughly convinced of the reputation of its author and the usefulness of the work to their particular library.

Despite Fletcher's warning, Evans did little to still this under-

---

[9] W. I. Fletcher to C. E., TLS, Jan. 20, 1902, TLS, March 13, 1902, and ALS, March 22, 1902. The quotation is from the letter of January 20, but the other letters reinforced Fletcher's admonition.

[10] George P. Winship to C. E., ALS, Jan. 16, 1904. C. E. to G. P. Winship, ALS, March 6, 1902, pasted in John Carter Brown Library copy of *American Bibliography*, I, acknowledges with thanks Winship's subscription to the work.

current of skepticism. Not until the appearance of the first volume did he follow his old friend's advice and print a circular with a list of 207 individuals and institutions who had subscribed for 218 copies of the bibliography.[11] Shortly after Evans published volume one, in November, 1903, Johnson Brigham, Librarian of the Iowa State Library, wrote Evans a letter which confirmed Fletcher's earlier advice. Brigham had made inquiry of two of the supposedly ablest and best informed librarians in the country to ask what they thought of Evans' bibliography. While one gave a favorable pronouncement, the other knew nothing about it and expressed grave doubt as to its value. However, Evans' latest circular, with its impressive list of subscribers, had stilled Brigham's doubts and he forthwith submitted the subscription of the Iowa State Library.

The subscription list of November, 1903, showed that most of the national libraries of the world and the important public, historical, and university libraries had subscribed. There had not been the hoped for response from American public libraries, but this was compensated by the heavy foreign subscriptions. Of the 218 subscriptions for volume one, foreign libraries accounted for fifty-three copies. While there had not been the minimum of 300 on which Evans had originally set his sights, he felt encouraged enough to go ahead with publication.

Almost two years had elapsed between the appearance of the first circular in January, 1902, and the second, with its impressive list of subscribers, in November, 1903. Evans had certainly not anticipated the intervening length of time. Much of this time was spent in trying to secure subscriptions, but the major difficulty was in finding an individual or institution to underwrite the publication cost. Lack of money, a factor which always loomed large in Evans' life, prevented his getting the manuscript to press earlier. Evans had noted in his first circular that no commercial publisher would have undertaken the publication of such a work "except on such terms as would make the labor of years a labor of love, wholly without profit." He had therefore determined to issue the *American Bibliography* as a privately printed work and to limit its sale strictly to subscribers. In his initial optimism he had hoped that advance payments would provide enough capital with which to print volume one. To encourage advance payment, he offered to ship all subsequent volumes free to any spot in the world. When this method

---

[11] *A. B., Circular*, Nov., 1903; Johnson Brigham to C. E., TLS, Nov. 13, 1903.

failed to obtain the desired results and when the librarians responded so slowly, Evans had far too little assurance of success to begin the venture in the summer of 1902 as he wished. Instead, he was forced to spend the rest of the year in an attempt to secure financial backing for the project. In his efforts to get the bibliography to press, Evans approached wealthy individuals in Chicago and elsewhere, manufacturing companies, banks, and the new Carnegie Institution in Washington.[12] In order to secure the capital for volume one, Evans offered to dedicate that volume to any man or institution which would underwrite publication costs. Turned down again and again, he then tried to secure a personal loan from several banks, and finally, as rejection followed rejection, three Indianapolis friends came to his rescue with an agreement to guarantee his personal note at the Union Trust Company, using subscriptions to the work as collateral. As J. C. Bay later remarked in noting Evans' dogged determination to succeed: "It is pathetic to think that Mr. Carnegie at one time dreamed of seeking out just such workers . . . and aimed 'to discover the exceptional man in every department of study whenever and wherever found . . . and enable him to make the work for which he seems especially designed his life work.' "[13] It is ironic that one of the institutions which turned down Evans' plea for publication funds was a creation of this same Carnegie.

The final contract, a loan of an unspecified amount to cover the cost of printing and distributing 500 copies of volume one of the *American Bibliography,* was executed on January 26, 1903.[14] Under the terms of this contract Evans agreed to pay the Union Trust Company of Indianapolis $100 for collecting the money from subscribers and to repay any amount he borrowed at a rate of 6 per cent per annum. This same agreement was the foundation stone for another seven volumes of Evans' bibliography. Accounts did

---

[12] Among the individuals contacted by Evans were the following men: Martin A. Ryerson, Marshall Field, Albert Dickinson, Thomas S. Wallin, A. B. Dick, Frank O. Lowden, Albert Keep, John H. Wrenn, Robert Todd Lincoln, and Stanley McCormick. During the latter part of 1902 it appeared that Stanley McCormick would back the project, but early in 1903 his personal secretary, H. P. Prentice, had him withdraw from the plan under conditions which baffled Holliday. John H. Holliday to C. E., TLS, Jan. 16, 21, and 24, 1903.

[13] J. C. Bay, "Charles Evans, 1850–1935," A. L. A. *Bulletin,* XXIX (March, 1935), 163.

[14] Carbon copy of formal agreement between Charles Evans of Chicago, Ill., and the Union Trust Company of Indianapolis, Ind., dated Jan. 26, 1903, signed by Charles Evans and John H. Holliday.

not always come out correctly. Sometimes there was a balance left from one volume, which Evans either paid from his own pocket or had carried over to be absorbed in the costs of the next book; but the basic agreement lasted for eight volumes, covering 25,074 titles and a period of eleven years. The three men who had been instrumental in guaranteeing funds for the work were John H. Holliday, President of the Union Trust Company; Addison C. Harris, prominent Republican lawyer and recent United States envoy to Austria-Hungary; and George T. Porter, also an Indianapolis lawyer and son of a former Indiana governor. All had been good friends of Charles Evans during his years as librarian in Indianapolis, and they had faith in his scholarly ability and his fiscal integrity.[15]

With the money in hand and the manuscript completed, Evans made arrangements with the Blakely Printing Company of Chicago to begin printing in the early spring, 1903.[16] He had bought his own paper and intended to exercise careful supervision over his volume's progress through the press. Through the Newberry Library he bought the necessary quantity of English red buckram and let a separate contract with Brock and Rankin, edition bookbinders, for the binding. As his own business manager, Evans secured bids from as many different companies as possible to obtain the lowest possible cost for the completed work. With each volume he followed the

[15] All vouchers, statements, correspondence, and so forth, for the first eight volumes of the *American Bibliography* are in a correspondence folder in the Evans Papers. Union Trust Company "Statement," Indianapolis, March 22, 1904, shows an overdraft of $65.57 for volume one as of that date. It should be noted that Evans put up as collateral only that number of subscriptions necessary to guarantee the actual money loaned by the Union Trust Company. For volume one the company advanced a total of $1,963.52, and charged Evans $151.60 for interest and collection costs. To this cost of volume one should be added $198.75 in initial advertising costs, plus miscellaneous costs of $41.20 and an indeterminate amount for postage. The known costs as revealed in Evans' "Ledger Book," I, amounted to $2,354.07. By the end of May, 1904, subscriptions had brought in $3,432.35. Up until the time volume two was published in March, 1905, Evans had collected $3,902.78 for volume one. That this $1,548.71 was not all profit can be seen in Charles Evans to J. K. Gill Co., MS draft of a reply to letter of April 26, 1905, "the publication is not yet on a paying basis."

[16] Exact date when printing began is unknown but the first bill of the Chicago Paper Company was dated March 5, 1903. The first bill of the Blakely Printing Company was dated May 9, 1903, for composition of 125 pages of the *American Bibliography*, indicating that the work had begun probably a month earlier. All of the information on the production of the volume is from the correspondence folder of the Union Trust Company and Charles Evans, "Ledger Book," I.

same routine: secured bids for various parts of the work, awarded the work to the best bidder on specific parts, supervised all the work carefully, then made arrangements with the express company and the post office for mailing the completed book. Using his home as a warehouse, Evans stacked the copies in the front hall until he could personally sign each one, wrap it, address the label, and arrange for its shipment. In two black ledgers he kept his accounts of receipts and expenditures. For each subscriber he set aside a separate page, designated by the number of the copy he was to receive, and on these pages Evans made such notations as seemed appropriate to him. Some checks went directly to the Indianapolis bank, others came to Pratt Avenue, but Evans kept a careful record of them all. The business details were undoubtedly the most tedious and uninteresting part of Evans' self-appointed tasks, and numerous letters tell of the petty annoyances and minor details that sorely tested his patience. On occasion there was the old Evans' temper to be reckoned with as he lost all patience.

However, to the business details and the physical make-up of his volume Evans devoted meticulous attention. He could point with a considerable degree of pride to the fact that he had used the finest paper, type, and binding for his bibliography. Nothing less seemed fitting for a work destined to record the outline history of printing in the United States. According to Evans' own account, he had spared no practical expense to make the first volume "in every way representative of the progress which has been made by the United States in Bibliothecal science, in the printing art and in the knowledge of book manufacture at the beginning of the twentieth century." [17] That he had been able to accomplish this without prohibitive expense had been due to his Yankee shrewdness in securing good terms for the various parts of book production.

Volume one was printed on specially made deckle-edged paper of durability and good writing quality so that bibliographers could later add notes and librarians who used it as a catalog could add shelf marks. Ample margins had been left for such notes, and a new font of bourgeois type had been made for the press work. Evans had set the body of the book in capital letters, with imprint information in italics. Lowercase letters were used for the numerous bibliographical notes. As an example of the treatment of the milestones in American printing, Evans' notes on his first entry, "The

---

[17] *A. B., Circular,* Jan., 1902, p. ii.

Oath of a Free-man," cover most of two pages. Similar treatment was given to such works as the first title of a printer, first collection of laws, controversial pamphlets, or items which especially attracted the censor's ire.

The first volume of the bibliography covered the years 1639 to 1729, almost a century of early American printing. In six pages of his preface Evans summarized the history of printing during the period, with comments upon the type of publications which came from the colonial press, the number of publications, and statements concerning his bibliographical technique. The entries were arranged chronologically, and, under each year, alphabetically by author, or title if the author were unknown. With typical Evans dogmatism, he had expressed his bibliographical creed in the preface:

The chronological arrangement has proved its perfect adaptability and superiority for reference, to an alphabetical arrangement of authors as the work proceeded. Its advantages are many. . . . The group of historical events and of subjects which evoke publication are to the student of literary history and to the historian of public affairs matters of first importance. To the bibliographical student, and all book lovers are such, the date of publication is the most important fact in the identification of books and editions; it is the key to all investigation. . . . For remembrance, we repeat, the fact of first importance in bibliographical research is the date—always the date! [18]

Each entry was given an Evans number, and the auction values were given for any book which had been sold for more than $10. At the end of the volume were detailed indexes of printers and publishers, subjects, and authors. His volume described 967 imprints for the seventeenth century, or about 30 per cent more than any previous bibliographer. The total number of titles described in the book came to 3,244.

To complete the volume Evans designed a spine with gilt lettering on a rich-colored crimson buckram. Clearly Charles Evans wanted the *American Bibliography* to be as perfect in design and production as it was in scholarship. No detail was too small to escape his personal attention.

Spring, summer, and fall of 1903 were spent in printing, proofreading, binding, and preparing the completed copies for shipment to the subscribers. The first copies were sent in early November to the three Indianapolis friends who had guaranteed the publication of the volume. As had been true in earlier centuries when literary

---

[18] Evans, *American Bibliography*, I, xi.

men dedicated their works to patrons, Evans had set aside a special page for his friends. Yet that page contained no perfunctory dedication nor is there reason to doubt the sincerity of his words. At a critical hour, when it seemed the work on which he so much depended would not be published, these men had generously backed their friend. In this act they had demonstrated for Evans a patriotism much in keeping with the finest traditions of the republic:

TO

    ADDISON CLAY HARRIS

    JOHN HAMPDEN HOLLIDAY

    GEORGE TOUSEY PORTER

    NOT ALONE AS A TRIBUTE OF PERSONAL FRIENDSHIP AND ESTEEM, BUT ALSO AS EVIDENCE THAT A REVERENTIAL REGARD FOR EARLY AMERICAN LITERATURE IS NOT CONFINED TO THE NARROW STRIP OF LAND WHICH GAVE IT BIRTH BUT IS THE PRECIOUS HERITAGE OF THAT GREATER REPUBLIC FOUNDED ON THE SPIRIT OF ITS TEACHINGS.

Holliday was quite overwhelmed by this dedication, and Porter touched by it. While no letter of Harris' survives, in view of his continued support of Evans' bibliography, it is obvious that he too was very pleased. Porter probably spoke for all of Evans' friends when he said, "I hope that you will reap that large measure of reputation which you deserve—& that along with it will come much gold." [19]

By late 1903, Evans needed both reputation and gold. If he had uttered a special "amen" to Porter's prayer, it certainly would not have been surprising. The result of any personality's having undergone the ego-shattering experiences Evans had known as a librarian could well have been defeat, despondency, and the lack of will to continue. The normal pattern after such defeats would have been for Evans to give up the thought of achieving bibliothecal distinction, take a secondary library position, and then retire with what honor he could. As a major library figure he had failed, and fifty-one, after all, is scarcely the age at which most men undertake ambitious projects, especially after twenty years of failure. However, Charles Evans was not an average man. He refused to admit

---

[19] J. H. Holliday to C. E., ALS, Nov. 11, 1903; G. T. Porter to C. E., ALS, Dec. 13, 1903.

defeat, and he was determined to achieve the longed-for recognition which he had so far not received. A strong individual with a violent temper and a Biblical sense of justification for the rightness of his actions, Evans was too stubborn to admit the thought of failure. He would show the bibliothecal world that there was a Charles Evans with whom to contend, and, thus, what had probably begun as conscious imitation of the great periodical index of Poole, now became the ruling passion of his life. With a persistence equaled by few, he had brought the first volume to the public; here was the project for which the bibliographical world had been hoping. With the right kind of luck, he would win both reputation and gold.

The initial response to the bibliography was laudatory. In a review for the Chicago *Evening Post,* John R. Young congratulated Evans on achieving an exceptionally difficult task, though Young's brief descriptive sketch might well have been expected from a local newspaper.[20] However, there followed a review in *The Bookseller,* a Chicago magazine of some national reputation, which called the bibliography a "valuable work" and spoke encouraging words about the physical make-up of the publication. Still, the editor felt called upon to add these cautious words at the end of the review: "As to the bibliographical value of the work, we are impatiently awaiting the judgment of competent critics, and hope for a review of it by some such an authority as Mr. Wilberforce Eames of the Lenox Library." [21] Newspapers as geographically separated as the New York *Tribune* and the Denver *News-Times* carried descriptive notices, and to this gratifying evidence of publicity could be added the favorable comments by letter of such midwestern librarians as C. W. Andrews of the John Crerar Library, Reuben G. Thwaites of the State Historical Society of Wisconsin, and J. T. Gerould of the University of Missouri. Nor did New York bookmen remain silent; Evans received congratulations from E. Dwight Church, noted collector of Americana, and from John Anderson, Jr., of the Anderson Auction Company. Such responses were sure to warm the heart of a man as starved for public recognition as Evans was.

The most important reaction in late 1903, not for its immediate value but for the future, came from a young librarian just completing his third year at the Rhode Island Historical Society.[22]

[20] Newspaper clipping, Chicago *Evening Post,* Nov. 21, 1903.
[21] "A Valuable Work," clipping from *The Bookseller,* Dec., 1903.
[22] C. S. B. to C. E., ALS, Nov. 17, 1903.

Only twenty-six at the time, Clarence Saunders Brigham had already published several bibliographical works, including a *Bibliography of Rhode Island History* the previous year. In a letter to Evans in mid-November, Brigham expressed enthusiasm for "such an unusually fine piece of book-making." Moreover, he was in hearty agreement with Evans' bibliographical creed: "There is no question but that the chronological arrangement is the most useful to students." Brigham also had praise for the alphabetical and subject indexes at the end of the volume, and a special commendation for that "novel feature," an index of booksellers. The introduction he had read with pleasure, taking exception to only one statement: Evans' doubt that the total of seventeenth-century imprints would ever go beyond the 1,000 mark. Brigham thought the publication of the first volume of the *American Bibliography,* which listed 967, would immediately bring to light at least another thirty titles. While Brigham was not yet one of the leading librarians, he was a bright young man who knew his way around in bibliography. To his general praise of Evans' efforts he added an offer to help on future volumes by checking the Providence imprints for him. In addition he would do what he could to supply information on other Rhode Island titles. In order to help him as efficiently as possible, would Evans tell him how much personal research he planned to do for future volumes?

That Evans was greatly encouraged by Brigham's "frankness and evident sincerity" is shown in his response of early December.[23] In the young librarian he recognized a man of kindred spirit, "one who has felt the fascination and charm of bibliographical research." If his plans worked out, he hoped to do much in the way of personal research for future volumes, and when he undertook these research trips, he would surely include Brigham's library in his itinerary. He gladly accepted the offer of help with Rhode Island imprints and would be happy to acknowledge such assistance. As for Brigham's criticism of his estimate of the number of seventeenth-century imprints, Evans could not conceal his confidence in his own judgment. Until such time as someone should prove differently, he stood by the original estimate.

Even earlier than this, Evans and Brigham had corresponded. When Evans was librarian of the Chicago Historical Society, he

---

[23] C. E. to C. S. B., ALS, Dec. 9, 1903, in R. I. H. S. Archives.

had managed to secure a partial file (1779–81) of the *American Journal and General Advertiser,* a newspaper published in Providence in the eighteenth century. A local workman had rescued this segment of the newspaper from a trash pile and wanted to sell it to Evans for the Chicago Historical Society. Evans had a strong desire to see such an item in its proper home and therefore had offered it to the Rhode Island Historical Society. Brigham had appreciated Evans' interest in the matter and was only too happy to secure the paper. In prophetic words he had written, "I only trust that I may some day repay the favor." [24] With his encouraging offer of help, he had now begun repaying Evans. Neither man could have foreseen that in the thirty-two years which lay ahead, Brigham would repay Evans many times, "good measure, pressed down . . . and running over."

The plaudits of the local people, of the midwestern librarians, of some easterners such as Brigham, Edward P. Van Duzee of the Grosvernor Library, and Albert S. Batchellor, Editor of the State Papers of New Hampshire, all encouraged Evans. However, the really prominent bibliographers had not yet been heard. Where were the comments of Wilberforce Eames of the Lenox Library and George Parker Winship of the John Carter Brown Library? These men were as yet silent, and no bibliographer, however promising, would be sure of his reward until they had rendered their judgment. What of the library press? Would it endorse the Evans bibliography?

When the January, 1904, issue of the *Library Journal* came from the press, Evans must have been angered at the condescending tone of the editor, who, in reviewing the past year noted: "In its bibliographical record the year was not unfruitful. Perhaps the most notable publication, in its purpose if not in its accomplishment, is the first volume of the 'American bibliography' in which Mr. Charles Evans has attempted the elaborate records of the beginnings of American book production." [25] This editorial was undoubtedly written by R. R. Bowker, editor of the journal, a bibliographer with several important works to his credit, and an associate of many eastern bibliographers. Evans, always sensitive to any slight, could not

[24] C. S. B. to C. E., ALS, Nov. 27, 1900.

[25] "Editorial," *Library Journal,* XXIX (Jan., 1904), 4. The Bowker family had controlled the journal since 1884. Although the *Library Journal* was still the official organ of the American Library Association, there was considerable ferment in professional circles for replacing it with a new association-edited journal.

have been pleased by this notice. Coming from such an important source, the review could only reinforce the skepticism of a number of potential subscribers.

In the same issue with Bowker's editorial note was a review of volume one by V. Lansing Collins, Princeton University professor, who acknowledged the importance of the volume to all who were interested in American literary history.[26] At the same time he was very critical of some of Evans' methodology and the latter's inaccuracy in some entries. The chief sin he found to be omission: "unconfessed omission from title-pages, insufficient auction records, and incomplete location details." While these were few in number, he thought they could have been so easily minimized that Evans must either have suffered from a lack of bibliographical apparatus or incomplete examination of well-known collections of Americana.

Both Bowker and Collins meant their criticisms to be helpful. Bowker wrote Evans the following month that he would gladly do his part "to forward in any way the monumental enterprise you have given yourself." [27] He had himself been interested in pushing the *American Catalogue* backward to cover the nineteenth century, but Evans now made that unnecessary. Moreover, in September, 1904, at the American Library Association conference in St. Louis, he pointed out that despite the severe criticism of the work by bibliographical scholars for "inaccuracies and omissions, and for lack of research in large and representative collections," it was on the whole a satisfactory work and should be in every important library in the world. Professor Collins, too, had closed his review by noting that his criticisms should not destroy the main fact: "this is one of *the* important bibliographies of Americana." Time alone would tell whether it would rank with Sabin, but Evans had a good opportunity for treating definitively the colonial press of America.

The Bowker editorial note and Collins' review were followed in mid-January by Winship's letter expressing doubt about Evans' estimate of the output of the seventeenth-century press, and the hope that he would not go to press with another volume until he had ransacked the major pamphlet collections. Winship, as the

---

[26] V. Lansing Collins, review of Charles Evans' *American Bibliography, Volume I, 1639–1729, Library Journal*, XXIX (Jan., 1904), 30–31.

[27] R. R. Bowker to C. E., TLS, Feb. 3, 1904; R. R. Bowker, "Recent National Bibliography in the United States," *Library Journal*, XXIX (Dec., 1904), C121–122. For a critical note on one of Evans' entries in volume one, see "Notes and Queries," *Library Journal*, XXIX (Sept., 1904), 500.

others, clearly had misgivings about the work, although he too closed with a wish for Evans' success. Certainly the early notices and letters from the major bibliographers did not constitute the sort of endorsement Evans needed to attract more subscribers.

Additional critical attention of volume one came in February, 1904, when *The Literary Collector,* "an illustrated monthly magazine of booklore and bibliography," published a four-page unsigned review.[28] Among the writers for this influential magazine were such bibliographers as A. W. Pollard and V. H. Paltsits. Presumably the review reflected the judgment of an equally competent man. Noting that the usefulness and accuracy of a book like Evans' could only be judged after much use, the reviewer directed his main attack at Evans' prefatory note in claiming completeness. Agreeing with Brigham and Winship, he thought the estimate of seventeenth-century imprints demonstrated a cocksureness which no bibliographer could have. As a small test of the bibliography's value, the reviewer had made a brief check against Wegelin's *Early American Poetry.* While his test was inconclusive, some titles appearing in Evans which were not in Wegelin and vice versa, he thought this indicated the difficulty in claiming completeness for any bibliographical effort. Even in a smaller field than Evans attempted to cover, completeness had been an elusive goal for the bibliographer, and the reviewer was not hesitant in saying that he doubted a perfect bibliography covering a century's time and a country's breadth could ever be accomplished. Therefore it irritated him to read Evans' prefatory "belief that the record here given is, at least, nearly complete." He also was disturbed about several minor conclusions of Evans, especially the latter's strong views against indicating the linear divisions of title pages. Basically, though, what the reviewer disliked about the bibliography was the author's lack of a decent sense of humility. This he attributed, incorrectly, to Evans' youth and inexperience in bibliographical matters. Nonetheless, when the critic remembered the necessity for overlooking personalities and giving broad-minded recognition where it was due, he had to admit that Charles Evans had produced a bibliography which filled a definite need; the work would "undoubtedly prove of inestimable value to all workers in the field of colonial history, literature, and bibliography."

Some of the criticisms voiced by the reviewers had been antici-

---

[28] "Book Reviews," *The Literary Collector,* VII (Feb., 1904), 113–116.

pated by Evans. Bibliographical format by no means followed a set
pattern in the early twentieth century,[29] and it was inevitable that
other scholars would criticize his methodology. After his first circular had appeared, Evans had received a letter from W. J. James,
Librarian of Wesleyan University, in which he had asked some
searching questions about the format of the proposed work.[30] James
was especially interested in full titles, citation of source of information, linear divisions of title pages, location of copies, and dis-
tinguishing titles which Evans had seen himself. Although Evans
was in hearty agreement with James about giving full titles (he
loved the lengthy titles coined by the New England worthies), and
the location of copies, he cared nothing for the "use of line-marks,
so dear to the heart of the young bibliographer" and thought they
accomplished little of value except for incunabula or books without
title pages.[31] He therefore purposely avoided their use.

In a subsequent letter James made his strongest plea for Evans
to indicate in some way those titles he had personally examined.
Would it not be wise to follow Hain's method and mark titles he
had personally examined with an asterisk? Closely allied to his
request for asterisks was his plea for citation of source of information. Recognizing that this might be impracticable, James noted
the utility of citing the source. Future researchers could weed out
errors in Evans' work more easily if they knew where he got his
information. Thanks to another bibliographer's citation of source,
James had only recently demonstrated how that man had misread
his authority and manufactured a seventeenth-century imprint. Al-

---

[29] Lawrence C. Wroth, "Evans's *American Bibliography*, a Matrix of Histories,"
in his *American Bibliography, 1639–1729, by Charles Evans, Illustrated with
Fifty-nine Original Leaves from Early American Books and an Historical Notice
of the Author and His Work* (Boston: Charles E. Goodspeed and Company,
1943). Cited hereafter as Wroth, "A Matrix of Histories." Wroth calls this
period the "horse and buggy days of bibliography in this country." In Lawrence
C. Wroth, *A History of Printing in Colonial Maryland* (Baltimore: Typothetae
of Baltimore, 1922), p. 160, Wroth comments upon Evans' early work and, incidentally, notes the lack of a standard pattern for such research at the turn
of the century: "The compiler wishes to make an especial acknowledgment of
the value to him of Charles Evans's *American Bibliography* in the preparation
of the following list of Maryland imprints. Mr. Evans's contribution to American
literary history has been of such character as to entitle him to the gratitude of
all students in that and related subjects. His diligence and courage and single-
minded devotion have cleared a high road through a wilderness in which, before his work was published, adventurers stumbled along uncertain trails."

[30] W. J. James to C. E., ALS, Jan. 17, 1902, and ALS, March 5, 1902.

[31] Evans, *American Bibliography*, I, xi.

though Evans was still weighing James's recommendation on the use of asterisks in late January, 1902, he later rejected it. This was rather unfortunate, for much of the later criticism of Evans' work would have been stilled if he had followed James's advice on the use of asterisks and citation of sources.

There were probably three reasons for not following the James recommendations: (1) Evans had immense, but mistaken, confidence in his ability not to make mistakes, (2) he thought the additional space required to give the source and to indicate the titles he had seen personally would add to the bulk of the book and thereby increase the already high cost of printing, and (3) the number of titles he had examined personally for volume one was probably relatively small. However, James was not the last person to urge Evans to mend his ways and identify those titles he had personally examined. As later volumes were published, Clarence S. Brigham continually sought to induce Evans to indicate his source. One can only wonder at that peculiar quirk of Evans' mind that saw in the asterisks a great addition to the cost of printing; [32] but Evans, once he had set a pattern, was not a man to change his mind. Except for some bibliographical notes on the landmark books in early American printing, citations and sources are notably lacking from the published volumes of the *American Bibliography*.[33]

Despite the reservations with which his work was received in some quarters, Evans could not have been wholly displeased with the results. The skepticism of the easterners was natural, and Evans would have been unusually imperceptive not to have known that there would be innuendoes, slights, and condescension. His first circular had noted that in the changing complexion of the library profession the name of Charles Evans meant little. Even a major bibliographical work which served a long-felt need would have to stand upon its own merits. If Evans felt the natural irritation of

---

[32] This was the argument Evans continually used with Brigham. Interview with C. S. Brigham, May 6, 1958. Another criticism of Brigham's which Evans also answered in terms of additional cost was his failure to indicate locations of copies when he actually knew the location. If the line of print ran to the edge of the page, Evans refused to add another line just for the purpose of giving location, since this cost him another line of composition. On this point he later yielded to Brigham's insistence, beginning with volume eight. C. S. B. to C. E., ALS, Sept. 30, 1913. C. E. to C. S. Brigham, ALS, Jan. 2, 1917, A. A. S. Archives.

[33] On major titles the notes furnish detailed information, including sources, but it is on the thousands of minor titles—the ones most likely to lead to confusion—that such information is lacking.

an author whose words had become sacred during the time devoted to their writing, still no one had attacked the bibliography directly. Friend and foe alike praised its good chronological arrangement, its typographical excellence, and the vast amount of work accomplished by the author. The general attitude was one of watchful waiting, to see if Evans could carry through in a splendid way what had been a fairly promising beginning.

By March, 1904, when the Union Trust Company had been reimbursed for the sum it had advanced for the printing of the first volume of the *American Bibliography,* Evans believed that he had begun a work which had within it the possibilities of greatness. Though the work was not yet a financial success, Evans had at least broken even, and not all the payments had been received.[34] There seemed a good possibility that Evans could make a reputation for himself and still support his family modesty by publishing a bibliography.

March was a good time for soul searching. Two years had passed since Evans' dismissal at the Chicago Historical Society and the intervening period had been a difficult one for the family. Added to the uncertainty of getting the manuscript published were the anxiety about the critical response of the bibliothecal world and the personal financial strain made inevitable when an impecunious librarian is without a job. However, the children were growing up and required less attention. In fact, Charles, Jr., soon to become widely known as a golfer nicknamed "Chick," was caddying at the Edgewater Golf Club and using some of the fees to help out at home. Lena had always been an efficient housewife, who saw that every penny for the household was spent wisely. Fortunately the local grocer extended credit easily, if sometimes anxiously. The Evans family had long since grown accustomed to financial uncertainty, but Charles Evans throughout his life still suffered great uneasiness about these matters. That he had persevered in the face of these difficulties augured well for his continuing his bibliographical enterprise.

One of the questions most frequently asked by Evans' early correspondents had been, "How much personal research do you plan to do for succeeding volumes?" Other bibliographers such as Win-

---

[34] Charles Evans, "Ledger Book," I. That Evans had "broken even" means that he had paid the actual costs of publication. As of March he had received no compensation for his own labors of two years. However, the ledger books do indicate that Evans probably made some money on volume one.

ship and Brigham believed that Evans must visit the large eastern libraries and personally examine their Americana collections if he expected to continue his bibliography with any degree of success. For his first volume Evans had worked primarily from the book catalogs in the Newberry Library and in his own personal collection. He had relied heavily upon the 1837 catalog of the American Antiquarian Society, Isaiah Thomas' *History of Printing in America* with Haven's appended bibliography which the society had published in 1874, Trumbull's manuscript additions to Haven which the society had copied for him, and other printed bibliographies.[35] For the most part examination of the books themselves was limited to those items available in the Newberry Library. While Evans had emphasized the importance of studying each item personally in his preface, he simply had not been able to do much of this for the titles in volume one. Despite his meticulous combing of printed catalogs and bibliographies, this method of collecting data of necessity left opportunity for incompleteness and inaccuracy.

However, this did provide a basic file. From the printed records Evans very carefully, in his neat legible hand, copied down the information for each title on three-by-five slips cut in half. At the top of each slip was the date, a testimony to Evans' creed of the date of publication being the most important fact in identifying a book. Then came the name of the author, followed by a complete transcription of the title, imprint, and notes. At the bottom

---

[35] Evidence from the Evans correspondence, especially in relation to bibliographic queries, leaves no doubt that Evans was thoroughly acquainted with the printed bibliographies of the day and that he used them heavily. No attempt is made here to list everything that Evans found useful, but two publications from abroad should be mentioned since he found them as useful as he did American bibliographies: the British Museum *Catalogue of Printed Books* (London: Clowes, 1881–1900), 95v, against which he checked his early imprints, and Robert Watt, *Bibliotheca Britannica* (Edinburgh: Constable, 1824), 4v. For his use of the American Antiquarian Society material, both in printed and manuscript form, see C. K. Shipton, "Report of the Librarian," A. A. S. *Proceedings*, n.s., LXVIII (Oct., 1958), 187–188, and Mary Robinson to C. E., ALS, Feb. 4, 1903. The Newberry Library, as has been noted before in chapters 8 and 9, was strong in Americana, having acquired among other items one of the best collections of American psalmody in existence. Poole was especially interested in collecting bibliography and library catalogs and his annual reports for 1888–94 give numerous titles of bibliographies which Evans undoubtedly combed thoroughly. He may even have cataloged some of them. The Newberry continued to strengthen its Americana collection after Poole's death, thanks largely to the generosity of trustee Edward E. Ayer, one of whose gifts was a copy of John Eliot's Indian Bible. Many of the most useful works Evans owned personally. See typewritten list of books in the library of Charles Evans, 1935.

of each card were the names of the libraries which owned copies, and any other bibliographical facts which Evans thought important.

These slips were made from all sorts of cards and papers. Some were discarded catalog cards he had picked up from his friends, some invitation cards, some mere slips of paper cut to the appropriate size. Evans stored these slips in corset boxes, for, as he later often explained, "nothing so well suited his needs as containers of this particular size, shape, and weight." [36] The boxes measured 16½ inches long, 2⅞ inches wide, and 3 inches high. Evans tied the boxes together with a leather shawl strap, and, as he visited libraries to collect his data, he placed the information on his cards and filed them away in the corset boxes. Later as he finished each volume, the information on the usable cards was scratched out, and the card turned over for use with another title. When the card was no longer usable, it was discarded.

Evans' failure to visit the large eastern libraries before publication of volume one stemmed not from any unawareness of the importance of such research nor from a desire to evade the amount of work involved, but rather from that familiar Evans obstacle: lack of money. When he had first approached the secretary of the wealthy Chicagoan, Stanley McCormick, with the proposal that the latter underwrite publication of volume one, Evans had asked that funds be advanced to enable him to visit eastern libraries and check his manuscript against the actual books themselves.[37] With McCormick's refusal to go along with this trip and his eventual declination to back the volume, Evans was forced to cancel his plans and proceed with the publication as rapidly as possible. Although he was distressed that he had not been able to make the contemplated journey, this was only another in a long series of disappointments, although it had insured an earlier publication date for volume one.

Now that the first volume was out of the way and with the prodding of Brigham and Winship to spur him on, Evans was determined to visit the eastern libraries to check his manuscript of volume two before he went to press. While the bulk of his work was done, he must see for himself the titles in doubt and assure himself that his claim to completeness was valid. Again Evans turned to his friends at the Union Trust Company, and again they responded. In May, 1904, using sixteen unpaid subscriptions to the bibliogra-

---

[36] L. C. Wroth, "A Matrix of Histories," p. [ii].

[37] John H. Holliday to C. E., TLS, Dec. 3, 1902.

phy as collateral, Evans borrowed $300 and headed East. His corset boxes tucked securely under his arms, he visited in turn the Northern Indiana Historical Society at South Bend, libraries in Cleveland, the New York State Library, the American Antiquarian Society, libraries in Boston, Providence, Newport, Hartford, New Haven, and New York. At each library he worked diligently, comparing his cards with the originals and searching out new material. It was a trip he thoroughly enjoyed. Going back to New England was going home, and Charlie could not help writing enthusiastic descriptions of the country to his wife in Chicago: "After leaving Albany you feel that you are in God's country. . . . There is such a difference in the mountains, hills, rivers, and running streams to the flat uninteresting scenery west of Albany. . . . I want you to see all these places some time 'when the ship comes in.' It will be a revelation to you. The West seems crude and unfinished along side of this older and stronger civilization." [38]

Besides the scenery there was much else to enjoy. While in Boston, he stayed with his brother John and renewed his acquaintances at the Farm School. During his trip there was also an opportunity to meet again a number of colleagues with whom he had worked at the Boston Athenaeum. However, the warmest welcome of all came from a totally unexpected quarter. One of the major stops on his itinerary was the American Antiquarian Society, founded in 1812 by Isaiah Thomas and the home of an excellent collection of early American printed books. Charles Evans arrived in Worcester on June 5, and, after a week there, could scarcely find words to express his delight with the city.[39] He was entertained royally by his colleague S. S. Green, who introduced him to Nathaniel Paine, Treasurer of the American Antiquarian Society, and Dr. Charles L. Nichols, member of the society and author of a Worcester bibliography. The latter two gentlemen took an immediate interest in Evans and his work, and ten days later he wrote Lena that this was the first evening he had spent by himself since coming to Worcester. There had been dinners, theater parties, a presidential reception for the graduating class at the Worcester Polytechnic Institute, and a Bohemian Club meeting, all very heady wine for a man, who as his wife remarked, had been in a shell for such a long time that he did not realize how much he needed a change. With a wifely "I told

---

[38] C. E. to L. E., ALS, June 5, 1904.
[39] C. E. to L. E., ALS, June 11, 15, and 19, 1904.

you so," Lena added, "I think by this time you are glad you did take those *evening clothes.*" [40]

Social life in Worcester was pleasant and the attentions of such important people as Dr. Nichols, Stephen Salisbury, President of the American Antiquarian Society, and Nathaniel Paine, flattering. The amazing part of the story is that despite such a program Evans actually managed to get some work done! However, working days limited by a 9:00 to 5:00 pattern were not in the typical Evans tradition, and later, from Boston, he had to scurry back to Worcester surreptitiously to complete his examination of the American Antiquarian Society's collections. This time he avoided all social contact so that he could press forward with vigor. Although he found little at the American Antiquarian Society which was totally new to him, he thought the corrections resulting from a personal examination of the books were of the utmost value in assuring the accuracy of the bibliography. In later years when Evans made additional trips to Worcester, he always found the same warm hospitality that he had found on his first visit. Of all the places Evans ever visited on research trips, he regarded Worcester as the best. There was good reason for this, for it was here that Evans first found the keen satisfaction of success, and in no other place was he ever treated with such sincere courtesy.

The remainder of the trip could not measure up to the weeks in Worcester, but he did make many corrections to titles for which he already had cards. There were also surprisingly good discoveries of new titles in a number of libraries including both Yale and Harvard. Since the early college material of the latter two places had been a special object of his journey, he was elated over such good results. There were also rewarding discoveries at the Boston Athenaeum, the Connecticut Historical Society, and the New York Public Library. His reception in New York by Wilberforce Eames, dean of American bibliographers and librarian of the Lenox section of the New York Public Library, was gracious and kind.[41] Although the library was open only from 9:00 until 6:00, Eames frequently remained overtime for Evans' sake and personally led him to many items he would otherwise have missed. The library's chronological arrangement of all books printed before 1800 was especially useful. The only obstacles to Evans' complete enjoyment

[40] L. E. to C. E., ALS, June 15, 1904.
[41] C. E. to L. E., ALS, July 29, Aug. 1, 6, and 12, 1904.

of that library were the expenses of living in New York City and the lack of time. After over two weeks' steady work at the Lenox Library, he left with great reluctance for Philadelphia.

Although there had been some disappointments on the trip, all had gone very well indeed, both personally and professionally. Thanks to his brother's generosity and hospitality in the Boston area, he had managed to make his money go twice as far as he had originally thought possible. There had been few incidental expenses, his clothes were still in presentable condition, and his health was excellent. The last he attributed to the fact that he took a bath "of some sort every morning." Staying at the cheapest boarding houses or hotels nearest his work, Evans used all sorts of strategems to economize on expenses. Breakfast was his only regular meal, and he seldom took lunch, except on the invitation of one of the local librarians. Usually operating as a lone wolf, he had occasion in New York to meet a fellow researcher, a Dr. Kurrelmeyer, young professor from Johns Hopkins University who was preparing an edition of the first German Bible. They became good friends, and through Kurrelmeyer, Evans was able to obtain a room at the student YMCA at a cost of only $2.50 per week. During long walks after working hours, they talked a great deal about their research. In describing his new-found friend to Lena, Charlie said he was "married, very temperate, does not drink, smoke, and apparently has no vices."

The only small pleasures Evans allowed himself during research trips were long walks, long rides on the trolley to some part of the city, or visits to art museums. All of these activities took place either at night after work was finished or on Sundays when the libraries were closed. Usually there was no kindred spirit like Kurrelmeyer, and Evans did these things by himself. They relieved the tedium of research and calmed him down before the night's rest.

One Sunday in New York was fairly typical. For want of anything better to do Evans went to Coney Island by boat (round trip: twenty-five cents) and then later took a trolley car for upper Manhattan. The antics of the crowd at Coney Island fascinated him and he described the scene vividly to Lena:

I went to Coney Island . . . and saw one of the sights of the country. Thousands were in bathing, and everything was wide open and the lid off. It was very brilliant of a servant girl, beer drinking kind, but no rowdyism that I could see. I left early, and by chance taking a car at New York marked "Fort George" which promised a long ride I went to nearly 200th street for 5¢ and found there another Coney Island without a beach, a little more noisy, a little lower in grade, crowded, good-natured, out for a good time and determined to have it. I staid a half an hour, and then returned, and went to bed. I doubt if any other City in the world could show you so much for 35 cents. And I suppose I had seen more in a day than most of New York sees in a year.[42]

Visits to such amusement parks later became an Evans custom when he went to a city to do research. They were usually located quite a distance from the downtown section of the city where he worked. Evans found the long streetcar rides restful and the milling crowds in the parks fascinating, but his interest in their activities was always limited to observation, never participation.

Except in the Boston Public Library, Evans had met with a good reception from the librarians. Philadelphia was another story. Arriving there on August 16, he found the Historical Society of Pennsylvania closed for the month, the manuscript Hildeburn material which he especially wanted to see not there, and the conditions in the Library Company of Philadelphia unpromising. Immediately he decided to leave for home. Although Lena had asked him if he should not go on to Washington before his return, Evans decided to pass up that opportunity on this trip. His money had run out, the family finances needed shoring up, the business side of the bibliography needed his attention, and volume two needed to go to press as soon as possible. Besides these factors, Evans had been gone from home for two and a half months. Under the most favorable circumstances research is both a tiring and a lonely business. Charles Evans was homesick. Stopping overnight only for the purpose of seeing two prospective subscribers, Evans left the next day for Chicago. It had been a good trip, and he had much to show for his efforts, but enough was enough. He would be glad to be home.

---

[42] C. E. to L. E., ALS, Aug. 1, 1904.

Through the Wilderness of
Early American Printing

11

Upon his return home Evans proceeded as rapidly as possible with the publication of volume two. In his 1903 circular he had announced his intention to publish the second volume in the fall of 1904 and to follow with the other five or six volumes at intervals of approximately a year. To achieve such a schedule would require effort of the most unstinting character. However, Evans had never been one to shirk hard work; indeed, he could be said to thrive on it. Therefore the thought of the prodigious labor involved in the next half-dozen years was no deterrent at all.

One of the most necessary tasks to be accomplished soon after his return to Chicago was the answering of some of the backlog of correspondence which had accumulated during the research trip. There were new orders to be filled, complaints about not receiving volume one or its damage in shipment, suggestions for the improvement of future volumes, and letters from librarians who wanted to know when to expect volume two. Some of the letters were petty, some were useful, but the duty of answering them all was annoying. Since Evans disdained the use of a typewriter, all replies had to be written in long hand, and such a task took a great amount of time. This was precious time that could have been used to prepare the manuscript for press, but when Evans had to do everything himself it was to be expected. Although Evans normally enjoyed writing letters, except for new orders which put money in his purse, he found even the correspondence with his friends irksome. Nonetheless, sometimes patiently, sometimes carefully, occasionally impatiently and disgustedly, Evans wrote his answers as quickly as he could, trying to sandwich them in between the important work of preparing volume two.

There were good reasons for proceeding immediately with the main job, but the major reason was familiar. Family finances, always low, were especially shaky at the end of 1904. While on his trip Evans did not want to be bothered with filling orders and so told his wife to let them wait until his return; however, Lena, in her anxiety, had urged him to let her fill the orders immediately since they needed the cash. They could forego the profit on volume one temporarily. What the family needed was cold hard cash, and that in a rather ample supply; moreover, anything Charlie could do to push the publication of volume two would be welcome.[1]

If Evans needed an additional reminder about the necessity for rapid production of volume two, he received it from John H. Holliday, who expressed the hope that the next volume could be printed and sold more rapidly than the first.[2] Harris had been approached in April about continuing his part of the guarantee, but Porter had gone to Greece in the late spring and was not to return for several months. While both he and Harris agreed to continue their sponsorship of Evans on the same terms as those for volume one, Porter's absence necessarily delayed the signing of new printing contracts. Not until October 24, 1904, did Evans finally affix his signature to the new instrument with the Union Trust Company.

In the interim Evans had not been idle. As early as July, from New York, he had written to Brock and Rankin, his bookbinders, and to the Blakely Printing Company about quotations for volume two. Both were interested in doing business with Evans again but Blakely had replied in vague terminology, and upon his return to Chicago Evans was to learn to his sorrow that the cost of materials and workmanship was rising. Still, the people at Blakely promised completion of the printing in sixty to seventy-five working days, once the contract was signed. Pressed as he was for finances and anxious to see the volume in press, Evans did something that he later regretted: he reduced the number of copies from 500 to 400.[3]

[1] L. E. to C. E., ALS, July 2, 1904.
[2] J. H. Holliday to C. E., TLS, Oct. 21, 1904.
[3] J. H. Holliday to C. E., TLS, Nov. 17, 1904. Charles Evans, "Ledger Book,"

At the time it undoubtedly seemed a wise decision. The cost of paper, printing, and binding for the additional 100 copies was considerable, and the prospect for ever selling 500 sets of the bibliography seemed remote. Evans' subscription list for both volumes one and two aggregated only 312 copies, and his canvass of all the major libraries had been very thorough.

Printing of volume two began late in the year, 1904, and the completed volume appeared in late March, 1905. An early copy went to the Boston Athenaeum, to whose past and present proprietors Evans had dedicated the volume. It was a gracious dedication, written with sincerity and affection for an institution which had started him on the road to bibliothecal success. He paid high tribute to the men of vision who had spurred the Athenaeum's efforts to preserve the records of early American literature. Upon receiving the volume C. K. Bolton, Librarian of the Boston Athenaeum, acknowledged the pleasure of the officers that "one of the Athenaeum sons" had been so thoughtful.[4]

Volume two of the *American Bibliography* contained 3,378 entries, only a slight increase over the number appearing in volume one. Yet the period covered had been reduced to twenty years, 1730–50, an indication of the acquisition of more printing presses in the colonies. During this period American printing spread southward, and a literature in the German language began to flourish. While the dominant religious outlook remained unchanged, the literature of the period began to assume a broader outlook. Religious revivals added to the volume of production and found expression in a variety of printed forms. Methodism's George Whitefield "awoke with alarm the conservative churches of the Atlantic Coast, from Savannah to Boston," and the eminent divine, Jonathan Edwards, pub-

---

II, 240, lists a payment to Evans' binder at $203.64. Since A. J. Cox and Company had agreed to bind volume two at forty-six cents per copy, Evans apparently received about 430 copies. Why he later insisted that this cut in numbers was due to a printer's blunder is unknown. C. E. to C. S. B., ALS, Oct. 3, 1930, A. A. S. Archives. Perhaps he confused volume two with volume five where he did suffer a loss of at least eighteen copies, and probably more, due to a printer's blunder. C. E. to J. Manz Engraving Company, MS draft, May 10, 1909. Eliot Evans recalled that his father told him several times the reason he could not supply additional sets in the early 1930's was a shortage of volumes two and five, which he attributed to a bookbinder's error. Eliot Evans to Charles Evans, Jr., TLS, March 11, 1935. However, the evidence above is conclusive on this point: volume two was purposely short and the shortage in volume five resulted from a printer's error.

[4] C. K. Bolton to C. E., ALS, March 28, 1905.

lished the first of his treatises, *God Glorified in the Work of Redemption,* in Boston, 1731. It was an exciting period in the history of the American press, covering as it did Benjamin Franklin's first work in Philadelphia, the trial of Peter Zenger on the issue of freedom of the press, and Christoph Sauer's *Biblia* in the German language. Evans chronicled all these events in his preface, giving a panoramic view of the history of printing during the twenty-year period. His lucid account of the subject matter and principal productions of the various presses is still excellent reading; in 1905 it was the most accurate account available.

The appearance of volume two brought a cordial response from the bibliothecal world. *The Nation* took the opportunity to review both volumes in a generally favorable critique in late June, although the reviewer's voice was added to that of a previous critic who took issue with Evans' lack of citation of source.[5] Encouragement came from a variety of sources. A bookseller in Puebla, Mexico, spoke of his pride that such a sumptious work came from an American, while Wilberforce Eames offered congratulations and Herbert O. Brigham, Librarian of the Rhode Island State Library, went on record "as heartily endorsing your work." [6]

As the favorable comments from librarians and bibliographers began to be received at Pratt Avenue, Charles Evans was pleased that his work was beginning to achieve some distinction. The letters expressed fewer criticisms and more admiration for Evans' pluck in attempting such a task. Yet he really had no basis on which to rest and enjoy some of the social pleasures which might have come from this recognition, as sales of the bibliography kept him busy at his desk during spring and summer. The only major social engagement Evans had permitted himself since his research trip to the East occurred on January 10, 1905, while volume two was still in press.

The lad upon whom he had looked so kindly during his early days in Indianapolis had summoned "that faith which removes mountains and bibliographers" and invited Evans to participate in the twenty-eighth anniversary celebration of the Indianapolis

---

[5] Review of *American Bibliography* by Charles Evans, *The Nation,* LXXX (June 29, 1905), 528.

[6] Francis S. Barton to C. E., ALS, May 10, 1905; Wilberforce Eames to C. E., ALS, April 3, 1905; Herbert O. Brigham to C. E., TLS, June 23, 1905. These are only samples of the favorable letters Evans received.

Literary Club.[7] To Meredith Nicholson's entreaty, Evans had responded that he would speak a few words on the subject "When We Were Very Young." The club had offered to pay his expenses, and Evans looked forward to renewing his Indianapolis acquaintances in person. It would be a welcome relief from the tension of producing volume two. However, whether from the excitement of the meeting itself, the pressure under which he had been laboring, or his own hesitation about speaking, Evans' speech was a failure. He managed to blurt out the first part and then forgot what he wanted to say. To his great embarrassment, he was forced to sit down without finishing his remarks. The effect of this failure upon Evans was so great that three months later he was still apologizing for it. Despite the advice of his friends to forget about it and just work hard memorizing anew for the next anniversary, the humiliation would not leave Evans' mind. He had always been noted for having a superb memory, and the failure to remember a speech gave him acute discomfort. That such should have happened before his Indianapolis peers bothered him considerably.

By midyear, despite the favorable scholarly response to volume two, financial success was by no means sure. That endorsement in the form of additional sales and quick payment for volume two was slow in arriving can be seen from the Evans balance sheet at the Union Trust Company. With volume two Evans had personally taken over the duty of collecting the money and forwarding it to Indianapolis. With the straitened circumstances at home, some of his early receipts were used to pay personal debts.[8] There was considerable difficulty also with several original subscribers who refused to continue purchase of the set and the normal difficulty with marginal accounts. Although Holliday had expressed the hope that they could clear up all accounts by midsummer, 1905, the process of collecting money dragged on through the fall and early winter. While he appreciated Evans' intense desire to go to press with volume three in the fall of 1905, Holliday stated that the executive committee of the Union Trust Company thought he ought to clear up all previous indebtedness before printing another book.[9] He was

---

[7] Meredith Nicholson to C. E., ALS, Dec. 7, 1904, TLS, Dec. 21, 1904, and ALS, Jan. 5, 1905; J. N. Hurty to C. E., TLS, Jan. 7, 1905.

[8] Charles Evans, "Ledger Book," I, 23–24. It is apparent that not all the receipts were going to Indianapolis.

[9] J. H. Holliday to C. E., TLS, Oct. 27, 1905.

still overdrawn in the amount of $240 in late October. There would be no trouble in arranging for the next volume provided Evans could push the collections and remit the amount due on volume two.

Sensing that the Indianapolis officers were adamant in their approach to the financial problem, Evans began to cast about for some way of raising the necessary $240. In desperation in early November, 1905, he approached Clement W. Andrews, Librarian of the John Crerar Library, for a personal loan.[10] When Andrews turned him down, Evans told his troubles to his friend William Stetson Merrill of the Newberry Library. Through additional payments for volume two Evans had been able to raise $140 by early December; then he could raise no more. Merrill was highly sympathetic to Evans' problem and a great admirer of his work. Through the Bibliographical Society of Chicago he had become acquainted with Dr. Frederic Ives Carpenter, a professor of history at the University of Chicago and a man of independent means. Merrill related Evans' plight to Carpenter and asked for his help. It seemed a shame that such an important work had to wait when only $100 would get it under way again.

Carpenter's response was prompt and favorable. Not only was he interested in Evans' work; he would advance the needed $100 and also subscribe for one set of the entire work. Evans could give him a personal note for the $100, without interest, to run for as long as five years if necessary. Needless to add, Evans was extremely grateful for Carpenter's loan. By January 8, 1906, he had forwarded the money to Union Trust Company and closed out the accounts for volume two. After a further wait of about two weeks to check with the guarantors, Harris and Porter, Holliday forwarded to Evans the contract for volume three. Time was pressing. Although he had promised volume three in the fall, 1905, there was some satisfaction that at last the obstacles had been removed and printing could get under way with a new publication date set for 1906.

By mid-January Evans had already drawn up a contract with the Blakely Printing Company and printing of volume three was begun soon thereafter. Already behind his original schedule, Evans pushed

---

[10] C. W. Andrews to C. E., ALS, Nov. 2, 1905; typed copies of W. S. Merrill to F. I. Carpenter, Dec. 15, 1905, and F. I. Carpenter to W. S. Merrill, Dec. 25, 1905. F. I. Carpenter to C. E., ALS, Dec. 30, 1905, enclosing check, and to Mr. Pratt [that is, Evans, his address was Pratt Avenue], ALS, Jan. 3, 1905 [should be 1906]. In his second letter Carpenter enclosed $45 to pay for his first three volumes of the *American Bibliography*.

the volume with all possible speed. Unhappily, during the printing there was difficulty with the Blakely Printing Company, which, according to Evans, had spent six weeks unnecessarily on the last eleven pages.[11] Despite these troubles Evans had the volumes in the mail by late May, 1906. This time the accounts were more promptly paid, and by mid-November he had cleared his debts with the Union Trust Company. At last the bibliography seemed on the road to financial as well as bibliographical success.

The dedication of volume three enabled Evans to pay his respects to the memory of William Frederick Poole, whose work on the *Index to Periodical Literature* and as administrator of so many libraries had inspired "his pupil and friend, the author." The period of coverage was smaller—thirteen years this time—from 1751 to 1764, with 3,276 entries. In his prefatory remarks Evans noted that the press had now been established in all thirteen original states, and he recapitulated in chronological order their record. Among other useful facts he recounted the number and place of newspapers published up to 1764, noted the presence of a matriarchy among colonial printers, summarized the literary record of the colonies and the influence of the colleges in that development, and, most interesting of all to historically minded librarians, he gave dates of the ten libraries which had issued catalogs up to that time. Evans was still writing good history, giving a record of some of the major problems in the various colonies and their chief cities. His prefaces so impressed two individuals that one asked to be put down for anything in the historical vein that Evans wrote, while later, another asked him to give the bibliographical world two other books: a short history of printing in America to the middle of the nineteenth century and a brief manual of bibliography.[12]

After the initial copies of volume three had gone to the subscribers and payment had been received from most of the major American libraries, Evans again strapped his corset boxes together and headed East for the research libraries. Shortly after publication

---

[11] Charles Evans to Blakely Printing Co., ALS, June 2, 1906. This letter was answered and returned on June 12, 1906; Charles Evans, "Ledger Book," I, 35.

[12] William Abbatt to C. E., ALS, Nov. 24, 1904; G. F. Winchester to C. E., ALS, Oct. 16, 1910. The latter's recommendations stemmed both from his appreciation for Evans' prefaces and a comment Evans made in the preface to volume five where he noted that there was a total absence of information on "exact description for the various forms used in issues from the printing press." He then proceeded to describe the five forms. *American Bibliography*, V, xiv–xv.

of his first volume, he had been chided by W. P. Cutter, Chief of
the Order Division at the Library of Congress, for his failure to
examine the materials in that institution.[13] In working his way
down the East Coast from Boston on his first research trip he had
run out of both time and money at Philadelphia. Now he was determined to see the materials in Washington before publishing another volume. Thus, late in July or early in August, 1906, he
boarded the train for Washington. This time he planned to reverse his itinerary and proceed northward up the coast since he
was especially desirous of visiting the Essex Institute in Salem. Such,
however, was not to be the case. When Evans got to the Library
of Congress, he found so much material that working twelve hours
a day for almost two months was insufficient to do justice to the
collections. Cutter's statement that the "largest library in the United
States, which contains an enormous collection of Americana, has
been ignored" was true. Evans quickly became the first to enter
the Library of Congress in the morning and the last to leave at
night. Descriptive of his daily efforts is a paragraph from a letter
to his wife: "I am usually the first reader to appear but leave about
quarter of ten so the assistants can get away in time. I haven't
found it necessary to take lunch but work steadily the twelve hours!
Then I usually take the electric car and ride to Georgetown—they
go swiftly and the ride is a good long one. Then back the same way,
and pick up a meal somewhere, and go to bed. My breakfast is my
one hearty, good meal every day. I seem to thrive on this plan. I
am in the best of health." [14]

Despite his disclaimer at first that he did not find much of which
he did not already have a record, Evans soon found a substantial
number of new titles. In late August he wrote to Lena that he had
examined all the almanacs and would soon finish his task of going
through 35,000 to 40,000 pamphlets. Beyond that he wanted to examine their old newspapers and check through the broadsides and
rare books. Almost weekly he underestimated the length of time it
would take him to finish examination of the Library of Congress
materials. He was so excited about the broadsides that he told
Lena it would have been a great blunder to go to press without
them and at one point confessed to an embarrassment over the
quantity of material. Moreover, W. C. Ford, Head of the Manu-

---

[13] W. P. Cutter to C. E., TLS, Nov. 11, 1904.
[14] C. E. to L. E., ALS, Aug. 18, 1906.

script Department, had made a list of the broadsides held by the New York Historical Society and placed that list at his disposal. Ford's generosity would probably make a trip to New York unnecessary. By early September he wrote that he believed that he had almost written another volume since he had been at the Library of Congress. In another two weeks, on September 23, after an exhausting but satisfying period of work in Washington, he left for Annapolis, where he spent two days. From there he moved on to Baltimore for a stay of four days, and finally to Philadelphia. Despite the fact that Evans always disliked Philadelphia, he had good reason to be pleased with his week's stay this time. Added to the materials from the Library of Congress, those from the Historical Society of Pennsylvania and the Library Company of Philadelphia rendered a trip to New York virtually useless, though he still wished that he could have gone on to Salem. Still it had been a "successful summer, and for every dollar I have spent, the value of my work in extent and accuracy has increased twenty fold at least." [15]

At home the usual business chores had piled up. Additional orders for the bibliography had arrived and money from the foreign libraries had been pouring in. It was fortunate for Evans that volume three seemed to be a financial success. He had made the trip East on faith, and, incidentally, on the Union Trust Company's money, for he had not informed Holliday of his trip. Lena forwarded all correspondence East, and Evans returned it to Chicago for mailing, since he wanted his bankers to think that he was home rather than "spending money in travel which should be applied to paying their account." [16] However, this time there was no real strain. By mid-November Evans had paid the Union Trust Company and even had a little surplus. The prospects for volume four seemed very bright.

Optimism over the prospects for a marginal operation like the *American Bibliography* can often be short-lived. In late November, 1906, Evans began his inquiries about prices for volume four, which he hoped to begin printing in December. Not only had Evans been at work garnering new titles and correcting his original data on his research trip, but he had also been able to get most of the material in good form for publication. Since the financial prospects seemed brighter than they had ever been, he wanted volume four to

---

[15] C. E. to L. E., ALS, Oct. 2, 1906.
[16] C. E. to L. E., ALS, Sept. 1, 1906.

go to press immediately. In late November, Evans wrote to the Blakely Printing Company requesting a contract for volume four similar to that for volume three. He evidently expected the price to be about the same. However, there had been some changes at the company, and the new manager wrote Evans that there would probably be an increase in the quotation because of an increase in the cost of labor.[17] The possibility of a rise in his costs outraged him. He was already operating on a shoestring; additional costs would probably absorb all the profit. In a lengthy letter to the manager he complained of the increase in costs over those of the last two volumes. Could not the manager see how good a business proposition the *American Bibliography* was for his company? Despite Evans' letter, the new manager was not content to let the matter rest on the basis of the old contract. He had the records looked up and was astonished to find that the company had actually lost money on both the second and third volumes of the work, even though the charges to Evans had been higher. The new manager of Blakely Printing Company was not the first to complain about doing business with Evans. The Chicago Paper Company in January, 1906, had complained that they had tied up money in paper stock for a year while they waited for Evans to publish volume three. However, the paper company was not inclined to charge additional costs since they had originally offered to hold the paper until he was ready to go to press. The story of the printing company was different. It was not a matter of tying up capital but one of actual loss. They refused to print volume four at a loss to themselves, and the manager suggested that if Evans remained obdurate, they would wish him well in the choice of another printing firm.

Again Evans lost precious time as he sought a cheaper method of producing his volumes. Finally, the only solution which appeared to him was one which he had originally suggested to Holliday, but which Harris had turned down at the time.[18] He would buy the

---

[17] E. F. Hamm to C. E., TLS, Dec. 1, 1906, plus MS drafts of Evans' reply on Dec. 3, 1906; E. F. Hamm to C. E., TLS, Dec. 7, 12, and 17, 1906. Both Charles Blakely and J. T. Oswald, with whom Evans had previously dealt, withdrew from the old firm to establish the firm of the Blakely-Oswald Printing Company in early December, 1906. J. T. Oswald to C. E., ALS, Dec. 4, 1906.

[18] J. H. Holliday to C. E., TLS, Nov. 7, 1902. "He [Mr. Harris] does not look with favor on your idea of buying type and supervising the printing yourself." For Evans' proposal see MS draft of a letter to Holliday in the Union Trust Company correspondence file, 1907, Evans Papers. This draft was probably written in January, 1907. There is no question that Evans pursued this method

types from the Blakely Printing Company, hire his own compositors for the make-up, rent space from the printing company, and let the company do the actual press work. By this method he hoped to save several hundred dollars on the cost.

At length Holliday approved the agreement and on March 20, 1907, the formal agreement for volume four was signed. With the printing of this volume came a new departure for Evans, one to which adjustment could not be made easily. First of all, Evans lost valuable time since he had to become familiar with the printing company and select his men for the work. The production of volume four occupied all the spring, summer, and much of the early fall of 1907. Not all of Evans' problems in getting this book printed can be discerned from his correspondence; probably he did not have time for much letter writing. However, his manuscript was apparently not so complete as he had thought, for there are several letters in early spring, 1907, providing him with answers to queries on specific titles covered in this group. In spite of the difficulty encountered in getting under way, Evans' optimism reasserted itself in late June when he wrote a New York book dealer that he hoped the volume would be ready in July. Troubles apparently accumulated and this date soon faded as the printers failed to meet the deadline.

Volume four finally went to the subscribers in early October, 1907. The volume covered the years 1765–73, the stormy pre-Revolutionary years, a period of pamphleteering by such firebrands as James Otis and Samuel Adams, Stephen Hopkins and John Dickinson; it contained exactly 3,200 entries. Evans continued his practice of sketching the colonial history for these years and highlighting it with the significant publications in the various areas of cultural, political, social, and religious life. It was the longest preface Evans wrote, comprising sixteen pages, and he wrote it with great feeling for the spirit of the times. His dedication honored the memory of his guardian Samuel Eliot, "scholar, educator, philanthropist," a man whose life was in the best tradition of his New England forebears.

The same chorus of approval which had greeted the previous volumes was showered upon the new one. By now, too, Evans had be-

for volume four. See Charles Evans, "Ledger Book," II, 240, 270. C. K. Shipton, in his preface to *The American Bibliography of Charles Evans*, XIII, v–vi, states that Evans began this practice with volume six, a reasonable assumption from the documents with which he worked. That the practice began with volume four is indisputable from the evidence in the Evans Papers.

come accustomed to the bibliographical queries which inevitably followed the production of one of the volumes. He was rapidly becoming a one-man reference bureau. The list of bibliographers with whom he corresponded climbed steadily as his work grew in reputation and influence.[19] By this time also Evans was receiving help from a number of bibliographers such as William Beer of New Orleans, for early Louisiana imprints; Franklin B. Dexter on the Yale theses; and George P. Winship of the John Carter Brown Library for the many imprints in that institution. The latter institution, especially, was a consistent source of support during these early years. Soon his help from the institution with the greatest amount of material for the period he was covering would be given in much greater degree when C. S. Brigham should go to the American Antiquarian Society as librarian. The very fact of Evans' work brought him offers from many people who were working in smaller areas such as early printing in Newburyport and Northampton, Massachusetts. With each offer of help, which Evans gratefully accepted, his work increased in usefulness and accuracy.

As soon as volume four was shipped to the subscribers and Evans had received a substantial number of payments, he made plans for another research trip. As in 1906, he proposed to go first to Washington and then up the coast to New York. Leaving Chicago by train, he arrived in the nation's capital on January 23, 1908, a cold and dreary day which was rendered further depressing by the social necessity of staying at an expensive hotel. George T. Porter had by this time moved to Washington, and Evans felt that he must have a proper address from which to call upon him. The unnecessary expense so upset him that he could not get any work done. For the first week he also spent part of his time visiting with the Porters and his niece Elise Lofton, who was attending the Martha Washington Seminary. Porter insisted on taking Evans to the capitol for a visit with Vice-President Fairbanks, an old Indianapolis acquaintance, and while he was there, he chatted with Edward Everett Hale, Senator Burrows of Michigan, and Congressman O. W. Gillespie, an old schoolmate of Lena's from Texas. After a few days of this unusual routine, Evans decided to risk the social stigma and move back to his old room in the Metropolitan Hotel.[20] Almost immedi-

---

[19] Among the correspondents who normally acknowledged each new volume were George Watson Cole, Sir William Osler, W. C. Ford, Albert Matthews, Wilberforce Eames, and George Parker Winship.

[20] C. E. to L. E., ALS, Jan 24, 26, 27, 30, and Feb. 8, 1908.

ately his attitude changed, and he settled down to his pleasant recluse ways, except for two succeeding Sundays when he had dinner with the Porters. Again he found more to do than he could possibly accomplish at the Library of Congress. The staff had been pleasant, one of them embarrassingly so, "as I prefer to do my digging in my own way." After almost three weeks of work, he left for Philadelphia, taking with him some 800 to 900 titles, fairly good work considering the social breaks in his normal routine.

If Evans could have avoided Philadelphia altogether, he would have been pleased, but that was impossible. Even the visits to Independence Hall and his use of James Logan's desk on which to work could not mitigate Evans' intense dislike for the city.[21] Yet Evans would endure anything for the progress of his bibliography, even the Ridgway Branch of the Library Company of Philadelphia with its mausoleumlike atmosphere. With a sigh of pity Evans noted that the place was largely a storehouse of rare and unused books and that no one had occupied the librarian's room since the death of his old friend Lloyd P. Smith. After nine days of fairly profitable copying, all at the Library Company, Evans left for New York.

Renewing his acquaintance with the Lenox Library was certainly a pleasure for Evans. Eames, the Lenox bibliographer, afforded him every convenience. Since the New York bibliographer often stayed late at his own work, he allowed Evans the privilege of staying to continue his. Nothing could have pleased the Chicago bibliographer more. To his wife he reported, "As we neither of us speak a word while we are alone together you can see it is quite chummy." [22] After their late hours of work, Evans would accompany Eames on a long brisk walk to the place where the latter caught the car for Brooklyn. Then Evans would proceed to some other area of the city to watch the night life before retiring. Each day he discovered more material and finally decided to take notes on everything in the Lenox printed up to 1800. To enrich his writing he visited some parts of the city where the people of the period had lived and worked. Despite the tall buildings in Wall Street, he imagined the scene as it must have been in the eighteenth century.

Toward the end of his six weeks in New York, Evans wearied of his work, especially since he was uncertain of the means for getting

---

[21] C. E. to L. E., ALS, Feb. 10, 14, and 16, 1908.
[22] C. E. to L. E., ALS, Feb. 23, 1908.

volume five to press after his return to Chicago. He still owed the Union Trust Company almost $600 for volume four, and the European accounts were slow in coming in. Despite his weariness he thought that he should go to Boston as long as he was this close, and Winship had been to the Lenox and urged him also to come to Providence before his return. Winship's entreaty was strong but time was running out, and the train schedule was not to Evans' liking. After spending a day in New Haven at Yale, he proceeded to Boston. Ten days there gave him excellent material from the Athenaeum, Massachusetts State Archives, Harvard, and the Essex Institute at Salem; but the loneliness of the city only increased his desire to return home. Evans thought there was no place quite so lonely as a large city. This might have been mitigated by pleasant visits with friends, but he felt that he had to forego the ordinary social rounds in order to get his work done. Even a trip out to Brockton to see his brother failed to lift his spirits. When a weekend with a Monday holiday following came along to interrupt his work, the thought of two days of enforced idleness was too much. On April 19, 1908, Charles Evans headed for Chicago to see if he could not find some means of getting volume five to press.

Financial uncertainty appears in the chronicle of Evans' life with almost monotonous regularity. By June, 1908, he was again casting about for some ready cash to clear up his indebtedness to the Union Trust Company so that he could get on with volume five.[23] Always hopeful that someone would eventually recognize the value of the work he was doing and provide some financial assistance, Evans was disappointed again and again. Support for individual researchers not attached to a library, university, or other like institution was virtually nonexistent. If Evans could have received a grant of as much as $1,000 for each volume, many of his financial anxieties and recurring domestic crises could have been avoided. However, the day of large "team" projects with thousands of dollars of support had not yet arrived.

Another possibility for funds appeared in late summer. As soon as he read of the death of A. R. Spofford, Chief Assistant Librarian of Congress, Charles Evans wrote to all of his friends who could bring political pressure to bear on the situation to secure his ap-

---

[23] A letter to F. I. Carpenter, whose timely help had enabled Evans to go to press with volume three, received a cordial but firm "no." F. I. Carpenter to C. E., ALS, June 15, 1908.

pointment as Spofford's successor.[24] Several of his friends responded to Evans' call, and even G. P. Winship wrote a rather perfunctory letter in Evans' behalf. Perhaps because he was on better terms with Evans than some others or perhaps because he was the dean of American bibliographers and could say what he pleased, Eames declined to endorse Evans' candidacy and told him why.[25] He understood that the position was created solely for Spofford and would cease with his death. Moreover, he did not think that Herbert Putnam, Librarian of Congress, wanted any more bibliographers around, especially since there was already a chief of the division of bibliography in the Library of Congress. Closing his letter, Eames expressed high regard for Evans' work as a bibliographer but absolutely refused to recommend him for the position.

Evans would have done well not to enter the lists, but he seemingly never learned his lesson. Even at sixty-seven when the librarianship of the Chicago Public Library was open, he tried to secure that position. As he grew older, Evans' lack of contacts with the outside library world seemed to make him more unrealistic than ever. In 1922 Evans privately approached Dr. Charles L. Nichols, a member of the committee of management of the John Carter Brown Library, to ask if he thought that age might be a barrier in becoming a candidate for the vacant librarianship there.[26] While there might have been more reason to hope for this position than the public library one, Nichols assured Evans that the committee felt the age limit was a necessary part of the candidate's qualifications. He tried to let Evans down gently, however. Evans had written to show that many librarians had made their greatest contribution after the age of seventy. Nichols admitted the truth of this but said, "What is the use? . . . Do you know what I want to live for? My friend—to grasp your hand—the day you write finis in the last volume of your work." Evans' efforts to obtain such positions were pathetic. One can only be amazed at his dogged persistence after he had been away from library administration for twenty-one years.

Disappointed as he must have been at his lack of success on the

[24] C. E. to G. P. Winship, ALS, Aug. 17, 1908, J. C. B. Archives. A. C. Harris to C. E., TLS, Aug. 14, 17, 19, and Sept. 23, 1908; G. P. Winship to C. E., TLS, Aug. 20, 1908; O. W. Gillespie to C. E., TLS, Aug. 28, Sept. 2, 1908; C. W. Fairbanks to C. E., Aug. 31, 1908.

[25] Wilberforce Eames to C. E., ALS, Aug. 26, 1908.

[26] Charles L. Nichols to C. E., ALS, Feb. 9, 1922; MS draft of C. E. to C. L. Nichols, ALS, Feb. 12, 1922; C. L. Nichols to C. E., ALS, Feb. 16, 1922.

Library of Congress matter, Evans had no time to grieve; he wanted to get volume five to press as soon as he could. He continued to work on his titles and requested information from several libraries. Despite his large overdraft on the previous volume he approached Holliday in early October about providing the money for the new one. The latter wanted to be sure that Harris and Porter understood the deficit situation before any new agreement was reached.[27] The purchase of type for volume four, delay in producing the volume, and the research trip had all taken their toll of Evans' finances. With the promises of Evans that he thought he could probably pull out of the hole with the publication of volume five, Harris and Porter cheerfully agreed to support his efforts once again. This time Evans changed from the Blakely Printing Company to the Hollister Press of the Manz Engraving Company. Contracts with the suppliers were signed in early December, and printing began soon thereafter. This management of his own printing was a worrisome business, and Evans had continual difficulties with the apprentice printers supplied by the Manz Engraving Company. Too, at one point in the production he became ill and his wife had to supervise the work. Both were constantly in trouble with the superintendent, trying as they were to get the volume out as quickly as possible. After it was completed, Evans had further difficulties with the company about the settlement of the bill. Late in the summer of 1909, Manz was as fed up with Evans as he was with them, and they agreed to accept his figures. Despite the unhappy experience Evans saved almost $400 on the cost of the volume.[28] Disagreeable as the procedure was, it offered some hope of keeping the bibliography going in the face of rising printing costs.

Volume five, covering the years 1774–78, appeared in early May, 1909. It contained somewhat fewer entries than the other volumes, but it was about the same length. Evans dedicated it "In Memoriam" to six distinguished collectors of Americana: Thomas Prince, Isaiah Thomas, Benjamin Franklin, John Carter Brown, George Brinley, and James Lenox. Again he wrote a historical preface, this to be his last, for the amount of time it took to compose these sketches was beginning to be a real problem. The era covered was a political

---

[27] J. H. Holliday to C. E., TLS, Oct. 19, 24, Nov. 12, and Dec. 1, 1908.
[28] See various MS drafts of C. E. to the Manz Engraving Company, May 10, 23, and 28, 1909, and Manz Engraving Company to C. E., TLS, May 17, 1909; W. C. Hollister to C. E., TLS, May 26, June 8, July 6, 9, 14, and 27, 1908, in Union Trust Company file. Also Charles Evans, "Ledger Book," II, 240, 245.

period, the time of the Declaration of Independence, the Boston Tea Party, and a variety of revolutionary battles. All of the turmoil of this period was reflected in the printing, which tended largely to political discourses, legislative acts, congresses, and addresses. Of all this and the part that the printers played in the events, Evans wrote as a good partisan of the American cause.

The remainder of the year 1909 Evans spent in bookkeeping for volume five, in preparing volume six for the press, and, for comic relief, in criticizing the Library of Congress, a favorite pastime of librarians and bibliographers then and now. Upset by the fact that the Library of Congress had made no attempt to issue a printed general catalog since 1864, Evans wrote to President Taft on November 21, 1909, and vented his spleen against the "present incumbent" who had neglected such an important matter.[29] Charles Evans never hesitated to write to the highest political figure for a hearing, if he felt strongly about a matter. The Evans Papers bear bulky testimony to his fondness for writing political officials about some policy with which he disagreed or suggesting his friends for political appointments. The President turned the letter over to Putnam, who pointed out that the Library of Congress was publishing a catalog of its holdings, two copies of which were available to Mr. Evans in Chicago. The only difference was that the current catalog was on cards instead of in a book, and Putnam did not hesitate to point out the wisdom of the card form. Accordingly, the President sent a reply to Evans with a copy of Putnam's memorandum attached. Evans was enraged and wrote another letter to the President pointing out the weaknesses in Putnam's arguments; but here the matter rested, an amusing interlude to the publication of bibliography.

In early March, 1910, Holliday gave the go-ahead signal for volume six, although there was still a deficit of $317.59.[30] In view of the fact that Evans was continuing to carry over the costs of previous volumes to each new one, the willingness of his Indianapolis friends to continue the old agreement is the more remarkable. While the sum of money may not seem large by present standards, it was considerable for that period. Later returns, however, justified their confidence; on volume six Evans was able to pay all overdrafts and clear completely his past indebtedness to the Union Trust Company.

[29] MS draft of Evans to the President and a copy of Herbert Putnam to the President, Nov. 26, 1909.
[30] Charles W. McBride to C. E., TLS, March 11, 1910.

Although Evans had set the pattern for future publication of his bibliography when he bought the types of the Blakely Printing Company in 1907, he had not been pleased with the quarters and service of either that press or the Hollister Press of the Manz Engraving Company. For volume six he began looking around for a press more suitable for his purposes. He finally settled upon the Columbia Printing Company, a small firm on the near north side. Evans' relationship with this firm must have been uniformly agreeable, for he used its facilities for the next seven volumes. Yet no one-man operation can be wholly satisfactory; there is just too much work to do. To show why he could not provide proof sheets for the American Antiquarian Society to check, Evans rendered his own account of his basic pattern with the Columbia Printing Company in a letter to Brigham in late March, 1910: "The difficulties in the way of financing my work have compelled me to purchase my own type and paper, employ my own (5) printers, do my own management, and be my own proof-reader. The press-work is under contract, and admits of no delay. Every hour is at my own expense after work has once been begun." [31] Only Evans' devotion to his self-appointed task kept him at this schedule. As if superintending the work were not enough, once the text was done, Evans had to make three indexes and send the volumes to the binder. When he had established the basic routine, Evans estimated that it took a minimum of four months to see a volume through the process. After that, he received the volumes at his home, wrapped each one separately, addressed it, and called the post office or express office to pick up the various bundles and ship them to his customers.[32] All of this work could obviously not be accomplished on an eight-hour day. The normal working day for Evans when he was seeing a volume through the press was eighteen hours, with absolutely no attention to personal or social engagements, even of the most pressing nature.[33] Letters, except for those providing information directly bearing upon the volume in press, went unanswered. Aside from the mental equip-

[31] C. E. to C. S. B., ALS, March 31, 1910, A. A. S. Archives. An excellent description of the pattern of Evans' work at the Columbia Printing Company is contained in John W. Bornhoeft, Jr., to Eliot Evans, typed copy, April 16, 1937, and Thomas B. Garrett to Eliot Evans, typed copy, April 27, 1937, A. A. S. Archives.

[32] Gertrude Evans Jones to the author, typed notes, Oct. 24, 1960. At first the boys had to carry the volumes to the post office but later the postmen agreed to pick the bundles up at Evans' home.

[33] C. E. to C. S. B., ALS, May 15, 1910, A. A. S. Archives.

ment necessary for such a mammoth project, Evans had to have a strong constitution. Only a rugged physical frame could stand such grueling pressure at the age of sixty.

Volume six came from the press in early May, 1910, and soon was on its way to the subscribers. The volume covered the years 1779–85, and with this volume the Evans entries almost reached the 20,000 mark. With a note of triumph Evans included on the title page the following quotation from Francis Bacon: "Before any thing is effected, we think it impossible; but when it is done, we stare— and wonder—why it was not done before. The mind then receives it with a degree of affinity, as if we had known it before." There were many who doubted that Charles Evans would ever reach six volumes, but now it had been achieved, and that at a high rate of scholarship. Evans' gloating had some point. Still he had underestimated his task, as should have been foreseen. The output of the American press increased at a rapid rate in the late eighteenth century, and each volume of the bibliography had to cover a smaller span of time in order not to grow beyond the 3,200 entries and 450 pages that were standard for volumes of the *American Bibliography*. He had reached the number of volumes he had originally estimated would be required for printing from 1639–1820 and had embraced only to the year 1785.

In the true spirit of his profession, Evans dedicated the volume "In Memoriam" to eight of his predecessors in the field of American bibliography: Samuel Foster Haven, Jr., James Hammond Trumbull, John Russell Bartlett, Henry Stevens, Joseph Sabin, Oswald Seidenstricker, Charles E. Hammett, Jr., and Charles Swift Riche Hildeburn. With its treatment of such momentous events as the end of the Revolutionary War, it was a volume well calculated to stand beside its predecessors on an Americana bookshelf.

The year 1910 was important for more than the appearance of volume six. Since the earliest days of active work on his compilation, Evans had from time to time received assistance from the American Antiquarian Society. At first he had asked the society to have the titles in Trumbull's manuscript addition to Haven's list of pre-Revolutionary imprints copied for him. For this task he paid a copyist at the rate of thirty cents per hour. Later, as already noted, he visited the society and examined its treasures himself. Then the correspondence began, with Evans both asking and answering bibliographical queries. However, the real assistance of the society to Evans' work began with the hiring of Clarence S. Brigham as librarian in October, 1907. By the time that Brigham had settled into his job, he was convinced that the society should move in the direction of collecting as many American imprints in the period before 1820 as it could.[34] This should be its major task, one made easier by the fact that the society already had a substantial body of material on which to build. In March, 1910, when Evans was seeing his volume six through the press, Brigham posed an important question for the Chicago bibliographer. He wanted to know if there were not some way that the society could help in making "this monumental work even more complete." [35] During the short period that he had been librarian the society had purchased nearly 4,000 American imprints dating before 1820, including a collection of Philadelphia imprints from 1785 to 1800 which the owner had intended to use in publishing a supplement to Hildeburn. Since Brigham's library planned to check the *American Bibliography* against its collection anyway, he thought it would be better if this could be done before publication rather than after, so that Evans could make his work more complete. His proposal was that Evans send the proof sheets for 1779–80; the staff would check them rapidly and return them immediately. To further this work, Brigham had already had the uncataloged pamphlets of the library arranged in chronological order up to 1820. To Brigham's query Evans responded immediately and favorably.[36] Added to Brigham's previous helpfulness in checking Providence imprints for Evans and loaning him his own lists, such a practical suggestion appealed strongly to the bibliographer-printer. However, proof sheets were out of the question because of his method of printing. As a counter suggestion he asked Brigham to send him a brief title list of imprints for the separate years. As quickly as possible, he would send back a list of lacunae for complete transcription of titles and collations and add the location symbol "A.A.S." to the entries in his manuscript. If Brigham could do this at once, Evans could catch the forms for the last half of the alphabet for 1779 and all of those for 1780. This procedure could be followed for all of volume six with decidedly more accuracy in the listings.

---

[34] C. S. Brigham, "Report of the Librarian," A. A. S. *Proceedings*, n.s., XX (Oct., 1909), 44. In his next report Brigham stated that random checking of three years of the *American Bibliography* revealed that the society owned about 39 per cent of the titles in that work. "Report of the Librarian," n.s., XX (Oct., 1910), 387.

[35] C. S. B. to C. E., TLS, March 25, 1910.

[36] C. E. to C. S. B., ALS, March 31, 1910, A. A. S. Archives.

Brigham's had not been the first practical suggestion, nor the first offer of help that Evans had received. Many had given him help through the mail and there had been much valuable assistance on his trips. However, this was the first offer to cover all the titles in a specific library. It was to be followed later by a similar proposal of Winship at the John Carter Brown Library, an offer Evans also accepted.[37] After the sixth volume was out of the way, in early September, 1910, Evans wrote to Brigham of his great appreciation for the encouraging words and the steady help that he had received. The letters of praise for Evans' work had been none too plentiful; and since Evans did not attend the usual meetings of the various bibliographical societies, he felt very keenly the lack of such encouragement. To Brigham he wrote: "You letters are very encouraging. When a man puts his heart into a work there is something in it more than the mere satisfaction of doing it. As I sometimes find myself wondering if it will only be posterity which will rise up and call me blessed, you will see that a little meed of praise now is appreciated by the worker." [38]

After answering some of Brigham's bibliographical queries, Evans then steered into another subject with some hesitation. If the opportunity ever arose, he would consider it an honor to be a member of the society. His work had been in line with the society's aims and their correspondence could then be carried on with greater freedom. In a manuscript addition to his reply, Brigham reported to Evans that he was personally very desirous of having such a prominent bibliographer among the membership, and he had already told the president of this.[39] Evans would probably have been elected at the society's meeting the preceding spring, except for the fact that the membership was limited to 175 and the new names had already been settled upon for the few vacancies. Rather fortuitously three members had died during the summer, and Evans' election to membership in October was virtually assured.

On October 20, 1910, George Parker Winship, Recording Secretary of the American Antiquarian Society, formally notified Evans of his election to membership. Such recognition was the first by a

---

[37] G. P. Winship to C. E., TLS, Jan. 7, June 13, July 16, and Aug. 11, 1913. C. E. to G. P. Winship, ALS, Jan. 9, 1913, J. C. B. Archives.

[38] C. E. to C. S. B., ALS, Sept. 4, 1910, A. A. S. Archives. See also MS draft, attached to A. C. Harris to C. E., TLS, Oct. 30, 1907, and C. E. to L. E., ALS, Jan. 24, 1908.

[39] C. S. B. to C. E., TLS and MS addition, Sept. 9, 1910.

learned body of the labors to which Evans had devoted some twenty years. Throughout the remainder of his life he regarded this honor as one of the two greatest tributes ever to be bestowed upon him.[40] Society membership and Evans' close association with Brigham were relationships of first importance, not only in terms of professional pride but also in the practical ways of improving the bibliography and getting it to press. From 1910 until his death, the amount of correspondence between the two was substantial. Added to the knowledge and resources at his command was Brigham's warmth of professional friendship and companionship such as he had not known since his early days in library work. Many times in the next two decades Evans would reciprocate by responding generously to the appeals of the society.[41]

Brigham wanted to send the titles for the next volume immediately since he was to be occupied during the winter moving the library into a new building. However, Evans wanted to hold him off because he was hoping to make another research trip soon after the first of the year; nevertheless, if it would help Brigham, he would undertake examination of the titles immediately. As matters turned out, Brigham did not send the titles for 1786–91 until late May, and problems at home kept Evans from beginning his trip early in 1911. This time he hoped to go South, a section whose libraries he had not yet covered, and he would work his way up the coast as spring advanced. Most of his time would be devoted to newspaper research which was "interesting, tiresome, and time-killing from the constant temptation it presents to stop and read." [42]

Evans was detained at home until mid-June and Brigham's lists were received just a few days before he left. He quickly checked the lists, and a comparison of the titles with his own manuscript gave him more positive than negative pleasure. As usual, he sent a list of incomplete titles for which he wanted more information. Then on June 13 he left Chicago, going directly to Savannah, Georgia, from where he proposed to work his way to Boston and Worcester in late July.

[40] The other was the Litt.D. degree conferred upon him by Brown University in 1934.

[41] In two society campaigns for funds Evans gave $100 for each, probably far more than he could afford at the time. "Report of the Treasurer," A. A. S. *Proceedings*, n.s., XXXIII (Oct., 1923), 252, and n.s., XXXVII (Oct., 1927), 191. Evans also frequently came to Brigham's aid in identifying titles, calling his attention to items for sale, and by occasional donations of books.

[42] C. E. to C. S. B., ALS, March 7, 1911, A. A. S. Archives.

Again Evans vastly underestimated the time necessary to visit so many libraries and copy their early American titles. As he had previously noted, the southern libraries were a virtually untapped treasure.[43] Spending only three days at the Georgia Historical Society, he then proceeded to Charleston, South Carolina, where he worked at the Charleston Society Library and the South Carolina Historical Society. He found more than he had anticipated in Charleston and was highly pleased with the helpfulness of the librarians. Although his first impression of the city itself was unfavorable, he soon yielded to its charm as he visited the old churches with the graves of Calhoun and Rutledge and saw the historic buildings dating from the eighteenth century. Despite the resources of the Charleston libraries, Evans felt that he must press on to Richmond. After a five-day visit during which time he received excellent help from the staff and learned about the problems of the Virginia State Library, he moved on to Washington and the Library of Congress. Dr. H. R. McIlwaine, Virginia State Librarian, had been impressed with Evans and later asked him to write something for the Richmond *Times-Dispatch* which would aid the state library in securing larger appropriations for its work.[44] This was a task which Evans undertook with relish, and he wrote a lengthy letter which the editor published with strong editorial endorsement. Evans' arguments did have an immediate effect, for after the appearance of his letter the governor wrote McIlwaine and asked him how much money the library would need from the next legislature.

The Library of Congress held Evans enslaved for nine weeks, instead of the three that he had originally intended.[45] The same pattern held throughout his entire trip. He was gone four months, and at each place he spent more time than he had planned. Since the next volume included the beginning of copyright entries, he had found the copyright division of the Library of Congress especially valuable. He allowed himself no social life inasmuch as that took time, and to him that was the same as money. While the Register of Copyrights was helpful, he found the rest of the staff practically uninterested in his work. The oppressive Washington heat and the indifference of the staff made Evans so testy that he poured out his

[43] *Ibid.*

[44] H. R. McIlwaine to C. E., TLS, July 18 and Aug. 3, 1911; newspaper clipping "Wanted—A City Library," Richmond *Times-Dispatch,* Aug. 3, 1911; C. E. to L. E., ALS, Aug. 5 and 12, 1911.

[45] C. E. to C. S. B., ALS, Nov. 13, 1911, A. A. S. Archives.

soul in bitterness to his wife. Later, in comparing the Library of Congress adversely to the New York Public, he wrote Lena that he had in mind taking up the shortcomings of Putnam upon his return home.[46] While Evans was not loath to take occasional pot shots at Putnam, his reaction to the library and the staff was far different from that of his previous experiences in Washington. One can only surmise that some changes in staff, the miserable Washington summer, and the long hard hours of work combined to make Evans judge the Library of Congress more harshly than it deserved. The money he had borrowed from the Union Trust Company was almost gone when he arrived in New York; he had just enough left for a week at the New York Public Library and the train ticket home.[47] His disappointment at having to forego visiting Worcester and meeting Brigham personally was keen, but his funds were so low that he even doubted that he could manage a week in New York. However, the profitable visits to the other places on his itinerary mitigated his sadness in missing Worcester. His corset boxes were bulging with perhaps enough material for three more volumes.

Upon returning home, he set about the laborious assimilation of the data collected on his trip into the manuscript for volume seven. This time finances did not stand in the way of immediate publication since he had made arrangements with Harris and Porter to sign the guarantee at the same time that he had borrowed the funds from the Union Trust Company for his eastern trip.[48] However, before he could get under way, Evans found it necessary to settle down to a revision of his manuscript. As he had noted to Brigham earlier, he no longer took the manuscript with him on his trips, both because of its bulk and also because of his fear of losing it.[49] Once during the early days his valise had ripped open; this near loss made him extremely careful after that. In August, with some apprehension, he had forwarded from 9,000 to 10,000 entries to Lena by mail because his notes were becoming too heavy to carry around. Naturally the research on his trips resulted in some duplication of effort he had already made at home, but Evans did not mind the extra work as long as he could make his volumes as

---

[46] C. E. to L. E., ALS, Sept. 9, 1911. See pp. 228–229, 232–233 for his reaction to the Library of Congress in 1906 and 1908.

[47] C. E. to L. E., ALS, Sept. 9, 1911.

[48] Charles S. McBride to C. E., TLS, April 21 and May 8, 1911.

[49] C. E. to C. S. B., ALS, April 15, 1911, A. A. S. Archives; C. E. to L. E., ALS, Aug. 26, 1911.

complete as possible. Frequently, he stated that he found almost as much pleasure in the negative results of checking as he did in the positive. In view of the voluminous notes he had made on his little cards, revising the manuscript after a research trip took considerable time. Because this period covered the origin of the national government, he was especially interested in being accurate about copyrighted material.

The winter of 1911–12 again found him in correspondence with Brigham on a number of problems, as he found the task of assimilating the great mass of notes taking more time than he had expected.[50] In early January, Holliday was pressing him for a date on which to begin publication, but, on the whole, he seemed satisfied with Evans' explanation for delay. As Brigham sent him additional data, though, the date for going to press receded. Also included in one shipment was a batch of undated pamphlets and in another some late eighteenth-century plays which Brigham had asked Evans to try to identify. All of this material excited Evans and he went to work with doubled fury, but it postponed the date of printing volume seven. Brigham kept up the shipment of packages of unidentified books and broadsides and lists of imprints throughout the late winter and early spring, 1912. As Evans received these items, he either identified them or hazarded a guess about their identity, noted the information on one of his cards, and shipped them back to Worcester. In later winter he expressed the hope, unfortunately to be thwarted, that he could complete volume seven in time to serve as a tribute to the American Antiquarian Society's centennial. In late May, Evans again expressed his gratitude to Brigham for his many courtesies when he accepted the latter's plan to send him all the books for the years 1792–96 rather than the titles.[51] This would enable Evans to examine each item personally and also look over the occasional book advertisements and other bibliographical information. The Chicago bibliographer was well aware of the importance of personal examination of an individual title, and the books of the society which Evans wanted to see went back and forth between Chicago and Worcester in a steady stream by express.

By the middle of June volume seven was at last ready for printing.

[50] C. E. to C. S. B., ALS, Nov. 13 and Dec. 5, 1911, Feb. 4, March 10, and May 26, 1912, A. A. S. Archives. J. H. Holliday to C. E., TLS, Jan. 16, 1912. C. S. B. to C. E., TLS, Jan. 2, March 9, and May 11, 1912.

[51] C. S. B. to C. E., TLS, May 11, 1912; C. E. to C. S. B., ALS, May 26, 1912, A. A. S. Archives.

This job, superintended by Evans personally and printed at the Columbia Printing Company, took all summer and fall. By mid-December, 1912, the new book was ready to be sent to the subscribers. In notifying Brigham of the birth of the new volume Evans sent him a copy of the proof of the dedication, which he hoped would be acceptable to the society.[52] It was one of his lengthy dedications, embodying as it did the "President, Vice-Presidents, Councillors, Officers and Members and to the Memory of their Predecessors and of the Founder of the AMERICAN ANTIQUARIAN SOCIETY of Worcester, Massachusetts, an institution whose collections are more nearly representative of the objects and purposes of this work than any other." The sincerity of Evans' recognition of the services rendered by the society is apparent from his well-chosen words. That he had had to forego the centennial celebration of the society had been an acute disappointment, but he partly made up for it by this dedication. As George Parker Winship wrote him from Providence, "The Dedication to Volume VII was very nice of you. It pleased the people at Worcester greatly." [53]

The dedication was not his only recognition of the society's helpfulness. In October he had presented the society with a set of the first six volumes of the *American Bibliography,* interleaved and specially bound, as a centennial gift. Brigham, in noting his delight with the gift, reminded Evans of the society's desire to help him with his life's work.[54] Since Brigham had been librarian, the society had acquired 7,565 American imprints published in the period before 1820, concentrating largely on the period yet to be covered by Evans.

Volume seven covered the years 1786–89, and, as Evans noted, "You can almost see the new Republic bursting forth into new life under its Constitution in it." [55] The birth of the new republic, the introduction of copyright, and the growing number of newspapers all made it a difficult volume to produce. He had worked through as many materials as he possibly could, but, as he told Brigham, "It is practically virgin literary soil we are delving in from now on." [56] The growth of governmental publishing would make

[52] C. E. to C. S. B., ALS, Dec. 8, 1912, A. A. S. Archives.
[53] G. P. Winship to C. E., TLS, Jan. 7, 1913.
[54] C. S. B. to C. E., TLS, Oct. 7, 1912.
[55] C. E. to C. S. B., ALS, Dec. 5, 1911.
[56] C. E. to C. S. B., ALS, Aug. 12, 1912, A. A. S. Archives.

the next volume equally difficult and almost as long a time would elapse before it appeared.

Even before Evans had put volume seven into the mail, he was laying the groundwork for its successor. Early in December, 1912, he wrote Brigham that he would be ready to take up the 1791 titles in the society's collections whenever it was convenient for him to send them.[57] He had already begun revision of his material for the next volume, and he expressed the hope that there would not be the long delay that there had been with the previous one.

In early January, Winship proposed sending Evans a brief check list of the John Carter Brown Library's collection of imprints for the period to be covered by volume eight.[58] The staff would send him not only a list of their holdings but also titles from the Brown University Library, the Rhode Island Historical Society, and the Providence Public Library. Where Evans' notes were incomplete they would supply the necessary data. Later in the year Winship was also to include photostats of broadsides which Evans did not know about. After checking these, Evans asked Winship to pass the photostats along to the American Antiquarian Society, since the next best thing to having the item itself was to have a photostat of it.[59] Between Brigham and Winship, Evans was kept supplied with titles throughout 1913 as he proceeded on his task of revising the manuscript of volume eight.

Late summer, 1913, is a difficult period of Evans' life to reconstruct. There is unmistakable evidence that he again went East to work in the large libraries, but the ones visited, the length of his visit, and the work accomplished are not discernible. The only letter of the period is written from Philadelphia, August 22, 1913.[60] Evans had been in the city for several days and had been working in the Library Company of Philadelphia. He mentioned to his wife that he also hoped while there to work in the Historical Society of Pennsylvania. In view of the material on which he was working for volume eight it seems probable that he went first to Washington to work on United States government publications and then to Philadelphia. It is apparent that neither Brigham nor Winship

---

[57] C. E. to C. S. B., ALS, Dec. 8, 1912.

[58] G. P. Winship to C. E., TLS, Jan. 7, June 13, July 16, and Aug. 11, 1913. C. E. to G. P. Winship, ALS, Jan. 9, July 1 and 24, 1913, J. C. B. Archives.

[59] C. E. to G. P. Winship, ALS, July 24, 1913, J. C. B. Archives.

[60] C. E. to L. E., ALS, Aug. 22, 1913; L. E. to C. E., ALS, Sept. 24, 1913.

knew about this trip, but Evans may have wanted to keep his journey to himself. If he had told them, they would have urged him to extend his trip north to Providence and Worcester, and he might have felt compelled to do so. As it was, he traveled as far as New York, for he was there in late September, 1913. Just what he accomplished during this late summer and early fall trip is not revealed in any of his correspondence, but a reasonable guess is that he worked largely on the early government publications.[61]

After his trip there occurs a long silence in his communication with his Providence and Worcester friends. Both Brigham and Winship worried about the reason for the silence and feared that he might be ill. Evans volunteered no information about his activities during the seven months when he did not write, except to say to Brigham that "other matters have so much engrossed my time that I have felt it would be better not to encroach on your time . . . until they were out of the way." [62] Surely out of common courtesy Evans owed Brigham more explanation than this. He had been holding the brief title list for 1791 imprints from the American Antiquarian Society for over half a year. Whatever it was that occupied Evans, he did not reveal it to his correspondents nor record it for his files.

In May, 1914, Evans again took up active work on volume eight and asked for titles from both Brigham and Winship. About mid-September he wrote J. H. Holliday that the manuscript was at last completed and ready for printing. Although the outbreak of war made Evans apprehensive about the financial success of this volume, he thought that there were enough American subscribers to pay the costs of production. Despite the loss of some European customers he wanted to keep on with his work as long as possible. He was still vigorous and unimpaired in both mental and physical faculties. Recalling that Dr. Osler, one of his subscribers, had expressed the idea that a man is useless above sixty years of age, Evans vigorously protested: "I think no man who has lived a cleanly life has reached

---

[61] There is no correspondence in the Evans Papers to indicate that other people knew about this trip, but the two letters in note 60 are incontrovertible. Evans' concern about scanning government publications for listing in volume eight is revealed in C. E. to G. P. Winship, ALS, Jan. 9, 1913, J. C. B. Archives. M. B. Stillwell to C. E., TLS, Aug. 21 and 26, 1913; C. S. B. to C. E., TLS, June 2, 1915.

[62] C. E. to C. S. B., ALS, May 23, 1914.

the full position of his power until he has reached the age of sixty at least. Then, only, is the mind a well ordered and disciplined machine, and capable of its best work." [63]

Although Holliday had thought that the bibliography was to be completed with volume seven, he was willing to enter the fray again as soon as he could secure consent of Harris and Porter. He had not the slightest doubt of Evans' ability to combat successfully Dr. Osler's theory. Fortunately there had been no increase in the cost of printing since the previous volume, and the charge for binding was slightly lower, but the scale of wages for composition was higher than ever. Nonetheless, the guarantee was signed and Evans advertised for a "COMPOSITOR-MAKEUP AND STONE man combined, for fine bookwork," in early October. By mid-November he had the printers hard at work.

Volume eight, covering the years 1790–92, came from the printers in mid-April, 1915. Because of the war and the financial uncertainty, Evans sent a printed circular to his subscribers notifying them that a new book was ready for delivery. To his foreign agents he wrote personal letters asking about the risk of shipment and the likelihood of payment. While he felt the same satisfaction of achievement as he did after publication of other volumes, Evans fully expected this one to be a financial failure.[64]

In return for the many courtesies he had received from the hand of George Parker Winship, Evans had decided to dedicate volume eight to the founders and committee of management of the John Carter Brown Library, "who have so admirably shown how private wealth intelligently directed and administered can aid the higher scholarship of the country." [65] The tribute came at a propitious time, for Winship was to leave the John Carter Brown Library that summer for a new position at Harvard and his departure would bring to a temporary end a long and profitable association. Winship, who had been one of the early skeptics, had become one of Evans' strongest supporters. While he still had reservations about

---

[63] C. E. to J. H. Holliday, MS draft, probably Sept. 15, 1914.

[64] C. E. to C. S. B., ALS, Jan. 15, 1915, A. A. S. Archives. Otto Harrassowitz to C. E., TLS, May 14, 1915; Henry J. Brown to C. E., TLS, May 25, 1915. *A. B. Circular*, 1914. This circular gives facsimile title page, dedication, and specimen page of volume eight and contains a plea for libraries to continue to support the bibliography.

[65] C. E. to G. P. Winship, ALS, March 21, 1915, J. C. B. Archives.

the technique, he admired the efforts Evans was making for American bibliography, and the two had come to have a mutual respect for each other.[66]

By 1914, with the publication of volume eight, Evans had set the pattern for the rest of his work. While his method of gathering material for his bibliography sometimes varied, he normally did not collect titles beyond the next volume or two. His adoption of the chronological arrangement, with indexes in each volume, assured the completeness of each book as it came from the press. If circumstances forced the discontinuance of the bibliography, each unit would stand as an entity in itself. Thus he had consciously followed the practice of completing each volume as he came to it. On his first research trip in 1904 he collected for volumes two and three, in 1906 for volume four, in 1908 for volumes five and six, and in 1911 and 1913 for volumes seven and eight respectively. If unusual circumstances occurred, which might render a repeat visit to a library improbable, he might yield to the temptation to collect titles considerably ahead of his next volume or two. Because the New York Public Library had arranged its collection of early American imprints chronologically, Evans took the opportunity in 1908 to copy all of these titles down to 1800. During the interruption which would be occasioned by World War I, he worked on volumes nine and ten, but did little on any titles beyond these volumes. Even in later years when he did not make his research trips East, he still worked on each unit by itself. For the as yet uncovered period, 1801–20, only a handful of titles remained at the time of his death.[67]

Under these circumstances it was inevitable that Evans would miss some titles for future volumes and also continually discover items that he had not included in his previously published work. He recognized these limitations, and an interleaved master copy of the *American Bibliography* testified to his intention to publish a final volume, including all titles he had missed along the way plus

[66] W. N. C. Carlton, review of *The John Carter Brown Library; A History,* by George P. Winship in Bibliographical Society of America *Proceedings and Papers,* VIII (1914), 137: "Mr. Winship considers Charles Evans' . . . *American Bibliography* as the most satisfactory of all bibliographical works from the point of view of the John Carter Brown Library." For another comment see Charles Henry Lincoln's appreciative review of volume six, Bibliographical Society of America *Bulletin,* II (July–Oct., 1910), 40–41.

[67] Interview with Clifford K. Shipton, May 12, 1958. For a description of Evans' year-by-year method of gathering titles see C. S. B. to Waldo Leland, carbon copy of TL, Dec. 5, 1930, A. A. S. Archives.

a master index to the set.[68] However, Evans was less concerned with earlier omissions and titles far in the future than he was with the current volume. Completeness depended upon his visiting the major collections or receiving brief title lists from those libraries before he sent each unit to press.

While there were certain limitations in his program, there were also advantages. The later volumes show a decided improvement over some of the earlier ones. As his techniques improved and as experience with earlier units demonstrated the need for improvement, Evans did change some practices, such as "shifting from personal to institutional entries for some kinds of materials." [69] Working with the actual books instead of depending upon other bibliographers gave his work greater accuracy. In the thirteen years since the publication announcing the monumental work Evans had become thoroughly immersed in his subject. Because of World War I and subsequent inflation, eleven more years would elapse before the publication of another volume. What had Evans achieved after eight volumes? Had it been worth the sacrifice, the endless struggle, the financial deprivation? How had he succeeded at his task?

Unquestionably Evans' work was a pioneering venture for his day. More than one contemporary called his work "trail-blazing" through a trackless mass of American printed books. From a reception which had been at best lukewarm and at worst highly skeptical, the contemporaries of Evans came to have respect for the man and his efforts. It would have been difficult not to appreciate such a conscientious attempt under such unpromising circumstances. As the other bibliographers took note of his work, they began to help him with information in the same manner as Winship and Brigham. Bibliographers of smaller scope also gave their help. This aid further helped Evans improve on his work as he went along. Too, there were the research trips, with their undoubted value of seeing each title that the bibliographer attempted to describe. While his techniques did not have the refinement of present-day bibliographers, he normally did not miss the important publications. That he was occasionally careless about such things as commas, periods, and use of brackets can perhaps be forgiven. There are more serious

[68] C. E. to C. S. B., ALS, March 31, 1910, A. A. S. Archives.
[69] C. K. Shipton, Preface to Roger Pattrell Bristol, *The American Bibliography of Charles Evans* (Worcester: American Antiquarian Society, 1959), XIV, p. iii.

errors, occasioned by his bibliographical imagination, but these are faults he shared with earlier practitioners, and they may well be less widespread than some have thought.

Despite these criticisms, Charles Evans was by 1915 one of America's leading bibliographers, and his work had received considerable renown. As volume was added to volume during the thirteen-year period, reviews in such respectable journals as *The Nation* and the Bibliographical Society of America *Bulletin* spoke highly of his endeavors.[70] Encouraging words came in the form of letters from some of the distinguished librarians, who not only praised his work but sometimes asked advice on bibliographical matters. Evans was still subject to occasional criticism by his peers—such men as Eames, Winship, and even Brigham; but younger bibliographers offered their criticism of Evans' work with great caution.[71] It mattered little that the sense of satisfaction which must have come to Charles Evans was tempered by financial failure and lack of contact with the outside world. He had set out to prove to the world the genuine worth of Charles Evans; by 1915 he had succeeded.

---

[70] Charles Henry Lincoln, Review of *American Bibliography*, VI, by Charles Evans, Bibliographical Society of America *Bulletin*, II (July–Oct., 1910), 40–41; "News for Bibliophiles," *The Nation*, LXXXIX (July 8, 1909), 31–32.

[71] Interview with L. C. Wroth, Providence, May 19, 1958, "It was not a pleasant experience to disagree with the leading American bibliographer [about 1726 date for Maryland imprints] but later Eames, Paltsits, and others agreed with me." See also L. C. Wroth to C. E., ALS, Nov. 24, 1919, Jan. 14, and Feb. 11, 1920, with MS drafts of Evans' replies.

Overlooking the Promised Land

12

The summer and fall of 1915 were filled with the usual clerical chores which came with the publication of another volume of the bibliography. Despite Evans' fears, the early receipts were promising, although, as he had anticipated, he lost a number of the foreign accounts. By late October he had reduced his Union Trust Company debt to $346.07, and early in the following year he was able to close out his Indianapolis account.[1] An adequate rate of exchange on English money was further encouragement, but the elimination of his customers in central Europe so affected his finances that continuation of the bibliography seemed impossible. There were just not enough American subscribers to pay the cost of printing, even at the old publishing cost, and the war inevitably brought a further rise in production costs.

In an attempt to produce some incidental income for his family Evans introduced to the library world in November the "Succedaneum Pamphlet Binder," a cardboard box 6½ inches long, 9¼ inches high, and ⅝ inch wide.[2] Its purpose, as stated by the inventor, was "for temporarily binding pamphlets, catalogues, or

---

[1] Charles Evans, "Ledger Book," II, 257–259; Union Trust Company, Indianapolis, "Statement," Feb. 1, 1916.

[2] A sample of this binder is in the Evans Papers. For detailed correspondence on the patent and some of the responses from libraries see the folder "Letters Patent for Pamphlet Binder and Correspondence Pertaining Thereto," Evans Papers. The United States Patent Office registered the Succedaneum Pamphlet Binder as number 110,344 on May 16, 1916.

printed matter of like nature" so that this class of material could stand on the shelf alongside classified books. To assure the up-rightness of the pamphlet within the box, Evans provided a wire down the middle of the open side of the box over which the leaves of the pamphlet could be passed. There were many advantages to his binder, but Evans thought the chief ones were the care and pres-ervation of a type of material that librarians did not know how to handle. He initially had the boxes made to fit anything smaller than octavo pamphlets, but he was fully prepared to provide larger or smaller sizes, depending upon the demand.

Samples of the Succedaneum Pamphlet Binder and a printed form letter went to the large public and university libraries which were likely to have a considerable number of pamphlets. The prod-uct was designed to sell at thirty cents and Evans hoped for sizable trial orders. His hope was again doomed to disappointment. From many, including his friends, he received a polite "no," and those who expressed interest did so in a mild way. Most libraries had already made other arrangements for their pamphlets which they not only regarded as satisfactory but cheaper than purchase of the Succedaneum would have been. The sale of only a few copies and the negative response did not quiet Charles Evans. To some of the more prominent librarians he persisted in citing the advantages of the Succedaneum. W. C. Lane, Librarian of Harvard University, was favored with an additional Evans epistle which Evans thought answered Lane's objections fully. With the cold hauteur of a man sure of his position, Lane responded in words which concluded the matter decisively: "I thank you for sending me a copy of your letter to Mr. Burrage, which, it seems to me, says all that there is to be said in regard to your ingenious pamphlet binder, and says it well." [3] Thus ended another futile effort of Charles Evans.

One other event occurring in late 1915 and early 1916 is worth noting because it demonstrates several of Evans' bibliographical characteristics: his willingness to help others, his defensiveness about his own mode of operation, and his general appreciation for others working in the field of Americana. In early December, 1915, the Americana bookdealer, Charles F. Heartman, sent Evans proof sheets of his bibliography of the *New England Primer,* with a re-quest for Evans to check the proof and make such corrections as he found necessary. Specifically, Heartman wanted Evans to note

---

[3] W. C. Lane to C. E., TLS, Dec. 2, 1915, Harvard Archives.

the authority for primer titles in his *American Bibliography* with particular comments where he had examined a copy himself. Some of Heartman's friends had argued strongly that he ought to leave out copies of the primer which Evans had included in his *American Bibliography* but of which no copy could be located. They had finally compromised by agreeing that such primers would be included but would be set in smaller type.

Because Evans liked Heartman and appreciated his work, he checked the proof thoroughly and then wrote him a letter stating his general practice on including such titles.[4] Since Evans' practice of including titles from advertisements had come in for considerable criticism, he was quite sensitive about this. His letter to Heartman is therefore especially interesting because it gives Evans' defense of a practice with which both his contemporaries and later critics found fault.

My dear Mr. Heartman,

I am returning, herewith, the proofs of your Bibliography of the New-England Primer which you sent me for correction and additions. As you will see, both are numerous. I know of no other work whose various undated editions have been subject to so much misinformation, regarding dates of publication, as the New-England Primer. Editions have been credited to Printers years before they began to print. A common error ascribes to the surviving member of a Firm an edition thirty years before the Firm dissolved, and nearly fifteen years before the edition issued by the Firm appeared. In other instances the approximate dates ascribed range from five to twenty-five years before publication was really made. Very few are given dates later than their actual issue. Probably from the erroneous idea entertained that age, and not comparative rarity, governs values. In the verification of undated editions, in your list, from my notes, the changes made in many instances may appear to you so radically different from the dates generally given as not to be followed. If there are any such instances I would be glad to be quoted as expressing an opinion differing from that expressed in your work.

I note what you say in your letter regarding your friends' advice to indicate any editions appearing in my American Bibliography, as are not known to them, by smaller type. I have no objection to your doing this, even with its implication discrediting the authority of that work. And in this connection, desire to relate the following incident, and to give my general practice followed by me some years ago when I was prosecuting bibliographical researches in a well-known Eastern Library. A lady entered and, in my hearing, said to the Librarian that she had an old book which she would like to sell. He replied that it would be useless for him to examine it, as his Board had decided to make no further purchases of old

---

[4] C. F. Heartman to C. E., TLS, Dec. 9, 1915, with Evans' MS reply attached.

books—along the lines for which the Library was noted. As she passed me in going out I asked her to permit me to examine the book, and she handed it to me wrapped in a newspaper. I found it to be an entirely unknown edition of the New-England Primer, in good condition, and she waited while I copied its title and collation, as given in Volume VII, Number 19816, of my work. As I do not make a practice of indicating individual ownership, owing to the uncertainty, no initials of ownership follow the title, and your advisory friends—one of whom I have reason to believe is the Librarian to whom it was offered—have consigned it to the category of editions which should bear the uncertainty of small type. As for the others so indicated from my work, I have never admitted unknown editions into my work, upon my sole authority, unless they were based upon advertisements which stated the edition could be obtained from the Printer, in quantity,—by the hundred, dozen, or single—incontrovertible evidence then, as now, that the Printer had printed an edition at the time and place where the advertisement appeared. This is the case in editions which are known, and there is no reason why it does not hold good for editions of which no copy is now known to be extant. This has been, and will continue to be my practice in my American Bibliography.

If the time given to the verification of the dates of undated editions, will clear the present muddled situation for the benefit of the buyer, the seller, and the Catalogue Maker, I will consider it well spent.

Thanking you for your interesting monograph of Phillis Wheatley; and for copies of your numerous excellent Catalogues with which you have favored me, I am

Y——

I do this the more willingly because your series of valuable monographs on early Americana, and your numerous excellently prepared Catalogues are doing much towards placing the trade in old books upon the plane of scholarly erudition it should hold to the cultured few who make up the bookbuying world.

Even though the likelihood of going to press with volume nine appeared dim, Evans wanted to start the year 1916 in the right way. Early he made plans for another research trip East. Although publication might have to await a more favorable time, he could at least collect the data for his manuscript. Beginning in late February he first went to his old familiar haunt, the Library of Congress. This time he found the service more to his liking; perhaps both the weather and the staff were more agreeable in midwinter, although the draftiness of the "detestable" main reading room made him consider putting his hat on while he was working there.[5] Except for a Sunday lunch with the Porters and an hour following

---

[5] C. E. to L. E., ALS, Feb. 27 and March 18, 1916. While Evans complained about the Washington weather, summer or winter, he seems to have fared better in his relations with the staff in the winter. See chap. 11.

at the Corcoran Art Gallery, Evans limited his outside activities to the usual streetcar rides in the evening after his research for the day was completed. He did vary the routine in the library enough to read the Chicago newspapers, which were taking considerable notice of son Chick, who was in 1916 to become the first American golfer to win both the National Open and Amateur championships in the same year.

A month at the Library of Congress found him still hard at work on a new batch of items he had discovered in the music division. In the midst of his work he was faced with a decision he disliked making. Both of the older children, Gertrude and Eliot, were to be married in late April. Since this would interrupt his plans for continuing the trip and be a very expensive undertaking, he hoped he would not have to go home for the weddings. Lena, always sensitive to Charlie's devotion to his work, consented to carry out the duties in Papa's absence.[6]

From Washington, Evans went first to Wilmington, Delaware, and then to Philadelphia for work at the Historical Society of Pennsylvania, the Library Company, and the Free Library of Philadelphia. Arriving on Sunday, he spent the day sight-seeing, ending with a trip to Fairmount Park. As he noted to Lena, he had made it a rule always "to see the Books and the animals." [7] A week was spent in Philadelphia and then he moved on to New York, where, in addition to visiting his usual headquarters, he spent almost three weeks writing over 1,200 titles at Union Theological Seminary. At the end of this two-and-a-half-month trip, he had over 5,000 titles, most for future volumes, but he was satisfied that he had a good plan to take everything that came his way. Tired of the "everlasting grind," he headed for home on May 11.

In the summer and early fall, with Lena accompanying Chick while he was winning his way to golfing fame, Charles Evans remained quietly at home, reading his newspapers to keep up with the matches and working on his ninth volume.[8] In early October,

[6] C. E. to L. E., ALS, March 16, 1916, and ALS, April 30, 1916. Eliot Evans was married to Hortense Gowing of Wilmette, Ill., on April 25, 1916, and Gertrude Evans to Donald Jones of Colorado Springs, Colo., on April 29, 1916, Charles Evans, Jr., *Chick Evans' Golf Book*, p. 22.

[7] C. E. to L. E., ALS, March 27, 1916.

[8] While Charles Evans was interested in Chick's golfing fame, he confined his interest to reading the accounts in the newspapers. Except when Chick won the Western Golf Championship in 1909 at Flossmoor, Illinois, his father did not watch him play golf. Charles Evans, Jr., *Chick Evans' Golf Book*, p. 115.

he wrote Brigham that his revision of the material for volume nine was almost completed, but he needed the finishing touches of the American Antiquarian Society material. Whenever it was convenient, he would be happy to receive all of the 1793 and 1794 titles.

In December, Brigham sent the list of titles with the suggestion that Evans check the slips and let him know what imprints he had not seen. He would then follow their usual procedure and send a box of books to Chicago. Expressing again his unhappiness with Evans' failure to give library location for titles which came out flush with the margin, he urged his friend to mend his ways.

Evans responded to Brigham's plea favorably, noting that he already had changed his old ways in volume eight by indicating the possession of specific titles of every library he knew, irrespective of whether it required another line.[9] Since he had always personally felt the importance of doing this, he regretted that his practice had not always been uniform. Brigham should certainly have felt a sense of triumph in these words. Charles Evans rarely admitted the error of his ways, and he had not agreeably changed his methodology at the insistence of someone else since his apprenticeship under Poole.

The books were sent to Evans in January, and he was occupied until March checking the eighteenth-century book catalogs. It took days to compare their titles with his manuscript records.[10] In despair he noted the inadequacies of early catalogs whose publishers seemed to regard titles and sizes as the chief things in their descriptions of books. Not until Samuel Campbell, New York bookseller, issued his 1794 catalog were place and date regarded as essential in the identification of books, and even then few followed his example. Drawing a moral from Campbell's practice, Evans remarked that bibliography as a progressive science had come a long way, with the end not yet in sight. The privilege of personal examination had been a great favor, for it insured accuracy of description and enabled Evans to clear up many well-established errors.

In late March there occurred an accident which gave Evans ten days of great anxiety.[11] The carelessness of the Antiquarian So-

However, Lena Evans frequently accompanied him on golfing trips and was one of his most loyal supporters.

[9] C. E. to C. S. B., ALS, Jan. 2, 1917, A. A. S. Archives.

[10] C. E. to C. S. B., ALS, March 7, 1917, A. A. S. Archives.

[11] C. E. to C. S. B., MS draft, on verso of C. S. B. to C. E., TLS, March 17, 1917. C. S. B. to C. E., telegram, March 27, 1917, and TLS, March 27, 1917. C. E. to C. S. B., ALS, April 10, 1917, A. A. S. Archives.

ciety's janitor resulted in the temporary misplacement of seventeen broadsides which Brigham had sent to Chicago. Upon their return to Worcester the janitor had unpacked the express box from the bottom rather than the top and simply left the broadsides in the loose packing. Fortunately the box had been kept and the broadsides were found. Both Brigham and Evans had been upset by this near calamity, and the former promised personally to oversee both the packing and unpacking of books in the future.

Since Evans wanted to have volume ten ready for the press so that it could be printed immediately after volume nine, he asked for the society's 1795 imprints in April. Early in 1917 he had reported to Brigham that the manuscripts for both volume nine and volume ten were in an advanced state for publication, except for checking the society's titles. When they would be published was a matter of conjecture since World War I had played so much havoc with his plans. Hoping against hope that the war would soon end and printing prices come down, Evans kept up his work.

His correspondence was heavy as he questioned other American bibliographers on points in dispute and answered their queries. To lift his spirits there were still occasional sales of sets to new subscribers. This pattern of activity—consulting his slips, writing for more information, and giving bibliographical advice—continued throughout the rest of his life.

By 1918 librarians were again asking when the next volume would appear. In August, Evans attempted to gain the interest of some American libraries which had not yet subscribed to the bibliography in order to secure enough funds with which to undertake publication of volume nine. In personal tones he stressed the service the *American Bibliography* had rendered to libraries and appealed to the professional pride of the librarians. While a few subscribers were added to the rolls, Evans' plea was generally unsuccessful. Although he was anxious to go to press, he simply could not afford to do so unless he could replace his foreign subscribers. Answering his loyal customers, Evans estimated that he would lose several thousand dollars if he attempted to go to press on the basis of the present subscription list.[12] While he could name numerous libraries which were able to subscribe, he had found that it was the individual librarian who counted, and most of them turned a deaf ear.

In late October, 1919, Johnson Brigham, the Iowa State librarian,

---

[12] C. E. to John D. Parsons, MS draft, attached to John D. Parsons to C. E., TLS, March 19, 1919.

an initial skeptic who had turned believer, wrote Evans to ask if the work were likely to be continued. His letter brought an immediate response from Evans, who told him that both volumes nine and ten had been ready for the press for several years and enumerated the difficulties standing in his way. Noting that his own efforts among American libraries had been unsuccessful, he added a typical Evans afterthought: "Whether a clarion call from you would rouse the slumberers, and accomplish more than I have been able to do, I do not know, but I would like to see you try and raise the dead—or the devil." [13]

Not a man to lose time, Brigham wrote to the editor of *Public Libraries* about the suspension of the bibliography and urged American librarians to rally to the cause. He suspected that many librarians had been prejudiced against the work because of the "uncharitable utterance in print by another bibliographer—who could not have information in advance of the work." [14] Just who this uncharitable bibliographer was is uncertain. A search of the periodicals in which his criticisms might normally have appeared fails to produce his name. However, in August, 1919, George Parker Winship had reviewed the Acorn Club's *List of Official Publications of Connecticut, 1774–1788* in the Bibliographical Society of America *Papers*.[15] In the course of his review he commented on the question of what proportion of the total output of the early press survived. Comparing the Connecticut list to the standard work in the field, Evans' *American Bibliography,* Winship observed that Evans had listed sixty imprints out of the 105 issues of the official Connecticut publications for these years. Moreover, he thought that this ratio of recorded to unrecorded titles might well apply to the remainder of the 25,074 entries in Evans. While evaluating the total output of a press was a complicated business, Winship considered his own estimates to be well below the actual number printed. If this were the utterance which Brigham regarded as uncharitable, he missed the point of Winship's review. Winship was by no means taking away from the value of Evans' work; he was merely stating an opin-

[13] C. E. to Johnson Brigham, MS draft, attached to Johnson Brigham to C. E., TLS, Nov. 11, 1919.

[14] "Interesting Things in Print," *Public Libraries,* XXIV (Nov., 1919), 386. Brigham is the unidentified "state librarian of more than ordinary discernment in bibliographies."

[15] George Parker Winship, "Recorded Versus Lost Titles," Bibliographical Society of America *Papers,* XIII (Aug., 1919), 82–85.

ion held by many: that a bibliographer working in a smaller area would necessarily add to the work of a man whose scope was as comprehensive as that of Charles Evans.

While Johnson Brigham's clarion call may have cheered Evans, it produced no tangible results. An organized campaign to get the volumes to press had to wait another five years for the energetic efforts of another midwestern librarian, Theodore Wesley Koch.

In late 1919, Evans was upset by another event which also struck close to the heart of his work. A young bibliographer who was assistant librarian of the Enoch Pratt Free Library had been working on the origin of printing in colonial Maryland. In his research he had come across irrefutable evidence that there was a press in Maryland before the date given by Evans. With the deference due an older bibliographer, Lawrence C. Wroth had written Evans a letter about his discovery and offered to send him the manuscript of his early chapters for comment.[16] Early in 1920 these chapters found their way into the hands of a disapproving Evans. Although Wroth had been courteous and careful in his letters to Evans, the same cannot be said of Evans' response. Evans tried to maintain a calm and dispassionate front, but his old resentment at being crossed reasserted itself. With a bibliographical sword unworthy of his better efforts he slashed Wroth's manuscript to pieces. Words such as "far fetched," "disingenious," "untenable," and "special pleading" described Evans' evaluation of Wroth's work. While he hesitated to dishearten the younger bibliographer by adverse criticism, he was more convinced than ever that the first printing press in Maryland dated from William Parks in 1726.

Wroth was not a man to be discouraged by such words, although he wanted to have the approval of one of America's leading bibliographers. It was not easy to disagree with Evans, but Wroth was convinced that after an examination of all the evidence, the average bibliographer and historian would reject Evans' interpretation of the documents. Those documents showed clearly that the Maryland press was established at least as early as 1686 by William Nuthead. Two years later when Wroth's book, *A History of Printing in Colo-*

---

[16] L. C. Wroth to C. E., ALS, Nov. 24, 1919, Jan. 14, 1920, and Feb. 11, 1920; C. E. to L. C. Wroth, MS drafts of answer to Jan. 14, 1920. Interview with L. C. Wroth, May 19, 1958. Wroth stated that despite their disagreement they remained friends. The author suspects that this was due to Wroth's courteous treatment of Evans and not the reverse.

nial Maryland 1686–1776, was printed by the Typothetae of Baltimore, it was hailed by bibliographers as a masterful work.[17] Despite
Evans' dogmatic opposition to the book, the latter did not use so
much as a footnote to cast doubt upon Evans' own efforts, but rather
paid tribute to the good work the older bibliographer had done.[18]
Evans might well have emulated his example. Aside from this controversy, 1920 was a quiet year. Evans was stymied until some means
of publishing the subsequent volumes could be found. Lena was
helping Chick write his golf book in between sessions on the links of
the Engineers Club on Long Island, where he again won the United
States Amateur crown.

The years were hastening on for Charles Evans, and he was a
frustrated man. Yet in 1921, just as he turned seventy-one, an opportunity appeared which promised to fulfill the dream of a bibliographical lifetime.[19] Item number one in the first volume of the
American Bibliography was "The Oath of a Free-man," a "half sheet
of small paper" which Governor Winthrop had said was the first
thing printed on Stephen Daye's press at Cambridge in March,
1639/40. Despite the evidence that this small broadside had once
existed, no copy of it had been known for nearly 300 years. A
quarter of a century before, when Evans had been searching the
British Museum catalog of printed books, he had come across this
entry which intrigued him: "The Oath of a Freeman. B. L. [Lon-
don, 1645?] s. sh. 12° 11, 626. aa. (1,2.)." As he meditated upon the
identity of this title, he became convinced that this entry revealed
the number one item in Americana. The brackets indicated the
cataloger's doubt about the place and date, and the latter could
easily have mistaken "small bodied English," the type used also on
the *Bay Psalm Book,* for English black letter. Knowing that there
is "no greater joy than that which fills the lover of books when his
long search for a rare book is rewarded," Evans had determined
some day to go to the British Museum and see this broadside for
himself.

In the spring of 1921, his son and a number of other American
golfers decided to try their luck in the British Amateur and Open
tournaments. When Chick asked his parents if they would like to

[17] George Parker Winship, "The Literature of the History of Printing in
the United States," *The Library,* ser. 4, III (March, 1923), 288–303.
[18] L. C. Wroth, *A History of Printing in Colonial Maryland, 1686–1776,* p. 160.
[19] This story is told with deep feeling by Charles Evans in, "Oaths of Allegiance
in Colonial New England," A. A. S. *Proceedings,* n.s., XXXI (Oct., 1921), 377–438.

accompany him, they were delighted, although his father did not intend to waste his time on the golf links when he could visit London libraries. Soon after their arrival in the British Isles, Lena went with Chick to watch the golf matches, and Charlie headed for the British Museum. As he walked up the steps to the huge building, he hid his rising anxiety as he approached what he thought surely would be the end of his search for the "Oath of a Free-man." With an elaborate casualness designed to mislead the attendants, he put in his slips for several books including the one he really wanted to see. When the attendant returned with the report that the broadside was missing, Charles Evans spent an anxious day. Early the next morning, having determined to go to the highest authority, he hurried to the shop of the bookdealer Henry N. Stevens and sought his help. As Evans unfolded the story, Stevens became equally excited and took him immediately to the office of the Keeper of Printed Books, A. W. Pollard. While Pollard did not agree with Evans that the missing broadside was the "Oath of Allegiance," largely because of its black letter designation, he did promise to bend every effort to find it. As day followed day without revealing the hoped-for item, Evans' misery increased. His account of his last day in London, as he sought again that for which he had waited twenty-five years, mingles Evans' pathos and sense of humor.

On my last day in London, I went again with Mr. Stevens to call on Mr. Pollard about the matter, and told him that I had made my arrangements to fly from London to Paris on the morrow, and asked him if these old eyes of mine were never to behold the holy grail. "In black-letter?" he queried, touching the weak spot in my armor. "In duodecimo!" I countered, pointing to the rent in his own. And the third interview ended with his assurance that the search would go on until the missing broadside was found.

And there the matter rests, very much in the condition of the story of the cook who asked the skipper, "Is anything lost when you know where it is?" And to the skipper's gruff response, "Of course not," he pleasantly replied: "I am glad to know that our only iron soup kettle wasn't lost when it fell overboard into the Bay." [20]

Despite his failure to find the broadside, Evans found his trip abroad both stimulating and profitable. Having no time for Chick's golf, he spent his days perusing the American imprints in various London and Paris libraries and transcribing their titles on the same type of cards he used on American research trips. He also enjoyed

---

[20] *Ibid.*, p. 404. To the author's knowledge, this broadside has never been located.

his conversations with some of the bookdealers such as Henry N. Stevens and Henry John Brown, the latter of the firm B. F. Stevens and Brown which had since the beginning distributed most of the copies of the *American Bibliography* in the British Isles, France, Holland, Norway, and Italy. He was immensely pleased that Lord Northcliffe, a friend of his son and the publisher of the London *Times,* offered one of his houses for the Evanses' use while they were in England.

To make 1921 an even more successful year, in July, Waldo Lincoln, President of the American Antiquarian Society, asked Evans to furnish a paper for the October meeting.[21] Such a request, coming from the society, was a summons to duty, and Evans accepted the assignment gladly. Since he had just returned from his two months' visit to Europe, "The Freeman's Oath" was still very much on his mind. What an excellent opportunity to share his adventures with his fellow members! Perhaps by October the British Museum would have found the lost broadside and what an exciting story that would make! At least initially, he wrote Lincoln, he thought he would talk on New England oaths of allegiance.

His first thought proved to be his best, and he set to work on the oaths with the same thoroughness which characterized his other bibliographical efforts. In mid-October Charles Evans boarded the train for Worcester. Meeting him at the station was Clarence S. Brigham, who put Evans up at the Worcester Club and gave him a week of activity that recalled the warmth of that earlier Worcester visit. The following night Evans and nineteen other distinguished members were guests at a dinner at Brigham's home. The dinner was a huge success, and Evans wrote Lena that he had not known such agreeable company since his old days in Indianapolis. Everyone, from President Lincoln down, made much of Evans' presence. After such a long absence from social life, Evans was exhilarated, and his letters home revealed the glow that always came to him when his work was properly recognized and appreciated.[22]

The following day surpassed even the previous night's festivities. It was the first time Evans had ever attended a meeting of the society, and he was prepared to be awed and excited. The first paper to be

[21] Waldo Lincoln to C. E., TLS, July 12 and 18, 1921. C. E. to Waldo Lincoln, ALS, July 15, 1921, A. A. S. Archives.
[22] C. E. to L. E., ALS, Oct. 19, 1921.

read was a lengthy treatise on the Monhegan Island. Since the author could not be present, it was read for him, and Evans reported that "a sigh of relief came at the end." Next on the docket was a short paper on "The Making of the Republic of Vermont," by James B. Wilbur, a wealthy and well-liked member. Although the latter was pleasantly received, Evans reported that when his own turn came, he really woke the crowd up. He was in good voice and determined to make a favorable impression. With a theatrical performance which did justice to his Indianapolis Literary Club training, he held up his right hand to heaven while he read "The Oath of a Free-man" with as much force and expression as he could put into it. The crowd responded jovially and listened to his story for the search for the still missing oath with rapt attention. Such attention was highly flattering, and both after the meeting and later at the luncheon at President Lincoln's home, everyone had a pleasant word for Evans' paper. The members also encouraged him to continue publication of his bibliography even at the increase in the price. They thought it a tremendously valuable work which ought to go on. Evans was like a little boy surrounded by toys on Christmas morning; he enjoyed being lionized and the folks in Worcester obliged him in this.

While in the East, Charlie spent some time with his brother, visited the Farm and Trades School, and called upon other friends in the Boston area. Foremost in his mind was the opportunity to search through the publications of the American Antiquarian Society for his future volumes; but this task was interrupted by dinner with Dr. Charles L. Nichols and a weekend trip with Brigham to Manchester, Vermont, where they were the guests of James B. Wilbur. Brigham hoped to be able to persuade Wilbur to finance the future publications, and, although this plan failed, Wilbur did see to it that the University of Vermont and another friend or two subscribed for sets. Despite the social breaks Evans managed to get much work done at the society. Most of the time he put in a twelve-hour day on the old newspapers. His health was excellent with the club's scales showing his weight at 172, about right for his height. After a ten-day visit he left for Chicago with many pleasant memories of Worcester and some hope for a continuation of his work.

Although Brigham had not been successful in getting Wilbur to finance future volumes of the bibliography, he was successful in selling additional sets. By late November, Brigham had talked four individuals into buying sets. He had also suggested that Evans increase the price of the subsequent volumes. Although Evans was receptive to this idea, he hoped to hold the cost to $20, even though society members had assured him that $25 would not be too much. Perhaps long experience and disappointment in moving volumes at $15 made him especially skeptical about the success of his efforts if the price had to be almost doubled.

During the winter Evans was engaged in proofing the galley of his paper, which was to appear in the *Proceedings*. Because of the facsimiles he wanted to use and certain other problems the matter took longer than anyone had anticipated. There was much correspondence with the editor. Meanwhile, Brigham kept pushing him to get his manuscript of volume nine to the press, and in the summer of 1922 asked if $1,000 would make any difference in enabling him to get started.[23] How any librarian could object to the price change was more than Brigham could see. Everyone with whom he had talked at the October meeting thought it was "absurd" to charge such a small sum anyway. He certainly shared the general opinion that the subscribers would be repaid many times over in the value of the completed work. Yet despite his own financial depression, Evans was able to scrape together enough for a $100 check for the society's building fund in October. He could not let their appeal go unanswered.

Despite his own eagerness to get the next two volumes under way, Evans was beyond the point where he could be pressured into the printing grind without some assurance that his efforts would meet with success. While he was also accustomed to being disappointed, he was not willing to risk almost certain failure. Both Harris and Holliday had died, the former in September, 1916, the latter in October, 1921. Evans felt their loss very keenly, and their deaths ruled out the continuation of the old relationship with the Union Trust Company of Indianapolis. Clearly some method would have to be found whereby Evans could finance the new volumes or he simply could not undertake publication. Though he lived in hope and saved every penny he had received from the sets sold by Brigham and Wilbur, he needed at least an additional $3,000 before he could consider going to press.

In late 1923, Evans was approached by Theodore Wesley Koch,

---

[23] C. S. B. to C. E., TLS, June 2, 1922.

Librarian of Northwestern University, who was concerned about the interruption in the publication of the *American Bibliography*.[24] A prominent member of the American Library Association, Koch had been active in numerous phases of the association's war libraries project. He suggested to Evans that the American Library Association make a canvass of its members with the hope that they could sell enough remaining sets to provide a revolving fund for printing the other volumes. Evans was entirely receptive to Koch's proposal, and at the midwinter meeting of the association in 1924 a committee was appointed to cooperate with Evans in circularizing the nonsubscribing libraries. The energetic Koch was assisted by George B. Utley, Librarian of the Newberry Library, who wrote a letter suggesting that the completion of the *American Bibliography* should be a very important part of the celebration of the association's fiftieth anniversary celebration in 1926. The committee concentrated first upon the academic libraries and then proceeded to bring pressure upon the large public libraries. Evans had promised the committee that if they sold thirty sets at $120 per set, he would be able to go to press.

With great hope for a successful completion of the committee's drive, Charles Evans in July, 1924, asked Dr. Charles L. Nichols, an old Worcester acquaintance and a member of the committee of management of the John Carter Brown Library, to use his good offices to secure for Evans verbatim transcripts of title pages, collations, and sizes of certain 1793 and 1794 publications in that library.[25] In earlier days when Winship had been librarian, the library had sent Evans photostats of such titles, with collations on the back. If he could be favored with this same type of service again, he would be happy to provide location symbols "J. C. B." by each entry in his new volume.

Nichols was away for the summer, but upon his return in September he immediately took up the matter with Lawrence C. Wroth, who only the year before had become librarian of the John Carter Brown Library. Nichols was very anxious to help Evans, and Wroth lost no time in sending Evans the 1793 items, which brought a characteristic note of gratitude from Evans and an offer to pay for the

[24] T. W. Koch to C. E., TLS, Feb. 19, March 3, May 23, June 18, July 18, Aug. 13, 21, 25, and 27, Sept. 9, 11, and 12, 1924; typed copy of committee report dated Sept. 12, 1924; G. B. Utley, printed letter, May 6, 1924; G. B. Utley to C. E., TLS, May 12, 1924.
[25] C. E. to C. L. Nichols, ALS, July 22, 1924, J. C. B. Archives.

cost of the photostats. In noting how typical of Evans this letter was, Nichols wrote Wroth: "I hope he will live long enough to finish the work, for we have in this world more half than wholly completed treatises—of all kinds." [26] Photostats of the other titles Evans wanted began to arrive in Chicago in late September as Wroth kept his staff hard at work filling Evans' requests. With both the American Antiquarian Society and the John Carter Brown Library collaborating on the volume Evans was certain of its success.

By the late summer Evans had become sufficiently infected with the enthusiasm of the committee to lower his requirements to the sale of twenty-five sets, and by Thanksgiving, Koch wrote Evans that he was enclosing order number 23, only two away from the new goal. Follow-up letters should tell the story. If Evans would let him display a set of the first eight volumes at the midwinter meeting, 1925, he thought he might be able to complete the job. Further good tidings came from New York during the Christmas season, when R. R. Bowker wrote that he would personally guarantee the two subscriptions so that Evans could begin publication at once. With the sale of an additional three sets at midwinter, Evans was close to the original goal he had set for the committee. In late January, 1925, Evans wrote Brigham that "the fat is on the fire" and "the pot of volume 9 will boil so soon as the frozen stream at Mittineague will run free enough to manufacture the paper." [27] As if to assure Brigham that this program really would go through, he added, "My health is excellent." The following month he wrote Brigham that the costs of printing were mounting, and if the latter still felt inclined to make a personal loan of $1,000, it would be useful. While the $4,000 he now had in the bank would have been sufficient for the other volumes, the expense of publishing volume nine would be about $6,000. By late March when he was looking around for compositors to set up the matter, Evans thought that the price of the new volume would have to be $25 if he were to clear costs. Why Evans did not sell the twenty-six sets for $20 per volume to allow a little leeway on his expenses is a mystery. It is improbable that any of the new subscribers would have quibbled over an additional five dollars per volume, and Charles Evans could certainly have used the $1,000 cushion. However, when it came to

[26] C. L. Nichols to L. C. Wroth, ALS, Sept. 26, 1924, J. C. B. Archives.

[27] C. E. to C. S. B., ALS, Jan. 30, 1925, A. A. S. Archives. See also C. E. to C. S. B., ALS, Feb. 13, March 29, and May 1, 1925, A. A. S. Archives.

the *American Bibliography,* Evans was willing to go to any lengths to help people secure a set, and he never tried to make money on the sets left on hand, even when he might have done so.[28] One of his wealthy friends later told him it was "an unusual pleasure to buy something now days for less than it is worth. I wish you had made this at $30 at least. It is worth more." [29]

Evans might have been less reluctant to announce an increase in the price of his volumes if he had known in January what the prospects were in terms of cost. At the time of the report of the Evans committee from the American Library Association in May, 1925, the committee quoted Evans on increases in cost of publication as follows:

90 per cent increase in the price of paper
100 per cent increase in the cost of composition—this item, alone equaling the entire cost of volume eight
100 per cent increase in the cost of press work
60 per cent increase in cost of rent
80 per cent increase in cost of binding [30]

To come out at all Evans would be forced to increase the price of volume nine to $25 per volume. He hated to do it, but he saw no other way, since the price would have to be even higher if he made any profit on it.

All through the late spring, summer, and fall, Evans worked on the publication of volume nine. In spite of his checking and re-checking the manuscript there were still minor matters to be cleared up, the business correspondence of the American Library Association committee to be done, and the arduous work of keeping the printing under way. Not many men at the age of seventy-five would begin anew on a project which demanded so much energy and involved so much personal hardship, but Charles Evans always wore his years with a light heart. As the printing of the 491 pages was completed in early November, Evans prepared to celebrate his

[28] M. B. Jones argued strenuously with Evans that he ought to be permitted to pay $200 for volumes three to ten, plus $25 additional for volume eleven, but Evans did not want to accept this amount even when his sets were becoming scarce and he desperately needed the money. See M. B. Jones to C. E., TLS, Nov. 21, 26, and 28, 1930, and ALS, Dec. 4, 1930. There are many letters in the Evans Papers indicating that Evans allowed some librarians to spread their payments over two or three fiscal years when they could not finance his bibliography any other way.
[29] J. B. Wilbur to C. E., ALS, Jan. 16, 1926.
[30] Evans Bibliography Committee, typed draft of report, May, 1925.

seventy-fifth birthday. From the staff of the Indianapolis Public Library on November 13 came birthday congratulations. With a sparkle of humor he responded with the following telegram: "Heartily reciprocate your good wishes. Like Cato, I hope to learn Greek at eighty and read the New Testament in the original." [31] While he occasionally noticed that he could not get as much work done in one day as he once did, he approached old age with undiminished vigor.[32]

When Evans finally announced in early November, 1925, that the printing of volume nine was completed and the pages were at the binders, he also had a little surprise for Brigham. Sending along a proof sheet of the dedication, he told his loyal and generous friend, "If the 'Dedication' gives you as much pleasure in receiving it as I have in making it, I will be glad." [33] "To My friend and fellow-worker in the pleasant and fruitful fields of American Bibliography, CLARENCE SAUNDERS BRIGHAM, A.M., Librarian of the American Antiquarian Society of Worcester, Massachusetts, Whose comprehensive Bibliography of American Newspapers, 1690–1820, so worthily crowns one of the main purposes of the founder of the venerable and noble institution which he ably administers."

In early January, Evans sent the first copy to Brigham, who had been deeply moved at the dedication. Expressing particular pleasure in the tremendous increase in the number of titles over those from previous years, the fullness of the entry of the government publications, and the fine showing of the American Antiquarian Society for this period, Brigham heartily congratulated Evans. Volume nine covered only two years, 1793–94, and yet had over 3,000 entries, an indication of how rapidly the American press had expanded. In this section Evans also paid tribute to the work of Koch and his committee from the American Library Association and included a list of the subscribers added since the publication of volume eight. As Evans had previously noted, the book covered an area of publish-

---

[31] Both telegrams are given in the notes section, *Public Libraries*, XXX (Dec., 1925), 599.

[32] Evans' explanation of not getting as much done in a day as formerly was that he was "no longer content with the title-pages merely, and read too much of what is in the books themselves." C. E. to Mary Robinson Reynolds, ALS, June 30, 1914, A. A. S. Archives.

[33] C. E. to C. S. B., ALS, Nov. 13, 1925, A. A. S. Archives. C. S. B. to C. E., TLS, Nov. 23, 1925, and Jan. 12, 1926; C. L. Nichols to C. E., ALS, Nov. 21, 1925.

ing activity which had lain fallow and almost untouched. He had been especially careful to get all the titles because it was a period which had been covered only lightly by Sabin's *Dictionary of Books Relating to America.*[34]

Brigham received his copy long before the other subscribers. Because Evans had been forced to raise the price per volume to $25, he sent a circular in early January, 1926, advising his subscribers of this decision. It was a reasonable and logical explanation of the necessity for such a drastic increase in price. From the first the bibliography had not been a paying proposition, and on several occasions it had even failed to meet the cost of production. However, Evans had persevered, and by the time volume eight was issued he could publish the volumes with some financial safety. Detailing his troubles with the loss of European subscribers during the war and the rising costs of printing, he asked his subscribers to remember that the proportionate increase was no greater than that of the average duodecimo novel. With the efforts of the American Library Association committee, enough new subscribers had been secured to offset the loss of the European libraries. Despite their best efforts, however, the committee had raised only a little less than half the amount necessary to finance volume nine. Under these conditions Evans thought it necessary to inform all his customers of the rise in cost; but, if he did not receive notification to discontinue their subscription soon after receipt of his circular, he would take it that they wanted subsequent volumes and he would send volume nine automatically.

These were the reasoned arguments. In the last paragraph Evans appealed to the librarians' pride. It was a convincing argument for the importance of getting the future volumes to press: "From the year 1790 this work enters a period in the literary and political history of this country which has long lain fallow and almost untouched by the bibliographer. Its importance in the formation and growth of national and state governments nearly equals that of the better known and more stirring periods of our history, and the historian and research worker will find much to enlarge or modify, change or confirm opinions formed from an imperfect knowledge of existing sources of information, in this and succeeding volumes." [35]

The results were about what Evans had expected. Remittances

[34] C. E. to L. C. Wroth, ALS, Oct. 5, 1929, J. C. B. Archives.
[35] *A. B., Circular,* 1925.

were slow, but on the whole there had not been many declinations. He did not know what the situation would be with respect to the foreign subscribers but, as always, hoped for the best. Brigham was anxious to know how the replies came in on the rise in price, although he could not imagine how anyone could object. He asked Evans to let him know the names of any libraries which turned him down, since he regarded such judgment as the result of a very narrow mind. Generous to a degree which Evans appreciated but could not accept, Brigham also offered to continue the $1,000 note to the period following volume ten, if that would be helpful. Evans was touched by Brigham's desire to help, and even though he declined the offer, he was grateful for it. Somewhat plaintively Evans added: "It is the first time in the entire preparation and printing of the work that anyone has, voluntarily, offered me a dollar of assistance. Heretofore I have had to beg for the money to carry on." [36]

By early summer he had sufficiently recovered from the clerical and business duties to undertake work on volume ten. In early June, Brigham sent him the 1795–96 almanac titles and a few books which Evans had not seen. The other titles for this period had been sent in 1922. Evans worked on them during the summer and cleaned up his business affairs. However, before starting another volume through the press, he thought it desirable to spend several weeks among the Antiquarian Society's newspapers and to gather up some loose ends in New York and Washington. As one of the few surviving founders of the American Library Association, he was expected to be in Philadelphia in early October for the celebration of the association's fiftieth anniversary. As he grew older, he found himself increasingly uninterested in travel, but some proprieties should be observed.

In September he made his trip to Worcester and had another delightful visit. Proceeding down the coast, he stopped briefly in New York, spent only one day in Philadelphia, and several days in Wilmington and Washington.[37] Materials in the latter two cities more than justified his trip, and he returned home optimistic about the production of volume ten. While Evans did not mention the anniversary celebration of the American Library Association to Brigham, he did make his perfunctory appearance. That the large crowds and

---

[36] C. E. to C. S. B., ALS, March 2, 1926, A. A. S. Archives.
[37] C. E. to C. S. B., ALS, Nov. 10, 1926, A. A. S. Archives. "Editorial," *Library Journal*, LI (Oct. 15, 1926), 917.

the festivities were not sufficiently interesting to hold him is demonstrated by the use he made of his time in Philadelphia. Out of this twenty-four-hour visit, he also managed time for trips to the Library Company and the Historical Society of Pennsylvania, where he compared a few titles.

However, Evans had reason to be grateful to the association and its members for reviving his work. In the very beginning of the committee's work, Bowker had lent strong support from the *Library Journal*, and he kept the project before his readers through editorial reminiscences which included Charles Evans. Whenever Bowker mentioned Evans by name, there was always a note about his work on the bibliography.[38] Such publicity was certainly useful since it kept his subscribers, both actual and potential, informed of his progress.

Bowker had also been one of the first to announce a change in Evans' goal. When the committee approached Evans about continuing his work, he was more than willing to undertake his labors again, but he was much more realistic than he had ever been about the prospects for its completion. He had originally set 1820 as the completion date, since this year would bridge the unfinished gap in American bibliography. As the number of titles printed each year increased, it had become apparent that he would never reach that magic date. His erstwhile supporter and critic, George Parker Winship, had suggested in 1923 that since Evans had already passed the logical stopping point—1789, when the present form of government was instituted—he should have no difficulty attaining 1800. However, Winship doubted that Evans would ever go beyond the century mark: "There are some considerations which might justify a hope that he may decide to stop at 1800. . . . If he had a fresh lifetime ahead of him, the work still to be done could not be finished on the scale and scheme of his earlier volumes, until the inevitable progress in standards would have relegated it to the museum of outgrown reference books." [39]

Evans was as well aware of the limitations of the human body as was Winship. To the committee he had estimated that it would

---

[38] "Editorial," *Library Journal*, XLIX (Jan. 15, 1924), 84; LII (May 1, 1927), 479; LIV (Jan. 1, 1929), 28; LIV (March 1, 1929), 219; LIV (Dec. 15, 1929), 1029; and LVII (Feb. 1, 1932), 120. All of these editorials were probably written by R. R. Bowker.

[39] George Parker Winship, "The Literature of the History of Printing in the United States," p. 295.

take another five volumes to bring the bibliography down to 1801. After that period the output of the press was so large that it would be impracticable to continue down to 1820. Not that Evans enjoyed the prospect of reducing his original goal, but as he wrote L. C. Wroth a few years later, "With my octogenarian friends falling around me, it would seem that the best that I can hope to do, is to complete one hundred and sixty years of my American Bibliography with the thirteenth volume, and the year 1800—the same number of volumes as the number of the original States; the end of the eighteenth century; and the death of Washington!" [40]

The publicity in library periodicals resulted not only in renewed American interest but in foreign interest as well. During 1925–26, Evans continued to sell occasionally a set of the previous eight volumes, even after the committee completed its work and was no longer actively soliciting subscriptions. His foreign agents reentered the picture, with the Germans being particularly interested in both volumes eight and nine, since they had never received the former. Despite the increase in price for volume nine, Evans managed to hold most of his old subscribers. With the money accumulated from all these sources, the prospect for publishing volume ten was very bright. Upon his return from the research trip and the anniversary celebration, Evans settled down to revision of his manuscript for publication.

Midwinter, 1927, provided a pleasant interruption to the grind of work on volume ten. The occasion was the fiftieth anniversary celebration of the Indianapolis Literary Club, and the group invited Evans to deliver an address on his recollections of the period when he was active. Embarking for Indianapolis on January 10, he carried with him a steel engraving of Sir Joshua Reynold's picture of the original literary club which he intended to present as a fiftieth anniversary gift. Evans had acquired this item in London, and it had long hung on his library wall.

This time he was not overcome with the emotion of the occasion but delivered an interesting and informative paper which he entitled "Looking Backward." As the only surviving charter member, he spoke of the beginnings of the club, some of its notable meetings, and its distinguished roll of members. His speech was enlivened with good anecdotes and vivid word pictures of some of the prom-

---

[40] C. E. to L. C. Wroth, ALS, Jan. 17, 1932, J. C. B. Archives. See also C. E. to C. S. B., ALS, Oct. 29, 1931, A. A. S. Archives.

inent members of his day. Evans closed his speech with a stirring peroration on the club: "I believe that the absent are present with us here tonight in spirit on this fiftieth anniversary meeting, to wish you God-speed on the threshold of another fifty years of interesting and beneficial companionship. And as I was near to them in the past, and am, perhaps, nearest to them now, I venture to give you their greeting: Hail; all Hail! and Farewell!" [41] The club members were so impressed with the address that they not only had it printed in the Indianapolis *News,* but also ordered additional copies on good paper for all club members. Evans was more than pleased by the expressions of gratification from the members, and he sent a copy of his address to Brigham with the remark that it might provide an interesting line for his obituary. [42]

The following summer was a busy one for Evans. Daily he made round trips of eighteen miles to the Newberry Library to verify in their copy of the British Museum catalog and other authorities some 6,000 titles he had in his manuscript for 1795–96. In the late summer he made heavy requests on both Brigham and Wroth for photostats and books which he used during the fall and winter. The material grew so voluminous that he thought he might have to use separate volumes for each year. [43]

Early spring, 1928, found him with distractions at home. Some of the family had to have hospital treatment, some were treated at home, and all had the "flu" followed by "the Springs." [44] While Evans' own attack was light, the worry and confusion around the house was necessarily bad for the progress of the bibliography.

On September 18, 1928, another event of importance to the family occurred when Chick married Esther Underwood at the Lake Placid Club in New York. This time his father did not have to make a decision about attending the ceremonies and continued his work unabated in Chicago. In fact Charles Evans was so busy during the remainder of the year that a promised paper for the Colonial Society of Massachusetts, of which he had recently become a member, had to be passed by. After a tedious year of

[41] Charles Evans, "Fifty Years of Literary Club History Recalled by Founder," reprint from Indianapolis *News,* Jan. 15, 1927. The original of the address is not in the family papers. This is the same as Charles Evans, "Looking Backward."

[42] C. E. to C. S. B., ALS, April 3, 1927, A. A. S. Archives.

[43] C. E. to C. S. B., ALS, July 17 and Oct. 19, 1927, A. A. S. Archives.

[44] C. E. to C. S. B., ALS, May 21 and June 25, 1928, A. A. S. Archives. "The Springs" refers to Excelsior Springs, Missouri, where Lena and Gertrude went to recuperate.

work, in early February, 1929, the book was sent to the subscribers.

As Evans had correctly anticipated, he could not cover both 1795 and 1796 in one volume. Instead he covered all of 1795 and through the letter *M* for 1796. The 451 pages included 2,687 titles. In his list of printers at the end of the volume, Evans still gave the date for the institution of printing in Maryland as 1726, a foible for which Wroth politely but firmly chided him.[45]

In his previous dedications Evans had always honored great bibliographers, historians, librarians, and institutions. For some years his older son Eliot had, without success, urged him to dedicate a volume to Lena Evans. While Charlie appreciated the contributions Lena had made to his work, he had in mind dedicating volume ten to the memory of Josiah Quincy. There would be time enough for his wife in the next one. Eliot, however, was insistent and pressed his father to recognize the wife who had "accepted this way of life with a sympathy and interest which sustained his spirits and his enthusiasm for the work when all else seemed to conspire against it." [46]

Evans made no promises to his son, but Eliot's persistence paid off. Just before the volume was published, the old gentleman one day handed his son a proof sheet of the dedication to volume ten. It read, "To my dear wife, devoted mother of our children—author of the following verses—but for whom this work would not have been undertaken; without whose aid and encouragement it could not have been continued, this volume is dedicated." There followed an eight-stanza verse written by Lena, entitled "Her Olden Book."

Lena Evans' poem puzzled at least one reader and probably others.[47] Despite the high tribute she received at her husband's hand, the poem expressed her thoughts that the bibliography had taken her place in Evans' affection. His decision to publish the verse indicates that he did not understand its subtle meaning, although he later admitted to a reporter that Mrs. Evans suffered more from the seclusion which his work on the bibliography demanded than anyone else.[48]

---

[45] Evans gave this date in his index of printers and publishers which appeared at the end of each volume. L. C. Wroth to C. E., TLS, Feb. 14, 1929.

[46] Shipton, *The American Bibliography of Charles Evans*, XIII, v.

[47] R. R. Bowker to C. E., TLS, Feb. 9, 1929.

[48] Gifford Ernest, "Aged Bibliographer Wins High Honor for His Labors on Twelve-Volume Work," newspaper clipping, Chicago *Daily News*, Aug. 16, 1934, in Eliot Evans, "Scrapbook."

Evans rejoiced in the new publication; it gave him immense satisfaction to be back in the publishing business with such good prospects for realizing his dreams. Added to his own personal satisfaction were the plaudits of men like Brigham, Eames, and Wroth.[49] It was the devout hope of these men that Evans would have the strength to continue the other three volumes. With data already collected for the latter part of the alphabet, 1796, another manuscript should be sent to the printer within a year.

The early part of 1929 was also a good time financially.[50] His subscribers had been prompt and the coffers were filling again, forcing Evans to spend most of the spring and early summer with the routines of messenger boy, delivery boy, and bookkeeper. However, in his anxiety to get the press rolling again, he could not rest from his labors.

In late June he began checking the 1797 slips from the American Antiquarian Society against his own findings. During Brigham's absence in Europe, two assistants at the society, Dorothea E. Nourse and Mary R. Reynolds, bent their efforts to supply Evans' requests for defective titles. In late September, Evans wrote Wroth that he had hoped to go East for the summer, but his checking of the society's slips and other chores had kept him at home. Perhaps, although he did not admit it, Evans' disinclination to travel had also overcome him. Anyway, it was too late to embark on such a journey, and he asked Wroth to send him the John Carter Brown Library slips for 1797 plus any 1796 titles the library might have added.

With everything running so smoothly, Evans could not have anticipated the financial difficulties which lay just around the corner. The stock market crash on October 29 would have far reaching implications for the subscribers to the next two volumes of his bibliography of which Evans did not even dream. It was fortunate that he had published volume ten in the early part of the year and had had time to receive almost all the checks for that volume before the crash. Even the foreign accounts had been paid by midsummer. With this cash in reserve for the printing of volume eleven, Evans was not too concerned about the crash. He was still hard at work in

---

[49] Wilberforce Eames to C. E., ALS, Feb. 13, 1929; L. C. Wroth to C. E., TLS, Feb. 14, 1929; C. S. B. to C. E., TLS, Feb. 26, 1929.

[50] Charles Evans, "Ledger Books," I and II, *passim*. While Evans ceased keeping a complete account for each volume with his eighth volume in 1914, he continued to record the receipts and date of receipts for each subscriber under the number he had assigned to that subscriber.

October, November, and December, corresponding with Wroth about printed music books in the eighteenth century, with Waldo Lincoln about a tribute to Brigham at the annual meeting of the American Antiquarian Society, and with Brigham himself about matters bibliographical. To the latter he had written in early September that after twenty-five years of effort the *American Bibliography* was over-subscribed.[51] If he had not reduced the number of copies of volume two, he would still have had some sets, but he had had to turn down both a private subscriber and the Library of Congress for an additional set. To show his good will and especially his appreciation for the efforts of their staffs he sent both Wroth and Brigham money with which to purchase "such sweets as Worcester [Providence] is famous for" to lighten the toil of the day for them.[52]

In late March, 1930, Evans was again making daily trips to the Newberry to check his manuscript against the basic bibliographies before his final revision for the press. He hoped to begin printing in the spring. Typically, he had underestimated the length of time to get his manuscript ready, but in July he was awaiting only the shipment of paper from the mill to begin printing. He looked forward to six months of daily visits to the printing office. As he pressed forward with his work, he more frequently neglected his correspondence, and an apology from Eames for the same weakness made him ashamed. As he wrote Brigham, "To men with one-track minds, like Eames and myself, it requires some extra effort to leave the beaten track we are following and write letters." [53]

By August, Evans was hard at work again on his printing procedure. The work went slowly and financial difficulties increased; by November 20, it appeared that he could not continue. Since the body of the work was completed, he discharged the printers. Just as he ran out of money a friend of his son Eliot offered him a loan of $750 (of which Evans used $500) in three installments, and he promptly put his best printer back to work. So, in late November the two of them were going forward with the indexes, "always a slow and tedious work."

At this point Brigham again entered the picture with a sugges-

[51] C. E. to C. S. B., ALS, Sept. 1, 1929, A. A. S. Archives.

[52] C. E. to C. S. B., ALS, Dec. 17, 1929, A. A. S. Archives. C. E. to L. C. Wroth, ALS, Dec. 17, 1929, J. C. B. Archives. Evans blamed the lack of copies of volume two on a binder's error but the real reason was the tight money situation. See chap. 11.

[53] C. E. to C. S. B., ALS, July 3, 1930, A. A. S. Archives.

tion that the American Antiquarian Society apply to the American Council of Learned Societies for a grant of $1,000 to aid in the completion of the manuscript.[54] Because of the nature and value of Evans' work, he had not the slightest doubt that the grant would be made. Brigham himself was a delegate of the Antiquarian Society to the council and was well acquainted with Waldo G. Leland, the permanent secretary.

Evans did not know how to reply to Brigham. He was in desperate straits with most of volume eleven published but no money to complete the process. He had borrowed all the money that he could and still it seemed insufficient to finish the work. Heretofore he had always regarded grants from foundations with distaste. With respect to the Carnegie Foundation grant for the continuation of Sabin's *Dictionary,* he had earlier noted that such a "dole" was always a curse and never a blessing; "the American spirit does not take kindly to the idea of letting dead men do the real work of the world." [55] Although the prospect of being able to pull out on volume eleven was very alluring, Charles Evans emphasized that he was not now nor had he ever been an object of charity. However, he closed on a hopeful note and thanked Brigham for his suggestion.

Brigham assured Evans that there was not the slightest thought of charity in an American Council of Learned Societies' grant.[56] The sole purpose of the council was to recognize scholarship. He intended to apply for the grant immediately, and he thought it would be very well received. Brigham knew very well that Evans' hesitation could be overcome for the sake of the work he loved, and he answered all of the latter's objections in a very firm manner. In early December, with information supplied by Evans, Brigham made formal application for the $1,000 grant. His application was a splendid summary of the difficulties Evans had encountered in publishing his work and a strong endorsement of its value to American scholarship. He was forthright in asking not for a loan but for a grant in aid of publication.

In early February, 1931, R. W. G. Vail, who had become librarian of the American Antiquarian Society the previous October when Brigham moved up to the directorship, wrote Evans the welcome news that at its January 31 meeting the council had approved the

---

[54] C. S. B. to C. E., TLS, Nov. 18, 1930.

[55] C. E. to C. S. B., ALS, July 3 and Nov. 20, 1930, A. A. S. Archives.

[56] C. S. B. to C. E., TLS, Nov. 24, 1930; C. S. B. to Waldo G. Leland, typed carbon, Dec. 2 and 5, 1930, A. A. S. Archives.

grant unanimously.[57] The money would be available late in February through the society. Later in the month Brigham reported to Evans that the American Council of Learned Societies had sent out letters and queries to about a dozen scholars and every one of them heartily endorsed the *American Bibliography* and its value to American scholarship. This good news brought the old twinkle to Evans' eyes and in a humorous vein he wrote to Vail:

> Your letter certainly was a bearer of good tidings. For months I have been nursing along a five pounder—my eleventh offspring—into life upon a diet of hope. In its waking moments it continuously cried for its bottle, then filled with the long green-like spinach—now with the three-quarter length you find when you open a "Mellon." And now I propose, on the strength of your information, to give him such a meal that he will either "bust" or burst forth into a healthy, happy, crimson kid, like his brothers, and, like them, no kidding, filled with the wisdom of the ages.[58]

With the promise of new money in hand, Evans in a final burst of speed discharged the volumes from the hands of the binder on February 24. While the progress through the press had been painfully slow, Evans was satisfied with the results. Immediately he began sending the volume to his subscribers.

A long expressed wish to dedicate one of the books to the memory of Josiah Quincy, 1772–1864, "scholar, patriot, statesman" and the "Cato of New England," was satisfied with publication of number eleven. Was Evans wistful as he included on the dedicatory page a paragraph from Quincy's *History of Harvard University?* To Quincy the study of history saved the republic of letters from the sin of ingratitude. The individual was like a man in an ancient temple, passing down amid the statues of the distinguished. He should pause a moment in the presence of each "doing justice to the humble, illustrating the obscure, placing in a true light the modest, and noting rapidly the moral and intellectual traits which time has spared." Was Charles Evans thinking of himself, the lack of recognition he had known, and the critical comments leveled at him as he penned these words to his manuscript?

This section covered from the letter *N* in 1796 through 1797 and contained 2,429 entries. Brigham was delighted with the volume and stayed up half the night, not examining but reading it just as if it were a novel.[59] His cheering words lifted Evans' spirits: "I

---

[57] R. W. G. Vail to C. E., ALS, Feb. 5, 1931; C. S. B. to C. E., TLS, Feb. 13, 1931.
[58] C. E. to R. W. G. Vail, ALS, Feb. 9, 1931, A. A. S. Archives.
[59] C. S. B. to C. E., TLS, March 3, 1931. See also C. S. B. to C. E., TLS, Feb. 7, 1934.

have never seen a work produced in this country which so notably represents a one man achievement as this great Bibliography." And from California, George Watson Cole, a fellow bibliographer who had always expressed appreciation for each volume, wrote that he hoped to receive many more before Evans laid down his pen. Despite the depression the sales were pretty good, and Evans had fair hope for volume twelve. The $1,000 grant from the American Council of Learned Societies was used to pay the $500 loan from Eliot's friend, the balance of $457.28 due for binding, and the cost of containers, paper, twine, and other materials for shipping. That Brigham contemplated further assistance from the American Council of Learned Societies for the remaining two volumes Evans regarded as "a consumation devoutly to be wished."

Difficulties of quite another kind, however, lay ahead. In early June, Lena Evans fell and fractured her right hip, necessitating a four-month stay in the hospital. Although Evans' own health and energy were unimpaired, the household cares and worry over Lena's health distracted him from the task. Despite these problems he managed to check the society's 1798 imprints and some of the actual books during the summer. However, when Lena came home from the hospital on October 10, Charlie had to serve as nurse and housekeeper. This left him no opportunity for correspondence, even with Brigham, nor for examining the case of books which had arrived from the society.

By late October, 1931, Mrs. Evans was progressing satisfactorily. With the help of a mechanical brace she was able to move about slowly and to sit up for short periods. However, her progress promised to be slow, and Evans was in despair about finishing his work. While his collections from volume eleven had been good and promised well for the next volume, the expenses for Lena's hospitalization had made a large dent in his bank account. The depression also brought some cancellations, and the moratorium had played havoc with his foreign subscribers. All of this was disheartening, for Evans knew that the time for his work was short. He would unquestionably need financial help if volume twelve were ever to see the light of day. With the prospects so dim, the need would be even greater than the grant he had received for the previous volume. Even then volume twelve would probably not appear before late 1932. Relating all this to Brigham, Evans noted that he had not intended to make his letter a "hard luck" story, but he found the subject a natural one. With a characteristic Evans footnote he added: "Of course I shall put everything I have into the work before asking help from anyone." [60]

Research trips were now out of the question, even if Evans had wanted to make them. His wife was to remain practically bedridden during the remainder of her life. Fortunately for Evans' work, the Library of Congress, the New York Public Library, the New York Historical Society, and even smaller places such as the New Hampshire Historical Society, now supplied him with photostats or collations of title pages when he needed them. Where they had shelf lists of their early American printed books, they also sent him brief title lists. Coupled with the unmatched assistance from the American Antiquarian Society and the John Carter Brown Library, they served adequately in lieu of Evans' personal visits. Brigham himself was Evans' right hand, digging into government documents at the Boston Athenaeum and other libraries in the Boston area as well as offering him continual encouragement to proceed with his great work. In a time when Evans needed an encouraging word to keep him going, Brigham's letters spurred him on. Knowing how concerned Evans was about financial matters, he tried to allay these fears with optimistic notes about the prospective help from the American Council of Learned Societies.[61] If Evans needed the money, he did not see why he should have to wait until the actual printing to receive part of it. Brigham would send a check along if he would let him know. Surely without Brigham's exhortations Evans would not have continued his work.

Winter proved to be an especially difficult time for Charles and Lena. To economize on household expenditures Charlie had discharged all outside help upon Lena's return from the hospital. He was now doing all of the housework, nursing his wife, and bending over the little cards whenever he could. Frequently, however, the cards were completely neglected. He complained to one of his sons that he was living only to finish the other two volumes, but since he did not know where the printing money was coming from, he had not been able to work much lately. Occasionally Chick would drop by to find him staring dejectedly into space. Time was catching up with Charles Evans. He was worn out and had lost the desire to continue.

[60] C. E. to C. S. B., ALS, Oct. 29, 1931, A. A. S. Archives.

[61] C. S. B. to C. E., TLS, Oct. 9, 27, and Nov. 2, 1931; Jan. 25, Feb. 2, and April 5, 1932; and Feb. 13, 1933.

When Evans' spirits were lowest, Chick Evans wrote to Waldo G. Leland, explaining the situation. Although Brigham had already made plans to ask for a grant from the council at the annual meeting late in January, 1932, Chick's letter undoubtedly confirmed Brigham's judgment about the critical financial situation.[62] Upon receiving it, Leland asked Brigham if he thought they were really doing enough for Evans.[63] Charles Evans knew nothing of his son's letter; he would have been furious if he had, for he had never knowingly begged a dollar from any man and he did not intend to start at the age of eighty-one. However, Brigham was anxious about the matter of volumes twelve and thirteen. Despite his advanced age Charles Evans was the man to complete the work, and Brigham wanted to see it finished. At the last minute after reading the letter from Chick to Leland, Brigham changed the amount of the request to $3,000. In a very strong letter to Leland he pointed out how much more money another bibliographical project and a biographical project of the same relative merit were receiving.

On February 1, Vail wrote Evans that after an eloquent tribute to the *American Bibliography* by Waldo G. Leland, the council had approved the $3,000 grant. Leland followed with a personal letter communicating the decision and the following resolution which had been passed unanimously by the council: "*Voted,* to extend to Mr. Charles Evans the thanks of the American Council of Learned Societies for his distinguished and self-sacrificing services to American scholarship." [64] The remainder of Leland's letter spoke of the high praise which he had heard on every hand for the work Evans had rendered American scholarship. The vote of the council feebly expressed their gratitude for the monumental research tool developed by Evans.

This news was received at the house on Pratt Avenue with great rejoicing.[65] Immediately upon receipt of the letter, Evans took it upstairs to Lena's bedroom. They were so excited about the good news that they could scarcely contain themselves. Over and over they exclaimed about their good fortune. When Chick came over

---

[62] Charles Evans, Jr., to Waldo Leland, typed carbon, Jan. 13 and 21, 1932.

[63] Waldo Leland to C. S. B., TLS, Jan. 23, 1932, and C. S. B. to Waldo Leland, typed carbon, Jan. 25, 1932, A. A. S. Archives. Waldo Leland to Charles Evans, Jr., TLS, Feb. 8, 1932.

[64] Waldo Leland to C. E., typed copy, Feb. 2, 1932. Original not in Evans papers.

[65] Charles Evans, Jr., to Waldo Leland, typed carbon, Feb. 5 and March 9, 1932.

for a visit in the evening, his mother whispered the good news to him—Charlie did not want any of the children to know. However, Chick could tell that the old gentleman was pleased, and he now felt sure that work would go on. Before this event he had been frankly skeptical, for his father had been as low in despair as he had ever seen him.

Unfortunately, soon after the news of the grant reached him, Evans became seriously ill with the "flu." Although it was his first real illness in years, he was so weak that the attack lingered. Again there appeared dejection, particularly over the loss of time which should have been spent on the bibliography. "What can we do?" he would ask Chick sadly and then stare desperately out the window or at the floor. In the midst of his attack Lena also became ill with his infection, and it appeared that all was lost.

However, the boost from the council, which meant as much psychologically as financially, carried him through. By early March he was back in the swing of things, hard at work on his cards. He spurned Chick's offer of a stenographer to speed up the production. By early April he wrote Wroth that he had thrown off "all the evil influences of that depressing malady" and was ready to receive the titles from the John Carter Brown Library. Such optimism, though praiseworthy, was ill founded. At eighty-one the body does not recover so quickly. In July, Evans apologized to Wroth for his tardiness in returning the 1800 slips, excusing his shortcomings on the basis of the depression following his illness. In his anxiety to speed up checking the materials from the other places he neglected his old friend Brigham, who, thinking he might be ill again, wrote to Chick. Chick responded that his father had slowed down and was neglecting his correspondence, but he would see what he could do. At the moment Evans was having difficulty with the Library of Congress since they were not so prompt as the American Antiquarian Society in supplying his wants.[66]

Although he worked with all the vigor of which he was capable, Evans was simply not getting the work done. Government documents, a very thorny problem for that period, as for the present, gave him great difficulty. He knew that somewhere there must be a complete set of executive documents and reports, but he did not know where.[67] Clearing up other bibliographical problems also

---

[66] C. S. B. to Charles Evans, Jr., TLS, May 5, 1932, and Charles Evans, Jr., to C. S. B., typed carbon, May 10 and 13, 1932.

[67] C. E. to L. C. Wroth, ALS, July 26, 1932, J. C. B. Archives. Evans tried hard

bothered him, and he spent almost a year revising his manuscript of volume twelve.

In a telegram to Vail for the annual meeting of the American Council of Learned Societies in January, 1933, Evans stated that the manuscript was virtually completed except for a few odds and ends. As a tentative publication date, he gave July, 1933, but he warned that financial returns both at home and abroad looked hazardous. It had been a hard year for the Evanses, but he promised Brigham a long letter about the new volume at the earliest opportunity. By the middle of March he had ordered the paper and his little band of three printers was anxious to get underway. He was still winding up loose ends after printing began; in fact, his desire for accuracy was so great that he even revised as the compositors set up the type.

Further difficulties loomed when President Roosevelt ordered all banks closed on March 6, 1933. The bank holiday held up the first installment from the American Antiquarian Society, but on March 27 the society opened an account in another bank, and Evans received a check for $1,500. In May, Evans was able to report that everything was moving satisfactorily. By July, he found the summer a drain on his vitality as well as his finances and, accordingly, asked Brigham to send along the rest of the money from the grant. Response was immediate, and Brigham, having previously noted that he had not missed a world's fair since 1893, expressed the hope to visit Chicago and talk with Evans personally. Evans urged him to come, promising that Chick would show him all the sights of the city: "I am pushing him forward in the matter because I am so 'shaky on my pins' as to be nearly useless as a chaperon. At my home, ten miles from the exposition, I live the life of a near recluse, with an invalid wife, going nowhere, knowing no one and no one knowing me. Charles Jr. goes everywhere, knows everyone, and everyone knows him." [68]

Brigham responded to Evans' invitation and made the trip to Chicago either in late July or early August. The highlight of the visit came when Evans took him to the press where his printers were working on volume twelve.[69] They had a long talk about the bibliography, and Brigham heartily encouraged Evans to continue his

---

to make sense out of the documents, but the press of publication and his physical location in Chicago never enabled him to clear up the confusion. Of all the titles in volume twelve the documents probably gave him the most trouble.

[68] C. E. to C. S. B., ALS, July 2, 1933, A. A. S. Archives.

[69] C. S. B. to C. E., TLS, Aug. 22, 1933.

fine work. It was a pleasant visit and it did much to enliven Evans' spirits.

Work moved steadily on during the early fall until tragedy struck. On October 5, 1933, Lena Evans died.[70] She had been an invalid since her fall in June, 1931, but her encouragement and aid had sustained Charlie during all the years of arduous work on the bibliography. So crushed was he by her death that he did not even answer the letter bearing Brigham's condolences. Private services were held in the chapel of the Graceland Cemetery on October 7 at 11:30 A.M.

With a fortitude reminiscent of some of the New Englanders he had written about, Evans resumed his task and saw the rest of volume twelve through the press. Although he could not have known it, this was the last volume that he would write. It pleased him that the press work was completed on January 5, 1934, the anniversary of Calvin Coolidge's death.[71] The latter had been president of the American Antiquarian Society from 1930 to 1933, and upon the occasion of Coolidge's election to that office Evans had written Waldo Lincoln that "There is no man in public office who more closely approaches the ideals of the sterling virtues which the Fathers, and Fore-Fathers of our Country strove to impress upon our national life." [72] Reflecting his high regard for the man, Evans used almost these same words in paying tribute to Coolidge in his dedication to volume twelve. He regarded Coolidge's presidency as "years of the greatest peace; the greatest prosperity; the greatest achievement in the arts and sciences; our national life has ever known." Not many people would agree with Evans' estimate, but that would not have bothered him.

Volume twelve was finally shipped to the subscribers early in February, 1934. It covered the year 1798 and through the letter *M* in 1799, containing 2,593 entries. As interested as he once was in this book and what it revealed about a little known period of American printing, Evans now found it hard to muster much enthusiasm. He had all the tedious chores of bookkeeping ahead of him. Lena's death, the printing tasks, and other difficulties of the year had sapped his strength, and he was tired. While the intensive work had

[70] " 'Chick Evans' Mother Dies of Old Injury," Chicago *Herald and Examiner,* Oct. 7, 1933, p. 17.

[71] Charles Evans, Jr., to C. S. B., TLS, Feb. 6, 1934, A. A. S. Archives.

[72] C. E. to Waldo Lincoln, ALS, Jan. 30, 1930, A. A. S. Archives.

temporarily helped to deaden his grief, he could not find the motivation to continue. The last book had dragged "woefully, both in printing and in shipping out." [73] Without Lena, Charles Evans had no real motivation or desire to publish again. Twenty-one years would elapse before Clifford K. Shipton and the American Antiquarian Society would bring out volume thirteen, covering the latter part of the alphabet for 1799 and the year 1800.

[73] C. E. to C. S. B., ALS, May 28, 1934, A. A. S. Archives.

The Man and His Reward

13

When Charles Evans began active work on the *American Bibliography* in 1902, that book became the core of his existence, the single consideration worthy of attention. All the ordinary social and familial obligations and pleasures which make life enjoyable for most people were ruthlessly subordinated to the main task. The bibliography took the place of association meetings (though he was never a joiner), of profession, of children, and of wife in his affections. One should not assume that this pattern began immediately at a set point or at a given date; it probably grew on him as the tight schedule involved in research and production of each volume of the bibliography made more and more demands on his time. One by one the ordinary social contacts fell by the wayside as he devoted his days and nights to his task. Not that Evans was brusque in his refusal to accept social invitations—he simply ignored them. Not even his closest friends and those who helped him on the bibliography could lure him from his lair at Pratt Avenue.[1]

---

[1] Even W. S. Mason of Evanston, Illinois, who had a large collection of Franklin imprints to offer as bait, sometimes found it difficult to lure Evans to his home for an afternoon chat and discussion of his Franklin material. See W. S. Mason to C. E., TLS, Dec. 13, 1917, with MS draft of Evans' reply, ALS, Jan. 9, 1918, TLS, Oct. 8, 1918, ALS, Feb. 11, 1923, with MS draft of Evans' reply, and TLS, Oct. 15, 1927. Charles Evans did visit Mason, but not often. In the 1927 letter Mason promised to drive down and pick him up, and to guarantee transportation back home if Evans would come. For Merrill's attempts to secure his presence at a meeting of the Chicago Library Club see W. S. Merrill to L. E., ALS, Feb. 9, 1910.

The pleadings, threats and promises of Merrill, even his sly attempts at blackmail through Lena, went unheeded. For the most part he viewed company with something less than hostility, but usually with nothing more than polite and stiff cordiality.[2] Except for a rare visit from Brigham or Emily Ellsworth Ford Skeel, fellow practitioners in the none-too-gentle art of bibliography, he cared nothing for callers. They took up time and impeded his work. He was willing enough for Lena to have company, so long as he was away in the East doing the work he loved. He even preferred to deal with his colleagues through the mail, though this chore, too, became burdensome as time went on. However, he was always polite enough in answering the numerous bibliographical queries which came his way, provided they did not imply criticism of his work.

In his mid-fifties Charles Evans was a very strong man, vigorous and virile. Seldom ill, he attributed his robust health to several rather diverse habits: regular bathing, a good breakfast, brisk walks, and hard work. When anyone mentioned the fact that older men seldom are able to do the work that they could do when they were younger, he would recall that maturity was a necessity for bibliographical endeavor.[3] His athletic build and good health past the age of sixty were reflections of his days at the Farm and Trades School, where he had been a good oarsman. The open outdoor life on Thompson's Island had given him the kind of rugged constitution to withstand any ordeal. Even on his eightieth birthday he was physically a very strong man.

Charles Evans was a tall man, just about six feet, and his quiet manner among strangers gave an appearance of dignity and competence.[4] Looking at his erect bearing, only slightly stooped from the shoulders in later years, his clear-cut features, his carefully clipped mustache, intense eyes, and white hair, one easily associated him with the New England worthies about whose publications he wrote. When he was in good trim, he weighed from 165 to 175 pounds, though with middle age he developed a spread around the middle that added a few pounds to this figure.[5] Not that he

---

[2] Interview with J. Christian Bay, Elmhurst, Ill., March 20, 1958.

[3] C. E. to C. L. Nichols, MS draft, Feb. 12, 1922.

[4] Emily E. F. Skeel to Gifford Ernest, copy of typed letter, Aug. 29, 1947, in possession of Gertrude Evans Jones.

[5] C. E. to L. E., ALS, Oct. 29, 1921. The best portrait of Evans for these years is the one used for the Brown University Commencement, which appears as *Figure 1*, facing p. 50, taken in Boston, probably in 1918.

was ever plump or out of proportion—the added weight detracted not at all from the dignity of his bearing.

Despite his sedentary habits, he had exceptional strength in his hands, his arms, and his legs. His daughter remembers that he could take an apple into his hands and break it into two pieces with little effort. Quite often the two rowdy boys felt the strength of those hands and arms, for Charles Evans was not a man to spare the rod.

His feet were rather large for his size, and occasionally his brother, who was associated with a shoe manufacturing association, would have shoes specially made for him. He always wore hightop shoes, a style he had adopted early in life, and he never wore nor liked oxfords. When he occasionally wore a hat, it was a derby, though sometimes on trips he would revert to a tweed cap. For dress he preferred a single-breasted suit with a vest, with the three front buttons always buttoned. Having discarded the neck-cloth and bow tie of earlier days, he wore a four-in-hand necktie under a high collar. Except for a slightly bald spot in the middle of his forehead which developed from parting his hair in the middle, Charles Evans had at the time of his death a good head of white hair.

Evans' routine at home fell into a comfortable pattern around 1902 and remained fixed, except for the period when a volume was in press or ready for delivery. Upon arising at seven, he had a leisurely breakfast, which always included oatmeal, heaped with sugar—a dish he considered particularly healthful. After breakfast he retired to his library, the one room in the house which was sacred to him, to spend an hour reading his morning newspaper. He enjoyed the newspaper thoroughly and read it completely from front to back. Occasionally when he was particularly unhappy with the state of the world or with something the newspaper had said, he would fire off a letter to the editor. After this ritual was completed, it was time to get down to work.

The library of the Pratt Avenue home was a large room, located on the first floor and connected to the parlor by a sliding door. A bay window, looking east, held a couch which usually was covered with old newspapers. The library was completely filled with book cases without glass, for Charles Evans believed a library with glass book cases was a definite sign that no one ever paid any attention to the books. In the library, facing the parlor, was an enormous hand-carved oak table, on which sat the corset boxes with the halved three-by-five cards. Looking down from one of the walls was a steel engraving of Sir Joshua Reynolds' portrait of the members of the original literary club which Charles Evans had picked up on his trip to London in 1877 and later gave to the Indianapolis group as a fiftieth anniversary present. The children were given strict instructions never to touch anything in the library on pain of severe punishment. One can imagine the anxiety when Gertrude once knocked over some things in the library, but her mother fixed them up for her and her father never knew that anything was amiss.

The books themselves were about what one would expect in a bibliographer's library.[6] It has already been suggested that Evans was not a collector, however, he did occasionally pick up an eighteenth-century work which interested him. Bibliography, library catalogs, the proceedings of the American Antiquarian Society and the Colonial Society of Massachusetts in which he held membership constituted the bulk. As Evans became more widely known, he did not have to buy bibliographies; the authors would send him complimentary copies of their work.[7] When he attempted to buy a copy of Pollard and Redgrave's *Short-Title Catalogue,* Henry Stevens' son suggested to the Bibliographical Society that they give him a copy. The society was happy to do so and sent an inscribed copy, autographed by the authors. Also included in Evans' library were such standard literary works as Tennyson's poems, Gibbon's *Decline and Fall of the Roman Empire,* Bacon's essays, and the histories of Prescott, Parkman, and Motley. His children do not remember that their father read much general literature except the newspaper in his later years. Always the emphasis was upon reading for his research and the topics that dealt with that. His knowledge of general works of literature was very good, but presumably it was acquired during the years when he was a public librarian or at the Boston Athenaeum. It was always Lena who read poetry to the children and told them stories about the authors.

Surrounded by these books, Charles Evans would work on his cards and answer his correspondence until lunch. Then more work and dinner followed, after which there was more work until about eleven, when he retired. However, during a particularly rushed period his light might be burning until well after midnight.

---

[6] Typewritten list of the books in the library of Charles Evans, 1935.

[7] C. K. Bolton to C. E., TLS, May 8, 1912; A. J. Wall to C. E., TLS, Dec. 31, 1921; Henry Stevens Son and Stiles, to C. E., TLS, May 30, 1927.

The dinner meal at the Evans household was a very formal affair. At the head of the table Charles Evans always carved. Conversation flowed in a quiet vein, with the children soon learning to be careful about reporting their activities for the day. If they talked about things of which their father disapproved, it would start him on a rampage. During the time when a volume would be stacked in the front hall, Evans used the dining room table on which to wrap his parcels for mailing to the subscribers. However, every scrap was carefully cleared away before each meal.

One of the tragedies of Charlie's life was that he never really knew his children. For the most part he ignored them. However, he had a violent temper that burst forth when his schedule and habits were interrupted. When he was angry, he raised his voice stridently and slammed doors until the house shook. The children, noisy as all children are, found it safer to stay out of the house most of the time. All the children developed great fondness for athletics under these conditions and their neighborhood was well adapted for this. There were many vacant lots in which to play ball, the lake was only a few blocks away, and for Chick there was the Edgewater Golf Club.

Charles Evans never talked about his work to his children. Whenever they wanted to know what their father was doing or wanted to find out how he felt about something, they asked their mother to intercede for them. Gertrude, asked by her friends about her father's occupation, could only give the answer that she did not know, until she finally felt compelled to ask her mother. Upon reporting that her father was compiling a bibliography of all books printed in the United States from 1639 to 1820, her friends looked at her quizzically and said, "Oh, very interesting." The matter was then dropped.

The only concession Evans ever made to his children's activities was his interest in Chick's golf. This was easy to do since he read the newspaper so religiously. Although he took an interest in the golfing matches, it was nearly always as a reader. Chick recalls only one instance in which his father ever attended a golf match in which he played. Even on the trip to England he never once ventured to the golf course with his son. While he was proud of his youngest child, as revealed in the following paragraph to Lena, he was not interested enough to watch the game, even when the matches were played in Chicago:

"I read to-day, with much pleasure, of Charlie's winning the City

Championship. . . . I love to think of him as he waved to us, and trotted off with a few sticks in an old bag to win his way to his present golfing fame." [8]

He had absolute disdain toward his older son's occupation. Perhaps his experience with lawyers had been such as to sour him on the breed forever, but this is somewhat strange in view of the fact that many of his Indianapolis friends and supporters were distinguished lawyers. Charles Evans knew nothing about law and very little about business. Yet he was not hesitant to give his son advice about legal matters. When Eliot Evans tried to recover a portion of his mother's inheritance in a Texas lawsuit in 1912, his father fired letters to him continually, advising him what course to take, what techniques to use, what questions to ask, and in what courts to practice.[9] Although he wrote to his old friend Captain Paddock of the "chivalrous" interest Eliot had taken in his mother's case, he lacked confidence in his son. Some years later, he disappeared for about six weeks, and afterwards the family discovered that he had gone to Fort Worth to check on the court records.[10] He was positive that Eliot had made some mistakes in prosecuting the case.

To all the children Charles Evans was a very difficult man. His working habits were particularly wearing on Gertrude, who was not allowed to entertain boy friends in her home lest they disturb the work on the bibliography. His attitude on this point was unyielding. Eventually, when Eliot was beginning to build up a little law

---

[8] C. E. to L. E., ALS, Aug. 5, 1911. Evans talked with his friends about Chick's golf and related some interesting details about Chick's early practice driving in the attic of the Evans' home to W. S. Merrill. Merrill, "Early Days at the Newberry Library," p. 26. Commenting upon Chick's golfing record, Merrill noted, "Striving for excellence and perfection in whatever they set out to do was a family trait. Evans told me that he read *through* Gibbon's 'Decline and Fall of the Roman Empire.'"

[9] For Evans' admission that he knew little about law and business see C. E. to C. S. B., ALS, May 28, 1934, A. A. S. Archives. Eliot Evans has confirmed this fact to the author. Charles Evans just was not interested in business or legal matters. He never congratulated his son, Eliot, upon passing his Illinois bar exams and was quite specific in his denunciation of lawyers as a sorry breed. For his directions to Eliot see MS draft, 12 pp., probably 1910 or 1911, and MS draft, 2 pp., about same date, plus Charles Evans to Eliot Evans, ALS, Nov. 23 and Dec. 6, 1910, and Feb. 1, 1911, all in possession of Eliot H. Evans. C. E. to B. B. Paddock, typed copy, Feb. 1, 1911. The letter to Paddock was never delivered.

[10] Interview with Eliot Evans, Chicago, March 20, 1958. See also typed report of the detective hired to trace Evans' whereabouts, dated Aug. 16 and 18, 1919.

practice, he rented an apartment elsewhere in Rogers Park where he and his sister lived until both were married in 1916. Later, the parents of Eliot's wife repeatedly asked to visit the house and meet the old gentleman, but he never permitted it and, in fact, never met them. However, he did develop some admiration for Hortense Evans, Eliot's wife. Mrs. Eliot Evans was a very plain spoken woman and did not mind in the least disagreeing with her father-in-law. Instead of provoking scenes as disagreement from the children inevitably did, Hortense's retorts amused him, and he seemed to admire her pluck.

Paradoxically, when he wanted to be, Charles Evans could be the most gracious and affable of men. He had wit, and his eyes fairly sparkled when he revealed his humorous side.[11] Although this trait was more often detected in the written word than in the spoken, it was nonetheless genuine. On one trip to Chicago, Brigham took him around the city in a taxi, showing him many sights that he had never seen before. Charlie was just like a little boy; he was so excited and filled with wonder about it all. Under the right conditions he was the soul of modesty, and his retiring, old-world deference to those who saw his good side was a memory to be cherished. Toward those who showed interest in his work he could be generous beyond their expectations. On a trip in 1932, when she and her companion dropped by Chicago unexpectedly upon the Evanses, Emily Skeel found him immersed in his bibliography. Yet he dropped everything and welcomed her so warmly that one would never have known that she had interrupted his work. Despite his advancing age, Mrs. Skeel found none of the less agreeable traits. "His friendly welcome, his chat and farewell alike, which still linger in our memory, deepened the impression of his lovable nature." [12]

More than one bibliographer associated with Charles Evans throughout the productive period of his life testified that he had a "lovable nature." [13] When Margaret B. Stillwell visited Chicago in

---

[11] Many of Evans' letters show his humorous side and more than one acquaintance commented upon his wit. See J. C. Bay, "Charles Evans, 1850–1935," *A. L. A. Bulletin*, XXIX (March, 1935), 164; Emily E. F. Skeel to Gifford Ernest, copy of typed letter, Aug. 29, 1947, in possession of Gertrude Evans Jones. For the impact of his humor on someone who did not know him personally see S. H. Fisher to C. E., TLS, March 15, 1933.

[12] Emily E. F. Skeel to Gifford Ernest, copy of typed letter, Aug. 29, 1947, in possession of Gertrude Evans Jones.

[13] Margaret B. Stillwell to C. E., ALS, June 22, 1923. Interview with J. C. Bay, Elmhurst, Ill., March 20, 1958. However, G. B. Utley, librarian of the

the early twenties, he met her at the Newberry Library, talked with her about his fruitless search for the "Oath of Allegiance" in the British Museum, and took her to the Art Institute to view the paintings. Miss Stillwell had the memory of a most enjoyable afternoon. Such pleasant memories were confined largely to out-of-town bibliographers, for not even a near-neighbor, J. Christian Bay, could talk him into showing his research slips to one of his colleagues.

On trips, as has been noted, Evans warmed to the courtesies and bonhomie of his fellows. Early in life he smoked cigars and occasionally took a drink. Long since, probably for financial reasons, he had given up these pleasures, but he never objected to other people indulging. As a dinner companion with Brigham, either in the East or in Chicago (Brigham took him out to dinner), Evans was enthusiastic, just like a boy. Under the pleasant banter of the dinner table Evans could be interesting and informative. Yet he was a very sensitive introverted person and could be easily piqued at nonrecognition. His shyness and retiring nature covered his resentments very well, but these characteristics were often mistaken for modesty and humility by those who did not know him.

Under these conditions, his wife did not have an easy life.[14] A slightly built woman, often ill, she still had the stamina to do for her family what had to be done. Invariably cheerful, even when in pain, she was devoted to her husband and the project on which he had based all his hopes. An attractive, highly cultured woman, she was the staff on which he leaned. Although she seldom helped him with the actual work on the bibliography, she kept the business affairs going at home when he was away, and in household matters she invariably took the initiative. And in a pinch, when Charlie became ill, she further showed her capabilities by supervising some pages through the press. Outgoing as her husband was not, Lena could meet the great and near-great with composure and assurance. Socially active and interested in others, she must have longed many times in her life for her husband to be just a bit more gregarious, but she never expressed such thoughts to him. She respected Charlie

Newberry Library, was one Chicago bibliographer who also found Evans "lovable." See G. B. Utley, "Charles Evans," *Library Journal*, LX (March 1, 1935), 198.

[14] L. E. to Eliot Evans, ALS, March 2, 1929, and March 9 and 13, 1930, in possession of Eliot H. Evans. Interview with Eliot Evans, Chicago, Jan. 29, 1959. Mrs. Bert Underwood to Charles Evans, Jr., ALS, Feb. 13, 1935. J. C. Bay, "Charles Evans, 1850–1935," A. L. A. *Bulletin*, XXIX (March, 1935), 164. See chap. 5.

for what he was, loved him as a wife should, and devoted as much of her energy and resources as she could spare from the rest of the family to the encouragement of his every undertaking. When everyone else failed and the prospect of publishing another volume would seem the blackest, Lena would encourage him to keep at his task. In his dedication to her he expressed gratitude for the aid and encouragement that had made it possible for him to continue.

This was a strange type of love, where the sacrifices were so obviously one-sided; and yet, there can be no doubt that Charles Evans in his own way was passionately devoted to his wife.[15] He was never so impatient as when he was away from her for a long period of time; she was absolutely essential to his happiness and to his success. While he recognized that she suffered more than anyone else from his seclusion, he did little to make her life more pleasant. When Eliot was preparing for the 1912 lawsuit, his father paid a great tribute to Lena Evans' integrity. "If a question of veracity comes up between Lora's [Mrs. Evans' younger sister] testimony and your mother's recollection of her statements: I would plainly tell her that your information of her conversations came from one, your mother, whom you had never known to make an untruthful statement in your life." [16] It is beside the point that such a declaration would have mattered little in court. Stated with all the dogmatism of which Charles Evans was capable, this sentence would have ended the matter. It would not have occurred to him that anyone could doubt the truth of his assertion.

Most of the joy Lena received in life came from another source. In addition to keeping her household on an even keel, she also enjoyed writing and from time to time submitted poems and prose pieces for publication in various Chicago newspapers.[17] When Chick began to become prominent in golfing circles, she accompanied him on his trips and used her talent to help him with stories for golfing magazines, with his syndicated column for the the Chicago *Daily Examiner,* and with his other journalistic work. As his mother, she enjoyed the attention and the hospitality of many famous people.

---

[15] C. E. to L. E., ALS, Aug. 26, Sept. 1, 8, 15, and 23, 1906. Gifford Ernest, "Aged Bibliographer Wins High Honor . . . ," newspaper clipping, Chicago *Daily News,* Aug. 16, 1934, Eliot Evans, "Scrapbook."

[16] C. E. to Eliot Evans, MS drafts, about 1910–11, in possession of Eliot Evans.

[17] There are some newspaper clippings of Lena Evans' poetry in Eliot Evans, "Scrapbook." For other references to her writing see the following letters: C. E. to L. E., ALS, Jan. 24 and Feb. 8, 1908, ALS, Jan. 20, 1912, ALS, May 2, 1913, ALS, May 16, 1914, ALS, April 20, 1915, and ALS, March 18, 1916.

Faithfully she followed her son around the golf courses, twice accompanying him to England for the British matches.[18] Adding to the glory of Chick's winning the double crown in 1916 was his mother's presence on the occasion. As reported in an evening paper: "When a slight, elderly woman under whose glasses tears of joy glistened came through the crowd, Chick threw his arms about her and kissed her and the crowd went wild with enthusiasm for it was his mother and all week she had followed her son over the course." [19]

Yet always back at home was the scholar, working on his cards, keeping up with the golf matches through his newspapers, and longing for his wife to come home. Difficult to everyone else, Charles Evans could be managed by his wife, and when there were family differences, she was the one who could smooth them out. It is not surprising that he lost all desire to continue his work after her death.

It is interesting, however, to find Charles Evans mellowing in later years toward his children as they grew up, married, and were successful themselves. In time they came to respect their father for his great achievement, though none of the three, with the possible exception of Chick, was ever very close to him. It was Evans' lifelong policy not to discuss family business matters with his children, and he retained this habit almost until the end. After Lena's death, he relented a little on the subject of the *American Bibliography* and discussed a few of the business details with Eliot. To the grandchildren he was rather distant, though after Evans Jones, Gertrude's older son, had learned to talk, they occasionally "conversed" together. Basically what his children or grandchildren did or did not do held little interest for him. Absorbed in a single, consuming endeavor as he was, the children had to become interested in what he was doing; it was not the other way around. Perhaps the increasing respect for his bibliographic work and the prospect of meeting the goal of 1800 eventually brought out his better traits to his children.

Although he had never gone out of his way to encourage personal interest in his work or attended society meetings where he might have received recognition, Evans was unhappy as the years

---

[18] Lena accompanied Chick to England in 1914 and again in 1921. See L. E. to C. E., ALS, May 15, 1914, for descriptions of some of the people she met. Among others whom she met on this trip was Lord Northcliffe, who later offered his home to the Evanses in 1921. See Charles Evans, Jr., *Chick Evans' Golf Book*, p. 227.

[19] *Ibid.*, p. 235.

rolled on and he received no formal testimonial to his scholarship. In early days he had been bitter about this; he finally became resigned to the fact that his great contribution to scholarship would have to wait for recognition by posterity.[20] It was all very well to work for posterity, but a little reward here and now would have lifted the spirit of the worker. It did not soothe his wounded pride that other bibliographers achieved recognition for less effort.

What Evans had really hoped and dreamed all his life was that some day a major American university would award him an honorary doctorate for his contribution. Acutely aware of his own lack of academic background, he would like to follow the path of his master W. F. Poole, whom Northwestern University had so honored in 1882. As the years passed, his dream seemed further from realization than ever. The only bright spots in the picture had been election to membership in the American Antiquarian Society in 1910 and in the Colonial Society of Massachusetts in 1926. He apparently regarded election to honorary membership in the American Library Association shortly after Lena's death of insufficient importance to merit comment, for no letter announcing this honor can be located.[21]

Just as Evans was completing his twelfth volume, he received a letter from Dr. Clarence A. Barbour, President of Brown University.[22] At the suggestion of Waldo Leland, the board of fellows had voted to confer upon Evans the honorary degree of Master of Arts, provided he would accept the degree and be present at the ceremonies in June, 1934. Happy as he was to be informed of this decision, Evans could not help being wistful in a letter to Brigham.[23] He had always hoped that one day he could receive an honorary doctorate, but he consoled himself that perhaps this was a stepping stone to the higher degree. Brigham, an alumnus of Brown, and also a choice for an honorary degree in June, thought it ridiculous for the university to award a scholar of Evans' age and attainments a master's degree. Saying nothing to Evans about it, he began a quiet campaign among Wroth, Leland, and some others to have President Barbour and the board change the degree to a doctorate.

[20] L. E. to C. E., ALS, Sept. 27, 1926; C. E. to A. C. Harris, MS draft, about 1908; C. E. to C. S. B., ALS, Sept. 4, 1910, A. A. S. Archives.

[21] C. H. Milam to C. E., TLS, Oct. 31, 1933. Other individuals so honored at the same time were R. R. Bowker, W. L. Clements, Wilberforce Eames, and Daniel B. Updike. "Honorary Memberships," *Library Journal*, LVIII (Nov. 15, 1933), 928.

[22] C. A. Barbour to C. E., TLS, Dec. 23, 1933.

[23] C. E. to C. S. B., ALS, Jan. 6, 1934, A. A. S. Archives.

By early March he had succeeded, and the president wrote Evans that "upon further deliberation and in accordance with my own recommendation" the board had decided to change the degree to be conferred to Doctor of Letters.[24] He was pleased to notify Evans that the latest affirmative vote in the matter had been received that very morning from the Chief Justice of the United States. Evans, of course, still knew nothing of Brigham's manipulations, but he knew that it was due to Brigham more than to anyone else that the doctorate would be added to his name.

President Barbour's letter simply overwhelmed Evans with joy. In the midst of the tiresome business of shipping out his volume twelve, it was a shot in the arm. For over fifty years he had tried to prove himself worthy of the degree and "as the years went by, without recognition from any learned body authorized to bestow it, the feeling has grown that I was working for posterity; and, in the long years which will surely come, others would evaluate my life work at its true worth to scholarship, as an indispensable aid to the understanding of American life and letters in the first two centuries of our history."[25] He asked Dr. Barbour if it were too presumptuous to suggest that the citation read for "a lifetime devoted to research and study in American Bibliography and bibliothecal pursuits." Barbour showed Evans' letter to Leland, who approved Evans' suggestion, but added that it would be appropriate to make the citation much stronger than Evans' modest phrase.[26]

Some of Evans' friends in the East, headed by Leland and Brigham, were concerned that he might be forced to forego the trip because of financial reasons. Since Brown never conferred a degree *in absentia,* it would be necessary for him to appear personally at commencement. Privately they communicated to him in the most tactful way possible that they would like "to give themselves the pleasure of meeting the expenses of your trip to Providence."[27] They would not press this matter upon Evans, but they were sin-

---

[24] C. S. B. to L. C. Wroth, TLS, Jan. 29, Feb. 2, 5, and 7, March 10, 1934, J. C. B. Archives. L. C. Wroth to C. S. B., TLS, Feb. 2, 1934, A. A. S. Archives. C. S. B. to C. E., TLS, Jan. 10, Feb. 7, and March 13, 1934. C. E. to C. S. B., ALS, Aug. 26, 1934, A. A. S. Archives.

[25] C. E. to C. A. Barbour, ALS, March 30, 1934, Brown University Archives.

[26] Waldo G. Leland to C. A. Barbour, TLS, April 4, 1934, Brown University Archives.

[27] Waldo Leland to C. E., TLS, Jan. 6, 1934, plus MS draft of Evans' reply; C. S. B. to C. E., TLS, March 13, 1934. Charles Evans, Jr., to C. S. B., ALS, March, 1934 (no day), A. A. S. Archives.

cere in their offer. As may have best foreseen, Evans rejected it, asking only that they "extend a friendly hand" to steer him on his way. However, he was so pleased with Brigham's letter, suggesting that Chick come along as his companion, that he showed it to his younger son. Chick described his father's happiness as that of a small boy, his only regret being that his wife was not alive to share the occasion with him.

The spring did not deal kindly with Charles Evans, and it was obvious to his family that the strain of Lena's death and the production of volume twelve had taken their toll. Additional bad news came from East Weymouth, Massachusetts, where his brother, John Evans, died on March 9, 1934, at the age of eighty-six. While Charlie and John corresponded and met infrequently in later years, John's death was one more reminder that Charlie's own days were about over. As Chick remarked to Brigham, "He is a pathetic figure, shuffling in and out amongst his books." [28] After Lena's death he had refused to have a housekeeper; he was living alone, with only his little Pomeranian dog "Atom" to keep him company. However, the family need not have been unduly concerned, for if sheer willpower could work the miracle, Charles Evans would answer *ad sum* when his name was called in Providence on June 18, 1934.

Toward the end of May as a final check on the design of the cap and gown he had asked E. R. Moore and Company to make for him, he wrote and asked Brigham about the chevrons on the sleeves. Such a detail had slipped Brigham's mind; consequently, and as a simpler solution, he suggested that Evans just borrow the university cap and gown. Such a casual attitude would certainly not do for Evans. He wanted his own cap and gown, for this was one of the red-letter days of his life. As the day approached, he became more and more excited. The letters from various Brown University officials added to his expectations.

At the last minute Chick found that he could not leave his business and accompany his father, but Eliot had occasion to go to New York for business purposes and could go on to Providence.[29] Although Brigham had offered to put them up at his house in Warwick Neck, Evans thought it would perhaps be better to join his son

[28] Charles Evans, Jr., to C. S. B., TLS, May 8, 1934, A. A. S. Archives. Gertrude Evans Jones to the author, typed notes, Oct. 24, 1960.

[29] C. E. to C. S. B., ALS, May 28 and June 12, 1934, A. A. S. Archives. Eliot H. Evans to C. E., TLS, June 12, 1934.

at the Biltmore Hotel in downtown Providence. Although it was necessary for Eliot to precede his father by a few days in order to take care of his other matters, he made all the arrangements for his father's departure from Chicago on Saturday morning, June 16. He met the old gentleman in New York on Sunday, and they arrived in Providence in the early afternoon of the same day. They were in time for the baccalaureate exercises, which were to take place in the First Baptist Meeting House, the oldest Baptist church in America. For generations the old church house, located at the foot of College Hill, had served Brown for commencement exercises. In earlier years Evans had stood at the foot of this hill and regarded the ascent to the libraries at the top as an ascent to Parnassus. Now, soon to be numbered among the Brown alumni, he, accompanied by Eliot, entered the meetinghouse to hear President Barbour's address on "vision." Both the Evanses were impressed with the speech, which the father called "easily the outstanding address of any College President"; but undoubtedly the part which had the most meaning for the aged bibliographer came at the end. Here Dr. Barbour declared that the widest and most useful visions come not by chance but "by steady perseverance and toilsome endeavor. Such visions help us to walk the ordinary way— and for most of us the way is ordinary, not extraordinary—in fortitude and high endeavor, until the day dawns and the shadows flee away." [30]

The long-awaited day dawned beautiful and cloudless. One of the longest processionals Brown had seen assembled at 9:00 A.M. for the march to the First Baptist Meeting House where the degrees for the one hundred and sixty-sixth annual commencement were to be conferred. Some 371 seniors and ten distinguished honorary degree candidates formed with the faculty. Included among the latter group, in addition to Evans and Brigham, were Newton D. Baker, former Secretary of War, and Dr. Ada Louise Comstock, President of Radcliffe College. The brilliant hot sun lent exceptional glitter to the processional, which was witnessed by an estimated 5,000 people.[31]

---

[30] "Useful Vision of Life Urged by Dr. Barbour," newspaper clipping, Providence *News-Tribune*, June 18, 1934, *Evening-Bulletin*, June 18, 1934, and *Journal*, June 19, 1934, all in Evans Papers, plus the *Brown Alumni Monthly*, XXV (July–Sept., 1934), 27–30.

[31] Interview with Eliot Evans, Chicago, Oct. 21, 1960. Description of the commencement exercises is from newspaper clippings, Providence *News-Tribune*,

To serve as Charles Evans' faculty escort Dr. Barbour had assigned Dr. Lawrence C. Wroth, his old friend and librarian of the
John Carter Brown Library. Hoping to relieve him of some of the
strain of the day, Wroth suggested before the procession started that
they have a quiet luncheon in the John Carter Brown Library instead of joining the general melée at Faunce House. To this suggestion Charles Evans added a vigorous dissent. "This is the greatest day
of my life, and I'm going to do everything I'm supposed to do if it
kills me." [32]

When Charles Evans took his place on the platform of the 159-
year-old meetinghouse and awaited the Latin pronouncement which
would add him to the roster of Brown's honorary alumni, he felt
that "it was the spirit of our seventeenth and eighteenth century
ancestors, among whom I had been living and working, which per-
vaded the scene. How beautifully the old church lends itself and
hallows it. . . ."

In solemn tones Dr. Barbour read the citation of Evans' honorary
degree:

> Distinguished figure in the field of the library and of bibliography, as-
> sociated with public libraries in Boston, Indianapolis, Baltimore, Omaha,
> Chicago, several of which he, himself, organized, such as the Public Library
> of Indianapolis and the Enoch Pratt Free Library of Baltimore; pioneer
> in the American Library Association, long identified with the Historical
> Society of Chicago and the American Antiquarian Society, author of Amer-
> ican Bibliography, herculean achievement, the chronological dictionary of
> all books, pamphlets and periodicals published in the United States from
> 1639 to 1820, unquestioned authority in that field; already having attained
> the age of fourscore years and three, long working in quiet willingness to
> serve the world of scholarship and to contribute to the understanding of
> American life and letters in the first two centuries of our national history:
> By authority of the Board of Fellows, I confer upon you, Charles Evans
> the honorary degree of Doctor of Letters.

So overwhelmed was he with this long-overdue reward that he
broke a 166-year tradition at Brown and spoke a few words of
appreciation for the great honor which had been bestowed upon
him.[33] As he wrote to his friend Brigham, the incident was entirely
unpremeditated; Evans himself did not know why he did it. The

June 18, 1934, *Evening-Bulletin,* June 18, 1934, and *Journal,* June 19, 1934, all in
Evans Papers, plus the *Brown Alumni Monthly,* XXV (July–Sept., 1934), 27–30.
    [32] Interview with L. C. Wroth, Providence, May 19, 1958.
    [33] C. E. to C. S. B., ALS, Aug. 26, 1934, A. A. S. Archives. The newspapers dis-
agreed about Evans' remarks, but the *Brown Alumni Monthly,* undoubtedly
quoting from the *Evening-Bulletin,* reported Evans' words as follows:

participants were so surprised that no one was quite sure what Evans said, but all agreed that it had been a moving expression of gratitude for this great honor.

The exercises over, the procession moved back up the hill to the formal luncheon, followed by the alumni meeting in Sayles Hall, where President Barbour, Governor Theodore Francis Green, and Secretary Baker delivered speeches. Following this meeting, Charles and Eliot Evans retired to the John Carter Brown Library for a rest. One of the women on the staff served the group some liquid refreshment, and Evans asked for ginger ale. Eliot, however, sensing that his father was very tired, asked her privately to put a little whiskey in it. Upon draining the glass of its contents, Evans pronounced it the best ginger ale he had ever drunk and asked for another glass. A number of important people came to the library to see Evans, including President Barbour and C. S. Brigham and his brother, Herbert Brigham. Leland hunted him up several times for short talks favorable to the continuation of his bibliography. To more than one person Charles Evans recorded his gratitude for the "happiest day of my life."

With these memories burned deeply into his soul, Charles Evans left for Chicago; the trip, long and tiring, was made more comfortable by the perfection of traveling on a silent, dustless, air-cooled Pullman car. As the train moved on toward home, he opened up as he had never done before to his son Eliot, even to the point of discussing some family business matters. He talked about the bibliography, about his wish that Lena could have lived to share his joy in the coveted degree, and above all about the commencement exercises through which they had just passed. It was an exhausted but happy Charles Evans who went back to his solitary existence in the big old house on Pratt Avenue.

In this grave presence to record my name
Something within me holds the hand and shrinks;
Dull were the soul without some joy in fame.
Yet here to claim remembrance were, methinks,
Like him who in the desert's awful fame
Notches his Cockney initials on the Sphinx.

Wroth does not remember these words, and another newspaper, the *News-Tribune*, reported that Evans had said, "In this great presence something within me holds me from an expression of full gratitude for the great honor which has been conferred upon me." The phrase "dull were the soul without some joy in fame" was an expression Evans had previously used in a letter to Brigham, but I have not been able to locate the source of the quotation. The occasion was recorded photographically and appeared in the alumni magazine.

The summer of 1934 was a tiring one and Evans' health continued to be none too good. The weather was hot and uncomfortable, and for two months he could not summon the energy even to answer Brigham's letter of early July. While he had been in Providence, Brigham had talked with him about his collection of American auction catalogs, and Evans had promised them for the American Antiquarian Society. Brigham was willing to pay for the packing and shipping of these items to Worcester, but Evans felt that their selection from among the debris stored in the attic by generations of Irish maids warranted his personal attention. Since the temperature had hovered around 100 degrees for months, to comply with Brigham's request would "tempt death in its most horrible form." [34]

Meanwhile, he worked desultorily, but not very hard, on several things. There were still checks arriving for volume twelve, but the ordinary household chores seemed to take most of his energy. In August he was interviewed by a reporter from the Chicago *Daily News*, who pleased Evans very much by his reference to the bibliographer as an "American Bardo de Bardi," the "father of Romola, the scholar devoted to his work, and blind to everything but the light within." [35]

When Evans sent Brigham a copy of the interview, Brigham agreed entirely with the journalist's thought, but he found most encouraging the word that Evans was working on the volume for 1799–1800. Brigham hoped that this was true. Evans' doubts about completing the work were implied in that part of Brigham's letter which sought to spur him on: "You can do it, no matter what misgivings you may have. No one can do it but you, so don't let any obstacle delay or deter you from completing this magnificent work. I will help you in every way in my power, so don't hesitate to put any work you wish upon the staff of this library." [36] Reversing the pattern and asking help from Chicago, Brigham had written to Chick of his anxiety about his father's health and the state of the bibliography. Since Chick was to be in Boston in September, Brigham wanted to talk with him at length about his father at that time.

---

[34] C. E. to C. S. B., ALS, Aug. 26, 1934.
[35] Gifford Ernest, "Aged Bibliographer Wins High Honor . . . ," Chicago *Daily News*, Aug. 16, 1934, newspaper clipping, Eliot Evans, "Scrapbook"; C. E. to Gifford Ernest, typed copy of ALS, Aug. 22, 1934, in Eliot Evans, "Scrapbook."
[36] C. S. B. to C. E., TLS, Aug. 31, 1934.

In early September two days of cool rainy weather sent Charles Evans into his attic to answer Brigham's second plea for the auction catalogs. He had not realized how many there were and he unearthed a veritable gold mine. Just as soon as he could find barrels to hold them, he would dispatch the several thousand catalogs to Worcester. He labored throughout the fall on this one project and finally shipped five barrels to Worcester just before Thanksgiving. His November letter showed some of the old vigor, and he promised Brigham that he would get to work on volume thirteen just as soon as he could get several other pressing matters out of the way.[37]

This promise was never realized. Rounding up the auction catalogs took the last ounce of Evans' energy. His family became concerned about him, but he absolutely refused either to move into an apartment with one of the children or to have a housekeeper.[38] Chick noticed that he kept putting off work that he had to do; this was unlike Charles Evans. More of a recluse than ever, he kept the house locked tight and refused to answer the door for pedlars. Gertrude brought him bread and cereals each day and Chick, his canned soups and pastry. The old man did not take anything solid, began to complain about his food, and toward the end even turned upon his oatmeal. At night he would go to sleep immediately after supper and then wake up at twelve, not to sleep anymore until dawn. Finding sleep impossible, he would go to Lena's room and sit in her chair until the milkman came. On one occasion when Gertrude came into the house, he was proceeding up the stairs and fell. She hurried to assist him, but he brushed her aside, saying, "I'm all right; I can take care of myself." Soon he began having trouble with his breathing. Chick tried to get him to have a doctor, but he absolutely forbade it. He did not want anyone to do anything for him.

On the last night before the brain hemorrhage which was to end his life, Chick had a long conversation with him in his library. He talked about many subjects and answered questions with a semblance of the same old vigorous voice. Everything on the oak table was in its precise position: pen, pencil, letter opener, letters, clips,

---

[37] C. E. to C. S. B., ALS, Sept. 7 and Nov. 25, 1934, A. A. S. Archives.

[38] After his father's death, Charles Evans, Jr., wrote Brigham a MS account in pencil of his father's last two or three months. This MS, dated Feb. 14, 1935, in A. A. S. Archives, provides an excellent basis for the two paragraphs which follow. Also interview with Gertrude Evans Jones, Chicago, Feb. 1, 1961.

and rubber bands. The only topic he avoided was the bibliography; he did not want to talk about the book.

The next afternoon Gertrude came to the house and found her father lying beside his bed, unconscious and breathing heavily. She called Eliot immediately, and they decided to move him to the Evanston Hospital, where he died the next day, February 8, 1935, at 1:22 P.M. Private funeral services were held the following day at the Graceland Cemetery Chapel with the Rev. R. Lester Mondale, Pastor of the Evanston Unitarian Church officiating.[39] His body was cremated and his ashes buried beside those of his wife Lena and his daughter Constance in the Lakeside section of Memorial Park Cemetery, Evanston, Illinois.

In death Charles Evans' fame spread as it had not in life, and newspapers throughout the country carried long obituaries.[40] He was hailed as a librarian, a great bibliographer, and a distinguished literary figure. The major professional journals responded with eulogies on his achievement. The commendation that Evans himself would have appreciated most, however, came from the pen of his friend Clarence Saunders Brigham, who wrote a biographical sketch for the *Proceedings* of the American Antiquarian Society. Concluding his tribute, Brigham said: "For the years to come, Charles Evans will be honored as the author of an invaluable historical reference work, but those who were privileged with his friendship will revere him most for his courage, his perseverance and his loyalty." [41] If Charles Evans could have read his friend's encomium, he would have said, with a twinkle in his eye, "a little meed of praise now and then is appreciated by the worker."

---

[39] A record of the services and the funeral oration are in Eliot Evans, "Scrapbook." Since Charles Evans was neither a member of a church nor a casual visitor to any church services, Eliot Evans asked the Rev. Mr. Mondale, whom he had heard preach occasionally, to conduct the services.

[40] Most of these are in Eliot Evans, "Scrapbook." Included are Chicago, Indianapolis, Baltimore, and Boston newspapers, but not the New York *Times*, Feb. 9, 1935, p. 15. Previously cited have been J. C. Bay, "Charles Evans, 1850–1935," A. L. A. *Bulletin*, XXIX (March, 1935), 163–164, and G. B. Utley, "Charles Evans," *Library Journal*, LX (March 1, 1935), 198.

[41] C. S. Brigham, "Charles Evans, 1850–1935," A. A. S. *Proceedings*, n.s., XXXXV (April, 1935), 21.

A Work of Enduring Usefulness

14

Toward the close of Evans' life, shortly after the publication of volume twelve, Lawrence C. Wroth, an especially valued correspondent, wrote a letter of appreciation and congratulation for the bibliographer's work: "I want to congratulate you most sincerely on the addition of another volume to the great series. It must be a very great satisfaction to you to look back upon the progress of this piece of work and to realize that you have accomplished, single handed, something that most men would have undertaken only with the support of a staff of trained workers. All of us who are working in Americana have cause to thank you every day of our lives." [1] Wroth recognized and paid tribute to a fact that subsequent scholars have also noted: the *American Bibliography* was uniquely the product of the devotion of one man. With a faithfulness that has few parallels, Charles Evans in three decades had published twelve massive volumes covering American printing from its beginning in 1639 almost to the end of the eighteenth century. The summarized record in Table 2 demonstrates clearly the perseverance of the bibliographer and the magnitude of his task.

In 1897, Richard Rogers Bowker had told the Second International Library Conference that "the wearied bibliographer, at work upon a book about books, has sometimes an overwhelming sense of the littleness of human endeavour"; and, in speaking of the un-

---

[1] L. C. Wroth to C. E., typed carbon, Feb. 27, 1934, J. C. B. Archives.

TABLE 2

The *American Bibliography* of Charles Evans

Volume	Period Covered	Printer	Date Published	Pagination
I	1639–1729	Blakely Press	November, 1903	446
II	1730–50	Blakely Press	March, 1905	448
III	1751–64	Blakely Press	May, 1906	446
IV	1765–73	Hollister Press	October, 1907	440
V	1774–78	Columbia Press	May, 1909	455
VI	1779–85	Columbia Press	May, 1910	445
VII	1786–89	Columbia Press	December, 1912	424
VIII	1790–92	Columbia Press	April, 1915	432
IX	1793–94	Columbia Press	January, 1926	491
X	1795–96, *M*	Columbia Press	February, 1929	451
XI	1796, *N*-97	Columbia Press	February, 1931	399
XII	1798–99, *M*	Columbia Press	February, 1934	419

requited labor of such nineteenth-century bibliographical giants as Lowndes, Watt, Leypoldt, and Poole, Raymond C. Davis noted that their pecuniary profit was practically nothing and their fame posthumous.[2] As a worthy successor in this tradition, Charles Evans felt both the weariness and the lack of fame and financial reward; but he had no regrets. His work had been a labor of love. As one of his friends had remarked, Charles Evans had done what he best liked to do, what was worthiest, and what would last.[3]

The record of such financial deprivation and solitary devotion to a single task can but excite the greatest admiration for Evans' pluck and endurance, but what of the value of the work? Was it worth all the toil, the sacrifice, the striving for an ever-receding goal? Alternately Evans' work has been praised and damned, sometimes by the same people: "great," "indispensable," "monumental," "full of errors," "incomplete," and "inaccurate." In view of the plaudits and the criticisms, what is the worth of Evans' *American Bibliography?* Was it really, as his friend Brigham called it, "one of the greatest bibliographical compilations of all time?"[4]

Generalizations about the quality of a bibliographical work are difficult to make, and an evaluation of Evans' bibliography could be made more easily if the American Antiquarian Society's "Evans

---

[2] R. R. Bowker, "Bibliographical Endeavors in America," in *Sec. Int. Lib. Conf.,* 1897, p. 150; Raymond C. Davis, "Unselfish Nature of Bibliographical Labor in the Last Century," *Public Libraries,* XXI (Jan., 1916), 1–3.

[3] G. T. Porter to C. E., ALS, Dec. 3, 1910.

[4] C. S. Brigham, "Report of the Council," A. A. S. *Proceedings,* n.s., LXV (April, 1955), 4.

Project" were completed. In 1954 the society entered into an agreement with the Readex Microprint Company to edit and to publish the full text of every book, pamphlet, and broadside listed in Evans' *American Bibliography*.[5] By this means the society hopes to make available for major research universities throughout the world copies of the priceless originals from a variety of institutions. As a basis for the project, the editor, C. K. Shipton, chose the chronological approach and planned to use the thirteen volumes of Evans as an index to the microprint edition. At the same time, the project would provide an excellent opportunity to publish corrections of the errors in Evans, provide a cumulative index to all the volumes, and publish a union list of additions which have been uncovered in the fifty years since the first volume of Evans appeared.[6] That the society and the company chose the *American Bibliography* as the skeletal outline for their project indicates a belief in its basic strength.

Since the original project was conceived, Shipton has made target cards for each Evans title to be reproduced, noting the probable source of error for those titles he could not locate. He had in 1961 produced all the nonserial titles in Evans through number 28,641 in volume ten. Eventually his target cards will provide the basis for a complete short-title revision of the entire *American Bibliography*.

Not originally a design of the project but now incorporated into the program is the cumulative author-subject-title index to the twelve volumes of Evans and the thirteenth of Shipton. Compiled by Roger P. Bristol, this index appeared in 1959.[7] In no sense is it a revision of the original work, and every title which appeared in Evans whether in error or not has been included. Compilation of this index offers further testimony to Evans' work. The *American Bibliography* has become so valuable that scholars have felt it desirable to have such a cumulative index, even when it includes titles that do not exist. The index does make one vital improve-

---

[5] C. K. Shipton, "Report of the Librarian," A. A. S. *Proceedings*, n.s., LXIV (Oct., 1954), 261–262.

[6] Actually the index was not a part of the project itself. Bristol had been working on the cumulative index for several years before the project began, but publication of the index fitted so well into the general plan that it, too, was published by the society. C. K. Shipton, "Report of the Librarian," A. A. S. *Proceedings*, n.s., LXVII (Oct., 1957), 117–118.

[7] E. G. Holley, review of *The American Bibliography of Charles Evans*, XIV, Index, by Roger P. Bristol, *Library Journal*, LXXXV (May 15, 1960), 1890.

ment on a deficiency in the original work. As a result of Evans' research on his titles, he sometimes assigned authors to anonymous titles. Since he did not prepare a title index for each volume, his ascriptions effectively hid many of the titles. Too, he used no device such as brackets to indicate that the author's name did not actually appear on the title page. Since Evans never used cross references, despite his being urged to do so, this ascribing of an anonymous work to an author has for years enabled book dealers to advertise an item as "not in Evans" when the title actually is there; it was effectively concealed under the name of the author to whom Evans assigned it.

Bristol has further added to the usefulness of Evans' original work by the publication of an *Index of Printers, Publishers, and Booksellers Indicated by Charles Evans in His American Bibliography*, which the Bibliographical Society of the University of Virginia issued late in 1961. As noted elsewhere, one of the distinctive features of Evans' work was a list of printers and publishers with pertinent addresses and dates at the end of each volume, though Evans' lists did not cite individual numbers attributed to each printer. Through the provision of this cumulative index Bristol's aim has been to help the librarian, bibliographer, or book dealer "in whose hand is a copy of a work printed in America before 1801 which is (or is it?) in Evans' American Bibliography." [8] Again he has not tried to revise Evans but has indexed the printers just as they appear in the original work.

Still a third part of the American Antiquarian Society project, also undertaken by Bristol, is the compilation of a union list of additions to the *American Bibliography*. Bristol has now accumulated some 9,000 additions to Evans.[9] In his compilation he has used the numerous bibliographies, imprint catalogs, and check lists which have appeared since the original volumes were published. This is a rather large number, considering the fact that the original twelve volumes of Evans contained 35,854 entries. However, L. C. Wroth estimates that the ratio between imprints recorded in bibliographies and pieces known to have come from the early American press is 1 to 4.7.[10] Using this ratio as a basis, there were approximately 168,514 pieces published during the period covered

[8] Roger P. Bristol, *Index of Printers, Publishers, and Booksellers Indicated by Charles Evans in His American Bibliography* (Charlottesville, Va.: Bibliographical Society of the University of Virginia, 1961), p. iii.

[9] R. P. Bristol to the author, TLS, Nov. 21, 1960.

[10] L. C. Wroth, *The Colonial Printer* (New York: The Grolier Club, 1931),

by Evans, though many of these unquestionably fell into the categories of invitations, tickets, circulars, and blank forms to be filled in on manuscript which Evans purposely omitted. Many bibliographers have been at work since Evans and it can be expected that they would uncover significant additions. As W. C. Ford many years ago told Evans, "No one has ever prepared a perfect bibliography and no one ever will." [11] While Charles Evans himself was too stubborn to admit this openly, he surely must have known that subsequent workers would add much to his bibliography. Again the comparison of Evans and Hain comes to mind: both gave to the world major bibliographical tools and provided bases upon which other bibliographers could build. It is a tribute to Evans that instead of scrapping his work and beginning anew, subsequent bibliographers are building upon his foundation.

Bristol plans for his check list of additions to appear in the near future. After its publication it will then be circulated to the major libraries of Americana for checking, and several years afterwards will appear as a printed volume. Since the short-title revision is scheduled to appear after the printed list of additions, it is safe to say that another decade will probably elapse before the up-to-date Evans reaches the public. Until all of these projects are completed, no definitive answer can be made to the question of the real value of Evans' work. However, a tentative evaluation can be given, based on other work that has attempted to supplement Evans, though none has been on the scale of the three current major projects.

At the beginning, it should be noted in fairness that Charles Evans himself was never pleased with his first volume. He recognized the deficiencies which are inevitable when a bibliographer cannot personally examine each item he attempts to describe. Let it be said in his defense that he very much wanted to visit eastern libraries before going to press with his first book, but the problem of money that persisted through all his future efforts kept him from doing so. Frequently Evans stated to his son Eliot that he regarded volume one as his poorest work, and, after he completed the entire

---

pp. 184–186. Wroth noted that printed blank forms were "unquestionably one of the staples of the American press." Following Evans' policy, Bristol has probably not included these forms either. Although he has not analyzed his "not in Evans" items, Bristol has said that many of them are variant imprints of Evans titles, many are broadsides, but many are also unknown in any other edition.

[11] W. C. Ford to C. E., TLS, Jan. 23, 1923. See also MS draft of Evans' reply attached to this letter.

work, he hoped to issue a revised edition of that first book.[12] This lends credence to Brigham's statement that Evans was aware of his own deficiencies, and if he had lived longer, he would have continued to revise and correct.[13] The interleaved master copy of volume one also supports Brigham's contention. Not counting the addition of locations and auction prices, Evans penned some 738 corrections to his entries and added 136 new titles. Many of these corrections were notes on sources, some were corrected titles, and a few were major errors.

For the seventeenth century, where Evans initially doubted any bibliographer would ever add as many as thirty-three titles to his original 967, he himself discovered an additional twenty-one. Recent information from the New York Public Library indicates that that library has added forty-eight seventeenth-century titles not in Evans.[14] How many more there are in other libraries will probably not be known until Bristol publishes his check list.

However, despite Evans' own statements that he had been overly confident about his early work, volume one as a whole still stands up rather well on the basis of a count made ten years ago by two outstanding libraries of Americana in this country: [15]

	Titles in Evans	Titles Not in Evans
Library of Congress	970	101
John Carter Brown Library	730	63

Although this count does not indicate whether or not the "not in Evans" titles are unique, even a combined total of the two libraries would be only 5 per cent of the 3,244 entries in the original Evans. The fact that these two major libraries have been able to uncover so few new titles indicates that Evans' basic work was creditable.

Data from two other large research libraries confirm the judgment based on the Library of Congress and John Carter Brown Library figures. The New York Public Library *Check-list of Additions to Evans* (1960) reveals 154 additions for volume one, still not a large number. Of this number, sixty-seven, or almost half, are broadsides, one of the categories in which W. C. Ford in 1922 dem-

---

[12] Interview with Eliot H. Evans, Chicago, Jan. 29, 1959.

[13] C. S. Brigham, "Report of the Council," A. A. S. *Proceedings*, n.s., LXV (April, 1955), 4.

[14] Lewis M. Stark and Maud D. Cole, comps., *Checklist of Additions to Evans' American Bibliography in the Rare Book Division of the New York Public Library* (New York: New York Public Library, 1960), pp. 1–4.

[15] L. C. Wroth to Eliot H. Evans, typed copy, Jan. 2, 1952.

onstrated that the *American Bibliography* was notably deficient.[16] An earlier supplement published by the Huntington Library in 1933 revealed eighty-nine additions to volume one.[17] As aids in evaluating Evans' work, these two check lists provide the best comparisons of additions now in print. The check lists appear in Table 3.

TABLE 3

Additions to the American Bibliography [a]

	Evans' Entries	NYPL Additions	Huntington Additions
Volume 1 (1639–1729)	3,244	154	89
Volume 2 (1730–50)	3,379	77	69
Volume 3 (1751–64)	3,267	127	105
Volume 4 (1765–73)	3,201	154	83
Volume 5 (1774–78)	3,085	174	86
Volume 6 (1779–85)	3,272	146	90
Volume 7 (1786–89)	2,849	113	61
Volume 8 (1790–92)	2,777	108	51
Volume 9 (1793–94)	3,071	73	34
Volume 10 (1795–96, M)	2,687	42	30
Volume 11 (1796, N-97)	2,429	46	42
Volume 12 (1798–99, M)	2,593	50	not included
Totals	35,854	1,264 (1289)	740 (736)

[a] Discrepancies in the numbers listed in columns two and three are caused by the fact that the NYPL list had assigned certain numbers which subsequently were not used and the Huntington list inserted items designating them 35a and 35b, etc. The numbers in parentheses represent the total numbers given by each list; the numbers not in parentheses represent the actual number of additions.

[16] W. C. Ford, *Broadsides, Ballads, etc., Printed in Massachusetts 1639–1800*, in Massachusetts Historical Society *Collections*, LXXV (1922), xiii. Cited hereafter as Ford, *Broadsides*. Evans was unhappy over Ford's comment "Pioneers in the field, they [Evans and Paine] did not go far in covering it." See C. E. to W. C. Ford, ALS, Jan. 19, 1923, M. H. S. Archives. W. C. Ford to C. E., TLS and MS draft of Evans' reply, Jan. 23, 1923.

[17] Willard O. Waters, "American Imprints, 1648–1797, in the Huntington Library, Supplementing Evans' *American Bibliography*," *The Huntington Library Bulletin*, no. 3 (Feb., 1933), 1–95. One should note that the Huntington

W. O. Waters, who compiled the Huntington Library *Supplement*, fifteen years later wrote that he had uncovered an additional 484 titles, of which ninty were not in Evans and the remainder of which were variations of Evans' entries.[18] This would bring the Huntington total almost to the same figure as the New York Public Library, though a difference of eleven years of research should still be remembered when comparing the two.

In another more specialized area, the National Library of Medicine has recently published Robert B. Austin's *Early American Medical Imprints: A Guide to Works Printed in the United States, 1668–1820*.[19] Austin's entries are very complete, with references and descriptive information following each entry, including the Evans number which facilitates checking. Of the 717 entries listed in his chronological index (including some duplicate entries) for the period covered by the twelve volumes of the *American Bibliography*, Evans listed 580, or about 81 per cent. An additional twenty-two entries are undoubtedly variants of Evans' entries. In an appendix Austin also lists some seventy-four entries from Evans which could not be verified or located. Again Evans' work stands up very well statistically.

Statistics, however, do not tell the entire story. What of the quality of the publications which Evans missed? Already mentioned is that fact that Evans was seriously deficient in broadsides. Many of the titles which Bristol has collected are these small but historically useful ephemera. Since they were used and then tossed away, broadsides have not survived in many copies. Later bibliographers from Ford, in 1922, to the present have delved into this special area with much improvement on Evans. Alden's *Rhode Island Imprints* (1949) lists 405 broadsides for Rhode Island, of which Evans secured fewer than half.[20] In view of his Rhode Island contacts, Brigham and Winship, it is difficult to see how Evans missed some

list is not solely additions but also includes significant variations from titles described by Evans.

[18] W. O. Waters to Gifford Ernest, photostat copy, Jan. 25, 1949.

[19] Robert B. Austin, *Early American Medical Imprints: A Guide to Works Printed in the United States, 1668–1820* (Washington, D.C.: Government Printing Office, 1961).

[20] John E. Alden, ed., *Rhode Island Imprints, 1727–1800* (New York: Published for the Bibliographical Society of America by Bowker, 1949). In his introduction, p. ix, Alden notes that he has added 610 items not recorded by Evans, or an increase of 50 per cent. On the broadside additions of Alden see C. S. Brigham, "Report of the Council," A. A. S. *Proceedings*, n.s., LX (April, 1950), 4–5.

of these. Some of the earlier omissions among broadsides were Harvard theses, which strangely enough Evans neglected, despite the fact that he secured most of the Yale theses, which were much harder to locate.[21] Yet, for these items, as Ford noted, "Intensive cultivation was needed to obtain the best results." [22] With Evans' technique and scope he simply could not do so well as those whose field was not so broad.

On the other hand, Evans did very well indeed with the eighteenth-century medical theses. Of the considerable number of published theses listed in Austin's *Early American Medical Imprints,* Evans missed only one, number 1,184, Ninian Magruder's *An Inaugural Dissertation on the Small-pox* (Philadelphia, 1792). These small pamphlets reflect the state of the medical art in their time and therefore are very important for the history of science. Austin's list also demonstrates how completely Evans recorded the inoculation pamphlets of the early eighteenth century, a point for which an Oxford University historian commended Evans in 1930.[23]

In addition to broadsides what else did Evans miss? Apparently he missed very little of importance. Shipton, who has perhaps mined this field more than anyone now living, in a 1954 report stated: "In defending the usefulness of Evans' American Bibliography we are accustomed to say that of the thousands of items discovered since his volumes went to press, only a handful have historical importance." [24] Presumably Shipton is here speaking primarily of books and did not have in mind the broadsides. Of this historically important handful, the American Antiquarian Society has secured its respectable share. Acquisition of such titles has always been so remarkable as to merit special attention in the society's annual reports, a practice lending weight to Shipton's statement.

On the other hand, in a recent provocative book, *The Books of a New Nation: United States Government Publications, 1774–1814* (1957), John H. Powell takes Evans and other early twentieth-century bibliographers seriously to task for their apparent neglect of the official documents of the new government. Complaining both of the quantity and quality of their treatment of such material, Powell is especially harsh about Evans' work and accuses the *Amer-*

---

[21] Interview with C. K. Shipton, Worcester, May 12, 1958.
[22] Ford, *Broadsides,* p. xiii.
[23] John Fulton to C. E., TLS, Jan. 25, 1930.
[24] C. K. Shipton, "Report of the Librarian," A. A. S. *Proceedings,* n.s., LXIV (Oct., 1954), 269.

ican Bibliography, among other things, of being "thinly representative" of official documents during that period of prolific publishing
beginning in 1789.[25] Throughout his work Powell takes an opportunity to point out what he believes are Evans' serious deficiencies,
and does not hesitate to call Evans' interest in government documents primitive and unawakened.[26]

However, a careful check of those items which Powell calls of
major importance for a study of the origin of United States government fails to substantiate his basic claim. Omissions, such as separate
bills, certainly exist; but time after time when Powell discusses an
item such as *The Association,* 1774, which he calls the "recorded
beginning of the American government," one finds the item recorded in the *American Bibliography* with the same notes used by
the historian.[27] Moreover, in the latter part of his second chapter,
which covers the period 1787–1800, Powell cites at least two dozen
important works by brief title, referring the reader to Evans' numbers for complete citation.[28] If Evans was as deficient as Powell
claims, it is not apparent in this book. Shipton's statement that
Evans missed few works of importance seems to hold true for government publications as well as trade books.

---

[25] John H. Powell, *The Books of a New Nation: United States Government
Publications, 1774–1814* (Philadelphia: University of Pennsylvania Press, 1957),
p. 101.

[26] *Ibid.,* p. 100. Evans' work may have been primitive, but his interest in government publications was not unawakened. A man spending weeks in the Library of Congress and the New York Public Library purposely looking for government publications is scarcely unaware of their importance. Evans' concern
for listing all of these publications accurately appears in many letters of which
the following are only samples: C. E. to Wilberforce Eames, ALS, Feb. 17, 1908,
in Wilberforce Eames Papers, New York Public Library; C. E. to G. P. Winship,
ALS, Jan. 9, 1913, J. C. B. Archives; C. S. B. to C. E., TLS, Jan. 12, 1926; C. E.
to Dorothea E. Nourse, ALS, June 25, 1929, A. A. S. Archives; C. E. to L. C.
Wroth, ALS, July 26, 1932, J. C. B. Archives. As for Evans' failure to use the
Checklist of 1911, I am as baffled as Powell, although Evans' volume seven was
well under way when the *Checklist* was published. A copy of the *First Checklist,*
1892, was in Evans' library. Typewritten list of the books in the library of
Charles Evans, 1935. However, one should remember that in the period when
Evans was doing his work on the earliest government publications, the Library
of Congress collections were far from being well organized.

There is a work on early United States documents under way by James B.
Childs. See also his recent article "The Story of the United States Senate Docu-
ments, 1st Congress, 1st Session, New York, 1789," Bibliographical Society of
America *Papers,* 56 (Second Quarter, 1962), 175–194.

[27] Powell, *Books of a New Nation,* p. 38; Evans, *American Bibliography,* no.
13703.

[28] Powell, *Books of a New Nation,* pp. 99–106, 159–160.

On the ground of importance, though, Powell takes issue with Evans on two documents of major concern to American historians: the Declaration of Independence and the United States Constitution. Of the former he notes that Paul Leicester Ford had listed five broadside editions in 1888 and Evans eleven in 1909; whereas Michael J. Walsh, who made a special study of the document, by 1949 had identified nineteen.[29] The increase does not seem surprising in view of forty years of research by persons working in a highly specialized area. In view of Julian P. Boyd's definitive study of the text of the Declaration of Independence one should expect his record to be a great improvement over Evans', who worked with limited tools in a day when collections were much less accessible.

The problem on the Constitution is much the same, despite Powell's warning to his readers to "not dismiss Evans' error lightly; it was the Constitution of the United States he was dealing with." [30] Evans had called the "first issue of the Constitution as agreed" the September 28, 1787, printing by Dunlap and Claypoole, an error Boyd decisively corrected when he found an August 6, 1787, document in the vaults of the Historical Society of Pennsylvania in 1937.[31] What Evans had recorded was the official text accepted by Congress and transmitted to the states for ratification. Again, it should surprise no one that historians working intensively on such a problem would add to Evans and provide the definitive statements on the documents. In view of the comprehensiveness of the *American Bibliography*, in which government publications play only a small part, it is amazing that Charles Evans did so well.

Important as the additions are in evaluating the work, what of the errors? Were there many and how significant were they? One of Evans' most reprehensible characteristics—perhaps an inevitable one under the circumstances—was his use of newspaper advertisements as a fact of publication.[32] When a colonial newspaper published an announcement that a book was "this day published," Evans understood the phrase to mean that the bookseller had just

---

[29] *Ibid.*, p. 33; Julian P. Boyd, *The Declaration of Independence, the Evolution of the Text as Shown in Facsimile of Various Drafts by Its Author* (Washington, D.C.: Library of Congress, 1943).

[30] Powell, *Books of a New Nation*, p. 65.

[31] *Ibid.*, pp. 62–65; Evans, *American Bibliography*, no. 20817.

[32] The best discussion of Evans' bibliographical ghosts is C. K. Shipton, "Report of the Librarian," A. A. S. *Proceedings*, n.s., LXVIII (Oct., 1958), 186–190.

issued it from his own press. Actually the bookseller frequently meant only that the book had just been received and was for sale. These titles were often of British origin. Copying as he did from other bibliographers who also did not understand this point, Evans created a number of American titles which did not exist. Yet Evans could not possibly have seen all the titles, and like any bibliographer, he often had to make some reasonable guesses. On these occasions his bibliographical imagination sometimes came into play, and it was not unknown for Evans to take an advertisement of a book title and reconstruct an entire title page, complete with name of printer. This introduction of titles on supposition has long been a criticism of Evans' work, and Evans would have mitigated the seriousness of his offense if he had done as W. J. James had suggested in 1902: cited his sources.

Another serious failing of Evans was his inconsistency in the use of punctuation. He sometimes used curved brackets to mean unnumbered pages, sometimes to mean that the pages themselves were numbered in curved brackets. Too, despite his love of long and involved title pages with their Latin or Greek phrases and their Biblical quotations, he was not always accurate in his transcription of punctuation in the titles. Meticulous in some details, he could be very careless about others. Somehow, when one considers the enormous amount of work involved, all of it done personally by Evans, this seems a carping criticism; but the bibliographers with a passion for accuracy think Evans should have been more careful.

An error which frequently bothered Shipton in securing materials for the microprint edition was Evans' assumption that if an almanac were printed in 1738 and again in 1758, it must of necessity have been printed every year in between.[33] This same type of error occurs with respect to newspapers. This is an almost inexcusable error and one finds it difficult to explain the peculiar quirk of Evans' mind which led him to such a conclusion.

Charles Evans knew as well as anyone else that there were some deficiencies in his methodology. He had an exalted conception of bibliography, but it was inevitable that he would not measure up to his own high standards. His belief in a science of bibliography was best expressed in a letter to Brigham in 1910, but Evans had ex-

---

[33] An early criticism of Evans' introduction of almanacs on supposition is Victor Hugo Paltsits, "The Almanacs of Roger Sherman," A. A. S. *Proceedings*, n.s., XVIII (April, 1907), 213.

pressed much the same thought to Wilberforce Eames some three years earlier: "It is tests like these which elevate Bibliography into one of the exact sciences. When an Agassiz from a single bone constructs an animal long extinct we wonder and applaud. It is a difference only in kind when a bibliographer from a single leaf, can determine with exactness, the authorship and title of a lost book; tell you where it was printed; and even designate the spot, now perhaps covered by a granite warehouse, or a towering office-building. . . ."[34] Throughout the long and difficult period of research and production, he had constantly sought to make his work ever more accurate and more comprehensive. The openhanded help of people like Brigham and Winship he received gladly, but at the best he remained politely silent to their suggestions for improvement. Once he had fixed his course, Charles Evans seldom changed direction. The politeness to his friends could turn to viciousness, and often did when the casual critic questioned his methodology. Knowing better than anyone else the defects of his work, Evans was totally unappreciative of efforts to change his pattern.[35]

Despite his belief in the science of bibliography, Charles Evans developed no great bibliographic techniques. Evans never regarded the mere mechanics of bibliography as particularly important. He was a compiler, not an innovator. Neither was he a collector, although he had high regard for that "gentlest and best of all human infirmities."[36] His particular form of bibliomania was to see the book, to describe it, and then to let it go. As he had one time remarked to Wroth, once he had described a book he had no desire

[34] C. E. to C. S. B., ALS, May 15, 1910, A. A. S. Archives. C. E. to Wilberforce Eames, ALS, Feb. 27, 1907, Eames Papers, New York Public Library.

[35] As related in chap. 12, Evans changed his procedures only once and that was to allow for the printing of location symbols despite the extra line involved. This was not a basic change in methodology, but in practice. For his vicious replies to the casual critic see W. J. Campbell to C. E., ALS, April 7, 1909, with MS draft of Evans' reply, and Harold Pierce to C. E., TLS, Aug. 31, 1926, with MS draft of Evans' reply. One of the simplest requests ever made to Evans was that he print a key to the library location symbols. Publication of this key was urged upon Evans repeatedly, but he would not accede. See Mary E. Hyde to C. E., TLS, Dec. 17, 1927, and ALS, Jan. 14, 1928. Evans obstinately refused to concede that his system was complicated and after his death a key to the location symbols was prepared by John C. Munger, "Evans's *American Bibliography,* Tentative Check List of the Library Location Symbols," New York Public Library *Bulletin,* XL (Aug., 1936), 665–668.

[36] L. C. Wroth, "A Matrix of Histories." Charles Evans, MS draft of a letter to the editor of the Chicago *Record-Herald* on the one-hundredth anniversary of the American Antiquarian Society, 1912.

to own it or even to see it again. However, until he had seen the work he would move heaven and earth to learn all he could about it.

That he succeeded in his work is apparent. Evans' *American Bibliography* has become so useful that some libraries use it as a second catalog of their holdings.[37] In 1956 after the rare books division of the Library of Congress checked its holdings of seventeenth- and eighteenth-century books, it was discovered that the library had more than 40 per cent of the titles listed in Evans. To facilitate research in this collection of early American material, the Library of Congress published a ditto list of all the Evans numbers held by them and distributed this document to the major research libraries in the world.[38]

Instead of being relegated to the museum of outgrown reference works, the *American Bibliography* is still being used heavily by scholars throughout the country. Anyone who has checked even casually the bibliographical writings on American printing cannot be unaware of the frequent citations of Evans, either for praise or blame. The most recent testimony to the use of Evans in this fashion occurs in *Sibley's Harvard Graduates,* volume eleven (1960). In his introduction C. K. Shipton, editor, notes that full texts of most of the graduates' works are now available in microprint form.[39] To aid in finding the text he has included the Evans number in the bibliographies. As was intended, the *American Bibliography* is a ready-made catalog for this Early American Imprints series. For what other work has anyone compiled two indexes which include the bibliographical ghosts?

After all has been said, the *American Bibliography* of Charles Evans stands, as Brigham called it, "one of the greatest bibliographical compilations of all time," despite ghosts and omissions, errors and inaccuracies, complexity and inconsistency. When one picks up a volume of Evans and reads the titles for a given year, he obtains a splendid picture of the cultural, intellectual, political, and social conditions of that period of American history.[40] Thirty-

---

[37] Brigham so regarded the *American Bibliography* and frequently mentioned this fact to Evans. See C. S. B. to C. E., TLS, Dec. 12, 1916. The John Carter Brown Library also checks holdings in the *American Bibliography*.

[38] U.S. Library of Congress, Rare Books Division, *Evans Titles in the Library of Congress*, ditto list (Washington, D.C.: Library of Congress, 1956).

[39] C. K. Shipton, *Sibley's Harvard Graduates* (Boston: Massachusetts Historical Society, 1960), XI.

[40] Evans himself expected this to happen and predicted such usefulness in

three years ago, L. C. Wroth, writing of recent bibliographical work in America, commented upon the resumption of printing of the *American Bibliography* with volume nine in these words: "Useful as it is and has been in libraries for many years, it will be long before its possibilities are fully realized. The opportunity it offers to the student of ideas, special and general, to the library investigator and to the social historian are limitless, and yet few members of these groups begin as they should with Evans or even end with him unless they are led to it by the hand. One wonders sometimes at certain characteristics of the scholarly mind." [41] With the various projects under way which are based upon Evans' framework it can be safely said that the possibilities of his work are still not realized, nor will they be for many years to come.

When the thirteenth volume of the *American Bibliography* was nearing completion under Shipton, Wroth again echoed his admiration for Evans' work in a letter to his son, Eliot H. Evans. There could be no better way to sum up his accomplishment than with a quotation from these encouraging words: "It must be a great satisfaction to you to feel that your father's work was one of enduring usefulness to historical and literary scholarship. All of us who knew him are proud of his achievement." [42]

American Bibliography, I, xi. Two subsequent scholars who have noted this particular value are John T. Winterich, *Early American Books and Printing* (Boston: Houghton Mifflin, 1935), pp. 63, 232, and L. C. Wroth, "A Matrix of Histories."

[41] L. C. Wroth, "Recent Bibliographical Work in America," *The Library,* ser. 4, IX (June, 1928), 61.

[42] L. C. Wroth to Eliot H. Evans, typed copy, Jan. 2, 1952.

Bibliography

Since the sources used in this study have been cited fully in the footnotes, they are not all repeated here. The materials which I have found most helpful are the autograph letters, scrapbooks, printed reports, and ledger books in the Evans family papers. These papers were presented to the University of Illinois Library by the Evans family in 1962.

The second most important source was the various interviews over the past four years with Charles Evans' surviving children: Mrs. Gertrude Evans Jones, Eliot H. Evans, and Charles Evans, Jr., all of Chicago. Interviews with Eliot H. Evans have been especially numerous and valuable.

Also in the possession of Eliot Evans are materials relating to the lawsuit between *Lena Young Evans et al.* v. *Lizzie Young et al.,* an important scrapbook "Charles Evans, 1850–1935," papers on the estate of Charles Evans, and some correspondence on the *American Bibliography*. All of these were made available in an openhanded way, which is a tribute to Mr. Evans' interest in the accuracy and completeness of the biography. Occasionally I have also received other papers from Mrs. Gertrude Evans Jones and Charles Evans, Jr.

Next in importance as source materials are the archives of the American Antiquarian Society and the John Carter Brown Library. Interviews with Dr. Clifford K. Shipton and Dr. Clarence S. Brigham from the former and Dr. Lawrence C. Wroth from the latter institution were invaluable to see the *American Bibliography* in perspective and in evaluating Charles Evans as a bibliographer.

Reports, both official and unofficial, of the Boston Farm and Trades School, the Boston Athenaeum, the Indianapolis Public Library, the Enoch Pratt Free Library, the Omaha Public Library, the Newberry Library, and the Chicago Historical Society have been very useful, and they have been cited fully in the footnotes.

The Poole Papers and the manuscript history of W. S. Merrill at the

Newberry Library, plus William L. Williamson's "William Frederick Poole and the Modern Library Movement," an unpublished doctoral thesis at the University of Chicago, have been especially fruitful sources in re-creating the relationship between Poole and Evans.

Printed articles and books relating either to Evans or to his time have been so numerous that to repeat them here would be pointless. Except for the unusually helpful titles, only the files of the most used journals and newspapers are listed in the bibliography. These are basic materials to which I have had occasion to refer over and over again.

A complete listing of Charles Evans' printed contributions is given at the beginning. Reports have been cited only if Evans could be credited with the substance of the document.

Printed Works of Charles Evans

Articles

Evans, Charles. "Oaths of Allegiance in Colonial New England," A. A. S. *Proceedings,* n.s., XXXI (Oct., 1921), 377–438.

————. "The Sizes of Printed Books," *Library Journal,* I (Nov. 30, 1876), 58–61.

Books

Evans, Charles. *The American Bibliography; a Chronological Dictionary of All Books, Pamphlets and Periodical Publications Printed in the United States of America from the Genesis of Printing in 1639 Down to and Including the Year 1820, with Bibliographical and Biographical Notes.* 12 vols. Chicago: Privately Printed for the Author, 1903–34.

Catalogs

Enoch Pratt Free Library, Baltimore. *Finding List of the Enoch Pratt Free Library of Baltimore City, Central Building.* 2nd ed. Feb., 1886. 1st Supp., May, 1886. 2nd Supp., Nov., 1886. Baltimore: The Sun Book and Job Printing Office, 1886.

Indianapolis Public Library. *Catalogue of the Public Library of Indianapolis, 1873.* Indianapolis: Press of Printing and Publishing House, 1873.

————. *A List of Books Added from November, 1873–January, 1876.* Indianapolis: Issued by the Library, 1876.

————. *A List of Books Added to the Public Library of Indianapolis from January, 1876–January, 1878.* Indianapolis: Issued by the Library, 1878.

————. *Finding-list of Books in the Classes of Biography, History, and Travels Belonging to the Public Library of Indianapolis.* Indianapolis: Carlon and Hollonbeck, 1891.

————. *Finding-list of Books in the Classes of Poetry and the Drama, Literature and Polygraphy Belonging to the Public Library of Indianapolis.* Indianapolis: The Library, 1891.

Omaha Public Library. *Finding List of the Books in the Omaha Public Library, 1888.* Omaha: Gibson, Miller and Richardson, 1888.

Reports

Chicago Historical Society. *Charter, Constitution, By-laws, Roll of Membership, MDCCCLVI–MDCCCCI, List of Officers and Members, MDCCCCI.* Chicago: Printed for the Society, 1901.

Indianapolis Public Library. *The First Annual Report of the Public Library of Indianapolis, 1873–4.* Indianapolis: Printing and Publishing House, 1874.

————. *The Second Annual Report of the Public Library of Indianapolis, 1874–8.* Indianapolis: Issued by the Library, 1878.

Reviews

Evans, Charles. Review of *Catalogue of Books in the Roxbury Branch Library of the Boston Public Library*, 2nd ed., in *Library Journal*, I (Sept. 30, 1876), 21.

————. Review of *Catalogue of the Mercantile Library of Brooklyn*, pt. I, A–C, in *Library Journal*, I (May 31, 1877), 330–331.

————. Review of *Fletcher Free Library of Burlington (Vt.) Catalogue* in *Library Journal*, III (April, 1878), 70.

Speeches

Evans, Charles. "Address," *The Farm and Trades School, 1814–1914; One Hundredth Anniversary.* Boston, 1914.

————. "Looking Backward," Indianapolis *News*, Jan. 15, 1927. The address was printed in full under the headline, "Fifty Years of Literary Club History Recalled by Founder," and separate copies were printed on good paper.

THE EVANS FAMILY PAPERS—MAJOR CATEGORIES

Letters

Charles Evans to Lena Evans, 1889, 1892–93, 1900, 1904, 1906, 1908, 1911–17, 1920–21, 1924, 1926, plus some undated.

Lena Evans to Charles Evans, 1904, 1906, 1908, 1911, 1913–14, 1926, plus some undated.

Correspondence with Mary Abbie Bean, 1869–72, 1876, 1878, 1883–85, 1890.

Correspondence with G. E. Channing, 1872, 1874–76.

Correspondence with Samuel Eliot, 1870, 1876, 1878, 1892, 1897, plus some undated.

Correspondence with T. J. Evans, 1877, 1889, 1895, 1897–98, 1904, 1910, 1918, 1926.

Correspondence with W. I. Fletcher, 1874, 1890–91, 1899–1900, 1902–03, 1909.

Correspondence with J. H. Holliday and the Union Trust Company of Indianapolis, 1902–14.

Correspondence with W. F. Poole, 1869–74, 1876, 1878, 1884–85, 1888–92.

Correspondence with Justin Winsor, 1878, 1894–95.

Other correspondence arranged chronologically, 1872–78, 1881, 1883–85, 1888–1934.

Unpublished Speeches

Evans, Charles. "Public Libraries," MS of speech delivered in Indianapolis, probably between April 9, 1874, and April 9, 1875. 75pp.

———. "An Evening with Dr. Johnson," MS of speech delivered before the Indianapolis Literary Club, Nov. 16, 1878. 49pp. plus quotation slips.

———. "John Lothrop Motley," MS of speech delivered before the Indianapolis Literary Club, Feb. 9, 1890. 58pp.

———. "The Bible of an Infidel; a Review of Lessing's 'Nathan the Wise,' " MS of speech delivered before the Indianapolis Literary Club, April 27, 1891. 34pp.

Other Unpublished Writings

Evans, Charles. "Fritz Deutscher's Beer Saloon," a satire in the vein of Hamlet, MS draft, probably Indianapolis, 1870's.

———. "The Meeting of the Bungtown School Committee," satire on school boards(?), MS draft, probably Chicago, late 1890's.

———. "A Plea for a Department of Peace in the Government of the United States," typed MS with Evans' autograph corrections, Chicago, between Aug. 2, 1923, and Feb. 3, 1924.

———. "Poems," with an allusion to Indianapolis Literary Club, 1878, MS draft, n.d.

———. MS draft of letter to the Editor of the Chicago *Record-Herald* on the one hundredth anniversary of the American Antiquarian Society, 1912.

———. MS draft of a story on simplified spelling, n.p., n.d., but sometime after 1906.

Miscellaneous Materials

Evans, Charles. *American Bibliography*, circulars and advertisements, MS draft for first three prefaces and other MSS, and research slips.

———. Bank books, 1871–72, 1882–83, 1890–92.

———. Boston Athenaeum, "Scrapbook."

———. Indianapolis Public Library, "Scrapbook."

———. Invitations, membership cards, tickets, etc.

———. "Ledger Books," I and II, MS, for the *American Bibliography*.

Boston Athenaeum file.

Boston Farm and Trades School file.

Charles Evans, Jr., file of condolences on his father's death.

Eliot Evans, file of correspondence with subscribers to the *American Bibliography*.

Enoch Pratt Free Library file.

Family photographs.

Indianapolis Literary Club file.

Newspaper clippings on Virginia Library of McCormick Theological Seminary.

Miscellaneous pamphlets such as public school directories, library annual reports, etc.

Typewritten list of books in the library of Charles Evans, 1935.

Other Manuscript Depositories

District of Columbia
    Library of Congress, Archives

Illinois
    American Library Association, "1876 Conference Scrapbook"
    Chicago Historical Society, Archives
    Newberry Library
        Administrative reports
        Merrill, W. S., MS history
        Poole Papers
        Blatchford Papers

Indiana
    Indianapolis Public Library, Archives

Maryland
    Enoch Pratt Free Library, Archives

Massachusetts
    American Antiquarian Society, Archives
    Boston Athenaeum, Archives
    Harvard University Library, Archives
    Massachusetts Historical Society, Archives

New York
    New York Historical Society, Archives
    New York Public Library
        Archives
        Wilberforce Eames Papers

Rhode Island
    John Carter Brown Library, Archives
    John Hay Library, Brown University, University Archives
    Rhode Island Historical Society, Archives

MATERIALS RELATING TO EVANS

Books

Angle, Paul M. *The Chicago Historical Society, 1856–1956; an Unconventional Chronicle.* Chicago: Rand McNally and Company, 1956.

Austin, Robert B. *Early American Imprints: A Guide to Works Printed in the United States, 1668–1810.* Washington, D.C.: Government Printing Office, 1961.

Boston Athenaeum. *The Athenaeum Centenary; the Influence and History* of the Boston Athenaeum from 1807 to 1907, with a Record of Its Officers and Benefactors and a Complete List of Proprietors. Boston: Boston Athenaeum, 1907.

Bristol, Roger P. *The American Bibliography of Charles Evans*. XIV: *Index*. Worcester: American Antiquarian Society, 1959.

————. *Index of Printers, Publishers, and Booksellers Indicated by Charles Evans in His American Bibliography*. Charlottesville: Bibliographical Society of the University of Virginia, 1961.

Chicago Library Club. *Libraries of the City of Chicago with an Historical Sketch of the Chicago Library Club*. Chicago: The Chicago Library Club, 1905.

Ditzion, Sidney H. *Arsenals of a Democratic Culture; a Social History of the American Public Library Movement in New England and the Middle States from 1850 to 1900*. Chicago: American Library Association, 1947.

Dunn, Jacob P. *Greater Indianapolis: The History, the Industries, the Institutions, and the People of a City of Homes*. 2 vols. Chicago: The Lewis Publishing Company, 1910.

Evans, Charles, Jr. *Chick Evans' Golf Book; the Story of the Sporting Battles of the Greatest of All Amateur Golfers*. Chicago: Thomas E. Wilson and Company, 1921.

Green, Samuel Swett. *The Public Library in the United States, 1853–1893*. Boston: The Boston Book Company, 1913.

Hart, Richard P. *Enoch Pratt, the Story of a Plain Man*. Baltimore: Enoch Pratt Library, 1935.

International Conference of Librarians. *Transactions and Proceedings of the Conference of Librarians Held in London October, 1877*. London: Printed at the Chiswick Press, 1878.

Noland, Stephen C. *Indianapolis Literary Club, Summarized Record, 1877–1934*. Indianapolis, Dec., 1934.

Powell, John H. *The Books of a New Nation; United States Government Publications, 1774–1814*. Philadelphia: University of Pennsylvania Press, 1957.

Shipton, Clifford K. *The American Bibliography of Charles Evans*. XIII: *1799–1800*. Worcester: American Antiquarian Society, 1955.

Stark, Lewis M. and Cole, Maud D., comps. *Checklist of Additions to Evans' American Bibliography in the Rare Book Division of the New York Public Library*. New York: New York Public Library, 1960.

Winterich, John T. *Early American Books and Printing*. Boston: Houghton Mifflin, 1935.

Wroth, Lawrence C. *The Colonial Printer*. New York: The Grolier Club, 1931.

————. *A History of Printing in Colonial Maryland*. Baltimore: Typothetae of Baltimore, 1922.

Articles

Bay, J. Christian. "Charles Evans, 1850–1935," A. L. A. *Bulletin,* XXIX (March, 1935), 163–164.

Bowker, Richard Rogers. "Bibliographical Endeavors in America," in *Transactions and Proceedings of the Second International Library Conference Held in London, July 13–16, 1897.* London: Printed for the Members of the Conference, 1898. Pp. 150–153.

Brigham, Clarence Saunders. "Charles Evans, 1850–1935," A. A. S. *Proceedings,* n.s., XXXXV (April, 1935), 14–21.

Utley, George B. "Charles Evans," *Library Journal,* LX (March 1, 1935), 198.

Waters, Willard O. "American Imprints, 1648–1797, in the Huntington Library, Supplementing Evans' *American Bibliography," The Huntington Library Bulletin,* no. 3 (Feb., 1933), 1–95.

Winship, George Parker. "The Literature of the History of Printing in the United States," *The Library,* ser. 4, III (March, 1923), 288–303.

Wroth, Lawrence C. "Evans's *American Bibliography,* a Matrix of Histories," in his *American Bibliography, 1639–1729, by Charles Evans, Illustrated with Fifty-nine Original Leaves from Early American Books and an Historical Notice of the Author and His Work.* Boston: Charles E. Goodspeed and Company, 1943.

——. "Recent Bibliographical Work in America," *The Library,* ser. 4, IX (June, 1928), 59–85.

Documents

Enoch Pratt Free Library, Baltimore. *The Enoch Pratt Free Library of Baltimore; Letters and Documents Relating to Its Foundation and Organization.* Baltimore, 1886.

U.S. Department of the Interior. Bureau of Education. *Public Libraries in the United States of America; Their History, Condition, and Management.* Special Report, pt. 1. Washington, D.C.: Government Printing Office, 1876.

U.S. Library of Congress. Rare Books Division. *Evans Titles in the Library of Congress.* Ditto list. Washington, D.C.: Library of Congress, 1956.

Unpublished Material

Hull, Thomas V. "The Origin and Development of the Indianapolis Public Library, 1873–1899." Unpublished M.A. thesis, University of Kentucky, 1956.

Merrill, William Stetson. "Early Days at the Newberry Library; Reminiscences of Persons and Events, 1889 to 1894." Typewritten MS, Oconomowoc, Wis., March, 1954. Newberry Library.

Rush, Charles E. "Historical Account of the Indianapolis Public Library from 1873 to 1893." Typewritten MS, Feb., 1925. Indianapolis Public Library.

Williamson, William L. "William Frederick Poole and the Modern Library Movement." Unpublished Ph.D. dissertation, University of Chicago, 1959.

Newspaper and Journal Files

American Antiquarian Society *Proceedings,* n.s., XVI–LXX, 1903–60.

Bibliographical Society of America *Bulletin,* I–IV, 1907/09–12.

Bibliographical Society of America *Papers,* I–LV, 1904/07–61.

Bibliographical Society of Chicago *Yearbook,* I–IV, 1899–1903.

Fort Worth *Democrat,* Sept. 19, 1880–Dec. 10, 1881.

Fort Worth *Democrat-Advance,* Dec. 11, 1881–June 30, 1882.

Fort Worth *Gazette,* Jan. 2, 1883–Sept. 30, 1883; Nov. 23, 1883–Jan. 5, 1885.

Indianapolis *News,* 1872–79, 1892.

Library Journal, I–LX, 1876–1935.

Index

Adams, Charles Francis: 20, 177; addresses Chicago Historical Society, 188; tribute to Evans, 189; urges Chicago as site for American Historical Association convention, 189–190

Adams, George E,, 165

Alden, John E.: *Rhode Island Imprints*, 314

Allan, Jessie, 114

American Antiquarian Society: 215, 247, 266, 270, 291, 315; aid to Evans increased, 239–240, 258–259, 268, 277–286; *American Bibliography*, vol. 7, dedicated to, 246; Brigham becomes librarian of, 239–240; centennial gift of Evans, 246; Evans elected to membership in, 241–242, 298; Evans' first visit to, 217–218; microprint project described, 308–309; Thomas' *History of Printing* with Haven and Trumbull's additions, 215, 239

American Bibliography: circulars announcing, 182, 184, 195–198, 201, 221; cumulative index to, 309–310; evaluation of, 307–321; financing of, 197, 200–204, 214, 222–223, 225–227, 229–231, 234, 236–237, 259, 265–266, 268–270, 278–281; index of printers in, 310; methodology, 212–216, 250–251, 255–256, 258, 310, 317–319; origin of, 181–186; reaction to circulars, 196–201; subscribers to, 199, 201, 223, 225, 270–272, 274, 278; summary of, Table 2, 308; vol. 1, 204–206, 208–211, 213–214; vol. 2, 223–224; vol. 3, 227; vol. 4, 230–231, 238; vol. 5, 236–237; vol. 6, 239; vol. 7, 245–246; vol. 8, 249; vol. 9, 269–272; vol. 10, 276; vol. 11, 278, 280; vol. 12, 285–287

American Council of Learned Societies: grants in aid of *American Bibliography*, vols. 11–12, 279–286; votes appreciation for Evans' work, 283

American Historical Association: invited to Chicago, 189–190

American Library Association: 70, 116, 128–129, 147, 151, 163, 179–180, 210, 267, 270–271; committee on Evans' *American Bibliography*, 267–269; conference, 1876, 1–2, 67; Dewey first member, 2; dues, 106–107; Evans elected to

331